The Bible and Spirituality

The Bible and Spirituality

Exploratory Essays in Reading Scripture Spiritually

Edited by Andrew T. Lincoln
J. Gordon McConville
and Lloyd K. Pietersen

 CASCADE *Books* • Eugene, Oregon

THE BIBLE AND SPIRITUALITY
Exploratory Essays in Reading Scripture Spiritually

Cover image:
The Crossing
by Sheona Beaumont
www.shospace.co.uk

Cascade Books
An Imprint of Wipf and Stock Publishers
199 W. 8th Ave., Suite 3
Eugene, OR 97401

www.wipfandstock.com

ISBN 13: 978-1-62032-709-8

Cataloguing-in-Publication data:

The Bible and spirituality : exploratory essays in reading Scripture spiritually / edited by Andrew T. Lincoln, J. Gordon McConville, and Lloyd K. Pietersen

xx + 294 pp. ; 23 cm. Includes bibliographical references and indices.

ISBN 13: 978-1-62032-709-8

1. Bible—Criticism, interpretation, etc. 2. Spirituality—Biblical teaching. 3. Bible—Hermeneutics. I. Lincoln, Andrew T. II. McConville, J. G. (J. Gordon). III. Pietersen, Lloyd. IV. Title.

BS543 L56 2013

Manufactured in the U.S.A.

Contents

Contributors

Stephen C. Barton, Honorary Fellow, Department of Theology and Religion, University of Durham, UK.

Richard S. Briggs, Lecturer in Old Testament and Director of Biblical Studies, Cranmer Hall, St John's College, University of Durham, UK.

Stephen B. Chapman, Associate Professor of Old Testament, Duke University, Durham, North Carolina.

Ellen F. Davis, Amos Ragan Kearns Distinguished Professor of Bible and Practical Theology, Duke University, Durham, North Carolina.

Michael J. Gorman, Raymond E. Brown Professor of Biblical Studies and Theology, St. Mary's Seminary and University, Baltimore, Maryland.

Barbara Green, Professor of Biblical Studies, Dominican School at the Graduate Theological Union, Berkeley, California.

Andrew T. Lincoln, Portland Professor of New Testament, University of Gloucestershire, UK.

J. Gordon McConville, Professor of Old Testament Theology, University of Gloucestershire, UK.

R. Walter L. Moberly, Professor of Theology and Biblical Interpretation, University of Durham, UK.

Lloyd K. Pietersen, Senior Lecturer in New Testament Studies, University of Gloucestershire, UK.

Contributors

Sandra M. Schneiders, Professor Emerita of New Testament Studies and Spirituality, Jesuit School of Theology of Santa Clara University, Berkeley, California.

Susannah Ticciati, Senior Lecturer in Systematic Theology, King's College London.

Pieter G. R. de Villiers, Professor Extraordinarius in Biblical Spirituality, University of the Free State, Bloemfontein.

Abbreviations

AB	Anchor Bible
ABR	*Australian Biblical Review*
ACCS	Ancient Christian Commentary on Scripture
ACNT	Augsburg Commentaries on the New Testament
AYB	Anchor Yale Bible
BCBC	Believers Church Bible Commentary
BJS	Brown Judaic Studies
BNTC	Black's New Testament Commentaries
BTB	*Biblical Theology Bulletin*
BZAW	Beihefte zur Zeitschrift für die alttestamentliche Wissenschaft
BZNW	Beihefte zur Zeitschrift für die neutestamentliche Wissenschaft
CBQ	*Catholic Biblical Quarterly*
CCSL	Corpus Christianorum: Series latina
CD	*Church Dogmatics*
DLNT	*Dictionary of the Later New Testament and Its Developments*
DOTPr	*Dictionary of the Old Testament Prophets*
FOTL	Forms of the Old Testament Literature
FRLANT	Forschungen zur Religion und Literatur des Alten und Neuen Testaments
HAT	Handbuch zum Alten Testament
HBT	*Horizons in Biblical Theology*
HSM	Harvard Semitic Monographs
HTR	*Harvard Theological Review*
ICC	International Critical Commentary
Int	*Interpretation*
JAAR	*Journal of the American Academy of Religion*
JBL	*Journal of Biblical Literature*
JBQ	*Jewish Bible Quarterly*
JES	*Journal of Ecumenical Studies*

Abbreviations

JETS	*Journal of the Evangelical Theological Society*
JSNT	*Journal for the Study of the New Testament*
JSNTSup	Journal for the Study of the New Testament: Supplement Series
JSOT	*Journal for the Study of the Old Testament*
JSOTSup	Journal for the Study of the Old Testament: Supplement Series
JSSCS	*Journal of the Society for the Study of Christian Spirituality*
JTI	*Journal of Theological Interpretation*
LHBOTS	The Library of Hebrew Bible/Old Testament Studies
LNTS	The Library of New Testament Studies
NCCS	New Covenant Commentary Series
NewDocs	*New Documents Illustrating Early Christianity*
NIB	*The New Interpreter's Bible*
NIBCNT	New International Biblical Commentary on the New Testament
NICNT	New International Commentary on the New Testament
NIDNTT	*New International Dictionary of New Testament Theology*
NIDOTTE	*New International Dictionary of Old Testament Theology and Exegesis*
NIGTC	New International Greek Testament Commentary
NTL	New Testament Library
OBS	Oxford Bible Series
OBT	Overtures to Biblical Theology
OTS	Old Testament Studies
PTMS	Pittsburgh Theological Monograph Series
RB	*Revue biblique*
SBLDS	Society of Biblical Literature Dissertation Series
SBLEJL	Society of Biblical Literature Early Judaism and Its Literature
SBLRBS	Society of Biblical Literature Resources for Biblical Study
SJT	*Scottish Journal of Theology*
SP	Sacra pagina
STAR	Studies in Theology and Religion
TDNT	*Theological Dictionary of the New Testament*
THNTC	Two Horizons New Testament Commentary Series
TNTC	Tyndale New Testament Commentaries
ThTo	*Theology Today*
UF	*Ugarit-Forschungen*
USQR	*Union Seminary Quarterly Review*
VTSup	Vetus Testamentum Supplements
WBC	Word Biblical Commentary
WUNT	Wissenschaftliche Untersuchungen zum Neuen Testament
WW	*Word and World*
ZAW	*Zeitschrift für die alttestamentliche Wissenschaft*

Introduction

A COLLECTION OF ESSAYS titled *The Bible and Spirituality* with a subtitle that speaks of "reading Scripture spiritually" is likely to produce a variety of expectations. It is important, then, at the outset, to be clear about what its contents are and what they are not. They do not constitute a study of how the Bible as a whole has functioned in the history of Christian spirituality or should function for contemporary Christians. Nor are they exercises in the kind of reading of Scripture that pays scant attention to critical study in order to be able to move immediately to application to one's personal devotional life. Instead the essays attempt, from within the context of the academy, responsible readings of Scripture that have as a major focus the study of how particular texts might contribute to a spirituality in which individual and communal flourishing is a major feature.

The essays began as papers produced for an international symposium on the Bible and spirituality at the end of May 2012, hosted by the Centre for the Study of the Bible and Spirituality in the School of Humanities at the University of Gloucestershire, UK. An explanation of this context and occasion may help clarify the nature of the essays. The Centre itself, by bringing together biblical scholars and colleagues from other subject areas within the University who share an interest in spirituality, aims to foster and develop biblical scholarship in relation to spirituality, to facilitate cross-disciplinary scholarship, and to engage in critical and constructive dialogue with contemporary perspectives on spirituality about what is necessary for human flourishing. The Centre was awarded a research grant from Bible Society for a project that pursues these aims and that runs from 2011 to 2014.

At the time the Centre was launched we were aware not only of the general widespread interest in spirituality, where in some parts of Western culture it is seen as replacing institutional religion, but also that the subject had become both an academic discipline in its own right with professional societies, conferences, and journals and a subdiscipline in a variety of other scholarly fields.[1] In regard to biblical studies, we were also aware that, although the Christian tradition has always nurtured an emphasis on spirituality rooted in the Bible and its interpretation, few biblical scholars pursued their work by making connections with either this religious tradition or present-day interest in the broader phenomenon of spirituality. This situation has begun to change and one can now find more works in biblical studies that have the term *spirituality* in their titles. This has been due in no small part to the influence of the pioneering work of Professor Sandra Schneiders, who has advocated readings of Scripture that respect contemporary criteria of interpretation and yet at the same time reflect Scripture's role in mediating the experience of faith.[2]

There is not the space here to document and provide an assessment of how far work in biblical spirituality has progressed and how it relates to another approach that has seen a recent resurgence, namely, theological interpretation of Scripture. It will have to suffice to assert that academic work in biblical spirituality is still in its relatively early stages and that, while there are considerable overlaps between theological and spiritual interpretation, what makes the latter distinctive is its focus on the wisdom of lived experience and practice. Instead, what may be just as helpful for understanding the approach in this volume is a brief further clarification of how thinking about biblical spirituality has developed in the early stages of our own research project. From the outset the writings of three major figures and their definitions of spirituality have been most influential on the shape of the project. Naturally we drew on the work of Sandra Schneiders, who states that "spirituality as lived experience can be defined as conscious involvement in the project of life integration through self-transcendence toward the ultimate value one perceives." She then moves from the general to the particular by making clear that "when the horizon of ultimate value is the triune God revealed in Jesus Christ and communicated through his Holy Spirit, and the project of self-transcendence is the living of the paschal mystery within the context of the church community, the spirituality is specifically Christian and involves the person with God, others and all reality according to the understanding of these realities that is characteristic of Christian faith."[3] We also soon discovered just how much there was to learn about spirituality as lived experience in the magisterial work by Kees Waaijman, *Spirituality: Forms, Foundations, Methods*, with its

---

1. K. Waaijman, "Spirituality—A Multi-faceted Phenomenon," surveyed work on spirituality in twelve different disciplines.

2. Cf. e.g., Schneiders, "*Written That You May Believe*"; "Biblical Spirituality."

3. Schneiders, "Christian Spirituality," 1.

complementary emphasis on transformation as the characteristic feature of this lived experience. For Waaijman the study of spirituality is a multidisciplinary enterprise that has as its object "the divine-human relational process as transformation."[4] Such transformation is operative on five levels, according to Waaijman: in creation, from non-being to being; in re-creation, from being mal-formed to being re-formed; in conformity to a particular model of transformation, say, Torah or Christ; in love and its intimacy; and in glory, a final, completely reciprocal and unhindered transformative relationship.[5]

While Waaijman claims that his use of the term *divine* need not be taken in an exclusively religious or theological sense,[6] in thinking about contemporary dialogue with those who have an interest in a spirituality that does not necessarily include a transcendent source of reality, it was another magisterial work, that of the Canadian philosopher Charles Taylor, in his *Secular Age*, that proved particularly helpful. While ostensibly a tracing of the rise of the secular, his book is at the same time a rich description of what has happened to the spiritual over the last five hundred years of Western civilization, as it illuminates how both believers and unbelievers, preferably in dialogue, have to negotiate the common conditions of a secular age. For Taylor, what both have to negotiate, whether against a transcendent background or within an immanent framework, is the spiritual in the sense of the aspiration for a flourishing existence, which he depicts in terms of "fullness": "Somewhere, in some activity, or condition, lies a fullness, a richness; that is, in that place (activity or condition), life is fuller, richer, deeper, more worthwhile, more admirable, more what it should be."[7] This generic notion of spirituality again has its more specific version within a Christian transcendent framework, and it lends itself to honest discussion and discovery of which perspective and lived experience can respond most profoundly to the aspirations for and dilemmas of human flourishing. It should be noted that the influence of these three thinkers has also made its mark on this volume in that its contributors all work within the parameters of the definitions of spirituality they have supplied and some of the essays offer their own nuancing of one or more of the definitions.

Another early discovery made by the Centre was the existence of two other major groups on the international scene doing research on the Bible and spirituality—one in South Africa with its centre at the University of the

4. Waaijman, *Spirituality*, 6, 312, 424.

5. Ibid., 425–82.

6. Ibid., 427–30.

7. Taylor, *Secular Age*, 5. For further discussion of the relevance of Taylor's work, see Lincoln, "Spirituality in a Secular Age," 61–80.

Free State, Bloemfontein, and the other in the Titus Brandsma Institute at the University of Nijmegen in the Netherlands. This resulted in our Centre, again with financial support from Bible Society, hosting a symposium with representatives from the other two groups at the beginning of May 2010 in order to explore common interests. This was extremely worthwhile, as discussion of papers allowed both overlaps and divergences in our approaches to emerge and we were fortunate to have Kees Waaijman himself as one of the participants and to be able to engage with his encyclopaedic knowledge and profound wisdom. The papers given were revised for publication as a supplement to the journal *Acta Theologica*.[8]

When it came to organizing an international symposium as part of the present research project, we were keen to secure the participation of a broader group of mainstream practitioners of biblical exegesis, interpretation and theology, whose work included the goal of showing how the Bible can be transformative for living, even though some of them might not have explicitly labelled what they do as "spiritual reading." This time we were extremely fortunate to obtain the participation of one of the other major influences on our work, Sandra Schneiders, and to engage with her about some of her more recent thinking. The papers for the symposium, which was held over three days, were distributed in advance to allow maximum time for discussion of each and for reflection on the occasion as a whole. There was a strong sense that we were all pursuing biblical spirituality at at least one of the levels that Schneiders outlines in her essay in this volume—the spirituality that produces the text, the spirituality in the text, and the spirituality that the text produces. At the same time there was enough diversity in approaches to ensure we were not short of convivial and rigorous questioning and debate. Some of the essays show the fruit of that stimulation in their revised forms. Schneiders' essay also reminds us of the crucial role of the imagination and of aesthetics in spirituality, and at the symposium further stimulation was provided by the artwork by which we were surrounded. This was produced by Sheona Beaumont, a professional artist[9] and a PhD student on the Centre's research project, who on the first evening of the symposium also talked about her work on display. Her dissertation will be on biblical imagery in contemporary photographic art, and one of her pieces features on the cover for this volume.

The arrangement of the essays in their revised form here follows a rough canonical ordering of their texts or themes. This means that they begin, somewhat disturbingly, with Stephen Chapman's reflections on

8. *The Spirit that Inspires: Perspectives on Biblical Spirituality*, edited by P. G. R. de Villiers and L. K. Pietersen, Acta Theologica Supplementum 15 (Bloemfontein, South Africa: University of the Free State Press, 2011).

9. See http://www.shospace.co.uk.

the Amalekite texts. Yet any spirituality that has its roots in the Bible will sooner or later need to confront questions about the nature of the God who is revealed there and with whom it claims to be in relationship. How do we read textual portrayals of God's violent side that sanctions Israel's eradication of its enemies? Chapman carefully lays out the evidence and presents some of the interpretative options for handling these texts in the context of how to respond to the presence of radical evil in our world. There follow two essays on Job, whose juxtaposition raises issues about the complex nature of spirituality. Walter Moberly looks at the initial presentation of Job's spirituality (his piety and flourishing), the suspicion raised about whether this is a spirituality that is only using fear of God for its own self-seeking ends, and how it fares when it is put to the test and no longer results in personal well-being. He goes on to argue that the later wisdom poem of Job 28 shows that the same fear of God that was operative when matters went well for Job is precisely what is needed when his life falls apart. Spiritual wisdom in the midst of incomprehensible tragedies consists in maintaining integrity and trust toward God. If Moberly focuses on the narrative presentation of Job and his patience, Susannah Ticciati complements this approach by her examination of the dialogue and Job's expressions of anger in his arguments with God. By focusing on Job's use of first- and second-person pronouns in comparison with the language of his friends, Ticciati proposes that Job eschews generalizations about suffering, refusing to give up on his irreducible identity in his particular inexplicable suffering, and that without his first-person angry complaint to God he would not have received the particular divine response that brings about his transformation. This proposal leads to reflections on the relation between traditional and irreducibly personal language about God within the dynamics of a genuinely transformative relationship. Gordon McConville also draws attention to first-person language, this time in relation to the Psalms where the "I" of the speaker draws the reader into imagining the life of the self before God. In reflecting on how the Psalms understand human flourishing, McConville examines their presentation of the person, that person's consciousness and its transformation. At the same time he indicates how the language of the Psalms has the capacity to transcend particular settings and to engage readers in their own unfinished project of formation, including for Christian readers conformity to the image of Christ.

Taking off from the injunction of one particular psalm to pray for the peace or well-being of Jerusalem (Ps 122), Ellen Davis offers reflections on the spiritual attraction and status of the city and its role both in Christian spirituality and interfaith engagement. Surveying Psalms, Prophets, and Luke-Acts, Davis finds a recurrent theme of lament over, compassion for, and commitment to Jerusalem and then makes the distinctive proposal, via discussion of Ephesians and four psalms, that a renewed Christian practice of singing about Zion with an awareness of global political realities can be a vehicle that enables Christians, alongside Jews and Muslims, to pray for the peace of the city. Barbara Green sees a spiritual reading as aiming to make visible characteristics of God and God's interaction with humans that believers need to ponder and practice. To this end she explores the quality of compassion in the book of Jeremiah in the context of whether and how the hearts of its various characters are changed. In particular, she asks how the prophet's ostensible failure to persuade Zedekiah of his option for survival might be seen as undergirded and overcome by divine and human compassion and as serving to catalyze compassion in readers. One reader of Jeremiah is the biblical character Daniel, and this enables Richard Briggs to pursue his study of the virtuous reader in terms of the sort of reader best placed to achieve spiritual insight and with specific reference to the portrayal of Daniel as a spiritual student of Scripture. After drawing out the nuances in the book of Daniel's characterization of its exemplar of wisdom, Briggs provides a close reading of Dan 9:1–4a, in which Daniel reads a prophecy from Jeremiah, perceives its significance, and is led to repentance and prayer. In the light of this he offers some important reflections about spiritual reading of Scripture.

Sandra Schneiders not only has pioneered work in the study of the Bible and spirituality but also has continually rethought its parameters in an attempt to move research forward. In her essay here she both provides the fruits of her reflections on what biblical spirituality entails and probes further how the encounter between readers and texts can be transformative within a Christian spirituality rooted in the resurrection of Christ. This takes her into a discussion of perception, the spiritual senses, believers' "sense of the faith," imagination, and corporeality that leads finally into reflections on the resurrection narratives as texts and their mediation of the experience of the risen Christ. Schneiders proposes that such texts are to be seen as "theopoetic" in the way that they imaginatively shape readers' experience of God and draw them into a transformative relationship with the Christ who is alive and present.

Spirituality in the popular mind is often thought to have a primarily otherworldly orientation. Michael Gorman tackles this perception head-on as he shows that the narration of even the most intense experiences of transcendence in the New Testament is related to a spirituality of life and mission within this world. He provides four worked examples—a brief analysis of the transfiguration accounts in the Synoptic Gospels, followed by more detailed readings of Paul's experience of the third heaven in 2 Cor

12, the exhortations to seek and set the mind on things above in Col 3, and the seer's vision of the heavenly throne room in Rev 4–5. Gorman indicates how in each case the text or its co-text highlights the implications of an encounter with the glorified Christ for this-worldly existence and summarizes the symbolic universe of New Testament spirituality as involving a pattern of glory/cruciformity/glory.

Stephen Barton's essay draws our attention to the role of the emotions in spirituality and in particular to the centrality of joy in the experience of the early Christian movement. After surveying some of the main features of joy and rejoicing in the Jewish Scriptures that were part of early Christians' inheritance, Barton turns to Luke-Acts and Paul's Letter to the Philippians for his exploration of what might be distinctive about articulations of joy in the New Testament. In the former, joy can be seen as the embodied delight resulting from discernment of and participation in the eschatological transformations of time, space, value, and persons consequent upon the coming of Christ and the Spirit. In the latter, Paul can be seen as offering a pedagogy in joy, where joy reflects an experience of spiritual and material partnership in the advance of the gospel that enables a distinct perspective on one's inhospitable social environment and is set against the vivid felt horizon of participation in the life of heaven. If spirituality is determined by one's ultimate value, Barton concludes by counting the ways in which joy expresses a sharing in the experience of that value understood as eschatological reality christologically defined and pneumatologically received.

By all accounts, not only joy but also love is essential to Christian spirituality. Pieter de Villiers investigates this spiritual quality in what at first sight does not appear to be among the more loving of Paul's communications—the Letter to the Galatians. While questioning whether, from our perspective, Paul always practises what he preaches, de Villiers traces how for the apostle love has its origin in the divine self-giving that brings about a personal participative response, in which Christ becomes a transforming and abiding presence in Paul's life. Christian existence is also shown to be a life of faith working through love, where love as the chief fruit of the Spirit paradoxically enables freedom to be both the fulfilment of the law and voluntary slavery to others and where it restores harmony in the midst of divisions.

With an eye on one of the research project's goals—dialogue between biblical perspectives on spirituality and those of contemporary culture—Andrew Lincoln attempts to see the spiritual wisdom of Colossians in its context in the ancient world as part of a broader discussion of spirituality as represented by the philosophical schools. Lincoln explores three common topics—cosmic spirituality, where alignment with the reality of the cosmos and its fullness is seen as essential for human well-being; the need to learn to die ahead of time if this present life is to be lived to the full; and the ascent to the world above in order to achieve perspective on the realities of earthly life. He proposes that Colossians engages some of the major aspirations for human flourishing of its day as it radically reconfigures and redirects them in the light of its own elaboration of the Pauline gospel of the crucified and risen Christ.

The volume began by relating spirituality to questions of violence and it ends similarly—this time with how spirituality might incorporate the violence that Christians may face as a result of their devotion to Christ. Lloyd Pietersen examines the spirituality of the Pastoral Epistles, particularly the way 2 Tim 3 gives expression to and has been received in a spirituality of persecution. After investigating the relationship of persecution to martyrdom, what can be known about persecution of Christians in the first century, and the invocation of the righteous sufferer of the Psalms, Pietersen turns to how 2 Tim 3:12 is handled in a variety of commentaries from the early centuries to more recent days. He finds a frequent softening of the notion of persecution to the general trials and afflictions Christians undergo and a lack of reflection on the type of spirituality required in the face of actual persecution. A striking exception, which, together with the first-century evidence, raises questions for present-day Christian spirituality, is the literature about the martyrdom of sixteenth-century Anabaptists in which references to 2 Tim 3 are particularly prominent in the narrations of lived experience and persecution is seen as a hallmark of discipleship.

While the essays found here are wide-ranging, they, of course, leave many areas and aspects of the Bible and spirituality to be probed further. These would include—to name but a few—different canonical texts, the relation between Old Testament and New Testament spiritualities, allegorizing in spiritual readings and the relation between contemporary and premodern spiritual readings, the role of gender in spiritual readings, the similarities and differences between theological interpretation and spiritual reading, and readings that contain more explicit interaction with the history of Christian spirituality and with contemporary perspectives on spirituality. Nevertheless, despite the exploratory and highly selective nature of these essays, it is hoped that collectively they demonstrate the importance and fruitfulness of spiritual interpretation for biblical studies and will provide stimulus for other scholars in their own explorations in this area.

Andrew Lincoln, Gordon McConville, and Lloyd Pietersen

1

Perpetual War

The Case of Amalek

Stephen B. Chapman
Duke University

IN THE YEARS FOLLOWING September 11, 2001, no one in the United States (and perhaps the world) has been left untouched by the events of that day. Questions still remain—not only about what took place then and why, but also how America has chosen to respond. Because of America's subsequent actions, the horror of that day has lengthened into a decade plus of war, a weakening of democratic decision-making at home, and an erosion of moral authority abroad. Whether Americans are safer continues to be debated.[1] A much asked question is therefore when or if the so-called "war on terror" *can* end—or whether this war has in fact become "perpetual,"[2] a necessary implicature of an insatiable need for fuels and raw materials at the expense of other nations, who have just as much need but more modest military budgets.[3]

The notion of perpetual war has a peculiar resonance within the Old Testament. Jewish tradition knows only two cases of what is called

---

1. For an official appraisal after the passage of a decade, see the U.S. Department of Homeland Security's report, "Implementing 9/11 Commission Recommendations." The National Security Preparedness Group of the Bipartisan Policy Center simultaneously issued its own, more critical, "Tenth Anniversary Report Card."

2. For descriptions and theories of "perpetual war," see Aravamudan, "Introduction"; Robbins, *Perpetual War*. For explorations of increased militarization in contemporary American life, see Bacevich, *American Militarism*; Wellman, "Is War Normal?"

3. For penetrating reflections on the necessity of perpetual war for modern empires and how capitalism drives militarism, see Hardt and Negri, *Multitude*.

"obligatory war" (*milḥemet miṣwâ*)—as opposed to "discretionary war" (*milḥemet rešût*) or war that may be prosecuted or not on the basis of reasoned deliberation and discerning God's will.[4] The two instances of obligatory war are: first, battle against the indigenous "seven nations" of Canaan, which is thought to remain theoretically in force but no longer be practicable;[5] and, second, perpetual battle against "Amalek," who continues to pose a genuine threat but is challenging to identify. It is this Amalekite tradition that I want to submit to renewed scrutiny in this essay. What are these Amalekite texts about? Is there any way to read them as Scripture in a manner that does not underwrite prejudice and promote genocide? How might these texts aid reflection about the reality of perpetual war in the contemporary world? There are four key texts: Exod 17:8–16; Num 14:39–45; Deut 25:17–19; and 1 Sam 15. I will briefly describe each of these texts in turn and then comment on their interpretation, both singly and in relationship with each other.[6]

In Exod 17 the people of Israel are moving through the wilderness, out of Egypt but not yet at the promised land. The first part of the chapter details internal quarreling within the community, the dissension arising from their lack of sufficient water. The people's criticism ultimately targets Moses, who voices his concern to God: "What shall I do with this people? Before long they will be stoning me" (v. 4). The people also doubt God's ability to care for them. But God arranges for Moses to locate water by striking a rock with his staff—the same staff with which he had parted the sea so that the Israelites could escape the Egyptian army (v. 5; cf. 14:16). In this way the motifs of staff and water recall the exodus even as they imply Israel's need for a further deliverance.[7]

In the second half of Exod 17 the narrative describes another threat to Israel in the wilderness. This time the threat is external rather than internal: the Amalekites attack Israel at Rephidim. No reason for this attack is given or even implied by the text. But again Moses and his staff (v. 9) provide what is needed. Moses climbs a hill and raises his hands

---

4. Carmy, "Origin of Nations," 64; Firestone, "Holy War," 959–60.

5. Thus Maimonides; see Carmy, "Origin of Nations," 65–66; Hunter, "(De)Nominating Amalek," 103.

6. For significant studies, see Allister, "Amalekite Genocide"; Cohen, "Remembrance of Amalek"; Feldman, *Remember Amalek*; Langner, "Remembering Amalek"; Levenson, "Is There a Counterpart?"; Lipton, "Remembering Amalek"; Noort, "Josua und Amalek"; Robinson, "Israel and Amalek"; Rooze, *Amalek*; Rudavsky, "Defense of Tradition"; Schmitt, "Geschichte vom Sieg"; Schuil, *Amalek*; Severin-Kaiser, "Gedenke dessen"; Stump, "Problem of Evil"; Tamir, "Remember Amalek"; Tanner, *Amalek*.

7. Coats, *Exodus*, 142.

(v. 11), apparently holding the staff. As long as he is able to do so, the men of Israel, led by Joshua down below, gain the advantage in the battle. Moses' arms tire, however, and so Aaron and Hur, who have accompanied him up the mountainside, sit him down and support his hands on either side, enabling an Israelite victory. Once more, then, the chapter illustrates how God employs Moses for the purpose of protecting the Israelites. The mention of Moses' staff and arm recall when he used them before, during the crossing of the sea (Exod 14:16, 21, 26–27).[8] This time Moses has needed the assistance of Joshua, Aaron, and Hur, but—just as in the previous story in this chapter—Moses and his staff represent and channel God's power. Only because of Moses' gestures on the hillside is Joshua eventually able to overcome the Amalekites. Even so, it is interesting that the Hebrew text describes Joshua's victory as "weakening" ($\sqrt{hl\check{s}}$) the Amalekites (Exod 17:13), not "defeating" them (as the NRSV has it). This "weakening" is still military in nature and apparently devastating, as the final phrase "by the sword" indicates (cf. Isa 14:12). But Israel's victory is oddly muted.

The major ethical difficulty comes at the conclusion of this battle account. God then tells Moses: "Write this as a remembrance [*zikkārôn*] in a book and make sure Joshua hears it: I will utterly erase the memory of Amalek from under heaven" (Exod 17:14). And so Moses builds an altar in response to what has transpired; he names the altar and explains it as meaning "the LORD will be at war with Amalek from generation to generation" (Exod 17:16). This is the verse in the Old Testament that immediately comes to mind in any discussion of perpetual war. What does it mean that God has apparently singled out one particular people for destruction? And why does God determine that this war will endure forever? Does this text really speak of divine genocide?

Numbers 14 is all the more important because it is frequently overlooked. Despite a divine warning not to approach the promised land through the territory belonging to the Amalekites and Canaanites (Num 14:25), and an additional Mosaic plea not to proceed (Num 14:41–43), the people make an ill-advised attempt to do so. They are cut down *'ad-haḥŏrmâ*, and while this expression most likely contains a place name,[9] it is also possible that *ḥŏrmâ* functions as some kind of modifier (= "to completion"?). The Hebrew root, at any rate, is the same as that of *ḥērem* or "the ban," the ancient military practice entailing the killing of non-combatants. It is also unclear how Num 14 is to be read in relation to Exod 17. Perhaps at one time Num 14 represented a parallel tradition regarding an Israelite–Amalekite battle.

8. Fretheim, *Exodus*, 192.
9. Deut 1:44; Judg 1:17.

3

However, its present placement in the pentateuchal narrative suggests that it depicts an inappropriate action by Israel—not only by attempting to enter the land prematurely but also in carrying out the divine enmity against Amalek set forth in Exod 17.

Deuteronomy 25 arguably makes the ethical challenge both better and worse. Deuteronomy emphasizes that responsibility for carrying out the divine judgment against Amalek belongs to every Israelite: "when the LORD your God gives you [sg.] rest from all your enemies around you in the land that LORD your God is giving you as a hereditary portion to possess, you [sg.] shall erase the memory of Amalek from under heaven; don't forget!" (v. 19).[10] The judgment against Amalek now becomes a commandment given to Israel, and not merely a description of enduring divine antagonism.

The Deuteronomy passage also offers information not included in Exodus. Amalek "did not fear God" (Deut 25:18). Amalek is said to have "happened upon" Israel (√qrh), a verb that underscores the unexpected nature of the attack. Moreover, Deuteronomy specifies that the attack occurred when Israel was "hungry and tired," and that Amalek "cut off" (√znb Piel; cf. Josh 10:19) the rear of the Israelite line. The use of the root √ḥšl (Niphal) in this passage, apparently for something like "stragglers," is a *hapax legomenon* and recalls the use of the similar root √ḥlš for Joshua's "weakening" of Amalek in Exod 17:13.[11] Yet there is no "perpetual war" in Deuteronomy; its version of the command to "erase the memory" of Amalek is tied to Israel's entry into the land. Curiously, however, the command is described as coming into force not during the process of Israel's battle for the land but afterwards, when Israel has been given "rest" from its enemies all around. Deuteronomy makes it seem as if Israel is fully justified in despising the Amalekite attack, and simultaneously that the divine command is one of observance rather than vengeance: viz., when you are finally at peace, do not forget to recall just how great the threat was and how God brought you to safety. One important point to stress is that neither Exod 17 nor Deut 25 uses the term *ḥērem* to describe how God or Israel is to respond to the Amalekites.

1 Sam 15 plays an important role in the discussion precisely because it does depict a response of *ḥērem* to an Amalekite threat. At the outset

---

10. The book of Deuteronomy switches frequently between singular and plural, so that one cannot lay too much stress on the difference in number. Still, I think there is a nuance to the use of the singular in this passage—similar to that within the Ten Commandments (Deut 5), in which the singular is used even though a group is being addressed.

11. Some interpreters (e.g., Cassuto) have suggested the possibility here of intentional wordplay between the two passages; in Deut 25 the term *hannehĕšālîm* seems somewhat parallel to the phrase *'āyēp wĕyāgēa'* or "faint and weary." For discussion, see Houtman, *Exodus*, 2:384–85; Novick, "Amaleq's Victims," 611–15.

of this chapter (15:2–3) the prophet Samuel reports God's intention to punish the Amalekites:

> Thus says the LORD of hosts, "I will punish the Amalekites for what they did in opposing the Israelites when they came up out of Egypt. Now go and attack Amalek, and proscribe [NJPS, √ḥrm Hiphil; NRSV: "utterly destroy"] all that they have; do not spare them, but kill both man and woman, child and infant, ox and sheep, camel and donkey.

Saul engages the Amalekites victoriously, but he does not do what he has been told. He spares Agag, the Amalekite king, as well as the best of the livestock and "all that was valuable" (15:9). Instead, Saul and the people only destroy what is "despised and worthless."[12] When challenged by Samuel, Saul makes excuses. Although the sincerity of these excuses is much debated exegetically,[13] Saul's patent disobedience is the last straw for Samuel and God, resulting in their rejection of his kingship.

Two points bear further mention: first, Samuel apparently rectifies Saul's omission by butchering Agag before the altar of the LORD. It must be acknowledged that the particular verb at issue in this action, often translated "hew" (√ššp, Piel; NRSV: "Samuel hewed Agag in pieces . . . "; NJPS: "cut down") is difficult and otherwise unknown.[14] But Samuel's preceding comment makes Agag's death likely: "As your sword has made women childless, so your mother shall be childless among women" (15:33). Second, the beginning of the chapter makes an explicit reference to the Amalekite attack upon Israel at the time of the exodus and enjoins ḥērem as the appropriate response. Forms of the root √ḥrm are used eight times throughout 1 Sam 15. Thus 1 Sam 15 appears to depict the very action warranted and commanded in Exod 17 and Deut 25. The commentary literature consistently construes the relationship between the three texts in this fashion. According to this commonly held perspective, both Exod 17 and Deut 25 command genocide, and 1 Sam 15 enacts it.

The moral problem emerging from this line of interpretation has been particularly acute within Judaism, since the stipulations of Deut 25 have secured a place within the 613 traditional religious laws (or *mitzvot*) of the Pentateuch, and since all of these passages form a regular part of the

---

12. Also in 1 Sam 15:9, the phrase is syntactically difficult; this translation is based on the Greek text of Vaticanus. See McCarter, *1 Samuel*, 262.

13. For a reading sympathetic to Saul, see Gunn, *King Saul*, 70–75.

14. However, the root √ššp does find attestation in post-biblical Hebrew, with the meaning "sever" or "dismember."

synagogue lectionary.[15] In fact the synagogue lectionary already moves in an interpretive and apologetic direction, assigning Deut 25 and 1 Sam 15 for the Sabbath before Purim. Purim remembers the story told in Esther, and the villain of Esther is "Haman son of Hammedatha the Agagite" (Esth 3:1). "Agagite" appears to refer to Agag, the Amalekite king whom Saul neglects to kill. So by a kind of transitive property of exegesis, one gains hermeneutical guidance for 1 Samuel from the book of Esther: viz., this is why it is in fact necessary for there to be perpetual war against Amalek, and in turn why Saul was wrong to relax the stricture, because Esther shows us only too well what these people are like when they get the chance.

Yet the really striking thing about traditional Jewish interpretation of the Amalekite texts is how seriously they are perceived to contravene Judaism's core humanitarian values.[16] Jewish tradition attempts to meet the challenge of these texts largely by moving in two directions: one realistic and one symbolic.[17] The realistic move searches for some reason or combination of reasons to fault the Amalekites and defend God's judgment against them. The symbolic reading extends the divine antagonism of these passages to other people, nations, or political forces that set themselves up against God, especially those that intend the destruction of the Jewish people. In this way the label "Amalek" is still used today as a characterization of antisemites and a justification for religiously based war, both spiritual and physical. At the same time, the prominence of these texts in the Jewish lectionary has stimulated searching moral reflection and generated many attempts to meet the ethical challenge of these texts while also retaining them as authoritative Scripture.

I find myself wondering whether the absence of the Amalekite texts from the Christian lectionary has by contrast contributed to a lack of resources within the church to engage the issue of perpetual war.[18] There was a time when these texts were very well known in Christianity; the story of Moses raising his arms is already treated in the Letter of Barnabas (12:2–3, 8) as a typological prefiguration of Jesus on the cross. Subsequent early church theologians ring the changes on the various features of the story in

15. Garber, "Amalek," 147, 152.

16. For further wrestling with Judaism's tradition of humanitarianism more broadly, particularly in light of contemporary political events in the Middle East, see Carmy, "Origin of Nations"; Eisen, *Peace and Violence*; Garber and Zuckerman, *Double Takes*; Leibowitz, *Judaism*; Schiffmann and Wolowelsky, *War and Peace*; Sprinzak, *Israel's Radical Right*.

17. Sagi, "Punishment of Amalek."

18. On the selectivity of the Revised Common Lectionary when it comes to biblical accounts of violence and warfare, see Jenkins, *Laying Down*, 201–8. As he notes, the Amalek texts do not appear at all.

figural terms, noting especially the similarity between the name of Joshua and that of Jesus (they are in fact identical in Greek):

> When the people waged war with Amalek, and the son of Nave, Jesus by name, led the fight, Moses himself prayed to God, stretching out both hands, and Aaron supported them the whole day. . . . For if he gave up any part of this sign, which was an imitation of the Cross, the people were beaten, but if he remained in this form Amalek was defeated, and he who prevailed, prevailed by the Cross. For it was not because Moses so prayed that the people were strong, but because while one who bore the name of Jesus was in the forefront of the battle, he himself made the sign of the Cross.[19]

As is already evident, sometimes this typology moved in an overtly supersessionistic direction, in which Joshua, as a type of Christ, is viewed as accomplishing what Moses was unable to do. For example, Irenaeus describes how "those who believed in him were put in possession of the heritage not by Moses, but by Jesus, who delivered us from Amalek and brings us to the Kingdom of the Father."[20] But the typology could also be employed without this same supersessionistic move. Justin, for example, treats the Amalek episode in Exodus as descriptive of

> the two advents of Christ . . . symbolically announced and told beforehand by what Moses and Joshua did. For the one of them, stretching out his hands, remained till evening on the hill, his hands being supported, and this reveals a type of nothing else than the Cross: the other, whose name was altered to Jesus, led the fight, and Israel conquered. Now this took place in both these holy men and prophets of God, that you may perceive how one of them could not bear up both the mysteries: I mean the type of the Cross and the type of the Name. For this is, was, and shall be, the strength of him alone, whose name every power dreads.[21]

In this instance Jesus still completes what neither Moses nor Joshua could fully accomplish, but both Moses and Joshua nevertheless partake in the reality of Christ and Christ's work in the world.

Further reflecting in this vein, Origen develops his own interpretation of Exod 17 as an illustration of Phil 2:9–11:

19. Justin Martyr, *Dialogue with Trypho*, 90.4–5. For convenience I cite this patristic passage and those following from the illuminating treatment found in Daniélou, *Shadows*, beginning at 233.

20. Irenaeus, *Demonstration*, 40, as cited in Daniélou, *Shadows*, 237.

21. Justin Martyr, *Dialogue with Trypho*, 111.2, as cited in Daniélou, *Shadows*, 235.

> God has given to our Lord and Saviour Jesus Christ a name which is above every name. That is why, at the name of Jesus every knee should bow, of those that are in heaven, on earth and under the earth. . . . We meet the name of Jesus for the first time when we see him as head of the army. From this first acquaintance with the name of Jesus I learn the mystery of its symbolism: Jesus is the leader of the army.[22]

What all of these Christian interpretations share, in addition to their basic typological impulse, is a symbolic understanding of Amalek as a representation of evil, and as such they possess common ground with the symbolic stream of Jewish interpretation.

With the advent of modernity this figural dimension of Christian interpretation was of course largely lost, which intensified efforts to find more realistic solutions—to the extent that the Amalekite texts were remembered at all. For example, some historical-critical scholars have postulated that Israel had likely already tangled with Amalek in the wilderness (e.g., Fritz) and that disputes over pastures and springs would have been common occurrences (e.g., Fensham).[23] But for all the apologetic speculation along these lines, other interpreters have countered with readings exacerbating Israel's own culpability. Already in the eighteenth century Reimarus treated Amalek as the victim of the story: the Amalekites were only trying to defend their territory against "the kind of thieving people who did not observe human rights and sought for themselves a dwelling place by force."[24] More recently Alastair Hunter has also fingered Israel as the guilty party: "even in the Bible's own terms the story is of a vast army of people making incursions into a territory which is not theirs and no doubt making huge demands on the economic resources of a region not famous for agricultural surpluses. The Amalekites' *defence* of their *home territory* is hardly surprising . . ."[25]

No wonder, then, that several recent publications have taken up the moral dilemmas presented by the Old Testament with renewed vigor, particularly with regard to the question of genocide. Paul Anderson compares genocide to the teaching of Jesus (some comparison!) and unsurprisingly finds Jesus preferable, leading Anderson to conclude that one

---

22. Origen, *Homilies on Exodus*, 1.1, 3, as cited in Daniélou, *Shadows*, 239. As Daniélou observes, Origen is noticing that the name Joshua first appears in the Bible at Exod 17:9.

23. For these and other examples, see Houtman, *Exodus*, 2:377.

24. German original: "ein solch räubrisches Volk das kein Völkerrecht achtete, und sich durch Gewalt einen Wohnsitz suchte," as reproduced in Houtman, *Exodus*, 2:377 n. 20.

25. Hunter, "(De)Nominating," 99. Hunter's emphasis.

must "recognize the anthropomorphic projections involved in the narrative traditions" of both testaments.[26] Eric Seibert goes even further, arguing for a thoroughgoing distinction between the "textual God" and the "real God."[27] And Thom Stark draws the logical conclusion to this line of thinking:

> [M]y contention is that God never did command the Israelites to slaughter entire peoples wholesale. These accounts reflect a standard imperialistic ideology that Israel shared with many of its ancient neighbors, and I read them as products of ancient culture, not as products of pure divine revelation. Therefore, my claim is not that I know better than God, but that, by God's design, we all know better than those who wrongly killed women and children in God's name.[28]

Here is accordingly the apparent shape of the interpretive dilemma at present: either affirming that the Bible commands genocide or dismissing certain portions of the Old Testament as inaccurate representations of God's character and will. Are there really no other options? Let us turn to the texts again.

With regard to Exod 17, some of its literary features already suggest a move in the direction of the symbolic interpretation well represented in Judaism and Christianity, particularly in premodern interpretation. For example, I have earlier called attention to the presence of Moses' staff, which not only links the Amalek story with the story of Massa and Meribah, but also relates back to Israel's crossing of the sea during the exodus. To my mind this detail alone provides strong evidence in favor of understanding Amalek as "Pharaoh redivivus," as Cornelis Houtman has argued.[29]

As Benno Jacob has also perceptively noted, "Amalek" is almost always called "Amalek" in these texts, and not "the children of Amalek" or "the Amalekites."[30] That rhetorical focus on the eponymous founder of the people group moves in the direction of a symbolic understanding, too. Furthermore, it is important to recall that human warfare is not actually commanded in Exod 17. Instead, Moses says that *God* will be at war with Amalek from generation to generation. This theocentric focus additionally

26. Anderson, "Genocide," 51.

27. Seibert, *Divine Behavior*, 169–81.

28. Stark, *Human Faces*, 150. Cf. Morriston, "Ethical Criticism," 133.

29. Houtman, *Exodus*, 2:377: "[I]t would seem that according to the writer it was not Amalek's fear of competition or violation of its territory that provoked the attack. He saw Amalek as the antagonist of the fulfillment of the promises to the patriarchs. Amalek is Pharaoh redivivus, even more, he is *the* enemy." (Houtman's emphasis.)

30. Jacob, *Exodus*, 505–6.

reinforces a symbolic reading.[31] Then one notes the description of the battle itself, which pays more attention to Moses' gestures than to the physical fighting. Indeed, the point of the story would seem to be that his gestures, however they are understood (magic? prayer? visual encouragement to the troops?), are more important than the size of his army or his tactics. In other words, the story actually turns on the superiority of piety over power, of gestures over weapons, of arms over armaments.

The divine judgment against Amalek is also highly metaphorical. God does *not* say that he will "kill" Amalekites. In Exodus God says: "I will utterly erase the memory of Amalek from under heaven" (Exod 17:14). In Deuteronomy the Israelites are similarly told "you shall erase the remembrance of Amalek from under heaven" (Deut 25:19). Both these texts use the verb √*mḥh*, which means to rinse off, wipe off, erase.[32] But what do these texts mean by "erasing a memory"?[33] To be sure, in Exodus the concluding statement of chapter 17 mentions "war" (*milḥamâ*), and an account of an actual battle with the Amalekites precedes this divine judgment. So the verb in this context probably does mean something like "obliterate," but still only indirectly and figuratively.[34]

31. As does the LXX rendering of Exod 17:16: "The war of the Lord shall be with Amalek from generation to generation with a secret power." The phrase "with a secret power" is not found in the MT.

32. The NRSV and the NJPS translations obscure the metaphor by translating "blot out," an English verb that they also sometimes use to translate verbs of killing; e.g., in Exod 23:23 for √*kḥd* Hiphil, "annihilate."

33. Stern, *Ḥērem*, 177–78, argues that the biblical writers have substituted "memory" for "name," given the established idiom "erase the name" (Akkadian: *šuma pašāṭu*) within the ancient Near East. According to Stern, this substitution occurs elsewhere in the Hebrew Bible, and thus ought to be reflected in modern translations: "the translation 'memory' misrepresents the idiom and obscures its background and true meaning." For Stern a command "not to forget to erase the memory" simply makes no sense. Stern understands the command instead to enjoin literal destruction and death. It should be noted, however, that Stern argues this point on the basis of an originalist hermeneutic: "The writers of Deut 25:19 and Exod 17:14 were not interested in memory but in Amalek's existence as a fighting force." By contrast I have no interest in guessing at an ancient writer's intention, particularly when such an intention is framed in opposition to the biblical texts we now have. I prefer in this instance to view the texts as making a more sophisticated theological point. The relationship between "memory" and existence is obviously a close one anyway; not to be remembered is sometimes clearly equivalent to destruction (e.g., Ezek 21:37; 25:10 [both references regarding the Ammonites]). "Memory" and "name" function as synonyms in Exod 3:15; Isa 26:8; Hos 12:6 [5]; Pss 102:13 [12]; 135:13; Prov 10:7; Job 18:17.

34. To the extent that some historical-critical scholars have viewed Exod 17:14–16 as a secondary addition to the narrative in 17:8–13, then the secondary addition would also appear to push in the direction of a more symbolic understanding; see Houtman, *Exodus*, 2:373–78. MacDonald, "Anticipations," 16, points out that √*mḥh* and *sēper*

The Amalekite verses in Deuteronomy come immediately after Deut 25:16, which concludes a discussion of dishonest weights by stating how "all who do such things, all who act dishonestly, are abhorrent to the LORD."[35] Within the context of this chapter, Amalek then seems to provide yet another example of abhorrent behavior. Some kind of comparison internal to the chapter is also suggested by the use of √*mḥh* in the discussion of levirate marriage in verses 5–10.[36] In these verses √*mḥh* describes the erasure of a man's name should he die without a son. Similarly, the appeal in verses 17–19 is primarily to memory rather than killing: "remember," the passage begins; "don't forget," it concludes.[37]

The same Hebrew verb √*mḥh* is used three times in the Flood account of Genesis (6:7; 7:4, 23), a context that clearly implies killing. But in these instances the verb is used without reference to *zēker*, "memory." The primary use of the verb √*mḥh* in the Old Testament is actually with reference to writing, not battle or killing. The two conceptions "writing down" and "wiping off" are related to each other as antonyms, both used in relation to texts (Num 5:23). What is being commanded in Exod 17 and Deut 25 is therefore suggestive of *textual* obliteration, but such erasure properly requires a written text. In order for Amalek to be erased, it first needs to be written down. There is thus a neat little irony at the center of this divine judgment on Amalek: Amalek must be remembered in order to be forgotten—or is it to be forgotten in order to be remembered? Either way, the implication is that such evil cannot finally be eliminated but only repeatedly renounced, and that such renunciation properly occurs literarily.

This viewpoint is not some overly clever, modern scholarly construal but in fact a living aspect of Jewish religious practice. At the beginning of his daily work, a Jewish scribe even today will write the name Amalek on a scrap-piece of paper and then draw several lines through the word, eliminating it.[38] Preserved in this action is not only the paradox of "remembering to forget," but also the close relationship between the Amalek story and text production. The book of Esther and the festival of Purim might be taken as another combined example of how forgetting ironically requires remembering, although

---

appear together in Exod 32:31 as well.

35. Abarbanel, *Commentary on the Torah*, on Deut 25:17.

36. So, too, Abarbanel, *Commentary*, on Deut 25:17; cf. Lipton, "Remembering," 150–51.

37. Robinson, "Israel," 18, offers the cogent point that this emphasis on memory may also stem from the absence of living Amalekites at the time the texts were put into their present form. 1 Chr 4:43 suggests that the Amalekites may have disappeared as a distinct people group during the reign of Hezekiah.

38. Lipton, "Remembering," 153.

an example focused more on textual use than textual production. Hamaan, descendant of Amalek, is remembered by name during Purim celebrations for the purpose of being denounced, that is, actively "forgotten."[39]

All of these features thus lend strength to a symbolic reading of the pentateuchal Amalekite texts. However, there is another feature that may provide help if one reads the story more realistically, something already mentioned: namely, that the texts provide no explicit explanation for Amalek's attack. Countless interpreters, Jewish and Christian, have attempted to fill in that silence in the text, but it seems to me that the silence is crucially important in its own right. In other words, the Amalekite attack may have been perceived as particularly egregious precisely because there was no cause for it. The Israelites were apparently not in fact seeking to enter Amalekite territory, nor were the Amalekites defending it.[40] Moreover, as Isaac Abarbanel already pointed out in the fifteenth century, Israel did not possess any land of its own yet, so the Amalekites could not have been motivated by territorial expansion.[41] They simply attacked to attack, without cause and without warning. The abruptness of this story's introduction into the Exodus narrative thus mirrors the abruptness of the Amalekite incursion, a feature which is then emphasized by Deut 25's use of √qrh. In the end this aspect of the tradition may well be the main reason why Amalek was considered deserving of especially harsh punishment.[42]

Of course, the entirely reasonable response to this suggestion, or to any suggestion that the Amalekites may have had it coming, is that no act, however despicable, justifies the slaughter of "man and woman, child and infant, ox and sheep, camel and donkey" (1 Sam 15:3). But this is where the relationship between 1 Sam 15 and the Amalekite texts also needs to be questioned rather than assumed. Because 1 Sam 15 explicitly characterizes God's command to Saul as punishment for the Amalekite attack on Israel during the exodus, interpreters have almost always used 1 Sam 15 in order to explain the meaning of Exod 17 and/or Deut 25, both of which, as we have seen, are actually somewhat vague. In a way, the move to read these passages together functions as a kind of "intertextual" or "canonical" interpretive

39. As Tanner, *Amalek*, 102–3, has suggested, there are considerable resources here for reflecting on post-traumatic stress disorder, particularly in treating soldiers returning from war. Traumatic memories cannot simply be blocked or ignored; healing involves handling memories productively, not ignoring or suppressing them. Cf. Siegel, "Zakhor."

40. Jacob, *Exodus*, 501–2. Numbers 14 is the exception, and in that case Israel is unsuccessful.

41. Abarbanel, *Commentary*, on Deut 25:17. Cf. Sagi, "Punishment," 325.

42. MacDonald, *Not Bread Alone*, 94–95, relates Amalek's violation to Deuteronomy's broader emphasis on hospitality toward Israel.

strategy, and it is therefore interesting to see how prevalent it is among histor-ical-critical scholars who otherwise sternly resist that sort of impulse.[43]

Yet there are exegetical reasons to question this intertextual associa-tion. Despite referring to an Amalekite *attack*, 1 Sam 15 does not actually allude to any divine *command* earlier than Samuel's directive to Saul. In other words, while God's judgment against the Amalekites at the outset of 1 Sam 15 is justified by reference to an earlier attack in the wilderness, Saul's duty is not portrayed as the fulfillment of any standing Mosaic directive. The logic of the Samuel text turns instead on Saul's successful enforcement of ḥērem, a word and concept absent from the pentateuchal Amalekite texts but quite prominent throughout 1 Sam 15. At issue is "Saul's disobedience, not Amalek's wickedness."[44] Rather than taking 1 Sam 15 as an illustration of what the pentateuchal Amalekite texts mean, it seems more appropriate to view 1 Sam 15 as independently employing the tradition of an Amalekite threat, and inflecting it according to the logic of ḥērem in order to demon-strate Saul's lack of fitness as king.

There is also a historical issue at stake: one cannot assume that Exod 17 and Deut 25 predate 1 Sam 15 as texts or even as traditions. As Philip Stern has argued, 1 Sam 15 may well predate the pentateuchal Amalekite texts, in which case it could be all the more significant that ḥērem is absent from them.[45] Instead of 1 Sam 15 making concrete the vague language of Exod 17 and Deut 25, it could well be that Exod 17 and Deut 25 have taken a legacy of animosity toward Amalek, portrayed especially in 1 Sam 15, and sought to make sense of that legacy by rendering it in more symbolic terms.

It is perhaps just as important to emphasize that even in 1 Sam 15, there is no sense that the divine command to annihilate the Amalekites is to be repeated, let alone become a "perpetual war." Moreover, identifying the Amalekites as appropriate objects of ḥērem serves again to limit ḥērem as well as to authorize it; for example, Saul and David do not invoke ḥērem against the Philistines or other people groups.[46] Finally, even Samuel's "hew-ing" of Agag (whatever it was) was apparently not thought to exterminate the Amalekites completely, because the Amalekites reappear later in the narrative.[47]

---

43. E.g., Edelman, "Saul's Battle," 75; Kang, *Divine War*, 125; McCarter, *1 Samuel*, 15.

44. Lipton, "Remembering," 150 n. 24.

45. Stern, Ḥērem, 176. Cf. his "1 Samuel 15," 414.

46. Goldingay, *OT Theology*, 3:571–72.

47. Amalek's repeated return within the biblical narrative is stressed by Knight, "Coming to Terms."

In 1 Sam 30 David pursues the Amalekites after their raid on Ziklag. David not only brings home all of the spoil from his victory, he makes sure that it is shared among those who have stayed at home as well as those who have participated in the raid. What David does not do is to invoke *ḥērem* against the Amalekites, as his appropriation of the spoil makes clear. There is no sense of a Mosaic injunction to kill every Amalekite in 1 or 2 Samuel. First Samuel 30:17 does say that "not one" of the Amalekites escaped, but then gamely adds "except four hundred young men, who mounted camels and fled." In a further irony, the first chapter of 2 Sam has a young Amalekite report to David that he has fled from Saul's defeat at Mount Gilboah, and that he was the one to deliver the death blow to Saul, at Saul's request, subsequently taking Saul's royal crown and armlet (2 Sam 1:10). Exegetes debate whether this Amalekite is telling the truth, since his account varies from that of the narrator in 1 Sam 31.[48] Be that as it may, significant for my present purpose is that David has the Amalekite killed for shedding the blood of the LORD's anointed, and not because he was an Amalekite and therefore stood under pain of death already.

There is no getting around the fact that all of these Amalekite texts offer a troubling portrait of God, Israel, and the life of faith. But I hope that my discussion of them has pinpointed several interpretive moves that can alleviate at least some of the difficulty. First, 1 Sam 15 does not have to be read, and probably should not be read, as an illustration of Exod 17 and Deut 25. Second, both Exod 17 and Deut 25 invite a symbolic interpretation of Amalek in which physical violence does not necessarily have a place. To be sure, these texts still entail the demonization of an "other,"[49] and the history of their interpretation reads in part like a catalogue of horrors. Catholics and Protestants have used these texts to incite violence against each other for centuries; Puritan New Englanders adapted the rhetoric to justify warfare against Native Americans; Afrikaaners used it of Zulus; Christians and Jews continue to use the term of Muslim Arabs; Hutu leaders invoked it against Tutsi victims in the Rwandan genocide; in recent years it has even been employed to smear homosexuals and liberal Jews in Israel; and so it goes.[50] But "Amalek" can also be understood as representing the same kind of primordial, spiritual resistance to God signaled by New Testament references to "rulers and powers" (Col 1:16; cf. Rom 8:38, "powers"; Eph

48. Andersson, *Untamable Texts*, 111–15, 179–98; Arnold, "Amalekite's Report."

49. Cromer, "Amalek as Other." Cromer helpfully distinguishes between primary and secondary "othering."

50. For these and other examples, see Corrigan, "Amalek"; Cromer, "Amalek," 195–98; and especially Jenkins, *Laying Down*.

6:12, "the cosmic powers of this present darkness").[51] The narrative account in Exod 17 already warrants this approach by depicting how the power of faith extends beyond military might. Later interpreters strengthened the approach by viewing Amalek's destruction eschatologically (*Barn.* 12:9), building on the cryptic reference in Num 24:20.[52]

Third, to the extent that Exod 17 and Deut 25 continue to be read realistically, as historical or historically oriented narratives, then their animosity toward Amalek needs to be viewed as most likely a response to Amalek's violation of accepted norms and conventions in the ancient world regarding warfare. Amalek attacked without warning, from the rear, targeting the weak. It was not defending itself or seeking material gain. It was seeking advantage without regard to the rules and customs of engagement.

Fourth, it is rather stunning to discover that Gen 36:12 traces Amalek's lineage to Esau.[53] Both Israel and Amalek are descendents of Abraham and Isaac![54] So although the demonization of Amalek is real, it carries with it an impulse toward self-examination. Is Israel finally completely different from Amalek? How could that be, since they both descend from common stock? What is the mysterious factor in history that turns one part of a single family into an "Israel" and another into an "Amalek"?[55] Such questions are intensified by the placement of the Amalek episode in Exodus directly after the account of communal rebellion at Massah and Meribah. Amalek's "chance" assault thus occurs opportunistically at a time when Israel has weakened itself through communal dissension. In this way the narrative may be placing some of the responsibility for Amalek's attack at Israel's own doorstep.[56]

Fifth, to the extent that this biblical tradition is understood as commending literal violence, it must be stressed that this violence, while real and troubling, is nevertheless characterized as self-defense and not as aggression. The proportionality and timing of that violence can continue to be questioned—can self-defense ever legitimately be "perpetual"?—but from this perspective the Amalek traditions can only be read as sanctioning defensive warfare in response to an attack, not as providing a warrant for military action against an enemy who has not yet attacked or represents

51. See Neufeld, *"Put On the Armour."* Stern, "1 Samuel 15," similarly explores the cosmic and mythic overtones of Amalek's behavior and identity in the Hebrew Bible.

52. For other examples, also within Jewish tradition, see Kugel, *Bible,* 364–65.

53. On later rabbinic debate regarding whether to include Amalek among the children of Esau, see Carmy, "Origin of Nations," 87 n. 54.

54. Cohen, "Remembering," 296–97.

55. The family link between Israel and Amalek also makes Amalek's hostility even worse because it is therefore fratricidal. See Carmy, "Origin of Nations," 81.

56. Severin-Kaiser, "Gedenke," 164.

some merely worrisome threat.[57] Numbers 14 points in the same direction by offering a cautionary tale of Israel's military overreaching.[58]

Benno Jacob emphasizes how Amalek's attack in Exodus transpires just before Israel is to arrive at Sinai, when Israel was in effect on a sacred pilgrimage. Jacob therefore understands the attack as an effort to keep Israel from becoming Israel, from becoming the people of God.[59] This interpretive logic helps to illuminate why Amalek has routinely been associated with antisemitism in Jewish tradition, and why Amalek has figured prominently in Jewish reflections on Hitler and the Holocaust.[60]

Christian reflection on these passages will also need to consider whether there is not in fact a radical evil present in the world, the kind of evil that opposes the merciful work of God, and ponder how that evil can best be "erased." For some Christians, such erasure is legitimately pursued through violence and the militarism of the nation-state. For my part, I fear instead that the U.S. response to 9/11 has looked more like that of Amalek—a "pre-emptive strike" that targeted the weak—than that of Moses, holding out his arms in faith. The crime of Amalek is precisely the sin of militarism, and the duty of the people of God is to oppose such militarism rather than to advance it. No biblical interpreter has perceived this inner logic better than Samson Raphael Hirsch, the leading figure of nineteenth-century Jewish neo-orthodoxy:

> Amalek alone did not fear God. . . . Amalek alone was heir to that spirit that chooses the sword as its lot, seeks renown in laurels of blood, and strives to realize the ambition . . . with which Nimrod began world history. This ambition is realized by destroying the welfare of nations and the happiness of men. This seeking renown by the force of arms is the first and last enemy of human happiness and Divine kingship on earth. The Pharaohs used ruthless force to further their own interests, and it was in their interest to keep their slaves alive. They were even capable of being friends of freedom, if this served their interest. But Amalek's glory-seeking sword knows no rest, as long as one free man's heart keeps beating and pays no homage to it; as long as one modest abode and happy home remains standing whose residents do not tremble before its might. Amalek does not hate nations that are its equal in power and armament, but, rather, regards their military preparedness as a sign of respect

57. Ibid., 166.

58. Tanner, *Amalek*, 86.

59. Jacob, *Exodus*, 503–4.

60. See further Carmy, "Origin of Nations," 66.

for its sword. Amalek fights them but honors them, since they acknowledge its power and share its principles. But Amalek harbors deadly hatred and scorn for those who dare to think the sword is dispensable, who dare to trust in spiritual and moral powers, which the sword does not perceive and cannot reach. In the representatives of peace and human nobility, Amalek sees only the mockery of its principles, its one real enemy, who hastens its downfall. With a sure instinct fed by hatred, Nimrod-Amalek rushed to crush the herald of spirituality, morality, peace and nobility, immediately upon its initial rise to the stage of world history.[61]

The fundamental question posed by these Amalekite texts is therefore whether we will follow the pattern of perpetual violence evident in the history of reception of these texts or learn to regard Amalek as the spirit of military aggression, and these Amalekite texts as calling to oppose violence instead of sponsoring it.

A number of recent works have directed attention to the "dark side" of the Bible, especially in relation to its portrayal of God.[62] I want to close by suggesting that this trend, on the whole, is probably a good thing. There are moral difficulties aplenty to be found within Scripture, and they are in need of a more thoughtful response than they often receive. As others have rightly insisted, *not* to attend to such features of the biblical witness also conveniently assists readers in thinking too well of themselves and disguising their own complicity in sin, not only in the past but in the present. Philip Jenkins has recently termed this phenomenon "holy amnesia."[63] Ronald Goetz once brought the same criticism to bear upon the relation between Christian faith and American national identity:

> Indeed we use the love of Christ as a façade behind which to hide, both from our critics and from ourselves—the fact that

61. Hirsch, *Hirsch Chumash*, 2:298. I reproduce this passage in full because it is too little known and not always easy to find. I owe my discovery of Hirsch to Diana Lipton, who makes reference to his work in her already cited essay. Hirsch is also mentioned in Sagi, "Punishment," 333.

62. See Barton, "Dark Side"; Copan, *Moral Monster?*; Davies, *Immoral Bible*; Dietrich and Link, *Die dunklen Seiten*; Jones, "Sacred Violence"; Lüdemann, *Unholy*; Metzger, "YHWH?"; Nysse, "Dark Side"; Peels, *Shadow Sides*; Penchansky, *Rough Beast?*; Sparks, *Sacred Word*. I would like to register my concern here that a term such as *dark side* may be racially insensitive or unhelpful. My black students and colleagues seem on the whole to be relatively untroubled about light-dark, white-black imagery in the Bible and within the Christian tradition; however, I worry about how such language reinforces feelings of inadequacy, suspicion, and disaffection, however subtly.

63. Jenkins, *Laying Down*, 13–15.

we have more in common with the ethics of Joshua than the ethics of Jesus. America is a nation of invaders who with the conviction of their own manifest destiny all but exterminated the Indian nations.[64]

Attending to the moral difficulties of the Bible is thus a necessary part of facing up to our own historical and contemporary complicities.

More positively, perhaps it is particularly important today to acknowledge and give expression to the monstrous, the wicked, and the tragic in the Bible—precisely because of what Anthony Giddens has termed the "sequestration of experience" in developed Western societies.[65] Paying attention to the objectionable and the horrific disrupts the pervasive consumerist patterns of modern life by naming aspects of human experience all too frequently pushed to the side and left unacknowledged. Such attention similarly works against the domestication of religious tradition and Scripture. Even when our moral inquiry into Scripture cannot locate definitive answers, the process of such questioning reminds us that Scripture is full of rough edges and still free of our efforts to control it.[66]

At the same time, however, there is an opposite danger that needs acknowledgement: a kind of emotional tourism that flirts with the exciting, the dangerous, and the transgressive in order to be titillated rather than to renounce what is wicked. To confess the existence of radical evil in the world is to concede the possibility that evil really does possess the power to infect and corrupt, and that it can successfully tempt believers away from God. For this reason, one must always be wary of too great an infatuation with the so-called dark side, in Scripture no less than in anything else. In his *Church Dogmatics* Karl Barth accordingly proposes only "a quick, sharp glance" in the direction of the demonic, adding that

> Sinister matters may be very real, but they must not be contemplated too long or studied too precisely or adopted too intensively. It has never been good for anyone . . . to look too frequently or lengthily or seriously or systematically at demons. . . . It does not make the slightest impression on the demons if we do so, and there is the imminent danger that in so doing we ourselves might become just a little or more than a little demonic. The very thing which the demons are waiting for, especially in

64. Goetz, "Joshua," 272.
65. Giddens, *Modernity*, 144–80.
66. See Magonet, *Subversive Bible*.

theology, is that we should find them dreadfully interesting and
give them our serious and perhaps systematic attention.[67]

The same could and should be said about treatments of "demonic" elements in the Bible and its portrait of God. The heart of the Bible's message is joy, and the work of discerning, learning, and expressing that joy is the proper task of a biblical interpreter, in the academy as well as in the synagogue and the church.[68]

67. Barth, *CD* III/3, 519.

68. It may be of interest to point out that I had concluded my conference paper with this appeal to joy prior to reading Stephen Barton's contribution, in which he skillfully explores the fundamental logic of joy within Christian theology and life.

2

"Where Shall Wisdom Be Found?"

(Job 1–2, 28)

Walter Moberly
University of Durham

1: The Nature of Wisdom

ONE OF THE PRIME categories of the Old Testament, and of the faiths rooted in it, is wisdom. Scholarly work often approaches wisdom as a phenomenon characteristic of certain books in the Old Testament—"wisdom literature." My concern here, however, is with the nature of wisdom as an existential reality: what might it mean and look like to be wise?[1]

Solomon is the Old Testament figure with most historic resonances in relation to wisdom. However, I want to argue here that the figure of Job valuably illustrates one primary dimension of wisdom. My argument will focus on two excerpts from the book of Job, which, taken together, offer a striking account of wisdom—an account which is a contribution to the larger study of the book of Job as a whole, but which is also meaningful in its own right. (The juxtaposition of this essay with that of Susannah Ticciati in certain ways replicates the dynamics of the biblical book, in which the portrayal of Job in differing modes in narrative and dialogue respectively is never explained, although both are to be held together and taken seriously. In general terms, it is surely the case that the integrity and trust displayed by Job in the narrative is a presupposition for his passionate speeches subsequently.)

1. This essay is an abbreviated version of a fuller discussion of Job 1–2, 28 in Moberly, *Old Testament*, and is used with permission.

The approach will be a close reading that takes the world of the text with full imaginative seriousness, so as to hear its voice and consider its implications for spiritual life today. Among other issues, we will consider what it is that makes goodness attractive, since piety is often considered to make for a dull life, and when it is a mark of wisdom to refuse to try to rationalize affliction and tragedy.

2: A Reading of Job 1:1—2:10[2]

> 1 There was once a man in the land of Uz whose name was Job. That man was blameless and upright, one who feared God and turned away from evil.

This initial depiction of Job, in which he has four strongly positive characteristics—blameless; upright; feared God; turned from evil—is the most glowing and positive character depiction in the whole Old Testament. The most closely comparable figure in this regard is Noah, though arguably his depiction is slightly less glowing: "Noah was a righteous man, blameless in his generation; Noah walked with God" (Gen 6:9). Particularly important among Job's qualities is the fact that he is "one who fears God" (*yĕrē' ĕlōhîm*), which is the prime term in the Old Testament for appropriate human response to God.

Given that Job is an outstanding example of right response to God, it is the more striking that he is from Uz. Wherever Uz might be located on a map, Uz is not Israel. That is, Job is not an Israelite, but someone who stands outside the chosen people. What difference does this make? In general terms, it is a reminder that true relationship with God is not restricted to the household of faith. In terms of the specifics of this narrative, the point is most likely that the dynamics of Job's story are not dependent upon the particularities of YHWH's dealings with Israel (election, covenant, *torah*, etc.) but represent that which is true or possible for the human condition as such.

Thus Job, though not an Israelite, is an exceptional human being, whose exceptional qualities are rooted in his relationship with God.

> 2 There were born to him seven sons and three daughters. 3 He had seven thousand sheep, three thousand camels, five hundred yoke of oxen, five hundred donkeys, and very many servants; so that this man was the greatest of all the people of the east.

---

2. I cite the NRSV throughout.

Job is fabulously well-off, in terms both of his family and his possessions. Since the groupings of numbers for both family and possessions all add up to ten (seven and three; five and five), they are presumably symbolic large numbers. Although large quantities of livestock in an apparently pastoral context may not say much to the imagination of many a modern urban/ suburban reader, the point in context—that Job is exceptionally wealthy— could easily be rendered in comparable contemporary categories (mansions, yachts, airplanes, offshore bank accounts, stock holdings . . .). Job enjoys the kind of prosperity about which most people can only dream.

Thus far we have been told two things about Job: that he is exceptional in piety/integrity, and that he is exceptional in prosperity. What we have not been told is the possible relationship between these; and it can often be an important principle of narrative interpretation to attend to what is not said as well as to what is said. The narrator has juxtaposed two facts about Job, and has left them uninterpreted, in silence. Such a silence, a "gap" in narratival terms, remains open to be filled; and this will be crucial to the story as it develops.

> 4 His sons used to go and hold feasts in one another's houses in turn; and they would send and invite their three sisters to eat and drink with them. 5 And when the feast days had run their course, Job would send and sanctify them, and he would rise early in the morning and offer burnt offerings according to the number of them all; for Job said, "It may be that my children have sinned, and cursed God in their hearts." This is what Job always did.

This fuller account of Job's family probably serves two purposes. One is to underline the delightful and enviable nature of Job's family, with its regular celebrations where all are included (v. 4). The other is to underline Job's piety, inasmuch as, in this pastoral/patriarchal context where there is apparently neither temple nor priesthood (as also in Gen 12–50), Job appropriately acts as a priest, in a way that brings together his concern for God with his concern for his family (v. 5). Although some modern interpreters have difficulty with such a portrayal of Job—on the grounds that it looks like neurosis and obsession rather than healthy piety—this is almost certainly to read against the grain of the text because of inhabiting a different frame of reference. The narrative's own concern is to portray the exemplary quality of all that Job has and does.

> 6 One day the heavenly beings came to present themselves before the LORD, and Satan [or the Accuser; Heb haśśāṭān] also came among them. 7 The LORD said to Satan, "Where have you come from?" Satan answered the LORD, "From going to

and from on the earth, and from walking up and down on it." 8
The LORD said to Satan, "Have you considered my servant Job?
There is no one like him on the earth, a blameless and upright
man who fears God and turns away from evil."

The scene shifts abruptly and dramatically, from earth to "heaven." Here a
dialogue takes place that is determinative for the whole story.

First, we must clarify the identity of YHWH's interlocutor. Here the
NRSV rendering "Satan" is seriously misleading,[3] because it implies that this
is a proper name, and consequently encourages readers to suppose that here
we have Satan who is the devil. This is wrong because of a simple rule of
Hebrew grammar: proper/personal names never take the definite article.
Yet here, as the NRSV marginal note reveals, we have the definite article
(*ha-*) before the Hebrew word *śāṭān*. So the Hebrew *haśśāṭān* designates
not a name but a function or role: "the Adversary/Opponent." In other
words, the heavenly being here is not Satan, the figure in much subsequent
Jewish and Christian theology, but an otherwise unknown member of the
heavenly court about whom we know only what we are told here: he gets
around on earth so as to be familiar with its inhabitants (vv. 7, 8a), and (as
we will see) asks awkward questions.[4]

YHWH, having initially established that the satan has been carrying
out his regular function of familiarizing himself with what is happening on
earth, then rhetorically commends Job as an exemplary person, of whom
the satan should be well aware. YHWH uses the same terminology as that
with which the narrator initially introduced Job, and underlines the truly
exceptional nature of Job's piety ("none like him on the earth"). YHWH
holds up Job as a model not just for consideration but also implicitly for
emulation. Although, within the constraints of the scenario depicted, the
implication about emulation is addressed to the satan, in all likelihood it is
intended for those overhearing the conversation, that is the reader/hearer
of the story. Job is being commended *to us* as an exemplary human being,
worthy of imitation.

9 Then the satan answered the LORD, "Does Job fear God for
nothing [*ḥinnām*]? 10 Have you not put a fence around him and
his house and all that he has, on every side? You have blessed the
work of his hands, and his possessions have increased in the land."

---

3. This occurs also in some other modern translations, e.g., NIV, ESV, perhaps out
of undue deference to the KJV and certain traditional readings of the text.

4. Henceforth I will replace "Satan" with "the satan" in citations of the NRSV.

Despite YHWH's commendation, the satan is not impressed; or, more precisely, he is suspicious. His suspicion is directed towards what we were told in the opening three verses. From Job's four commended qualities the satan naturally focuses on the weightiest of them, his "fear of God," and puts his question with regard to it: the satan fixes on the silence about the relationship between Job's outstanding piety and his outstanding prosperity. Where the narrator was silent, the satan is suspicious. He does not deny that, in a real sense, Job fears God; but he wonders about what is going on under the surface, what is Job's motivation. Although it is possible that there is no relationship between Job's piety and his prosperity (it just happens that both are the case), it is also possible to read the narrator's silence as implying that Job's prosperity is a *consequence* of his piety (YHWH blesses Job *because* he is faithful). However, the satan asks whether the real relationship is not in fact that of *purpose* (Job is faithful *so that* YHWH will bless him). Job's piety, though formally directed towards God, is at heart directed to what Job receives from God. Indeed, he does so well out of his piety that his piety is hardly surprising—rather, he would presumably be foolish not to fear God, given the extensive protection and prosperity he receives from God. In short, Job's in it for what he gets out of it.

One could reframe the satan's suspicion by saying that he is suggesting that Job is the religious equivalent of someone who marries for money. Whatever the declarations of love, and whatever the apparently loving gestures and actions, the insidious purpose of it all is not to love but to *exploit* someone—to proclaim love for the person, yet in reality to be in love with their possessions. Although to love is to be self-giving towards another, this is a matter of being self-seeking, of using someone else as a means to one's own ends. Such self-seeking is the more reprehensible when it is disguised by language and actions that purport to be its opposite. But is this in fact the reality of Job?

How should this suspicious question be heard? What is its tone and tenor? Robert Alter, for example, remarks that "the dialogue suggests . . . an element of jealousy (when God lavishes praise on Job) and cynical mean-spiritedness."[5] Certainly the question can be taken this way. But need it be? After all, is it not legitimate to want to know if a person is really what he appears to be? Especially when someone is held up as exemplary, is it not appropriate to seek assurance that this person is genuine? To raise such a question may not leave the questioner sounding "nice," but that is beside the point.

In this context, it is worth recollecting the former practice of the Roman Catholic Church with regard to the procedures for the canonization

5. Alter, *Wisdom Books*, 12.

of saints. The Vatican used to employ someone who, with nice irony, was entitled "the devil's advocate," whose role was to ask hard questions of someone proposed for sainthood. To recognize someone as a saint means, among other things, that their life is held up as exemplary, a trustworthy model for the faithful to emulate, whose name they can take for their children, and so on. The role of the devil's advocate was "quality control." For, should the Church proceed hastily and proclaim someone to be a saint without first checking carefully, it is possible that an investigative reporter could then do some homework and discover, say, Mafia links, money laundering, and a mistress, and the resultant publication of the findings would bring shame, confusion, and turmoil to the Church that had precipitately declared a plausible crook to be a saint. The devil's advocate had to do the investigating, and establish whether or not there were hitherto-unknown difficulties in the life of the proposed saint; if there was dirt to dig, it was his responsibility to dig it. Interestingly, the role of devil's advocate was abolished by Pope John Paul II, precisely to try to speed up the process of canonization, which traditionally was notoriously slow, not least because of the devil's advocate (though the politics of canonization could, and still can, be complex). He wanted to have more saints whose lives were still known in living memory, saints who could serve as, among other things, contemporary role models to commend the faith. It may be that these revised procedures will work well, and that the old ones were unduly cumbersome. Nonetheless, the concern represented by the devil's advocate remains a valid one: the greater the claim made on behalf of someone, the greater the importance of rigorous validation of the grounds for the claim.

If, as I have suggested, YHWH's commendation of Job to the satan as exemplary is implicitly a commendation to the audience of the book, then the audience in every generation can recognize their own legitimate concern being voiced by the satan: Is this apparently exemplary person really what she or he appears to be? If Job is being commended as, as it were, a "saint" even while he is still alive, then can this commendation withstand rigorous validation?

Once the suspicion is voiced—that Job's apparently exemplary fear of God may in reality be a self-seeking using of God—how best can it be dealt with? It is clear that mere reaffirmation of the initial commendation would get nowhere, as it would not take seriously the nature of the objection raised; it could lead to a fruitless "Yes, he does," "No, he doesn't." A different way of handling the issue is needed, if progress is to be made: Job must be tested.

> 11 "But stretch out your hand now, and touch all that he has,
> and he will curse you to your face." 12 The LORD said to the

25

satan, "Very well, all that he has is in your power; only do not stretch out your hand against him!" So the satan went out from the presence of the LORD.

If the suspicion is that "he's in it for what he gets out of it," then the only sure test is to remove "what he gets out of it" and then see whether or not he remains "in it." If Job is deprived of the protection and blessing of God, will he retain his fear of God or not? The satan expresses his expectation in the negative: Job's piety will turn into profanity. And since there is no way of YHWH's genuinely showing that his commendation of Job is right other than by acceding to the proposed stripping from Job of all that he has, the testing sequence of events to follow is set in train without more ado—other than that, since the suspicion has been expressed with regard to all Job has, as enumerated in verses 2–3, it is to these alone, and not Job's person, that what happens next must be directed.

> 13 One day when his sons and daughters were eating and drinking wine in the eldest brother's house, 14 a messenger came to Job and said, "The oxen were ploughing and the donkeys were feeding beside them, 15 and the Sabaeans fell on them and carried them off, and killed the servants with the edge of the sword; I alone have escaped to tell you." 16 While he was still speaking, another came and said, "The fire of God fell from heaven and burned up the sheep and the servants, and consumed them; I alone have escaped to tell you." 17 While he was still speaking, another came and said, "The Chaldeans formed three columns, made a raid on the camels and carried them off, and killed the servants with the edge of the sword; I alone have escaped to tell you." 18 While he was still speaking, another came and said, "Your sons and daughters were eating and drinking wine in their eldest brother's house, 19 and suddenly a great wind came across the desert, struck the four corners of the house, and it fell on the young people, and they are dead; I alone have escaped to tell you." 20 Then Job arose, tore his robe, shaved his head, and fell on the ground . . .

In a stylized and somewhat breathless sequence Job loses everything. To be precise, everything and everyone specified in verses 2–3 is either killed or carried off by others (apart from the four who escaped to tell Job!). That which Job had got "out of" God is gone—so will he remain "into" God? The moment of truth has come. Job initially responds with the common actions of grief in response to death and disaster. He embarks on presumably time-honored rituals of mourning, in such a way that the next thing we expect is to hear him speak, presumably to utter a lament of some kind or other in which he will bewail his situation—a lament that could easily degenerate into cursing.

> . . . and [he] worshipped. 21 He said, "Naked I came from my mother's womb, and naked shall I return there; the LORD gave, and the LORD has taken away; blessed be the name of the LORD." 22 In all this Job did not sin or charge God with wrongdoing.

Job speaks memorable words of creaturely acceptance of finitude and loss. He ignores the human agents of his disaster and focuses instead on God, whose sovereign will he affirms, and whose name he blesses. Indeed, although he is not an Israelite, at this key moment he uses language characteristic of Israel's praise of God (the wording of Ps 113:2a, "blessed be the name of the Lord," is identical to Job's wording in verse 21b). He even, uniquely in the book, names God as Israel knows God, YHWH, a name that otherwise is reserved to the narrator. Perhaps Job's usage underlines the congruence of his knowledge of God as here displayed with Israel's knowledge of God.[6]

In other words, because Job blesses and does not curse, he defies the satan's suspicion and proves it to be unfounded. His fear of God is shown to be a genuine fear *of God*, and not disguised self-seeking. He has passed the test with flying colors.

Or has he?

> 2:1 One day the heavenly beings came to present themselves before the LORD, and the satan also came among them to present himself before the LORD. 2 The LORD said to the satan, "Where have you come from?" The satan answered the LORD, "From going to and fro on the earth, and from walking up and down on it." 3 The LORD said to the satan, "Have you considered my servant Job? There is no one like him on the earth, a blameless and upright man who fears God and turns away from evil . . ."

Thus far the scenario and the wording (with two minor and insignificant variations in the Hebrew) are identical to the previous occasion.

> ". . . He still persists in his integrity [*tummātô*], although you incited me against him, to destroy him for no reason [*ḥinnām*]."

---

6. The narrator's note in verse 22 in one sense states the obvious and would not be needed in the context of this narrative alone. It has presumably been included because of what Job says later in the book, and Job's possible reputation as someone who does, more or less, charge God with wrongdoing—as, notably, in his speeches in Job 21 and 24. Thus the narrator is clarifying that, even if some of what Job says later may be open to question in certain ways, no such reservation applies at this point in the book.

YHWH continues to commend Job to the satan as exemplary, and now includes reference to what has taken place since first they spoke, in effect commenting on Job's demeanor and words in 1:20–21. He changes the leading category for depicting Job from his "fear" to his "integrity," where the Hebrew noun for "integrity" (*tummâ*) is formed from the same root as the adjective "blameless" (*tām*) that has been repeatedly used to describe Job (1:1, 8; 2:3); so one might render it "blamelessness" to keep the verbal continuity, though "integrity" better captures the sense in English. But the point is unchanged: Job continues to display those qualities for which he has been commended as exemplary, despite their not "benefitting" him.

Moreover, YHWH depicts what has happened to Job with the same term with which the satan articulated his suspicion of Job: "for no reason/ for nothing" (*ḥinnām*). The point is not that there was no reason at all for what happened to Job—for the concern to test was explicit—but that there was nothing deficient in Job himself or in his relationship with YHWH that gave rise to what happened. The fact that Job really does fear God "for nothing," as has become apparent, underlines that what happened to him in some sense corresponds to this— the rightness of his disinterested ("for nothing") relationship with God is shown in the unrelatedness to his way of living of what has happened to him ("for no reason").

> 4 Then the satan answered the LORD, "Skin for skin! All that people have they will give to save their lives. 5 But stretch out your hand now and touch his bone and his flesh, and he will curse you to your face."

The satan, however, is unpersuaded, and that for a simple reason. The terms of the previous test related only to all that Job had (1:2–3) and explicitly excluded his own person (1:12). But this exclusion allows the suspicion to be expressed again in severer form. Job is not only self-seeking, but he is nasty, indeed ruthless, about it: he will sacrifice anyone and anything in the cause of self-preservation. What does he ultimately care if his family, servants, and livestock perish as long as he himself is preserved unscathed? The initial test was not sufficiently searching and therefore must be renewed so as to include Job himself. He must experience devastation and desolation in his own person. When this happens, and Job's piety no longer results in his personal well-being, then at last the true nature of Job as indeed unscrupulously self-seeking in relation to God will be revealed. This time, his piety really will turn to profanity.

Whether or not the satan's suspicion is a "fair" response to Job's words and deeds so far is beside the point. It is the fact that it remains a *possible* construal of what is going on that is all-important. So something further must happen to Job that will lead him to reveal and express his inner reality.

> 6 The LORD said to the satan, "Very well, he is in your power; only spare his life." 7 So the satan went out from the presence of the LORD, and inflicted loathsome sores on Job from the sole of his foot to the crown of his head. 8 Job took a potsherd with which to scrape himself, and sat among the ashes.

The terms of the further test dictate themselves. Job's life must be deprived of all that makes it worthwhile, and become deathlike; but he must remain alive. This necessary reservation is not, as in the first test, restricting the scope of the test, but is simply so that Job remains able to respond to his situation. So he is afflicted in the kind of way that is agonizing and makes him an object of disgust to himself as much as to others; and the point of these loathsome sores covering him from bottom to top is that *all of him* is afflicted with no part left as some kind of comfort zone, where he might still feel all right. His consequent sitting among ashes—ashes being the useless and unlovely remnants of that which once was living and/or had shape and purpose but is now located at the rubbish tip—is an eloquent symbol of his new situation.

> 9 Then his wife said to him, "Do you still persist in your integrity [*tummâ*]? Curse God, and die." 10 But he said to her, "You speak as any foolish woman would speak. Shall we receive the good at the hand of God, and not receive the bad?" In all this Job did not sin with his lips.

Job's wife now articulates in her own way the issue at the heart of the satan's suspicion. What is the point of integrity, if this is what integrity leads to? Once you see that nothing good comes of it, why bother with it? So be done with it: give up on God, say what you must surely now think about him, and perhaps thereby hasten the end which is now welcome and which must surely be coming soon anyway.

Job's response (again differentiated in a subsequent aside from his later poetic speeches) is simple and clear. After reproving his wife for speaking "foolishly," presumably because of her assumption about the "point" of integrity, he articulates his own understanding of his integrity/fear of God. In essence, it is no good being a fairweather friend; true relationship is sustained through the hard times as well as the good times. Indeed, if one reflects on all that Job has been through, then it is appropriate to depict his relationship with God in time-honored and hallowed language: "for better, for worse; for richer, for poorer; in sickness, and in health," for these marriage vows both describe and constitute true relationship. Job's integrity/

fear of God has the dynamics of true love. It thereby becomes fully clear that the content of "fear of God" is far from being "frightened of God lest God do something unpleasant," for the worst that could happen to Job has happened, and he sustains his fear of God regardless. In terms of the narrative, it is as final a refutation as there could be of the suspicion that Job was self-seeking, that his piety was merely instrumental, or that he did not relate to God for God's own sake.

3: A Reading of Job 28:1–28

We turn now to a famous and beautiful poem, located later in the book towards the end of the speeches of Job and his friends. It is here that the question, "Where shall wisdom be found?" is explicitly raised.

One introductory clarification: Whose voice is speaking in this poem? My proposal is that the voice in the poem is that of the narrator whom we have already heard in 1:1—2:10.

1 Surely there is a mine for silver,[7]
and a place for gold to be refined.
2 Iron is taken out of the earth,
and copper is smelted from ore.
3 Miners put an end to darkness,
and search out to the farthest bound
the ore in gloom and deep darkness.
4 They open shafts in a valley away from human habitation;
they are forgotten by travellers,
they sway suspended, remote from people.
5 As for the earth, out of it comes bread;
but underneath it is turned up as by fire.
6 Its stones are the places of sapphires,
and its dust contains gold.
7 That path no bird of prey knows,
and the falcon's eye has not seen it.
8 The proud wild animals have not trodden it;
the lion has not passed over it.
9 They put their hand to the flinty rock,
and overturn mountains by the roots.
10 They cut channels in the rocks,

---

7. NRSV prefaces this line, as it prefaces the start of each paragraph of the poem, with an inverted comma, which indicates that the poem is being construed as on the lips of Job. Since I am taking the poem to be a contribution by the narrator, and not a speech, I omit the inverted commas throughout.

and their eyes see every precious thing.
11 The sources of the rivers they probe;
hidden things they bring to light.

The poem begins with an elaborate account of human ability to discover that which is widely held to be supremely precious: silver and gold. Human ingenuity is represented by mining underground in remote and difficult locations where precious stones of many different kinds (iron and sapphires as well as silver and gold) can be found (vv. 1–6). To penetrate underground means that humans can get to places inaccessible to birds and beasts, who are restricted to what is above ground (vv. 7–8). Humans who delve for precious metals are not only bold in undertaking (v. 9b) but also successful in execution—they see, they bring to light (vv. 10, 11). Human ingenuity and ability is wonderful.

Yet it is precisely this wondrous resourcefulness that poses the issue of the poem:

12 But where shall wisdom be found?
And where is the place of understanding?
13 Mortals do not know the way to it,
and it is not found in the land of the living.
14 The deep says, "It is not in me,"
and the sea says, "It is not with me."

The ability to discover precious stones does not suffice to discover that quality which, by clear implication, is even more precious than such precious stones: wisdom. This cannot be found in the way that humans find other things (v. 13). Even if they delved under sea rather than under land, it would make no difference—wisdom is no more in the one place than the other (v. 14). In the places and by the means whereby they discover and get hold of other things, humans cannot get hold of wisdom.

15 It cannot be bought for gold,
and silver cannot be weighed out as its price.
16 It cannot be valued in the gold of Ophir,
in precious onyx or sapphire.
17 Gold and glass cannot equal it,
nor can it be exchanged for jewels of fine gold.
18 No mention shall be made of coral or of crystal;
the price of wisdom is above pearls.
19 The chrysolite of Ethiopia cannot compare with it,
nor can it be valued in pure gold.

The thought changes from the possibility of discovering wisdom to that of buying it. If ingenuity fails, might wealth, especially exceptional wealth, succeed? Might the precious stones dug out from the earth be used to acquire wisdom? To which the answer—in a series of elegant variations on precious materials the precise identity of which is not always clear, but which unfailingly represent high value—is simply no. Wisdom is indeed supremely valuable, but its value is incommensurate with financial value. Wisdom cannot be bought; it is not that kind of thing.

> 20 Where then does wisdom come from?
> And where is the place of understanding?
> 21 It is hidden from the eyes of all living,
> and concealed from the birds of the air.
> 22 Abaddon and Death say,
> "We have heard a rumor of it with our ears."

And so the poet repeats, with variation, the refrain of verses 12–14. If one cannot get wisdom by the prime means that humans use to acquire things— ingenuity, discovery, wealth—then where on earth is it to be found? To which the answer is: nowhere on earth. Those on the earth, above the earth, or below the earth alike agree that it is not there.

But where then is wisdom?

> 23 God understands the way to it,
> and he knows its place.
> 24 For he looks to the ends of the earth,
> and sees everything under the heavens.
> 25 When he gave to the wind its weight,
> and apportioned out the waters by measure;
> 26 when he made a decree for the rain,
> and a way for the thunderbolt;
> 27 then he saw it and declared it;
> he established it, and searched it out.
> 28 And he said to humankind [*ʾādām*],
> "Truly, the fear of the Lord [*yirʾat ʾădōnay*], that is wisdom;
> and to depart from evil [*sûr mērāʿ*] is understanding."

That which is beyond humans is not beyond God. Where wisdom is, and how to get there, is known to God (v. 23); and God is able to see what no one else can (v. 24; contrast vv. 13, 21). When at creation he regulated wind and rain (vv. 25–26), then he established what wisdom is and where it is to be found (v. 27). God, however, did not keep this knowledge of wisdom to himself, but rather declared it to his human creation (*ʾādām*), to those who would have the capacity to understand it and for whom it would be of fundamental importance. The content of this primordial revelation is that wisdom and understanding is in fact constituted by the fear of the Lord and departing from evil (v. 28).

These key terms that define wisdom are, however, precisely those qualities which have been seen to characterize Job in the opening narrative. Not only did the narrative introduce Job as "one who feared God [*yĕrē' 'ĕlōhîm*] and departed from evil [*sār mērā'*],"[8] but the narrative probed the meaning of this "fear" and showed that it means true relationship with God, a relationship to be sustained even when the worst that could happen does happen. If the opening narrative establishes a meaning for "fear of God," and the poem of chapter 28 identifies such "fear of God" with "wisdom," then Job in the narrative exemplifies that of which the poem speaks. Job's unswerving adherence to God in the midst of disaster and desolation represents true wisdom and understanding. If, then, we, the readers/hearers, want to know what wisdom looks like, we should look at Job—and, in principle, emulate him.

Why then does the poem so stress the inaccessibility of wisdom? This is surely in part because, in an important sense, wisdom is like God himself. On the one hand, God is impossible to find within the world—in a postbiblical formulation, "God is not an item in an inventory of the universe," for anything thus discovered would by definition be a creature rather than the Creator. Nor is God accessible by those means with which humans regularly attain their goals (ingenuity, hard work, wealth). On the other hand, it is the common testimony of countless people down the ages that God is accessible both here and now. The way God is "accessed" is different in kind from the way that things that humans commonly value are accessed; so too wisdom.

This general point receives specific focus in the context of Job: How should one live, when life itself falls apart? When things go wrong, it is common either to rationalize or to resent, or to do both. Job does neither. Although we the readers/hearers know the rationale for what Job goes through, he does not when he makes his responses in 1:21 and 2:10, nor

---

8. The wording of "depart from evil" is identical in 1:1, 8, 2:3, and 28:28, except that in the former context *sār* is a participle, appropriate to the narrative description, while in the latter *sûr* is an infinitive, appropriate to a definitional use. More surprising is that 28:28 uses "Lord" (*'ădōnay*) rather than "God" *'ĕlōhîm*, when the use of "God" would be expected, because of "God" in both immediate (28:23) and more distant (1:1, 8; 2:3) context. Although some manuscripts have *yhwh* instead of *'ădōnay*, none have the expected (*'ĕlōhîm*). I see no good explanation for this (the suggestion that verse 28 may be an addition resolves nothing, for one could expect someone to make the wording of the addition appropriate to its new context), although of course the present wording appropriately emphasizes the intrinsic lordship of God over his creation. The LXX irons this out by using *theosebeia* in 28:28, which lines up perfectly with the adjective *theosebēs* in 1:1, 8; 2:3.

does he ever; and Job does not resent, but rather maintains his stance of trust in God (which then becomes the premise for his passionate questioning). So where is wisdom in a world in which there are incomprehensible tragedies and disasters? It is found in "fearing God and turning away from evil," in maintaining integrity and trust towards God even *in extremis*. This is both hopelessly hard and elusive (as evidenced by the many down the ages who have responded otherwise) and entirely possible (as evidenced by the many down the ages who have displayed Job-like qualities).

One corollary of this construal is surely that the poem is using "wisdom" in a specific sense, appropriate to the concern of the book—knowing how to live well in extreme situations. "Wisdom" as defined here is not the ability to utilize knowledge in such a way as to live well in general, which is the consistent concern in Proverbs. Hence a difference of formulation. In Proverbs "the fear of YHWH is the beginning of wisdom" (9:10; cf. 1:7; 15:33), which most likely means that "fear of YHWH" constitutes access to the high road by which wisdom is attained, has a didactic import appropriate to the young person whose life is being shaped: first learn to live in the fear of God, and thereby you will be enabled to live wisely. In Job 28 wisdom is *equated with* "fear of the Lord," rather than being the result of it, because it is a construal of Job's fear of God, maintained in extreme adversity, as being the wise way to respond to apparently random affliction.

4: Concluding Reflections

By way of conclusion I will reflect a little on the way in which the understanding and possible appropriation of the substantive content of the biblical text relates to how one reads it.

One of the keys to my reading has been attentiveness to literary context, the relationship between the fear of God that Job displays in the opening narrative and the fear of God that is defined as wisdom. Many interpreters either do not notice the linkage or leave its interpretive potential more or less unexploited. Yet even a recognition of its substantive significance does not necessarily lead to the reading offered here. David Robertson, who thinks that attempts to read Job in its received form are generative of irony, comments on 28:28: "This is precisely the wisdom Job has followed all his life (chs. 1–2) and where has it got him: the ash-heap. Some wisdom!"[9] Comparably, David Clines comments: "It is hard not to see the relation between these sentences [28:28 and 1:1] as ironic. If fearing God and turning aside from evil is what

---

9. Robertson, *Literary Critic*, 33–34, 46.

has got Job into this unhappy condition (and that is the thrust of the pro-logue), the value of this prescription for life is seriously undermined."[10]

These seem to me instructive examples of non-attuned readings, which in effect score a point at the expense of taking the text seriously.[11] On the one hand, the thrust of the prologue is *not* that Job's fear of God and turning from evil got him into misery. To be sure, had he not had these qualities there could have been no question of testing their authenticity. But had there been no test, there would have been no misery. His qualities as such were not the problem, and there is no implication whatever in the text that fear of God in itself engenders an "unhappy condition."

On the other hand, the implicit assumptions in the way that Robertson and Clines formulate their critiques are surely open to question. To be sure, there is indeed a clear "prescription for life" in Job's fear of God and its construal as wisdom. Or, to put it differently, despite the narrative's rejection of the suspicion that Job's piety may be essentially instrumental in relation to God, there are various ways in which piety may have consequences that need not be problematic; the proposition that to live with faith and integrity should lead to a good life, and that that is a legitimate reason for living with faith and integrity, should be uncontroversial, at least for any (would-be) believer—although of course the notion of a "good life" needs considerable discussion as to what it does, and does not, mean. The problem arises if one construes faith and integrity in instrumental terms, such that if they do not lead to the attainment of a "good life" then it is pointless to maintain them. It is the difference between faith and integrity having intrinsic value with an expectation of certain consequences, and their having solely or predominantly instrumental value. It is suspicion that the latter may be the case that prompts the satan to speak up.

To generalize the issue somewhat, the priorities that are surely present within the Job texts we have looked at are shared widely within the biblical canon. Elsewhere within the Old Testament Habakkuk famously depicts the righteous person, in a context of affliction and puzzlement and scorn, living by "faithfulness" (*ĕmûnā*), and ends with a personal testimony of comparable faithfulness in time of overwhelming disaster (Hab 2:4; 3:17–19). Within the book of Isaiah, an unnamed voice asks a searching question about how people are to respond to the servant of YHWH, whose repeated afflictions have just been recounted (Isa 50:4–9, 10):

10. Clines, "Job 28:28," 84.

11. Contemporary biblical scholarship affords all-too-regular occasion to ponder the sentiment succinctly expressed by Robert Alter: "the language of criticism now often reflects an emotional alienation from the imaginative life of the text under discussion." Alter, *Pleasures of Reading*, 15.

> Who among you fears the LORD
> and obeys the voice of his servant,
> who walks in darkness
> and has no light,
> yet trusts in the name of the LORD
> and relies upon his God?

Within the New Testament it is supremely Jesus in his passion who displays comparable qualities. Whatever his own hopes and preferences, his bottom line is to be faithful to his Father: "My Father, if it is possible, let this cup pass from me; yet not what I want but what you want" (Matt 26:39). Just as Jesus is not swayed by the thought that "if being Son of God does not make your life obviously better or easier for you, then what is the point of it?" nor should (would-be) believers be swayed either.

If I may venture a summary generalization, my reading of the literature on Job 1–2 and 28 has left me with a sense that the interpretive thesis for which I am arguing here—that the maintenance of faith and integrity *in extremis* is wisdom—gets little, if any, hearing for one reason above all others: it is considered dull, shallow, simplistic, boring. It represents "conventional piety," and (by implication) the conventionally pious lead predictably dull and intellectually unstimulating lives, all of which is (by implication) generative of no more than boredom or perhaps suspicion[12]—how different from the Job of the speeches who is interesting precisely because he abandons the conventions of piety and speaks with unrestrained passion. To be sure, piety can be dull. But need it be so? As Michael Gorman pointed out in discussion of this essay, people who bear great hardship with faithful patience and courage are deeply admirable if one has the privilege, often a humbling privilege, of knowing them in the flesh.

So perhaps the issue is to some extent the age-old problem of how to make goodness appear *imaginatively* interesting, when encountered not in the flesh but in a story or picture. In medieval murals of heaven and hell, for example, the angels and saints regularly seem less interesting than the demons and the damned. In many a classic novel, such as those of Dickens, the dubious characters and villains (Scrooge, Fagin, Wackford Squeers) are usually more memorable than the heroes. Contemporary film goes much the same way; for example, in Peter Jackson's big-screen rendering

---

12. David Penchansky comments that the "legendary Job" (i.e., the Job of the narrative, who is commended by 28:28) functions to "confirm the easy piety of the superficially religious, reaffirming the control of the religious establishment." Penchansky, *Betrayal of God*, 32.

of J. R. R. Tolkien's *The Lord of the Rings* the elves, who epitomize patience and wisdom, are duller than the orcs, who epitomize violence.[13]

But the problem is also surely to some degree one of perspective—the extent and nature of one's own comfort or affliction may make a marked difference to one's evaluations of moral and spiritual stability in both self and others. In all fundamental issues of life, how and where we stand affects how and what we see. Part of the challenge of the Job material that we have considered is to learn when life may be going well, and Job's situation may seem remote, how best to respond if life goes badly.

13. It is interesting to compare Jackson's construal with Tolkien's original. In Jackson's rendering Frodo for a while loses trust in Sam, Aragorn displays self-doubt, Faramir wavers, and Elrond inclines to despair of Middle-Earth and pressures Arwen to break faith with Aragorn, which for a while she goes along with. In Tolkien's own portrayal Frodo, Aragorn, Faramir, Elrond, and Arwen display unwavering integrity and resolve to resist faithlessness and to oppose Sauron to the end, come what may, and, because of Tolkien's imaginative genius, this is consistently engaging. Jackson, however, presumably considered this potentially unappealing and decided that the story would be more interesting cinematically if its main characters were less consistent.

3

Theology in the Second Person

Job's Indexical Spirituality

Susannah Ticciati
King's College London

For the arrows of the Almighty are in me;
my spirit drinks their poison;
the terrors of God are arrayed against me.

Job 6:4 (NRSV[1])

JOB IS WELL KNOWN not only for his patience (as exhibited in the prologue of the book of Job), but also for the anger he expresses as one who argues with God (in the much longer poetic section of the book). As such he offers a compelling and liberating model for the Christian believer, who is not confined in relationship with God to a stance of submission and uninterrupted praise, but is given permission to cry out in the face of the darkest and most painful corners of life. These can be confronted with as much truthfulness and integrity as those aspects that more obviously manifest the goodness and love of God. God is in the heights and the depths, being no stranger to suffering. And like the friends, tradition often finds itself on the wrong side of that suffering, misrepresenting God in its inability to hear and suffer alongside those who are suffering—sometimes at its hands.

1. English translations are taken from the NRSV throughout the essay, unless otherwise stated.

But such a description subtly avoids the real challenge of Job. Job does not just confront the dark parts of creation, or expose the falsehoods of tradition. He argues *with God*, and attempts thereby to expose the injustice of God. It is perhaps for this reason that however much attention his example has attracted, he has always remained an exceptional figure, marginal or peripheral in respect of the dominant tradition. Within the Hebrew Bible itself he may bring into question the doctrine of retribution; but the weight of the Deuteronomic literature keeps him in his place as the exception that proves the rule. His marginal nature within Christian tradition (with which I will primarily be concerned in this essay[2]) is of a slightly different kind. His rebellious stance towards God was, until relatively recently, an embarrassment to be minimized.[3] And while it becomes an important focus for positive attention in the interpretations of Kierkegaard and Barth, it does so in a qualified way.[4] Moreover, even the daring exhibited here is overshadowed by the predominant modern treatment of the book as a theodicy, which ultimately shifts attention away from Job's confrontation of God to his nature as an innocent sufferer, such that he becomes paradigmatic for undeserved suffering throughout history.[5] His rebellion against God is once again overlooked.

In the present essay I seek to tackle Job's angry complaint head on. Moreover, I will argue that Job, in his argument with God, need not be treated as exceptional, but to the contrary can be regarded as normative for Christian tradition. In doing so I do not want to suggest that anger or

2. I am not qualified to comment on his place within Jewish tradition.

3. In his *Moralia in Iob*, Gregory the Great reads Job as a patient sufferer by focusing on the interior meaning of his words; Aquinas, in *Expositio super Iob*, attributes to Job correct doctrine but intellectual pride; and Calvin, in his *Sermons on Job*, makes Elihu instead of Job his hero, unable to countenance Job's angry impatience. See Schreiner, *Where Shall Wisdom Be Found?*, for an excellent account of these interpretations.

4. Kierkegaard offers interpretations of Job in two works: *Repetition*, 124–231, and *Eighteen Upbuilding Discourses*, 109–24 (in a discourse titled "The Lord Gave, and the Lord Took Away; Blessed Be the Name of the Lord"). Kierkegaard's praise of Job in the former is complicated by the work's layers of pseudonymity, and the latter reads the whole book through the lens of 1:20–21. The commendability of Job's complaint is secret and paradoxical. Barth's interpretation can be found in *Church Dogmatics* IV.3, 383–88, 398–408, 421–34, and 453–61. For him, Job is simultaneously in the right and the wrong in his complaint. I do not disagree with these readings in the following, but I do hope to offer a slightly different kind of justification for Job's arguing with God.

5. This characterization includes a large number of the historical-critical treatments of Job, some of which I engage with below. Moreover, exceptions to the pattern (e.g., Zuckerman's *Job the Silent*) tend to be ones which do not read Job as religiously normative, such that the particular challenge for Christian belief is not confronted.

argument *as such* are normative (making praise and thanksgiving marginal). Rather, I will argue that in his complaint Job offers us a model of *indexical theology*. Job, I hope to demonstrate, is an indexical theologian *par excellence*. The term "indexical" will need to be defined, and its usage in this context explained. But a preliminary descriptive paraphrase can be offered: Job eschews relationship with a "God in general," speaking of and to God from out of his own very particular experience, finding and wrestling with him in it and thereby being transformed.

1. Indexicality

This essay borrows the term *indexical* from its linguistic usage. Indexical expressions are those whose reference is a function of their context of utterance, and whose meaning helps pick out the relevant aspect of the context. Paradigmatic examples are the first and second person pronouns, "I" and "you," the demonstratives, "this" and "that," and the temporal and spatial adverbs, "now" and "then," "here" and "now."[6] While all language is contextual, some referential expressions have their usefulness in their constancy across contexts, such as proper names (e.g., Job, Israel, and the earth) or definite descriptions (e.g., the first book of the Bible). Indexical expressions are contextual in the further, more specific sense that their reference changes depending (variously) on the exact time and place of the utterance, and on the identity of the utterer; and their usefulness lies in the fact that they do so (when Job says "I" he does not refer to the same person as when one of the friends says "I").[7]

The claim that Job's theology is indexical uses the word *indexical* in an analogous sense: the purchase of Job's language on God is a function of its context. In other words, just as the referent of the word "I" changes depending on who says it, so the purchase of Job's words would change if they were to be put in the mouth of another. They are not generalizable. Unlike the friends, Job does not attempt to express universal truths. The controversial claim of the essay, however, is the further one that Job is normative in his eschewal of generalization; or in other words, that the truth of theological

---

6. For a standard, authoritative account, see Levinson, *Pragmatics*, 54–96. For a more intricate and critical discussion, see Nunberg, "Indexicality and Deixis." Strictly speaking, according to Nunberg, it is the *usage* of words that is indexical rather than the words themselves (ibid., 2–3, 33).

7. Cf. Ricoeur, *Oneself as Another*, 28–30, for this subclassification of referential expressions or "designators," with indexicals or "indicators" as one subclass.

language is indexical at its core, generalization being possible only around the edges.

In the following analysis we will find that Job's theology is indexical in a further, more than analogous, sense. It is rooted in his frequent and special use of the pronoun "I" (most often expressed by verbal inflection or in suffixes, but occasionally also occurring as the separate pronoun *ănî*). This is complemented by his use of the pronoun "you" in relation to the friends (again, usually in verbal inflections or suffixes), as well as his sporadic switches from reference to God in the third person to second person address. For this reason the title refers to Job's theology "in the second person," in implicit contrast with the friends' theology, which might be said to be in the third person. This contrast is not to be understood at the literal grammatical level. The friends frequently use the first and second person, just as Job often uses the third person. However, we will find that Job's use of first and second person pronouns differs markedly from the usage of the friends.

The next section will therefore be devoted to tracking shifts in pronoun use in Job's dialogue with the friends. An exhaustive treatment will be impossible, so I will attempt to identify the distinctive pattern with reference to chapters 4 to 15 (where it is borne out with repetitive clarity), drawing on supplementary passages from later in the book, which strikingly corroborate the thesis. This analysis will provide the context for an assessment of Job's characterizations of God, including the essay's epigram—chosen for its affront to any traditional Christian doctrine of God. My aim will be to identify their indexical significance and truth.

2. Pronouns in the Book of Job

Eliphaz the Temanite addresses Job directly in response to Job's outburst of chapter 3: "If one ventures a word with you [*ēleykā*], will you be offended [*til'eh*]?" (4:2). But as he continues Job becomes the opportunity for the lessons of wisdom, and even when Eliphaz makes further use of the second person, he no longer singles out Job in particular, but speaks to him increasingly as an illustration of his wisdom theology: "Think now [*zĕkor-nā'*], who that was innocent ever perished?" (4:7); "Call now [*qĕrā'-nā'*]; is there anyone who will answer you [*ônekā*]?" (5:1); "How happy is the one whom God reproves; therefore do not despise [*'al-timās*] the discipline of the Almighty. . . . He will deliver you [*yaṣṣîlekā*] from six troubles; in seven no harm shall touch you [*bĕkā*]" (5:17, 19). By the end of his speech Job has disappeared entirely into Eliphaz's traditional wisdom; "you" has become "you in general" (the English "one"). It is only left for Job to apply it: "See, we have searched this out; it is true. Hear, and know it for yourself [šĕmā'ennâ wĕattâ da'-lāk]" (5:27). The generalized "you" is complemented by Eliphaz's increasingly rhetorical "I." While Eliphaz still shimmers behind his report of a night-vision (4:12–21),[8] the first person has become entirely proverbial in the following: "I have seen [ănî-rā'îtî] fools taking root, but suddenly I cursed [wā'eqqôb] their dwelling" (5:3); "As for me ['ûlām ănî], I would seek [edrōš] God, and to God I would commit my cause [ăśîm dibrātî]" (5:8).

Job's response comes as a bombshell: "O that my vexation were weighed [lû šāqōl yiššāqēl ka'aśî], and all my calamity laid in the balances! For then it would be heavier than the sand of the sea; therefore my words [dĕbāray] have been rash" (6:2–3). Eliphaz's generalizations crack and disintegrate under the weight of Job's singular vexation. Job's forceful rhetoric (note the intensifying infinitive absolute) draws attention again to Job's irreducible individuality. All the weight of the tradition cannot outweigh *his vexation*. In other words, he is more than an instance of Eliphaz's wisdom. He cannot be weighed. This is brought home all the more poignantly by the fact that Job's use of "vexation" (ka'aś) picks up on Eliphaz's own use of it in 5:2: "Surely vexation kills the fool." As Habel points out, Eliphaz did not necessarily have Job in mind there, but Job appropriates Eliphaz's generalizing words to himself, pulling them out of their traditional alignment.[9] Job continues by speaking out of his singular experience, characterizing God in the light of it. This is the context for the shocking words with which we prefaced the essay, to whose significance we will return. But for now we will continue to track the use of first and second person pronouns.

While Eliphaz's use of "you" became more and more generic, Job's becomes more and more targeted. The friends first emerge out of the third person of 6:14–20 in the second person of 6:21, which locates the failure so far described in them. Job continues with a series of interrogatives designed to demonstrate further their uselessness, culminating in a direct appeal to them: "but now, be pleased to look at me [hô'îlû pĕnû bî]; for I will not lie to your face [wĕ'al-pĕnêkem 'im-ăkazzēb]. Turn, I pray [šubû-nā'], let no wrong

8. Habel comments on the fact that Eliphaz's revelatory vision is characterized in untraditional terms, but that its content is nevertheless traditional (*Book of Job*, 127–28). Commenting later on 15:17, Habel draws attention to Eliphaz's emphasis on the importance of personal experience (257). One might think that this would go hand in hand with an ability to speak to Job in his particularity—with a genuine use of the second person—but Eliphaz's experience is rendered stock by the entirely traditional nature of its content (whether in 4:17–21 or 15:18–35; indeed, in 15:18 Eliphaz equates his "experience" with "what sages have told").

9. Ibid., 131 and 144–45. Clines, by contrast, denies that Job is picking up on Eliphaz's words, given that his ka'aś is entirely excusable (*Job 1–20*, 169).

be done. Turn now [*wĕšubî*], my vindication is at stake" (6:28–29). While for Eliphaz Job becomes more and more typical, Job renders the friends' presence more and more intensely personal. And his request is that they regard him as the person he is before them. Job's appeal to the friends becomes, in turn, a prelude to his first address to God in the second person: "Am I the Sea [*hăyām 'ănî*], or the Dragon, that you set [*kî-tāśîm*] a guard over me [*'ălay mišmār*]? . . . If I sin [*hātā'tî*], what do I do to you [*lāk*], you watcher of humanity? Why have you made me [*śamtanî*] your target?" (7:12, 20).[10] By contrast with the friends, God will not let go of Job in his singularity. The intensity of his personal presence to God is unbearable.

Like Eliphaz, Bildad seeks to contain Job's lack of restraint, at first addressing him directly but almost immediately absorbing him into a string of platitudes, thereby taking the bite out of his words. The following verses are almost an articulation of Bildad's strategy: "For inquire now of bygone generations, and consider what their ancestors have found; for we [*'ănahnû*] are but of yesterday, and we know nothing, for our days on earth are but a shadow" (8:8–9). If Job's vexation outweighed Eliphaz's traditional wisdom, Bildad can only reassert the incomparable longevity of tradition to put Job back in his place. The rhetorical effect is heightened by his emphatic use of "we" to conceal Job's individuality even further.

Job's response to Bildad is the beginning of his well-known attempt to frame his complaint against God in legal terms, with God as his adversary. It is the opening of his *rîb* or trial against God.[11] But it is a trial condemned to paradox, since Job is calling God to account precisely for his unaccountability (9:3–12).[12] What is remarkable for our purposes, however, is Job's (albeit fleeting) discovery and declaration of his innocence: "Though I am innocent, my own mouth would condemn me; though I am blameless [*tām-'ănî*], he would prove me perverse. I am blameless [*tām-'ănî*]; I do not know

10. Between these verses is Job's parody of Psalm 8 (Job 7:17–18). Yamm is the sea god of Canaanite mythology, and Tannin is also a mythical monster. Good comments: "The god is dealing with him not as if he were a cloud that evaporates but as if he were the enemy in a cosmic combat myth" (*In Turns of Tempest*, 216). And Habel suggests that the significance of Job's use of these myths "lies in the individualization of the chaos symbols . . . the direct appropriation of key images from the cosmic domain to the personal domain of Job's life" (*Book of Job*, 162). While Job wishes at this point to be left alone by God, it is his characterization of the relationship in these terms that both resists Eliphaz's placid and pacifying wisdom and prepares Job for his trial against God. His identity is as irreducible as that of the chaos monsters.

11. Cf. Gemser, "*RIB-* or Controversy-Pattern," 120–37; Zuckerman, *Job the Silent*, 104–17. Job arguably begins to use legal language already in 6:24–30 (esp. vv. 25–26 and 29); cf. Good, *In Turns of Tempest*, 214–15.

12. For a fuller account of this paradox, see Ticciati, *Job and the Disruption of Identity*, ch. 5, 119–37.

myself; I loathe my life" (9:20–21). His repetition of *tām-ʾānî* gives dramatic emphasis to the first person nature of his speech. By way of his trial Job breaks free from the friends' attempted reductions, giving expression to his irreducible identity. But as these verses show, his experience of the latter is inextricably caught up in a dialectic of innocence and perversion.[13]

The trial begins and continues for some time to put God in the third person, as if to manifest Job's inability to call God to account—God remains at one remove. But almost imperceptibly Job shifts into the second person (9:28–31), at first only to switch back (vv. 32–35), but then as if gathering momentum, to sustain it for the remainder of his speech (10:2–22). The intensity that builds up is once again diffused, this time by Zophar, and with somewhat more difficulty. Zophar does not just declaim and interrogate, but appeals to God in the optative: "But oh, that God would speak, and open his lips to you [*ʿimmāk*], and that he would tell you [*wĕyagged-lĕkā*] the secrets of wisdom!" (11:5–6). Job's individuality is an affront to the friends, and the more he discovers the resources to assert it in the face of their silencing, the harder they have to fight to keep it at bay. Nevertheless, the same thing follows with Zophar as before, Job being subsumed by a toothless proverbial "you": "Can you find out [*timṣāʾ*] the deep things of God? Can you find out [*timṣāʾ*] the limit of the Almighty?" (11:7).

Job must clear aside the friends' worthless sayings (13:12) in order to clear the way for the resumption of his purpose: "But I [*ʾûlām ʾānî*] would speak to the Almighty [*ʾel-šadday*], and I desire to argue my case with God" (13:3). This he does with gathering confidence, again turning from third to second person, and continuing to address God even as his more defiant attitude fades into the more melancholic (14:1–22). In response, Eliphaz takes up a harsher tone than in his first speech. Moreover, in order to tame Job this time, he must move into the register of the mythic (as Job has done already, for example in 7:12, but to the opposite end). If Job has taken on mythic proportions for him, then Job can only be written off by the mocking classification of him in mythical terms: "Are you the firstborn of the human race? Were you brought forth before the hills? Have you listened in the council of God? And do you limit wisdom to yourself?" (15:7–8).[14]

By now the pattern of the dynamic between Job and the friends should have come clearly into view. As Job becomes more and more confident and

13. For a fuller account of the dynamics of Job's trial, especially as it comes to expression in these verses, see Ticciati, *Job and the Disruption of Identity*, ch. 6, 138–57.

14. That Eliphaz is drawing on a well-known myth (the myth of the Primal Human) is generally agreed upon, even if its precise significance is disputed. Gordis equates the mythic first human with the Adam of the paradise narrative of Gen 2–3 (*Book of Job*, 160), while Habel queries this identification (*Book of Job*, 253).

vehement in his assertion of his irreducible identity, out of which he turns to and addresses God, the friends must work harder and harder to keep Job under control, subsuming him within their platitudes and generalizations. Instead of tracking the pattern further, I will highlight some pertinent verses within the developing trajectory.

What is at stake for the friends is expressed forcefully by Bildad in his second speech: "You who tear yourself in your anger—shall the earth be forsaken because of you [*halĕma'anĕkā*], or the rock be removed out of its place?" (18:4). Job, in his desire not to be counted as just another statistic within his friends' wisdom theology, threatens the very foundations of this theology. And for the friends this is tantamount to overturning the earth. Their theology is their world: it is that in which everything coheres. There is no sense outside of this world; thus anything which resists being made sense of in its terms threatens its comprehensive explanatory power, which means to threaten world order. It is for this reason that the friends can only deal in the general "you," since they cannot be addressed anew by a particular "you." Their system is effectively one in the third person, which cannot make room for a genuine second person (even while they make grammatical use of the second person).

But if anything, Job's resolve is strengthened by the friends' inability to hear him. We have seen how he resists their sense-making by his entrenchment within the orbit of first and second persons, appealing first to the friends in their personal presence and then to God, whose tormenting presence he refuses to let go of; and finally how he pits his own sense-making against that of the friends, in the form of a trial against God—albeit a paradoxical sense in which he calls God to account for his unaccountability, and renders himself simultaneously innocent and wretched. Further on in the dialogue, after several twists and turns, Job is goaded by the friends' persistent obtuseness into a yet more dramatic declaration of his refusal to give in to their cheap resolutions: "Why do you, like God, pursue me [*tirdĕpunî*], never satisfied with my flesh? O that my words were written down! Oh that they were inscribed [*wĕyuḥāqû*] in a book [*bassēper*]! O that with an iron pen and with lead they were engraved [*yēḥāṣĕbûn*] on a rock for ever!" (19:22–24). In this Job gives expression, on the one hand, to his desire for a permanent, written record of his trial against God (cf. 31:35–37).[15] But on the other hand, his desire for permanence is his desire

---

15. Clines follows Gordis by translating *sēper* as "monument," pointing out that the verbs *ḥāqaq* and *ḥāṣab* emphasize the durability of the testimony. He notes the judicial language of the strophe and suggests that the words Job has in mind are his depositions referred to throughout chapter 13 (Clines, *Job 1–20*, 428 and 455–56; cf. Gordis, *Book of Job*, 196 and 204). Cf. Habel, *Book of Job*, 303, for a similar rendition.

never to be silenced by the friends' theology. His written words would stand as a testimony to his refusal to acquiesce or submit, and therefore to his irreducible identity.

Job then continues: "For I know [*waănî yāda'tî*] that my Redeemer [*gōălî*] lives, and that at the last he will stand [*yāqûm*] upon the earth; and after my skin has been destroyed, then in my flesh I shall see God, whom I shall see on my side [*ănî 'eḥĕzeh-lî*], and my eyes shall behold, and not another" (19:25–27). Here we arrive at that most memorable passage within Job, most of whose complexities I cannot hope to explore here. Striking, however, is Job's emphatic use of the first person. The passage is dense with first person reference, but Job also twice uses the separate first person pronoun, *ănî*. Further, the vocabulary Job uses (*gōēl* and *qûm*) suggests that he envisages legal vindication.[16] If we take seriously the trajectory we plotted in earlier chapters, it is no coincidence that legal victory before God is accompanied by this first person emphasis: Job is emboldened in his relationship with God to just the extent that he has clung onto his irreducible identity in the face of the friends' attempted reductions.

We cannot move on to an assessment of our findings in this section without looking at the culmination of Job's dialogue with the friends (after Elihu's interruption) in God's speeches out of the whirlwind. We will do so only briefly from the point of view of our particular question regarding the use of pronouns; and without further reflection on the dynamics of the poem as a whole, our interpretation can only be suggestive. The opening of God's response to Job runs as follows: "Who is this [*mî zeh*] that darkens counsel by words without knowledge? Gird up [*ĕzor-nā'*] your loins like a man, I will question you [*wĕ'ešālĕkā*], and you shall declare to me [*wĕhôdî'ēnî*]" (38:2–3). God, by contrast with the friends, appears here to be addressing Job directly—looking him in the eye, as it were. Moreover, while the content of what follows is not an answer to Job on his own terms (and can even be read as being utterly irrelevant to Job's complaint[17]), God seems to continue to engage Job in particular. This impression is informed by the care with which God describes his creatures, each one in particular and for its own sake. No general lessons are drawn, and thus no attempt is made to

16. The *gōēl* is the next of kin who defended the family by avenging blood or redeeming from bondage, but the term is also used in extension of God as one who delivers from bondage or exile (e.g., Habel, *Book of Job*, 304). Habel comments on the legal context of the verse, linking the *gōēl* to the witness of 16:19–21, and understanding *qûm* as an expression for "rising up in court to testify" (*Book of Job*, 293).

17. See Good for a characterization and listing of readings along these lines (*In Turns of Tempest*, 339 and 435 n. 5).

fit Job into a preconceived theology. If Job's categories are irrelevant, then so are those of the friends.[18]

That Job hears God in this way is suggested by both of his responses. After God's first speech he answers: "See, I am of small account; what shall I answer you [*ǎšîbekā*]? I lay my hand on my mouth" (40:4). What has happened to his desire for a permanent written record of his words? Surely Job's willingness to fall silent is a result of the fact that God has spoken to him not in general but in particular, evoking the particularity of his many creatures. But the transformation that results in Job is profound. Job's irreducible identity is no longer something to be clung to and ferociously asserted, because it is no longer threatened by an anaemic third person theology. Job is among the many creatures of God, each of whom has its own divine rationale, untranslatable into human terms. Job's identity is guaranteed by God such that he need no longer fight for it.[19] After God's second speech Job claims: "I had heard of you by the hearing of the ear, but now my eye sees you" (42:5). This, again, is suggestive of the shift from third to second person. Job has persistently demanded that God hear his personal complaint, not by fitting him into a predetermined scheme as would the god of the friends, a mere orderer of the cosmos, but by attending to him in his irreducible identity. Insofar as the whirlwind speeches meet this need, they manifest God to him not as an impersonal deity but as a God who listens and responds. In sum, God addresses Job out of the whirlwind as a thou, and as a result becomes himself a Thou to Job.

3. Job as Indexical Theologian

I claimed in the introduction that Job is an indexical theologian *par excellence*. It is now possible to flesh out what I meant by this—with reference to the exegetical findings of the last section. In the first place, we have found that Job's ability to speak of and sporadically to address God is rooted in the fact that he continues to say "I" where the friends would desire that he become a mere instance of a more general theology. In other words, Job's words about and to God are spoken from within his own unique context.

18. This interpretation has some resonance with that of Gordis, who emphasizes God's joy in the beauty of his creatures, for whom he cares and provides, but who are beyond the control of human beings. However, Gordis understands the speeches to be pointing by analogy with the natural order to a moral order which is beyond human comprehension (*Book of Job*, 435 and 558–60). I would argue that this imports too much purpose into the speeches, whose point is rather to eschew generalizing lessons.

19. For a fuller account of the transformation brought about by the whirlwind speeches, see Ticciati, *Job and the Disruption of Identity*, 101–15.

They are not general declarations or universal truth claims, but personal utterances that gain their purchase from their particular situatedness. They arise out of Job's peculiar relationship with God as embodied in his extreme and inexplicable suffering.

But we can say more about the particular situatedness of Job's utterances by considering, in the light of the above exegesis, their place within the trajectory of Job's transformation. In other words, just as Job's situation is not static, nor is the context for his words. Job begins with outcries of pain and anger which depict God as his hostile enemy. This anguished note does not go away, but it is overlaid and interwoven with a legal language that gives new articulation to his relationship with God in the terms of a trial. Job no longer simply cries out in desperation; he calls God to account. And from within his legal challenge Job begins to sound yet another note: one of confidence that God will ultimately vindicate him (as we saw in chapter 19, but this note is also prefigured in chapter 16[20]). Job, full of confidence in his innocence, utters his final challenge in the oath of chapter 31.

In relation to this, God's responses out of the whirlwind and the change they bring about in Job appear to be a complete volte-face. But I suggest that the clue to their interpretation lies precisely in their connection with Job's own argument. It is only because Job has so relentlessly pursued the God at the root of his experience, caring not for the friends' wisdom, that Job is prepared for an encounter with the God who cannot be captured by platitudes. Job, unlike the friends, has not been blinded by generalizations. Moreover, while his "I" is exploded and decentered in his encounter with God, having been at the center of his own discourse, it is only because he refused to be reduced to a cipher that the multifarious creatures of God's creation can appear for him in all *their* irreducibility. Even if he did not know it, Job had all the while been clinging to his creaturehood before God. This is what is affirmed in the whirlwind speeches via the extravagant spectacle of God's creation as a whole.

These creational terms were not available to Job in his dialogue with the friends, for their creation theology was a domesticated one that emphasized order over particularity. His only recourse was a legal discourse that resisted the friends, but simultaneously constrained Job to paradox: the paradox of God's unaccountable accountability and of his own simultaneous innocence and perversity. This paradox is recontextualized rather than overcome by God's response: the fact of God's response vindicates Job's lawsuit—God is called to account; but the content of the response blows apart the terms of Job's case, showing God to be unaccountable in respect of them. God, as

20. With Gordis (*Book of Job*, 526–27), but against Pope (*Job*, 125 and 146), Habel (*Book of Job*, 274–75), and Clines (*Job 1–20*, 459), I would argue that Job's heavenly witness (16:8) or vindicator (19:25) can only be God himself.

creator, transcends the law, even while holding the law in place. Likewise, Job is heard by God not in terms of his legal status, but as God's creature.

In sum, we can say that God's response is something that could not have been given or heard had it not been for Job's argument. But at the same time it does not automatically follow from Job's argument. It is both the genuine insight of Job and the gift of God.

Job's utterances cannot be understood apart from their place within this radical transformation undergone by Job, a transformation which works itself out gradually during Job's dialogue with the friends and reaches climactic and dramatic reversal in the change wrought in Job by God's speeches out of the whirlwind. They gain their significance from their contribution to this transformation, outside of which they could not give expression to the living God who holds Job dynamically in being—the God who is at the root of his transformation. Before considering, in a final section, how this indexical claim makes sense with respect to particular utterances of Job (on the basis of which we will be able to offer, in turn, a more general argument for the nature of theological truth), there is another layer of indexicality within the Joban text which must be brought to light. More precisely, we are now in a position to understand why Job's theology is indexical in the more than analogous sense mentioned in the first section—why his use of the first and second person gains the pronounced character it does.

The reason is as follows. Job does not merely speak persistently from his own context in defiance of the friends; he makes the need for contextualization his theme. In other words, he does not simply do indexical theology, he articulates the indexical nature of theology. He is an indexical theologian to the second degree. This can be seen, in the first place, in his criticisms of and appeals to the friends. Consider, for example, the following: "Do you think that you can reprove words, as if the speech of the desperate were wind? You would even cast lots over the orphan, and bargain over your friend. But now, be pleased to look at me; for I will not lie to your face" (6:26–28). "As for you, you whitewash with lies; all of you are worthless physicians. If you would only keep silent, that would be your wisdom! Hear now my reasoning, and listen to the pleadings of my lips. . . . Your maxims are proverbs of ashes, your defenses are defenses of clay" (13:4–6; 12). In both cases Job's complaint is that the friends are not listening to and regarding Job as a person—an irreplaceable individual—but have fitted him into their preconceived maxims, reducing his value to the measurable. They have no regard for Job as the context for his and their words. Their theology, as blandly generalizing and contextless, is non-indexical, and as such cannot be challenged or resisted by new particulars. Their responses in 8:8–9 and 18:4 (cited above) abundantly confirm Job's accusation: Job's lifespan pales into comparison with the generations gone by (8:8–9), and as such his claim to be an exception is tantamount to the desire to overturn the earth (18:4). Their message is clear: the second person does not and must not stand out from the third. There can be no indexical theology.

Second, as we have seen, Job's response is to stress his "I"—his irreducible identity. But this is precisely to reassert the indexical nature of his speech (against the friends' contextless claims). Thus he expresses *his* vexation (6:2), *his* innocence (9:20–21), *his* desire to argue with God (13:3), and that *he* with *his own* eyes will behold God (19:27). He cannot be weighed; the law is brought to paradoxical breaking point under the weight of his irreducible identity; he will not content himself with God in the third person, but pleads to be granted God's listening ear; and speaking out of his "I" he foresees such face-to-face meeting. In this way Job does not merely speak from his context but argues for the right to do so—clamors that he be heard in first-to-second person encounter.

4. The Indexical Nature of Theological Truth

In this final section the aim will be to ask more specifically after the significance of particular utterances of Job within their context. On this basis it will be possible to ask more generally after the nature of theological truth. If Job's utterances about and to God gain their significance indexically, is this true for all utterances concerning God?

Let us return, in the first instance, to our opening citation: "For the arrows of the Almighty are in me; my spirit drinks their poison; the terrors of God are arrayed against me" (6:4). Job's characterization of God as his hostile enemy is, as we have seen, a note that (while overlaid by other notes) is only deepened during the course of the dialogue. Consider, for example, the even more extreme utterance of 16:9: "He has torn me in his wrath, and hated me; my adversary sharpens his eyes against me." But would it be right to infer from these utterances as they accumulate over the course of Job's speech the claim "God is (sometimes) hostile"? To do so would be to generalize from Job's individual utterances a general truth claim about God. Is this warranted?

The argument of this essay is that to extract general truth claims in this way is to ignore the indexical nature of Job's speech. We have seen how Job's angry and violent outbursts, with their concomitant portrayals of God, arise within the context of his defiant assertions (against the friends) of his irreducibility. 6:4 follows on directly from Job's exclamation, "O that my vexation were weighed . . ." (6:2). As the counterpart of Job's pain, God as hostile enemy is an index of Job's inability to be circumscribed by the friends' teaching. But more than this, God as enemy is a prelude to Job's characterization of God as adversary-at-law. Job's legal challenge of God becomes the performative context for all of Job's ensuing utterances, by which he seeks not to describe God in general but to call God to account. And the ultimate upshot, as we have seen, is Job's radical transformation, which causes him to put away his earlier words (40:5 and 42:3). This must not be understood to render Job's earlier words invalid; emphatically not. Rather, as the endpoint of the transformation they helped to bring about, it gives them their context of significance. In sum, Job in his speech enacts a relationship with God which ushers in transformation and thus precludes neutrality. His speech is significant precisely insofar as it contributes to this transformation.

To test this conclusion, let us consider the very different words uttered by Job in his responses to God's speech. On the first occasion they include the following: "See, I am of small account; what shall I answer you? I lay my hand on my mouth" (40:4). On the second occasion Job utters amongst other things: "Therefore I have uttered what I did not understand, things too wonderful for me, which I did not know" (42:3). It would be easy to think that it is here that Job reaches genuine insight, and therefore here that his words come to possess generalizable truth, his earlier words being inferior, if necessary, words along the way which can now be left behind. But the adequacy of this reading is sharply brought in question when we consider how these later words would sound if uttered to the friends in response to some of their earlier arguments. Zophar has asked Job: "Can you find out the deep things of God? Can you find out the limit of the Almighty? It is higher than heaven—what can you do? Deeper than Sheol—what can you know?" (11:7–8). For Job to have responded with 42:3 would have been to capitulate entirely to Zophar's argument, conceding his right to be heard and his irreducibility to an instance of proverbial wisdom. Again, Eliphaz has asked, "Are you the firstborn of the human race? Were you brought forth before the hills? Have you listened in the council of God? And do you limit wisdom to yourself?" (15:7–8). Suppose Job were to have answered with 40:4. This would likewise have been to throw in the towel—to relinquish his determination to speak with God, and thus to vindicate the friends' impersonal theology.

In other words, Job's utterances in response to God are not detachable, context-free insights. They are not insights he could have come to more quickly had he only been more spiritually wise or mature. They depend for their meaning on the utterances that have preceded and made way for them. If those earlier utterances gain their significance from their contribution to Job's transformation, the culminating utterances gain theirs from the fact that they are the outcome of this transformation. Moreover, that Job's particular relationship with God led him along this transformative trajectory does not mean that everyone should end up just there where he did. Others with different starting points are in need of different kinds of transformation. Thus his culminating words are no truer in themselves than his earlier words. Submission to God in the abstract is no better (or worse) than rage against God in the abstract. What is demanded on a particular occasion depends entirely on that occasion and the dynamic of the relationship with God it participates in.

Can this conclusion be generalized to all language about God? Is it impossible, for example, to make the general truth claim "God is good"? The argument thus far would suggest that such a claim only becomes appropriate when used to contribute to transformation in relationship with God, in which case it might be said to gain "indexical truth." Outside this transformation it has no purchase. This is shown negatively by the friends' use of such would-be truth claims. Take the claim "God is just," and consider Bildad's utterance: "Does God pervert justice? Or does the Almighty pervert the right?" (8:3). Or take "God is wise" and contemplate Zophar's exclamation: "But oh, that God would speak and open his lips to you, and that he would tell you the secrets of wisdom!" (11:5–6). In both cases, any would-be truth claim is rendered void by the inappropriate use to which they are put in relation to Job.

We could draw the weaker conclusion that no truth claim is free from falsification: any truth claim can be undermined by its insensitive or unloving application, since the act contradicts the words and thereby renders them void. But this weaker conclusion fails to make sense of Job's appropriate use of obviously ungeneralizable claims such as "God is hostile." That noteworthy fact invites the stronger conclusion that God language is indexical through and through, "indexically true" when it contributes to transformation, and "indexically false" when it hinders such transformation.

But this leaves us with the uncomfortable conclusion that the claim "God is good" is on all fours with the claim "God is hostile," or worse still, "God is evil"—since each has the capacity to be rendered both indexically true and indexically false. Such a conclusion need not follow, however. We have argued above that Job's utterances gain their significance from their contribution to his transformation in relation to God. But we have simply assumed that this transformation is good, or in keeping with God's will. While we have described Job's transformation, we have not drawn any normative conclusions about the shape of such divinely willed transformations. However, without anything to guide us in this respect we would be left anchorless in our language about God. By contrast, both the friends and Job are drawing on traditional wisdom in their speech about God, even if they are doing so in radically different ways and to radically different effect. I suggest that it is at this level—the level of tradition (or in a Christian context we might say, more specifically, of church doctrine)—that the language of divine goodness has its privileged context. More specifically, it is within this context that the claim "God is good" is true while the claim "God is evil" is false, or better, that the former is consistently appropriate while the latter is consistently inappropriate. At this level, in other words, the claims remain fundamentally asymmetrical.

This introduction of tradition may seem to tone down the radicality of the earlier claims made with regard to Job's indexical language. But what we learn from the book of Job is that tradition must be put to the service of transformation. Traditional language does not, contrary to what the friends believe, tell us all we need to know about God in advance. Rather, as Job demonstrates, it provides the matrix within which encounter with God might take place. More specifically, it tells you where to look for God's transformative presence. While in the hands of the friends tradition becomes a non-negotiable set of answers, for Job it is a resource for the continual discovery of God anew in the new circumstances life brings. We might put this differently by distinguishing between tradition and its performance. Job's performance makes use of a traditional repertoire, albeit shocking use. Without it he would have nothing to perform—no resources with which to put his case before God. The trouble with the friends, however, is that they cannot distinguish between the resources and the performance. Their performance is thus a stale repetition of tradition. Their mistake is to treat tradition as if it were the primary mode of discourse in relation to God, rather than that which serves transformation in relationship with God.

What conclusions does this allow us to draw regarding the nature of theological truth? If traditional language is not indexical in the way that its performance is (being consistent across contexts), its purchase nevertheless comes ultimately from the transformation it serves. We can legitimately conclude, therefore, that all speech about God ultimately gains its significance indexically, whether by directly contributing to human transformation within particular contexts, or by resourcing this transformation across particular contexts.

5. Concluding Questions

The book of Job shows us indexical theology at work. We have seen not only how Job's utterances gain their significance and truth from their contribution to his transformation, but also how the lack of truth in the friends' utterances is contextually rooted—paradoxically in their denial of the importance of context. We drew from these interpretive findings the tentative wider conclusion that all speech about God is indexical—that it gains its truth from its context of utterance, or more specifically from the transformation to which it contributes. We went on to qualify this conclusion by distinguishing between traditional language and its performative use. While we were not able to claim indexicality for the former, we were nevertheless able to claim that its ultimate purchase comes from the transformations it resources.

We could end the essay here. But the interrogative mood of the book of Job invites us instead to end with a question—a question that will unsettle the comprehensiveness of the conclusions we have drawn regarding language about God. These conclusions have been reached in interpretation of the book of Job: might different conclusions have been reached had another biblical book been the subject of inquiry? We claimed in the introduction that Job "need not be treated as exceptional, but to the contrary can be regarded as normative for Christian tradition." And the essay has demonstrated that Job's use of language both about God and in relationship with God can be generalized without making Job's angry complaint the norm *per se*. But this raises the further question of whether it *should* be so generalized. Is the relationship between tradition and performance exhibited by Job—despite its theoretical generalizability—in fact a result of the extremity of his circumstances? Does tradition only come under this kind of strain and require such radical interrogation in situations of comparable extremity?

If this question is to be answered in the affirmative, then other biblical books are given room to display different understandings of the role and dynamics of God language. The role of the book of Job within the canon would then need to be explored in relation to these alternatives. However, before pursuing this wider exploration, we might ask an analogous, but more immediate, question in respect of the diverse aspects of the book of Job itself—a question invited by Walter Moberly's reading of Job in this volume, which focuses on parts of the book that have not entered at all into the present essay's treatment. With its alternative focus, Moberly's reading arrives at a very compelling—but very different—portrait of Job in his relationship with God. The Job of chapters 1 and 2 (read as Moberly reads them in conjunction with chapter 28) offers an entirely different model of response to situations of extremity. The radical interrogation of the tradition we found within the dialogue (for which we claimed normative status) is nowhere to be found in the prologue. Indeed, Job might even be said, in Job 1:21 and 2:10, to enact the kind of repetition of tradition of which we have accused the friends. In other words, if interpretation of the book of Job is complicated by its presence in a larger canon, it is first and foremost complicated by the different voices that can be heard between its own covers: how is the dialogue of Job and its culmination in the whirlwind speeches to be interpreted in the light of the prologue and the Hymn to Wisdom?

These are questions that lie beyond the scope of this essay. But they are invited by the place of the present essay within this larger volume, which in its wide range of essays manifests the intriguing diversity not only within the book of Job but also within the canon.[21]

21. I am most grateful to Harriet Publicover for her transliteration of the Hebrew in this essay.

4

Spiritual Formation in the Psalms

Gordon McConville
University of Gloucestershire

1. Aim and Definitions

MY AIM IN WHAT follows is to consider in what ways the Psalms may be a resource for the reader who seeks to use them for spiritual formation or growth. This opening heralds one of the underlying questions, namely the search for an appropriate metaphor. To speak of "formation" runs the risk of appearing to propose a formulaic program of change, but may perhaps be adopted with the strictures of Dietrich Bonhoeffer in mind, that it should be understood as formation in Christ, or indeed the formation of Christ in the believer and the church. This "formation," with its by-forms in "conformation" and "transformation," is nothing other than the rediscovery of a person's true humanity.[1] The Christian reader who seeks to identify with the worshipping subject in the Psalms cannot avoid the christological implication of this.

Having said that, the Psalms themselves provide further metaphors for the spiritual life of the faithful, notably the first psalm's "flourishing" like a well-watered tree (Ps 1:3), as well as the prominent "walking in the

---

1. Bonhoeffer, *Ethics*, 61–62. Bonhoeffer means "transformation in the image of Christ" and refers to 2 Cor 3:18; Phil 3:10; Rom 8:29; 12:2. Transformation is also a crucial concept in the magisterial study of Kees Waaijman. Waaijman sees spirituality as encompassing a "divine-human relational process," which is "a process of transformation." Waaijman, *Spirituality*, 426–84 (426).

ways" of YHWH.[2] The topic of the person's transformation is thus bound up closely with language, and I will return below to the Psalms' use of metaphorical language in particular as central to the understanding of the human subject's transformation.

2. Spiritual Growth in the Old Testament

Regardless of quests for a "center" of Old Testament Theology, the human subject is evidently in focus throughout,[3] in a richly varied portrayal that consistently puts the question about character and the spiritual quality of human life. Josipovici, referring to the canonical shaping that brings the "historical" books under the rubric of the Prophets, says, "the tradition seems to imply that what is important is not so much the historical continuum of conquest, exile and return, as the spiritual link between Moses, the first prophet ('by a prophet the LORD brought Israel out of Egypt,' says Hosea 12:13), Samuel, David and Elijah, and the so-called 'writing prophets' like Isaiah and Jeremiah."[4]

Throughout the Old Testament, there is an assumption of the possibility of spiritual flourishing. A narrative such as that of Joseph and his brothers (Gen 37–50) displays this possibility, even if the extent to which either Joseph or any of his brothers actually undergoes spiritual change is a matter of how one reads the key moments in the narrative.[5] One of the striking features of Old Testament narrative's depiction of character, however, is its resistance to any notion of simple progression. The boy Samuel can hear the word of the LORD, whereas the aged priest Eli cannot, or can no longer, and has become a helpless spectator of the moral and spiritual decline of his house. The story's reversal of what ought to be the case is pointed up in 1 Sam 2:18, with a certain ironic wonderment at this boy-priest implied in its circumstantial clauses: *ûšmû'ēl mĕšārēt 'et pĕnê yhwh na'ar ḥāgûr 'ēpôd* ("Samuel was ministering before the LORD, a boy wearing a linen ephod," NRSV). Here, as often in Hebrew narrative, irony serves as a tool

2. For the metaphor of "pathway," see Brown, *Seeing the Psalms*, 31–53.

3. Gabriel Josipovici, writing about the thematic unity of the Bible, says, "As in any narrative, the same protagonists, God, man and Israel, run through the entire story." Josipovici, *Book of God*, 12.

4. Ibid., 43.

5. This involves judgments about whether the characters speak truthfully or expediently, and so whether they truly disclose their character. Barbara Green has expressed reservations about the sincerity of Reuben in Gen 42:22 (Green, *What Profit for Us?*, 123), *contra* Sternberg, *Poetics of Biblical Narrative*, 291. I have also explored this in "Forgiveness."

for alerting the reader against complacency of expectation. The boy Samuel is indeed said more than once to be growing in maturity, in respect of both God and people (1 Sam 2:21b, 26; 3:19), as the contrast with Eli is pursued. Yet in the fully developed portrayal of his life, for all his greatness, a certain shadow falls over it, with the implication that he eventually succumbs to a destructive favoritism for his own sons that is one of the marks of spiritual weakness in the wider narrative of Judges-Samuel (1 Sam 8:1–3).

The reading of Old Testament narrative with an interest in learning the spiritual life, therefore, does not postulate characters who offer simple paradigms for imitation. The reading process is hermeneutically complex. As readers, we perceive that the narratives place their characters under a judgment, variously a judgment of God, the narrator and the reader, a judgment which then falls in turn back on the reader. Richard Briggs, in his portrait of "the virtuous reader," puts it thus:

> implicit in the Old Testament's handling of a wide range of moral and ethical categories, we find a rich and thought-provoking portrait (or perhaps series of portraits) of the kind of character most eagerly to be sought after, and this in turn is the implied character of the one who would read these texts, especially one in search of their own purposes and values.[6]

The same point holds in principle for the different divisions of the Hebrew Bible. Torah, Prophets, Wisdom, and Psalms project in their own ways images of the person who is open to being transformed by the Word of God.

3. The Person in the Psalms

In the Psalms, the human subject appears most directly in the voice of the psalmist, especially when speaking in the first person singular. This speaking subject is not identifiable with any historical person, as form-critical approaches to the Psalms have long recognized. There are, of course, intimations of royalty in a number of psalms, as in Ps 2, where a voice addresses the speaker in language from the lexicon of Davidic kingship: "You are my son, today I have begotten you" (Ps 2:7 NRSV; cf. Isa 9:5[EVV6]), and where connections are made between particular psalms and the life of David, as in Ps 18 (cf. 2 Sam 22), and in a number of superscriptions (e.g., Ps 51:1–2). These testify in different ways to a kind of theological reflection on the memory of King David, embedded in the editing and shaping of the Psalter, which is itself part of the spiritual reception of the Psalms. If

6. Briggs, *Virtuous Reader*, 17.

there are parts of the Psalter where the king is depicted as conforming to a pattern of righteousness, this, according to Patrick Miller on Pss 15–24, is because he is presented as a kind of "ideal Israelite."[7] This is, then, not the historical David, but a projection of a righteous individual, and we might add, a "virtuous reader." The significance of the speaking subject as "I," on this view, is its capacity for the reader's identification with it. The singular has sometimes been understood to represent a plurality, such as the people of Israel or the worshipping community, in a particular extension of the Davidic persona. But be that as it may, the predominance of the speaker as "I" is of paramount importance in itself, I believe, for engaging the individual reader in imagining the life of the human self before God.

3.1 A Unified Portrayal of the Person?

Is there, then, a unified or coherent portrayal of the righteous person in the Psalms? There are suggestions of this, for example in the formal features that are recognized in the modern tendency to read the Psalms "canonically," both in respect of the book as a whole, and of sub-sections of it (as in Miller's reading of Pss 15–24). The voice that leads the creation in praise at the end of the Psalter (Ps 150) arguably embodies a kind of fulfilment of the project at the outset (Ps 1), where the one who delighted in the LORD's *torah*[8] was pronounced "happy." Thus the possibility of "happiness" is sustained throughout, in spite of the many trials and tribulations encountered along the way, and all nurtured by that delight in *torah* that finds its most intense expression in Ps 119.[9] Yet the canonical project has not led to unanimity on the interpretation of the Psalms' message. G. H. Wilson's classic account of the canonical shaping of the Psalter, with its conclusion that a Wisdom framework predominated over a Davidic-messianic one,[10] has been challenged by others who maintain that a Davidic eschatological hope remains paramount.[11] The canonical approach does not overcome the problem of diversity.

Indeed, however one seeks to unify the Psalter, the diversity of voices remains one of its unavoidable features. While the Lament form is perhaps

---

7. Miller, "Kingship."

8. Where the term *torah* appears in this form, it stands, not for the division of the Hebrew Bible (Torah), but for the phenomenon of *torah*, that is, law or instruction, more broadly. It is a rendering of the Hebrew *tôrâ*, but refers to a concept represented by a range of vocabulary, as in Ps 119. See further below, n. 33 and context.

9. I have argued along these lines in "Happiness in the Psalms."

10. Wilson, *Editing of the Hebrew Psalter.*

11. For an account, see Howard, "The Psalms," 23–29.

the most prominent expression of the human experience in the Psalter, with its many examples of a return to trust and praise following doubt, attack or distress, it does not exhibit an inexorable linear forward movement. The classic theory of an "oracle of assurance" tended to a false harmonization in this respect. Many psalms sustain a tension in experience between trust and besetting anxieties. The cyclical pattern of Pss 42–43 is just one example of this. There is no systematic way of integrating the many expressions of the self in the Psalms into a coherent or prescriptive picture of the spiritual life.

The Psalms' portrayal of human "flourishing," therefore, is distinct from those modern accounts that lay strong emphasis on the analogy of health. Many in the health disciplines have recognized a "spiritual" dimension in the human being and the healing process.[12] The trend known as "positive psychology" is based on the premise that human beings have often-untapped resources to improve their lives.[13] Such analyses often recognize a spiritual dimension in the quest for well-being. For C. Robert Cloninger, what he calls "positive philosophy" is essentially a belief in the innate capacity of the person, through their "psyche," to intuit their unity with universal reality. People can choose to progress along a path of consciousness in a process of growth. The language at this point is quite "religious":

> we contemplate what is good (as well as true and beautiful), so that we can grow in the depth of our love of the Truth[;] . . . we grow in our love of what is—that is, reality, Truth, God—which is eternal, light, and good, not what is transient, heavy, and selfish.[14]

However, it is questionable whether the Psalms will bear an interpretation of flourishing in terms of health (or even "well-being"). David Kelsey calls the "health/well-being" model of flourishing into question, arguing that human flourishing depends radically on the person's relation to God, and the belief that the world that the person inhabits has a future in the renewal of all things. This does not have the effect of minimizing the harsh actualities of life. Rather, it accommodates an approach to life which can face up to its many vicissitudes.[15] Charles Taylor says something similar, and points to the eschatological dimension of the life of faith:

12. See Tournier, *Médecine de la personne*. Tournier's work has spawned a literature in itself; see Cox et al., *Medicine of the Person*.

13. E.g., Seligman, *Flourish*.

14. Cloninger, *Feeling Good*, 91–92.

15. Kelsey, "On Human Flourishing," 15. For Kelsey, "a theological account of human flourishing cannot identify suffering as a decisive criterion of a human being's non-flourishing, even though it is a criterion of severe ill-health and non-well being, nor can it imply that the elimination of suffering, even horrendous suffering, is a necessary condition for any human flourishing theocentrically understood" (ibid.).

> Although Christian faith has incorporated and at times elabo-
> rated different conceptions of the natural order of things, it
> focuses on another dimension, the eschatological. We are called
> to live a quite transformed life, one in which death has been
> overcome. This transformation calls for our living for some-
> thing beyond the human flourishing, as defined by the natural
> order, whatever it be.[16]

This view of the spiritual life accords with the Psalms' portraits of persons in relationship with God, rather than programs for self-improvement.[17]

3.2 The Person and Consciousness

The question of the person's coherence arises in a further way. This has to do with consciousness itself. The point is fundamental for any prospect of a reader being able to associate somehow with the person who is projected in the Psalms. The modern reader, confronted with "I," knows immediately that this is problematical. Ordinary experience tells us of the unsettling limitations of self-knowledge that attend the most sincere declarations of intent. Conscious-ness, under the microscope, seems a poor guide to who we "really" are. The novelist Iris Murdoch sees an inescapable relation between the problem of consciousness and the moral life: "how can there be moral responsibility in view of the brokenness of consciousness?" and "Can there be felicity . . . in the moral life?"[18] Postmodern thinking about the instability of the self is evident here, characterized by Terry Eagleton, with typical panache, as "merely a function of power, a congeries of sense-impressions, a purely phenomenal entity, a discontinuous process, an outcrop of the unconscious."[19]

Such questions pose a challenge to the psalmists' postulate of the self as thinking, willing subject. But how do we make sense of this in relation to the infirmities of will and intention that we experience? It is a false trail, I think, to look for the true self in some inner core of the being, or to suppose that a term such as *nepeš* (often rendered as "soul") designates a kind of inner life that can be distinguished clearly from the person's public demeanor.[20]

---

16. Taylor, *Secular Age*, 66.

17. It also broadly accords with what might be called an Augustinian understand-ing of "happiness." For Augustine, as Ellen Charry puts it, "life's goal is to enjoy God utterly." Charry, *God and the Art of Happiness*, 51.

18. Murdoch, *Black Prince*, 189–90. The speaker is her central character, the story's narrator. Self-knowledge is here something more profound than "self-awareness."

19. Eagleton, *Event of Literature*, 6.

20. Thus far, I agree with DiVito, "Old Testament Anthropology."

This is not to deny interiority. The psalmists were, indeed, aware of some kind of inwardness, as suggested, for example, by Ps 103:1 (where *napší* is in parallel with *kol qĕrābay*, "all that is within me"). Elsewhere the psalmist speaks of *God's* knowledge of him in his full complexity, a thing that is too "wonderful" for the psalmist himself to know (Ps 139). DiVito goes too far when he argues that Old Testament people, in contrast to modern people, had no sense of "inner depths," by which he means that "the subject is relatively transparent, socialized and embodied."[21] If we are to make sense of the Psalms' depiction of the self, it will not consist in distinctions between inner and outer aspects of the subject. Rather, the language of the self, as in uses of the term *nepeš*, should be understood to express the psalmists' longing to be truly human. This makes best sense of the trope of the poet's address to his *nepeš* in texts like Ps 103:1, as well as of the pervasive psalmic prayer that the LORD should lead and teach him his "ways" (Ps 25), or indeed of the notion that the psalmist delights in the LORD's *torah* (Ps 1; 119). There may be mysteries in the depths of the psalmist's being, but self-knowledge will be contingent on the person's knowledge of God, and so a matter of faith.

The unsuspected force of the psalmist's predication of the self in the ubiquitous "I," indeed, is an assertion that there is such a thing as "humanity." The point is not as obvious as it may appear. It implies the reality of a human nature that takes its existence and meaning from God. Human subjects find their individuality in relation to this common nature.[22] And this has implications in turn for the relation of the human subject, not only to God, but to the created order. That is, there is such a thing as "the good," and this is the proper object of human desire.[23]

Right desire is at the heart of the Psalms' portrayal of the human being. As for what constitutes the desirable, or the good, we have broached this above, with reference to the ultimate orientation of human longing towards

21. DiVito, "Old Testament Anthropology," 221.

22. By "human nature" in this context is meant the idea that there is something essentially human, such that individuals recognizably belong to the category "human." This is in contrast to the idea that humans (or any other entity) are irreducibly particular. Eagleton writes that "humans are the distinctive individuals they are by virtue of their participation in a specific form of 'species-being,' and that the process of individuation is itself a power or capacity of this common nature." *Event of Literature*, 8. (He is referring to the early Marx in the context, but the point is part of his own argument).

23. Fergus Kerr, writing about Aquinas, puts it thus: "The exercise of the will is more like consenting to the good that one most deeply desires, rather than imposing oneself on something different or recalcitrant . . . [it] is aligned conceptually with desire, consent, delighted acquiescence, in short, with love." Kerr, *Thomas Aquinas*, 69, 48; cited in Eagleton, *Event of Literature*, 13. The context of Eagleton's remarks is a discussion of philosophical nominalism and realism.

God. The Psalms maintain a certain earthiness alongside their desire for God in their conception of the good. In Ps 16, the LORD is the psalmist's "portion" and "cup" (*měnat ḥelqî wěkôsî*, v. 5, cf. v. 2), yet there is a this-worldly horizon in his trust that his body (*běśārî*) will dwell secure, and that he will be delivered from death (vv. 9–10). The "good" is unthinkable apart from God (v. 2), but the sense of a good and favored life has a reality in the actual world (v. 6). Psalm 23 also maintains a connection between the psalmist's relationship with God and the facts of earthly life in the metaphors of the shepherd's negotiation of physical dangers and of the table laid before enemies (Ps 23:4–5). The essential point, however, may not lie in whether the "good" is located in this life or beyond, but rather in the psalmist's longing for a restitution of created harmonies between the person and God and the external relations that constitute the person's world.

4. The Psalms and Transformation

If the person in the Psalms exhibits a desire to become fully human, this is predicated upon the possibility of change, or transformation.[24] The desire for change is everywhere apparent in the Psalms, especially in the forms of Lament or Petition. What kind of transformation is meant here? I have suggested already that the person must be understood in their wholeness, and take this to include, at least, the interrelatedness of inner disposition, intellect, emotion, and social relations.[25] The desire for transformation, furthermore, cannot be detached from the location of the person in a tradition. The person's orientation to the future is inseparable from the factor of memory.

Some of this is illustrated by Ps 42–43, a poem that seems to presuppose that the psalmist has been somehow separated from the temple and its worship.[26] The keynote of desire is struck in the opening words of the poem,

24. See above, n. 16, on transformation according to Charles Taylor, *Secular Age*.

25. To attempt to describe human wholeness comprehensively would be an enormous task. John Swinton identifies the aspects of the physical, intellectual, emotional, social, and spiritual—where "spiritual" includes notions of transcendence, meaning, value, hope, and purpose. Swinton, *Spirituality and Mental Health Care*, 36–37. He bases his analysis on Peplau, *Interpersonal Relations in Nursing*.

26. See Schaefer, *Psalms*, 107. Michael Goulder thought the temple in question might be the sanctuary at Dan, citing the northern geographical references. Goulder, *Sons of Korah*, 23–37. This has some support from Seybold, *Die Psalmen*, 174. But the language hardly has the force to determine a setting in a cult other than that of Jerusalem, and need not even require a situation of exile, but any circumstances in which the psalmist has been prevented from participating in worship; see Craigie, *Psalms 1–50*, 325.

where the longing of the "soul" (*nepeš*) is likened to the craving of a thirsty deer for water (42:1[2]). The metaphor of thirst and the vivid physical image of a large animal to convey the person's deepest desire show that the person's whole being is the subject of this desire. And the object of it is no less than God; the psalmist yearns to come and be in God's presence (v. 2[3]). God is not just an undefined ultimate reality, but the God of Israel, about whom a very particular story may be told, with whom persons relate, and about whom they use passionate language. This is a God whom the psalmist already knows in experience and memory. The adversaries say, "Where is your God?" with its implication of an existing bond between God and the psalmist, together with a set of expectations on the psalmist's part. Memory and desire are inseparable, as in 42:4[5], where "remembering these things" is paired, in a close syntactical relationship, with "pouring out my soul." There is also a close connection between the psalmist's relationship with God and his relationship with other people. His remembered joy and gladness in the worship of God is in the context of the physical act of walking to a place, in company with others. The person here is not only embodied, but also essentially in relationship. Moreover, the unity of memory and desire is such that memory also discloses the desired future, the end of a trajectory in fulfilment, as the rediscovery of joyful communion in worship of the God who is known.

Connected with this expression of deep desire, expressed through memory, are aspects of renewed understanding, and the engagement of the will. The psalmist's view of her present reality has an underlying rationale. God is the God who saves the psalmist (42:5[6]); characterized by "steadfast love" (*ḥesed*) (42:8[9]), God is the one in whom the psalmist can take refuge (43:2), who gives judgment in her favor against those who deal unjustly with her (43:3), who leads her by his light and truth (43:3). The adversaries, who keep saying "Where is your God?" see a discrepancy between the psalmist's expectations of God and her present situation, and the psalm may be seen as a response to their taunt. At one point, the psalmist expresses her own perplexity at her abandonment by the one whom she trusts (43:2). Yet taken as a whole, and especially in the refrain in 42:5[6], 11[12]; 43:5, the psalm is an affirmation that her trust in God will in the end be vindicated.

Finally, the psalm itself is an act of the psalmist's will, notably in the poetic device in which the poet repeatedly exhorts her *nepeš* to "hope in God." The will thus plays a crucial part in the restoration of the psalmist to a right mind. If this is "free will," it is a contested freedom, for the psalmist is challenging her own propensity to give up. Why does she "go about mourning"? Is not the "casting down of her soul" itself a failure of the will that needs to be addressed? Here is an act of the will in the furtherance of the realization of desire, as the psalmist seeks to enter a virtuous circle. And if the psalm represents a triumph of the will, what hidden factors brought about this triumph? How far may it have been due to a recovery of true perspective owed to the operations of memory and participation that belong to the psalm's vision of the person's integration? If the psalmist had her adversaries, she will also have had her friends, who may have been indispensable to her renewal.

5. The Psalms and Transcendence

If the Psalms testify to the possibility of human transformation, there is also an implication of their capacity to transcend the life circumstances in which the psalmists find themselves. The point just made about the connection between desire and the specific memory that belongs within a tradition raises the important question of situatedness. If we are to maintain our ability as modern readers to associate ourselves with the speaker in the Psalms on the grounds of a common human nature, and thus the possibility of transformation in our various situations, we may not underestimate the contingencies of time and place that must be reckoned with in all reading. The possibility of change, or transcendence, can be addressed by considering, first, the nature of hope as expressed in the Psalms, and second, by examining further the capacity of language itself to express the desire for change.

The Psalms, like all the biblical literature, have a context in the life and thought of ancient Israel, and it follows that every kind of study of that context, be it historical, literary, psychological, sociological, or ideological, is in principle relevant to their understanding. And these disciplines in their various ways stress the distance between the biblical writers and audiences and the modern reader.[27] Modern treatments of the Psalms are concerned with their location, as a post-exilic work that aims to come to terms with the crises of 587 BCE and after, and wrestles with questions such as how God's ancient promises to the Davidic king can be understood in the light of the violent end brought to that dynasty.

Yet it is a function of the form of the Psalter that it is impossible to make its meaning depend on its specific historical situation. As already

27. DiVito's perception of the distinct psychology of ancient Israelites compared with moderns, for example, is incontrovertible, and finds an echo in Charles Taylor's contrast of the "porous" person of antiquity with the modern "buffered" individual. Taylor, *Secular Age*, 37–38. For psychological readings of the Old Testament, see also Brueggemann, "Psychological Criticism." For ideological particularity, Erin Runions puts it thus: "the reader comes to a text already formed as a subject within ideology." Runions, *Changing Subjects*, 250.

noted, the Psalms have, as separate compositions and as a whole, precisely been extricated from specific situations. The overarching Davidic rubric has the curious effect of signalling disjunction from putatively original settings. It is therefore intrinsically difficult to make the Psalms subservient to some specific religious or political program. It might still be supposed that by virtue of their general historical and theological situation, they represent a "conservative" view of the world, exhibiting and reinforcing certain "binaries," such as male versus female, or humanity versus nature. Some of the imagery for creation found in the Old Testament and Psalms, for example, in which God appears as a warrior, has been thought to express a kind of violence towards the earth, even if this can also be said to be subverted or redeemed in places.[28] The predominance of male voices and interests in particular has represented for some an obstruction to the Psalms' capacity to speak positively to feminine experience.[29]

It seems to me, however, that the Psalms' extrication from situation is of their essence, and that consequently they have a capacity for transcendence that enables them to escape limitations of meaning that might be imposed on them by specific situations. First and most obviously, they are predicated upon profound disturbance of worldview. A number of psalms face up to the deconstruction of the Israelite-Judean symbolic map. Psalm 89 is a prominent example of this, because it addresses the problem so directly, and because of its position at the close of Book 3. It rehearses in a lengthy hymn the ancient promise of an everlasting dynasty to David (vv. 1–37[Heb 2–38]), only to put to it the jarring existential question that arises from the LORD's own "rejection" of his "anointed" (měšîḥekā) (vv. 38–51[39–52]), presumably referring to the disappearance of the dynasty from history following the Babylonian conquest. The agonized questioning is relieved in the end only by the doxology: "Blessed be the LORD for ever, Amen and Amen" (v. 52[53]) NRSV. The prospect here is entirely open, containing both praise and perplexity, and even shifting the notion of permanence that was characteristic of the Davidic covenant (lě'ôlām, "for ever," cf. vv. 1–4[2–5] and 2 Sam 7:13) to the continuance of the LORD himself and his praise. This feature, in one sense ironic, in another indicating a kind of resilience, is found also in lāneṣaḥ in v. 46[47]. (See also Ps 103:9,

28. Walker-Jones, *Green Psalter*, 151–54.

29. Carleen Mandolfo has documented this in a paper given at SBL, San Francisco, 2011: "Feminist Enquiry into the Psalms and Book of Lamentations," now forthcoming in a volume edited by Susanne Scholz and F. Rachel Magdalene. For Mandolfo, the difficulties are not entirely insurmountable. She outlines ways in which features of the Psalms may permit constructive feminine receptions "in front of the text." I am grateful to Professor Mandolfo for a preview of the published form of the paper.

where *lāneṣaḥ* is in parallel with *lĕʿôlām*, in an affirmation that YHWH's anger would not be permanent.)

Another psalm of profound disturbance is Ps 74, which laments the destruction of the sanctuary, in terms which once again ironically evoke the promise of permanence ("the perpetual ruins," NRSV, *lĕmaššuʾôt neṣaḥ*, 74:3). This notion of permanence persists to the closing word of Ps 74, in which the clamor of the LORD's enemies' goes up "continually" (*tāmîd*, v. 23) in the psalmist's present time. The query about the promise is thus put pointedly once again. The psalm sets its questioning in the context of an affirmation of the LORD's kingship in creation, in terms which (as in Second Isaiah) declare his superiority to the gods of Babylon (74:12–17). Thus hope is reaffirmed in the midst of extreme disorientation, and without any articulated outcome.

Finally, Ps 73, which, as the opening psalm of Book 3 brackets the book together with Ps 89, is especially significant for an understanding of the Psalter as a whole. The psalm follows the pattern of the Lament, in the sense of traversing the ground of doubt and fundamental questioning, before returning to a place of repose. But what exactly is reaffirmed here? The opening statement (v. 1) puts the psalm in a tradition of affirmation, and we recognize at once a rereading of inherited creed. The beginning anticipates the ending, placing the intense questioning of God's justice that forms the core of the psalm under the rubric of faith. Yet there is something unsettling in it, signalled by the textual uncertainty felt by commentators and translators over whether to read "Truly God is good to Israel" (with MT) or "Truly God is good to the upright" (NRSV), on the grounds of the inner parallelism of the line and the theme of the psalm as a whole.[30] The unexpectedness of "Israel" in this line suggests that the psalmist is not only considering the hard issue of God's apparent preference for the wicked, but also what it is to speak of Israel. (The meaning of "Israel" is always in question in the Psalms. Who is meant, for example, in Ps 118:2; 124:1?).[31] The resolution of the psalm, too, though evidently a return to confidence, is entirely open in relation to the manner in which God will demonstrate his goodness to the upright (or "Israel"). Rather, it rests on a restored belief in

30. The reading of NRSV is supported by Kraus, who thinks that MT "is hardly possible in view of the inner division of verses and also in consideration of syntax." Kraus, *Psalms 60–150*, 83. There is no support from the ancient versions for the emendation.

31. The term tends to be taken in a rather general sense of "the community," allowing for settings that are no longer national. According to Allen, Ps 124 had a long history, form-critically speaking, and may reflect the adaptation of a group's song of thanksgiving to communal praise. Allen, *Psalms 101–150*, 164. This presupposes the capacity of "Israel" as a concept to be adapted in the light of experience, while retaining its power to evoke YHWH's saving in the past. For the many possible meanings of "Israel" in the Hebrew Bible generally, see Davies, *"Ancient Israel,"* 48.

God's presence with the psalmist (v. 23), which however cannot specify the form of the vindication ("receive me with honor" [NRSV], or "receive me to glory" [RSV]), nor the time of it, beyond an indeterminate "afterwards" (v. 24). The ambiguity of this language is apparently of the essence of its meaning. In this rereading of traditional theology, no present actuality can be taken for granted, only a radical trust in God remains.[32]

I have introduced the idea of the Psalms as rereading, and we have observed that it is reflected in the language itself. Within the context of worship, the psalmists are taking into their thinking the possibility that entire frames of reference may have to be reimagined. Not only the core concepts of David and Israel have been summoned for recharacterization, but even Moses and Torah are not exempt. In the great meditation on *torah* in Ps 119, there are clear echoes of Moses and the covenant at Sinai, with its wide semantic range of "law." But the referent of the term *torah* (*tôrâ*) and its analogs is elusive. Is it a body of written law? Is it oral teaching of the law? Is it Priestly, or Deuteronomic? In fact, I think there is no answer to this. The question is of the same order as: Who was David?—a concept that has been thrown open for reevaluation, as we have seen. The focus of Ps 119 is on the piety of the believer; this hearing of the Word/*torah* of the LORD implies a knowledge of that Word that belongs within the believer's life before God, but does not specify it as an object.[33]

5.1 Transcendence and Language

In drawing attention to the Psalms' transformation of tradition, we have begun to see how this is partly carried by their language. Walter Brueggemann recognized the power of language to transform in his well-known analysis of trajectories in the Psalms in terms of disorientation and reorientation. His model of reorientation does not imply a simple return to a previous state, but allows for the radically new. For example, the "declarative hymns and songs of thanksgiving" (e.g., Ps 124), understand

32. Psalm 17 might also be included here, with its "waking" to behold the face of God (17:15). Despite attempts to concretize this into, for example, an account of a night-vigil in the temple and a ritualized "waking," the nature of the experience and the content of the vision remain elusive; see McConville, "Psalm 17."

33. Cf. Freedman, *Psalm 119*, 89. Freedman thinks that while the Psalm apparently presupposes the existence of written Torah, it "never specifies the actual contents of *tôrâ*. . . . Moses, Sinai and covenant have all disappeared; nor is anything known of its setting or the identity of its speaker" (94). Waaijman focuses on the experience of reading the Psalm as a spiritual act in itself, and one that, by its pervasive allusiveness, opens up "the full space of Scripture as a whole." Waaijman, *Spirituality*, 717.

that "a newness has been given which is not achieved, not automatic, not derived from the old, but is a genuine newness wrought by gift."[34]

The Psalms rest on the tacit premise that speech is effective, and linguistic acts change things. B. A. and B. D. Strawn, writing about the effect of language on the different psychologies of ancient and modern audiences, say that "psychological effects are taking place in the working of the literature itself—in both its writing and its reading," and they cite Holland, Kugler, and Grimaud: "Consciousness is continually being imagined (imaged, in-formed) by the metaphors in the very text it is writing or reading."[35] This perception points to the significance of the act of language as a component of the Psalms' capacity to transform. It is another caution against a sharp distinction between the inward and the external in a person, as when the performance of ritual acts—including speech-acts—is regarded as separate from a truer inward disposition.[36] Such acts, indeed, can produce a change in a person's disposition.[37] The power of utterance itself, in the context of prayer, may sufficiently explain the "change of mood" in the psalms of Lament, that is, without recourse to other special factors (such as a prophetic "word of assurance"). For Josipovici, prayer is analogous to speech between human persons, that is, in language that has meaning "in the linguistic and social usages of the community" and is "what mediates between inner and outer"; there is no prayer without words. He goes on to reflect on the significance of uttering the pronoun "I":

> By entering language and the community of men I find myself. To speak to God is to acknowledge this, that in speaking I trust that I will find myself. That is why the poems of Herbert, the English poet most deeply imbued with the Psalms, so often exhibit a profound change at the end; for it is the act of making the poem, of uttering it, that leads to change, to an unblocking, and so to a new simplicity, a new clarity, "something understood."[38]

34. Brueggemann, "Psalms and the Life of Faith," 14. For his view of language, he refers to Ricoeur, *Conflict of Interpretations*, e.g., 96.

35. Strawn and Strawn, "Prophecy and Psychology"; Holland et al., "Psychological Criticism," 1000.

36. See the critical remarks of Josipovici on Friedrich Heiler, *Prayer* (1918), in which Josipovici resists a distinction between "prayer of the heart" and "formal literary prayers." *Book of God*, 159, cf. 161.

37. So argues Lapsley, "Feeling Our Way," who also cites Anderson, *A Time to Mourn*.

38. Josipovici, *Book of God*, 163. He also refers to Samuel Beckett's *Not I*, and the character there who cannot say "I." There is in this a kind of refusal of personal responsibility; ibid., 162–63.

And again, language "[enables] us to outer ourselves and thus become fully alive."[39]

5.2 Transcendence and Ambiguity

The power of the language of the Psalms to transform is inseparable from its specific poetic qualities. We began to notice the suggestive power of the psalmists' language above, in ironic allusions to God's promise that the Davidic dynasty would last "for ever." W. P. Brown points to the close relationship between metaphor and the imagination. Its play with the spoken and the visual enables the seeing of "several things at once, in order to create something new." And this new creation involves a passage from the known to the unknown.[40] The capacity of the Psalms' language to suggest both concrete realities and something not quite contained by these may be exemplified by Ps 23, where the phrase *lĕmaʿgĕlê ṣedeq* rests on an interplay between "right paths" (safe for shepherding) and "paths of righteousness," as part of a sustained interpenetration of physical and spiritual sustenance. The point could be illustrated at length. I will consider here just one further example, necessarily briefly.

Psalm 84 is ostensibly a psalm of pilgrimage. An older hypothesis saw the psalm as a "liturgy of the temple gates," that is, the prayer of a pilgrim who has arrived in Jerusalem and recalls the arduous journey now finished.[41] But the modern tendency is to think of a setting far from Jerusalem, perhaps in the Diaspora, expressing a longing for the presence of YHWH felt by communities far from home.[42] In favor of the latter view is the mood of deep longing, which seems to suggest that temple worship is something lost, remembered and yearned for. In this respect the psalm has some kinship with Ps 42–43 (another psalm of Korah).[43] I want to suggest that the linguistic features that suggest separation from the temple also serve to construct a view of the psalmist and the life before God that is characterized by this absence.

39. Josipovici, *Book of God*, 165. Iris Murdoch says something similar, when she speaks (again through her narrator) of "the redemptive role of words in the lives of those without identity." *Black Prince*, 199.

40. Brown, *Seeing the Psalms*, 9. On the passage from the known to the unknown, he cites Gillingham, *The Poems*, 15–16.

41. Kraus, *Psalms 60–150*, 167.

42. Gerstenberger, *Psalms*, 126; Hossfeld and Zenger, *Psalms 2*, 350–51.

43. Psalm 84 has even been thought to be based on Psalm 42–43. Hossfeld and Zenger, *Psalms 2*, 351.

A first striking feature is the plural forms that are used to evoke the temple and its precincts, namely "thy dwelling-places" and "courts of the LORD" (vv. 1–2[Heb 2–3]), and "thy altars" (v. 3[4]). This may indeed be a plural of splendor, that is, not a true plural, but its effect is to shift the attention away from the temple in its concrete singularity, and evoke instead the atmosphere and experience of the presence of God. It is closeness to God that the psalmist wishes to experience, as is borne out by the language of longing itself, with its involvement of the psalmist's whole being in the combination of *nepeš* ("soul"), *lēb* ("heart-mind"), and *bāśār* ("flesh").[44]

In vv. 5–7[6–8] there is a progression from the happiness of "those who dwell in thy house" to images of the journey. Happiness is now predicated of those "whose strength is in thee" (*'ōz lô bāk*), which is immediately qualified by *měsillôt bilbābām*, (literally) "in whose hearts are highways." The odd phrase caused uncertainty in the textual tradition, and some modern translations supply "to Zion" (NRSV), or adopt other expediencies.[45] But the phrase can make sense as an internalization of the idea of pilgrimage, and may be read, for example, as: "who have the paths of pilgrimage in their hearts."[46] The absence of Zion is thus offered to the interpreter for pondering. And the phrase is a striking case of the ambiguity between what might be an actual pilgrimage route and a metaphorical sense of a pathway to the presence of God.

The ambiguities continue with the image of the "valley of Baca" (v. 6[7]), an unknown place, whose echoes of *bākâ*, "weep," have long been observed. With or without that particular echo, the image here is of dryness converted to life-giving waters.[47] The natural image of rain goes closely together with "blessings" (*běrākôt*).[48] How, indeed, might the passing pilgrims make a dry valley a place of springs? The thought here may begin with the idea of a pilgrimage at the time of the early rains, but it travels on to an evocation of blessing in a broader sense, an accompaniment of the worshipper's longing for God.[49]

---

44. Ibid., 355.

45. Kraus emends *měsillôt* to *kěsillôt*, and takes the phrase as "trust in their heart." *Psalms 60–150*, 166.

46. Hossfeld and Zenger, *Psalms 2*, 348.

47. The Hebrew *bākā'* denotes a kind of shrub that grows in dry places. The term is associated in the ancient versions with *bākâ*, "weeping" (Vg. *vallis lacrimarum*). Hossfeld-Zenger, *Psalms 2*, 349. Their interpretation of the line rightly shows, however, that an extended sense of the term does not depend on this echo (355).

48. Wordplays on *môreh* ("rain" or "teacher") and between *běrākôt*, "blessings," and *běrēkôt*, "pools," have also been observed. Goldingay, *Psalms*, 2:594.

49. Cf. Brown, *Seeing the Psalms*, 41.

The image of a progression continues with the phrase *mēḥayil ʾel ḥayil*, which could hint at fortified cities along the way,[50] but is more familiarly taken as "from strength to strength," intimating a personal strength that comes from the worshipper's seeking of God. It is the vision of God that is the desired culmination of the journey. The latter verses of the psalm, like its beginning, are based on an imagining of Jerusalem, the home of the vision of God (v. 7b[8b]). The LORD's "anointed" (*mĕšîḥekā*) is also invoked, and so a memory of the Davidic king. The referent of the "anointed" is not quite clear, however,[51] and the allusion to "our shield" (*māginnēnû*, v. 9[10], elsewhere David) is transferred to God himself in v. 11[12]). The "courts" of the LORD reappear, again in a plural, corresponding to the plural "tents of wickedness," and the poet taking a position not quite within them. The psalm concludes with the declaration that human happiness (*ʾašrê ʾādām*) consists in trusting in YHWH (v. 12[13]), so that the final note is not limited to Zion, and takes in the broad scope of human happiness.

There are, therefore, indications throughout the psalm that it depicts a piety that has roots in, but is not dependent on, the temple worship. Hossfeld and Zenger conclude their commentary on verses 10–11[11–12] thus: "the 'Temple piety' of Ps 84 is not restricted to the cult, but rather projects a comprehensive spirituality of daily life (Wisdom perspective!)."[52] They rightly perceive that the psalm is not a simple iteration of a Zion-pilgrimage perspective, though its assignment to another category ("Wisdom"), may underestimate its creative power to engage the imagination for the transformation of the life before God in the context of profound threat to a person's deepest sense of their identity.

6. Conclusions

We began by thinking of what is involved in reading the Bible in accordance with the Bible's own projections of the person who hears the Word of God. In the case of the Psalms, this has proved to lay down a profound challenge. The Psalms do not feature characters or situations in the way that narratives do. The persona who is presented everywhere is detached from identifiable situations and employs many voices, so that the reader cannot readily perceive a pattern of "formation." Yet there is here a peculiarly powerful presentation of the human subject, which challenges the reader to a profound self-knowledge and engagement. The reader is invoked in the entirety

50. Schaefer, *Psalms*, 207.
51. Hossfeld and Zenger, *Psalms 2*, 356.
52. Ibid.

of their being. This includes not only the "inner" dispositions of mind and heart, but also the more visible outcomes of purpose and desire, in social relations and public attitude and participation. This public aspect extends to an active engagement with themes associated with the prophets but which also arouse the passion of the psalmists, namely truth and justice (Pss 12; 50:16–23), as well as the more overtly "religious" dimension of participation in the words and acts of worship.

The formation of the persona of the Psalms is not finished, but the reader catches it in the act, and recognizes their own participation in an unfinished project of formation. This involves a kind of bi-focal view, in which the reader participates fully in the concrete world of their physical and social existence, yet is sustained in it by a vision of a humanity that is still in the making. This bi-focal view emerges strongly in the longing that characterizes so many of the psalms, even in those that express great confidence, such as Pss 16 and 23, where the possibilities of harm and death cast their shadow. This rooting of the Psalms in the reality of earthly existence gives them their immense credibility, while at the same time lending meaning to that reality by the vision of God.

Spiritual formation, therefore, is a realization of what it is to be fully human within the constraints of earthly existence, made possible by the reader's identification with the psalmist's active life of faith and worship. To speak of full humanity in Christian perspective is to invoke that model of it that is Christ. The specifically Christic color of this humanity is entailed in the narrative of Christ's earthly life, and his death on the cross as the condition of resurrection to the glorified life of the kingdom of God. In Christian perspective, therefore, the Psalms' tension between the realities of human life and the eschatological vision takes its meaning from that narrative. Taylor, correspondingly, characterizes the tension in Christianity in terms of the disciple's commitment to love God as far as the cross, or death, while also affirming ordinary life, and the possibility of ordinary human flourishing.[53] Spiritual formation in the Psalms, for the Christian reader, is by definition christological, the conformation to Christ adumbrated at the beginning of this essay. Important strands of Christian spirituality have assimilated the Psalms to the wider project of transformation into the likeness of Christ (2 Cor 3:18). In doing so, however, they have been able to adopt the language and potential meanings of the Psalms in themselves for that project. The use of the Trinitarian Gloria in liturgical practice such

---

53. Taylor, *Secular Age*, 80. Similar notes are struck by Bonhoeffer, *Ethics*, whose ethics drove him to the extremity of opposition to what he saw as the manifestation of hostility to God in the public sphere, and by Jacques Ellul, with his combination of eschatological hope and revolutionary Christianity. Ellul, *The Presence of the Kingdom*.

as the Anglican and Benedictine embraces the Psalms within Christian worship, without further commentary. In Benedictine practice the regular liturgical reading of the Psalms is the primary content of the Divine Office, permeating the monastic life, and in itself an act of testimony and devotion to Christ.[54] The Benedictine handbook puts it thus:

> the psalms were not only an external discipline but also a help to the internal life. Little by little, when combined with silence and *lectio*, external words, the words of the world, are gradually abandoned, until all that is heard is the Word of God. When that Word is all that there is to shape the mind, the thought, the conversation of the disciple, then it has begun to be internalized, and it can begin the work of transforming the heart, what Paul calls "having the mind in you that was in Christ Jesus" (Phil 2:5).[55]

Such reception of the Psalms calls for the work of theological interpretation, rather than rendering it superfluous. But for the Christian disciple, the learning of Christ is various and unfinished, and the language of the Psalms lends its unique accents to it. The Psalms' performance of the realization of the human self in the life lived in relation to God contributes for the Christian reader to their growing experience of what conformity to Christ might mean in the particularity of their own life.

54. I am grateful to Sandra Schneiders for making this point at the Cheltenham Symposium, and for pointers to the literature.

55. *Benedictine Handbook*, 132. See also Chittister, *Rule of Benedict*, 84–89, who shows how the Psalms were the focus of Benedictine daily spiritual practice.

5

Singing for the Peace of Jerusalem
Songs of Zion in the Twenty-First Century

Ellen F. Davis
Duke Divinity School

"Pray for the peace of Jerusalem—may those who love you be at rest."

(Ps 122:6)

Truly, "Jerusalem" name we that shore,
City of peace that brings joy evermore;
Wish and fulfillment are not severed there,
Nor do things prayed for come short of the prayer.

(PETER ABELARD, TRANS. J. M. NEALE)

For all your songs, I am a violin.

("JERUSALEM OF GOLD," NAOMI SHEMER)

1. The Mystery of Jerusalem

THIS ESSAY IS MY first exploration of a mystery upon which I stumbled more than forty years ago, as a student in Jerusalem, and with which I have lived more or less closely ever since, namely the *numen*, the spiritual weight or attraction of that place. "Glorious things [*nikbādôt*] are spoken of you, City of God," says the psalmist (Ps 87:3)[1]—*nikbādôt*, things invested with weight and consequence. The unique spiritual status of Jerusalem or Zion is presented to us as a profound mystery, a mystery that lies at the heart of history and possibly of the created order itself.[2] Elements of that mystery are asserted countless times in the Old Testament, especially in the two great poetic corpora of Psalms and Prophets; its reality is both assumed and affirmed by some New Testament writers, mostly notably Luke and John the Divine. On that basis, it would seem that Jerusalem and what happens there is a necessary focus for Christian thought, prayer, and action. Indeed, the Psalms, the backbone of the church's prayer, address everyone who has ears to hear with an unparalleled directive to "pray for the *shalom*, the well-being, of Jerusalem" (Ps 122:6).[3]

History demonstrates that Jerusalem's *mysterium fascinans*[4] has been compelling for Christians, although too often in the wrong way, as the long and deep tragedy of the Crusades attests. A very recent instance of the highly politicized affirmation of Jerusalem's special spiritual status by a Christian occurred on December 7, 2011, when Newt Gingrich promised a group of Jewish Republicans that if elected, he would immediately move the

---

1. All translations are the author's own.

2. While the Bible does not state explicitly that Zion was the starting point for creation of the world, the Talmud does make that assertion, based on a reading of Ps 50:1–2: "The Sages said: 'The world was created from Zion, as it is said: "A Psalm of Asaph, God, God, the Lord hath spoken," whereupon it reads on: "Out of Zion, the perfection of the world"; that means from Zion was the beauty of the world perfected'" (b. Yoma 54b). A possible allusion to such a mythos is Ezekiel's reference to a people (Israel) living secure "at the *ṭabbûr* of the earth" (38:12); following Talmudic usage, Jon Levenson renders the uncertain word as "navel" (*Sinai and Zion*, 115–17).

3. The only similar injunction to prayer for the well-being of a city is the instruction to the exiles in Babylon to "seek the *shalom* of the city to which I [YHWH] have exiled you" (Jer 29:7). However, the fact that the imperative here (in contrast to that in Ps 122) is addressed to a specific group in a particular historical situation would seem to narrow its potential scope.

4. In his seminal work on the phenomenon of the numinous, Rudolf Otto distinguished the twin (and inseparable) elements of *mysterium tremendum* and *mysterium fascinans*, the dual power that is experienced as a "daunting 'awefulness'" and at the same time entrances and compels us "to make it somehow [one's] own" (Otto, *Idea of the Holy*, 31).

American Embassy from Tel Aviv to Jerusalem. I do not warm to Gingrich's politics, nor probably to most of his theology (if there be such). But still I wonder: Is it possible that statements such as his become more potent and volatile in significant part because the matter of the special sanctity of Jerusalem receives too little critical attention in contemporary Christian theology and spirituality? Especially the spiritual weight of Jerusalem may be overlooked or denied by those who identify with the so-called mainstream church (however misleading that designation may now be). I recall a brief exchange over lunch in a "mainstream" seminary cafeteria one day, when a student said to me (in what connection I have forgotten), "I simply don't believe that Jerusalem is different from every other place." My response probably sounded more glib than I intended: "Well, that's one thing that makes you different from nearly every one of the biblical writers."

This essay is an attempt to test my own response by asking a critical question, or rather a small set of questions:

- Should Christians acknowledge, as most of the biblical writers do, the special spiritual quality of Jerusalem?

- What is the theological reasoning that might underlie a practice of praying for the peace of Jerusalem?

- If we pray for the peace of Jerusalem, then how should we do it?

My exploration here focuses on three things: *first*, on the biblical doctrine of the holiness of Zion, as set forth in Psalms and submitted to critique by the Prophets; *second*, on how the burden of Jerusalem's spiritual weight has been borne by those who love her—that is, by those whom the psalmist charges to pray for her—including Jeremiah and the Lukan Jesus; *third*, on singing as the primary vehicle whereby the unique spiritual standing of Jerusalem has impressed itself (however obliquely) on Christian awareness through the centuries, and as a possible locus for a healthy practice of prayer for the peace of Jerusalem.

In all this I am seeking the basis on which a spiritual practice that is almost universally neglected by Christians might be (re)established. As we are all aware, the sheer political significance of Jerusalem in our time is probably greater than it has been in centuries, maybe ever, and so prayer for the peace of Jerusalem is potentially a politically significant act. Therefore I must be explicit at the outset in saying that I offer this with the hope of eliciting interfaith engagement in such a practice, which might itself stimulate critical theological thinking among Muslims, Jews, and Christians. Perhaps that is one contribution that might belong distinctively to twenty-first-century spirituality.

1.2 The Doctrine of Jerusalem and the Prophetic Critique

The biblical witness to Jerusalem's special character shows a strong awareness of complexity and even contradiction. On the one hand, it is a political
entity, the seat of kings who were for the most part no better than the norm
for rulers in the ancient Near East and probably every time and place. On
the other hand, Jerusalem remains throughout the Bible, for both Jews and
Christians, possibly the most powerful symbol of religious aspiration, pointing to what God has yet to accomplish and what humans have yet to achieve.
Both the Jewish and the Christian canons end with images of aspiration
focusing on Jerusalem. *Tanakh*, the canon of Hebrew Scriptures, concludes
with Cyrus the Persian's self-proclaimed charge to build a house for YHWH
in Jerusalem and the call to any one of God's people who might be living in
exile, "Let him go up [to Jerusalem]!" (2 Chr 36:23). For centuries Jews have
prayed for the opportunity and the will to answer that call. The Christian
Bible likewise ends with a vision of Jerusalem restored for habitation by the
faithful. However, in John's Revelation there is no going up to Jerusalem,
but rather the great descent of "the holy city of Jerusalem, coming down out
of heaven from God" (21:10). This is the Jerusalem that the Isaiah tradition
imagined, illumined solely by the glory of God, shedding light by which
the nations walk—and tellingly, it has no Temple apart from God Almighty
(21:22–24), so there can be no imperial appropriation of religious power.
That there is a mutual attraction between Jerusalem and the faithful, long-
suffering people of God would seem to be a crowning affirmation of biblical
theology in both forms of the canon.

If there is in the Bible what a later mode of theology might call a
doctrine of Jerusalem, then surely we find it in the Psalms, and probably
there is no clearer statement than this, from Ps 46:

> There is a river whose streams gladden the city of God,
> the holy habitation of the Most High.

(This is love language; the geophysical Jerusalem is a rather arid place.)

> God is in her midst; she shall not be shaken;
> God will help her at the break of day.
> Nations are in tumult; kingdoms shake;
> he sends forth his voice; the earth melts.
> YHWH of Hosts is with us;
> the God of Jacob is a stronghold for us. (Ps 46:5–8 [EVV 4–7])

An even bolder statement of the *numen* of the place is this one:

> Walk around Zion; go all the way round her;

count her towers.
Take note of her strength;
pass among her great buildings;
so you may recount to the last generation,
that this is God,
our God forever and ever.
He will lead us forevermore. (Ps 48:13–15)

"This is God"—to this psalmist, Zion is the place where God's presence is palpable; for all practical purposes, it is visible. Thus walking about Jerusalem becomes something like a sacrament: an outward, physical, and symbolically enacted encounter with God's real and gracious presence to humans—"this is God." The experiences of God recorded in these psalms are closely akin to Isaiah's great Temple vision, where God's long robes flow all the way down the *axis mundorum*, the straight line that runs from the heavenly throne room into the Holy of Holies. Mount Zion, the Temple mount, is the closest we can get to heaven while still on earth. That is the root affirmation of the biblical doctrine of Jerusalem.

Yet as my first theology professor laid down the principle, every orthodox teaching has its concomitant heresy, the perversion to which it is liable. In the Bible, it is mostly the work of the Prophets to expose such perversions, as Micah does with a devastating oracle in which he explicitly cites the songs of Zion:

Hear this, you heads of the house of Jacob,
and leaders of the house of Israel,
who abhor justice
and pervert all that is straight,
building up Zion with blood-crimes,
and Jerusalem with wrongdoing—
her heads sit in judgment for a bribe,
and her priests give instruction for a price,
and her prophets tell fortunes for silver.
But they lean on God, saying:
"Is YHWH not in our midst?
Evil will not come upon us!"
Therefore because of you,
Zion is a field that will be ploughed,
and Jerusalem will be a ruin,
and the Temple mount, a shrine in the forest. (Mic 3:9–12)

The people have been gulled by their leaders; Zion without justice and truth-telling is a mockery of God; the city has become a deathtrap for leaders and people alike.

Yet that does not mean the ideal is hollow. Rather, the very next verse proclaims Jerusalem's exaltation "at the end of days," when all nations will stream to her, go up to the mountain of YHWH for instruction:

> For from Zion will go forth *tôrâ*, true teaching,
> and the word of YHWH from Jerusalem.
> And he will judge among many peoples,
> and mediate for powerful nations [far away],
> and they will beat their swords into ploughshares
> and their spears into pruning hooks,
> and nation to nation will not lift up swords,
> and they will not learn war anymore. (4:2–4)

This same oracle appears also among the words of Isaiah of Jerusalem (2:2–5) and is likely an editorial addition here; thus the two nearly contemporaneous traditions work together to make the point that the prophet is responsible for holding up the vision of what Zion could be and in the deepest sense has always been: the meeting place of heaven and earth—and not the royal acropolis.

The order in which the oracles appear in the Micah tradition is crucial: first the statement of abject failure by the religious and political leadership, and only then the vision of a world without war, of peace proceeding from Zion. If one heeds that order, then the doctrine of Jerusalem can indeed be maintained, yet neither naïvely nor narrowly. This oracle goes beyond any delusory notion that God is present or perceptible in Zion merely to guarantee the safety of one special nation. To the contrary, Micah foresees Jerusalem ploughed as a field, and the very first chapter of Isaiah shows Zion abandoned like a harvesters' shack in a cucumber field (Isa 1:8) or, changing the metaphor, like the harlot the once-faithful city has become (1:21). The Micah and Isaiah traditions join forces to assert unambiguously what is in fact the much larger claim of Ps 46, that the God who is in the midst of Zion is at work even now, and from that place,

> making wars to cease to the end of the *'ereṣ*, the earth . . .
> Let go [your weapons] and know that I am God;
> I am exalted among the nations, exalted upon the earth.
> YHWH of Hosts is with us;
> the God of Jacob is a stronghold for us.
> (Ps 46:10–11 [EVV 9–10])

Those who pray for the peace of Jerusalem are constrained to bear in mind the larger vision and promise of this song of Zion: If YHWH of Hosts is "with us" in this one place, it is for the sake of the peace of the whole world.

2. Bearing the Burden of Jerusalem

The most obvious reason to pray for the peace of Jerusalem is that Jerusalem is not a very peaceful place, and there is no biblical or historical evidence that it ever has been so. "Jerusalem stone is the only stone that can / feel pain," says the city's greatest modern poet, Yehuda Amichai. "It has a network of nerves." This portion of an extended poem, "Jerusalem 1967," goes on to image the city as the tower of Babel, beaten down by God, its houses and walls flattened:

> and afterward the city disperses, muttering
> prayers of complaint and sporadic screams from churches
> and synagogues and loud-moaning mosques.
> Each to his own place.[5]

Having been reared in an Orthodox Jewish family, with German and Hebrew as his mother tongues, the adult Amichai was not religious. Yet through his poems he remained in steady conversation with the poets of the Bible, while articulating a kind of personal doctrine of Jerusalem:

> I and Jerusalem are like a blind man and a cripple.
> She sees for me
> out to the Dead Sea, to the End of Days.
> And I hoist her up on my shoulders
> and walk blind in my darkness underneath.[6]

"The End of Days"—'aḥărît hayyāmîm: the phrase echoes the Zion oracles of Isaiah (2:2) and Micah (4:1) and other Prophets—is no less visible from Jerusalem than is the Dead Sea on a clear day, looking out from the Mount of Olives to the eastern wilderness, which is the direction from which God always enters Jerusalem (Isa 63:1; Ezek 43:2; Zech 14:1–5; cf. Luke 19:28–44). For Amichai, Jerusalem is a necessary burden; it is the source of both immediate darkness and long-distance vision.

The tone of Amichai's poems of Jerusalem is distinctly reminiscent of the prophet Jeremiah—in his sadness, his inability to lay down the burden

5. Amichai, "Jerusalem 1967," 51.
6. Ibid., 55.

of Jerusalem, and his deeply personal laments over the city, whose tortured existence determines the character of his own:

> My joy is gone; grief is upon me;
> my heart is sick.
> Hark, the loud cry of my dear-people
> from the far corners of the land:
> "Could it be that YHWH is absent from Zion?
> That her King is not in her [midst]?" . . .
> For the brokenness of my dear-people I am broken;
> I go in mourning; desolation has taken hold of me.
> Healing-balm—is there none in Gilead?
> No doctor there?
> So why is the open sore of my dear-people not healed?
> If only my head were water
> and my eyes a fount of tears,
> so I could weep day and night
> for the slain of my dear-people!
> (Jer 8:18–19, 21–23 [EVV 8:18–19, 22; 9:1])

"My dear-people" is a (necessarily inadequate) rendering of the Hebrew phrase that expresses the tragedy in which Jeremiah is enmeshed: *bat-ʿammî*, literally "my daughter-people." It is a term of affiliation, perhaps a pet name. Yet spoken in such terrible circumstances—Judah, God's wayward daughter (Jer 31:22), is facing or about to face her enemies and will not escape whole—it underscores or even heightens the prophet's (or God's) anguish. He sees clearly what they do not yet see, that they are doomed. With his tears Jeremiah models the grief over the people's faithlessness—grief that they themselves should feel, but cannot.

Jeremiah articulates the terrible possibility that Zion's King has abandoned her, and he never fully allays that fear. A generation later an anonymous poet, who evidently knows Jeremiah's prophecy well, brings to the fore the question of abandonment and denies it categorically.[7] Known to us as the Second Isaiah, this prophet-poet offers the most exquisite biblical statement of God's unshakable commitment to Jerusalem:

> Zion says, "YHWH has abandoned me,
> and my Lord has forgotten me."
> Does a woman forget her suckling from her own womb,
> the child of her body?
> Even these might forget,
> but I, I will not forget you.

7. On Second Isaiah's use of Jeremiah, see Sommer, *A Prophet Reads Scripture.*

Look, I have engraved you on my palms;
your walls are before me always. (Isa 49:14–16)

God, too, bears the burden of Jerusalem, or rather God wears Zion like a tattoo—a scar deliberately, painfully, and indelibly inscribed; however the bearer might come to regret the image, it is there forever. Jerusalem is ineluctably part of God's person, even God's body, imaginatively speaking.

The Evangelist Luke places Jesus of Nazareth firmly in this tradition of anguished commitment—both prophetic and divine—to Jerusalem. The city and its Temple are the epicenter of the drama of Jesus' life, the goal and consummation of his earthly mission. Alone among the New Testament writers, Luke represents the Temple and its ceremony in wholly positive terms. The Gospel opens with a scene in the inner precinct, where just to the right of the altar of incense the angel of the Lord appeared to Zechariah, a priest from the division of Abijah (Luke 1:5, 11). With such details Luke recreates for his readers the distinctively Jewish milieu in which Jesus lived. Likewise in the second chapter, we learn that Mary and Joseph fulfilled the law of Moses in taking their infant son to the Temple, to present the prescribed offering following the birth of a male child (Luke 2:22–24; cf. Lev 12:1–8). The parents, and presumably Jesus himself, were among the pilgrims coming to Jerusalem every Passover (Luke 2:41). It was there, at the age of twelve, that Jesus first attracted public attention with his skill in the back-and-forth dynamic of Torah study, "[his] Father's business" (2:49). This was no hostile disputation; in the manner of Jewish prodigies through the ages, Jesus learned from and with the most respected sages of his generation. Thus, as Luke says, "he advanced in wisdom and stature and favor with God and people" (2:52; cf. 1 Sam 2:26).

So it was in Jerusalem, at the Temple, that the adolescent Jesus first manifested his mastery of God's word; the grown man Jesus was later brought there by the devil, where he withstood the final temptation, refusing to put God to the test (4:12). It is against this long history of Jesus' spiritual maturation and strengthening, always with reference to Jerusalem, that we must understand the distinctive Lukan theme of Jesus "setting his face" to go there, as the time drew near for him to be "taken up" from the earth (9:51, cf. 9:53; 13:22; 17:11; 18:31; 19:11, 28). The most telling passage is the account of his exchange with the Pharisees who come to him on the way and warn him:

"Leave and go someplace else, because Herod wants to kill you."
And he said to them, "You go and say to that fox, 'Look, I am casting out demons and performing healings, today and tomorrow, and on the third day I shall bring it to completion. But it

> is necessary that today and tomorrow and the next I journey
> on, for it is impossible that a prophet should perish outside
> Jerusalem.' Jerusalem, Jerusalem, who kills the prophets and
> stones those who have been sent to her—how many times have
> I wanted to gather your children as a hen [gathers] her brood
> under her wings, and you did not want it. Behold, your house
> is abandoned to you. I tell you, you will not see me until you
> say, "Blessed is the one who comes in the name of the Lord" [Ps
> 118:26]. (Luke 13:31–35)

Judith Lieu observes that here "*Jerusalem* stands for people who have experienced blessing and responded with disobedience," following upon the Old Testament tradition (e.g., Neh 9:26) that "the prophets met their death at the hands not of outsiders, but of those they came to warn."[8] Yet she points out that, unlike later Christian writers who saw the destruction of Jerusalem as divine punishment for the Jews' refusal to recognize Jesus, Luke "distinguishes between the city and the various groups within it, and he also emphasizes Jesus' yearning for the city."[9]

Both his yearning and the distinction among the inhabitants of Jerusalem are evident in another scene closely related to this one, of Jesus coming to Jerusalem for the last time. He weeps as he descends the Mount of Olives and sees the city that still does not know "the things that make for peace" (19:42). In a chapter that directly cites sayings about the Temple from both Isaiah and Jeremiah (Luke 19:46; cf. Isa 56:7; Jer 7:11), Jesus' tears evoke both these prophets, who wept over *bat-'ammî*, "my dear-people" (Isa 22:4; Jer 8:22f). And what is more, they suggest God's own anguish for the city. In this portion of the narrative, Jesus' action and person is fully transparent to God's own. As the throng of disciples greeting him proclaimed, Jesus enters the city as her King, "in the name of the Lord [*kurios*]" (Luke 19:38); three times in the chapter Jesus himself is called *ho kurios*, "the Lord" (19:8, 31, 34).[10] David Tiede suggestively compares Luke's unique portrait of the weeping Jesus with this passage from 2 *Baruch*, which alludes to grief in the heavenly realm: "Do you think that there is not mourning among the angels before Mighty One, that Zion is delivered up in this way? Behold, the nations rejoice in their hearts. . . . Do you think that the Most High rejoices in these things or that his name has been glorified?" (2 *Bar* 67:1–3).[11] The

8. Lieu, *Gospel of Luke*, 112.

9. Ibid., 157.

10. C. Kavin Rowe has argued persuasively that the appellation *ho kurios* for Jesus points to Luke's high Christology; see his *Early Narrative Christology*.

11. Tiede, *Luke*, 332.

poignancy of this final visit is intense, and the people's response to Jesus contrasts sharply with that of their leaders. He went daily to teach in the Temple where he had once listened to the wisest teachers of the age, and while the chief priests and other leaders of the city plotted his demise, "the whole people [*laos*][12] hung upon his words" (Luke 19:48).

This time Jesus has come back to the city, willing and intending to die there, "for it is impossible that a prophet should perish outside Jerusalem" (Luke 13:33). This saying, unique to Luke,[13] is a crucial theological assertion. Marshall rightly notes that "the force of the verb [*ouk endechetai*] should not be pressed to produce the false general rule that all prophets perished in Jerusalem." Yet his own interpretation is still too generalized: "Rather, since Jerusalem does kill prophets (v. 34), it is appropriate that Jesus as a prophet should die there too."[14] Luke is emphatic that it is not just appropriate but *necessary* for Jesus to die there, and the necessity for this particular death in Jerusalem is underscored by the further statement—an allusion to Jeremiah 12:7 and 22:5—"Behold, your house is abandoned to you" (Luke 13:35). Thus Jesus obliquely raises the same question that Jeremiah and Isaiah posed directly: "Is it possible that God has abandoned Jerusalem?" Jesus' determination to die in Jerusalem and nowhere else is itself the unequivocal and prophetically informed answer to that question.

Jerusalem has often killed the true prophets, yet God has long refused to give up on the beloved city. Zechariah speaks of the great burning jealousy God feels for Jerusalem (Zech 8:1), the unquenchable passion that moves God to bring the people back out of exile in Babylon to dwell in the holy city. The concluding chapters of that book envision its restoration, indeed its elevation to total sanctity, right down to the last holy cooking pot (Zech 14:21). One verse in that concluding section has particular importance for understanding Jesus' death: "And I shall pour out on the house of David and on the inhabitants of Jerusalem a spirit of grace and supplication, and they will look upon the one whom they pierced, and mourn over him as one mourns over their only child, and weep bitterly over him, like the bitterness over their first-born" (Zech 12:10). This is the kind of weeping that Isaiah and Jeremiah model for the Jerusalemites, and that Jesus, God's "only child," enjoins upon the women who follow him to the place of crucifixion (Luke 23:27). Such weeping denotes a clear understanding of one's own desperate situation, a return to sanity and to God after a time of profound alienation.

12. I. Howard Marshall notes that *ho laos* denotes for Luke "the Jewish people as God's people, the nation apart from its leaders" (*Gospel of Luke,* 722).

13. The statement does not appear with Matthew's version of the lament over Jerusalem, 23:37–39.

14. Marshall, *Gospel of Luke,* 573.

Later Christian tradition, recognizing the transformative capacity of deeply sane weeping, would come to call it "the gift of tears."[15] Some of us know the bitter yet grace-filled experience of being recalled to ourselves, not by the anger of someone whom we have wounded, but rather by their patent suffering and simple refusal to leave us. That is how Jesus' death in Jerusalem works, as Luke sees it, and why it is impossible, from a prophetic perspective, that he should die outside Jerusalem. His final, willing walk to "the place called the Skull" (23:33) is the fullest affirmation of God's unswerving commitment to Zion and Jesus' own desire that God's will should be accomplished through him (22:42).

Thus in Luke's eyes the crucifixion does not diminish the spiritual significance of Jerusalem but rather enhances it, as his account of the events that follow demonstrates. Is it merely convention that "Peace" should be the resurrected Lord's first word to his disciples gathered in Jerusalem (24:36)? Or is the standard greeting rendered more meaningful here, since not long before Jesus had wept over the city's failure to recognize the things that make for peace? Now the peace-making gospel of "repentance [directed] toward forgiveness of sins is to be proclaimed in [the Messiah's] name to all the nations, beginning from Jerusalem" (24:47). It is exactly as declared through Isaiah and Micah, that the word of the Lord—the Father's word now embodied in the life, death, and resurrection of Jesus—goes forth from Jerusalem, the place where God's promises from every age begin to be fulfilled. Everything in Luke's account of the immediate post-resurrection events points in that direction: Jesus' word of peace perhaps, and certainly his further words of blessing as he is taken up into heaven (24:50–51), his injunction to "stay in the city until [the disciples] are clothed with power from on high" (24:49), and the fulfillment of that promise when the Holy Spirit is poured out on Pentecost. Significantly, fulfillment comes in the form of mutual understanding, and leads to repentance (Acts 2:1–39). These several events bring the story back to where Luke's Gospel began: in the Temple and its immediate environs, with faithful Jews witnessing to God's transformative action and offering their praise.

So what have we seen? In Prophets and Psalms, and in Luke-Acts, which is so deeply informed by both, there is a recurrent theme of lament over Jerusalem, compassion for Jerusalem, and commitment to Jerusalem, evinced by both God and humans. All these biblical books express the conviction that in some way Jerusalem exists for the sake of the world; it is the point from which true religious witness ("Torah") radiates outward "to the

15. On the importance of weeping in multiple religious traditions, including Eastern and Western Christianity, classical Sufism, and Judaism, see Patton and Hawley, *Holy Tears*.

ends of the earth" (Acts 1:8). Likewise, this is the place where the mutual fidelity[16] between God and Israel is tested and proven, as evidenced in Jesus' faithful suffering but also in the suffering and witness of the apostles (Acts 5:40–42) and the martyrdom of Stephen (Acts 7). And what does this mean for us? If we heed the psalmist and pray for the *shalom* of Jerusalem, then we shall necessarily assume some of the burden of its pain, its violence, and its confusion, as the Israeli poet Yehuda Amichai so vividly expresses. I take it as no coincidence that all these writers, ancient and modern, religious and secular, use poetry (or poetically informed prose, such as Luke's) to explore the "open secret"—or, as David Ford defines *musterion*, holy mystery[17]—of Jerusalem's special spiritual status.

3. Singing of and for Zion

Through the generations in the church, singing is the way that Christians have most commonly articulated a theological understanding of Jerusalem, whether or not they were conscious of doing so. Save only the theme of divine sovereignty, there may be no element of Old Testament theology or spirituality that has so much stimulated the musical imagination of the church as has that of Zion. For most of the history of the church, hymnody may be the only healthy way that Western Christians have remembered Jerusalem. An outstanding example is Peter Abelard's *O Quanta Qualia* ("O what their joy and their glory must be," in John Mason Neale's felicitous translation) composed late in his life, long after his own deep humiliation, for the nuns at Abbess Heloise's Convent of the Paraclete. Although this Jerusalem hymn was written during the Crusader period, it is wholly free of Christian triumphalism. Rather, in this extended expression of longing for the heavenly Jerusalem, conceived as *patria*, "dear native land,"[18] Abelard identifies himself with the Israelite experience of "long exile on Babylon's strand." Although it would be too much to see Abelard as deeply sympathetic with his Jewish contemporaries, nonetheless he is able to represent their suffering without caricature or defamation. On one occasion he even uses a Jewish voice to express the experience of being despised and hounded (an

16. The theme of God's fidelity to the people Israel as evidenced in Jerusalem is a central concern of Luke Timothy Johnson in his study, *Prophetic Jesus, Prophetic Church*.

17. David F. Ford evokes the notion of "open secret" in relation to the "daring identification of the *musterion* . . . of Christ with the reconciliation of Jews and Gentiles" in Ephesians; this particular application might well be connected with the "open secret" that this essay explores. See Ford, *Self and Salvation*, 114.

18. The theme of Jerusalem as a homeland for those who were not literally born there may reflect Ps 87.

experience he himself knew well, for very different reasons): "We are confined and oppressed, as if the whole world had conspired against us alone. It's a wonder we are allowed to live."[19] Remarkably, Abelard uses the voice of a Jew to express his own understanding of what it is to be humiliated (setting aside the vexed question of the degree to which Abelard invited his own humiliation). M. T. Clanchy observes: "Abelard is one of the few medieval churchmen who shows any understanding of what the Jews suffered at the hands of Christians."[20]

In this final section, I want to consider how the Christian practice of singing about Zion/Jerusalem, which likely began with the earliest years of the church, might prove to be theologically productive in our generation, and perhaps in some new ways. Specifically, I wonder whether singing might be a vehicle whereby Christians might pray alongside Jews and Muslims —together, or separately yet in awareness of each other—for the peace of that most holy place, Zion, Jerusalem, Al-Kuds.

If Zion-oriented hymnody is to address the critical ethical and theological problems we currently face, then it must overcome a limitation that has characterized such hymnody in the past, namely that it ignores Jerusalem as a geopolitical entity. Christians have sung about the eschatological reality of the heavenly city, or they have imaged as Zion the church or some sector of it, often a marginalized or oppressed sector.[21] In this way Christian hymnody has created a distinction between Jerusalem the city and Jerusalem the symbol or locus of religious aspiration, a distinction the Bible itself does not observe. When it comes to the land of Israel and especially Jerusalem, the realities of geophysical space and concrete social events are acknowledged, even as they are invested with meanings—often simultaneously theological and political—that stretch from creation and Eden to the historical past to the measurable future to the eschaton. As we have already seen, the "songs of Zion"[22] is one set of texts that offers much evidence of

19. Abelard, *Dialogue of a Philosopher*, cited by Clanchy, *Abelard*, 17.

20. Clanchy, *Abelard*, 17.

21. For example, many Dissenting churches in late seventeenth- and eighteenth-century England were named "Zion" (Fountain, *Isaac Watts Remembered*, 60), and Zion is repeatedly evoked in hymns written by Isaac Watts for "non-conforming" congregations. The name has strong resonance also in multiple strands of African-American religious experience, and it is no coincidence that Watts' "Marching to Zion" became inspirational for the American civil rights movement.

22. I follow the psalmist in using "songs of Zion" (Ps 137:3) as a non-technical designation for those psalms that give central attention to Jerusalem.

such an "all-inclusive simultaneity [that] opens up endless worlds to explore and, at the same time, presents daunting challenges."[23]

Here I am describing biblical conceptions of Jerusalem in terms of the concept of "Thirdspace," developed by political geographer Edward Soja. Drawing on the work of Henri Lefebvre, Soja defines Thirdspace as

> the space where all places are, capable of being seen from every angle, each standing clear; but also a secret and conjectured object, filled with illusions and allusions, a space that is common to all of us yet never able to be completely seen and understood, an "unimaginable universe," or as Lefebvre would put it, "the most general of products."[24]

Granted, Soja is thinking in the first instance of his own city of Los Angeles, yet his notion of Thirdspace as uniting "the real and the imagined, . . . everyday life and unending history"[25] would seem especially apt for considering what Jerusalem means for the psalmists and perhaps for everyone who has ever sung the psalms, or hymns based upon them, with spiritual attentiveness. The relatively new area of critical spatial theory might help biblical scholars consider the ethical dimensions of two interrelated phenomena: on the one hand, how space is symbolically represented and inhabited, and on the other hand, how space is ordered and utilized through concrete social and political practices.[26]

As a preface to considering the importance of the biblical songs of Zion for Christian prayer, it is apt to note the encouragement offered to the young church in Ephesus to make psalm-singing (presumably of biblical psalms) a central part of what they do together: "Be filled with the Spirit, speaking among yourselves in psalms and hymns and spiritual songs, singing and praising the Lord from your [plural] heart, giving thanks always for everything in the name of our Lord Jesus Christ to God the Father, [thus] being subject to one another in reverence for Christ" (Eph 5:18–21). In a highly suggestive study, David Ford points to the ethical and even salvific significance of such singing in community, in which "there can be a filling of space with sound in ways that draw more and more voices to take part, yet with no sense of crowding. . . . The inclusive, uncrowded space of song therefore embodies a distinctive unity" in which "each singer can be valued and have something distinctive to offer while yet being given to the complex

23. Soja, *Thirdspace*, 56.

24. Ibid..

25. Ibid., 56–57.

26. Biblical scholars are in fact beginning to make use of critical spatial theory; for the study of Jerusalem, see Berquist and Camp, *Constructions of Space II*.

unity of the singing."[27] Because it is the nature of singing in community to be alert to one another, to wait upon and yield to one another, it may lead to "a transformed notion of power which is in tension with domination. . . . The picture by the end of the letter is of an energetic, resilient gentleness growing in members of a community who can sing to each other and to God as they resist whatever evils come."[28]

We must suppose that if the Ephesians followed the author's instruction, they would have been singing songs of Zion, especially since the larger goal of the Letter is to help these Gentile Christians grasp the import of their unity in Christ with the "commonwealth [*politeia*] of Israel" (2:12). Which songs of Zion might we imagine on their lips, and how could those have advanced the proclamation of peace between Jew and Gentile (2:17)? Guided by the several related principles laid down in the Letter—unity, mutual gentleness (4:2), and resistance to domination through selfless love (5:21–25)—I would offer the following non-exclusionary shortlist, as a way of prompting thought about how the songs of Zion could be instrumental for peacemaking:

1. Psalm 87 comes first to mind because it inspired what may be altogether the most sophisticated Christian statement of Zion theology, John Newton's eighteenth-century hymn, "Glorious Things of Thee Are Spoken." Apt for my imagined group of singers in ancient Asia Minor is the fact that the psalm speaks of peoples alienated and/or physically distant from Jerusalem: Rahab (probably Egypt), Babylon, Philistia, Tyre, and Cush (Ethiopia/Sudan). In a remarkable statement that has no clear parallel elsewhere, it affirms of them all: "This one was born there" (vv. 4, 6)—that is, in Zion; "each one is born in it/her,[29] and he establishes it/her, the Most High" (v. 5). The poetic claim of "native" identity for all might well be taken as affirming the vision of Isaiah and Micah, with peoples streaming to the mountain of YHWH, to be instructed in his ways. As Robert Alter suggests, "all who come up to Zion to acclaim God's kingship there are considered to be reborn in Zion."[30] The Septuagint makes the implied maternal imagery explicit with its reference to "*Mother* Zion" in verse 5.

   As Christl Maier observes, the song "envisions the nations living peacefully together as fellow citizens of Israel because of their common

---

27. Ford, *Self and Salvation*, 121. Ford considers it probable that the author of the Letter to the Ephesians intends the biblical psalms to be sung (126).

28. Ibid., 124.

29. The pronominal suffixes here and in the next phrase are feminine.

30. Alter, *Book of Psalms*, 307.

origin."[31] It could be seen as the most extreme version of the vision in Ps 122, of Jerusalem "as a city whose parts are bound tightly together" (v. 3). Yet when singing for the sake of peace, it is well to heed David Ford's caution that "the singing self . . . needs to be suspected," namely of totalitarianism. His question about the rhetoric of Ephesians could equally be posed of each of these Zion-oriented texts: "Does its repeated advocacy of unity not call to mind the many regimes of domination that thrive on the suppression of difference? What about those who do not share this particular vision of God . . . ?"[32] Other psalms on my shortlist must speak to this crucial question.

2. Therefore I mention next Ps 131—not explicitly a song of Zion, yet it is included among the fifteen Songs of Ascent (Pss 120–34), some ten of which do refer to Jerusalem or its Temple.[33] Scholars often suppose this small collection to have been sung by pilgrims to the Temple. Although this psalm has no overt connection with any aspect of Israel's cult, what makes it suitable for someone preparing to encounter God, and likewise merits it a place on this shortlist of Zion songs, is the fact that the psalmist's sole spiritual claim is of humility: "I have not occupied myself with great things, nor with things too marvelous for me" (v. 1). Like a weaned child in its mother's arms, the psalmist calls on Israel to "wait for YHWH, now and forevermore" (v. 3). The image is a powerful disclaimer of triumphalism, of totalitarianism, of claiming to know beyond the shadow of a doubt *what* or (even more dangerously) *whom* God hates.

3. Another example of a biblical song of Zion that invites an anti-totalitarian reading is Ps 72, a prayer that the king may exercise justice over a realm far-reaching in space and time: "May righteousness flower in his days, and abundance of peace until the moon is no more" (v. 7). I treat this as a song of Zion, since it is one of only two psalms (cf. Ps 127) whose superscription associates it with Solomon, and its imaginative setting is the crown of the hill country (v. 16), where Jerusalem is located. A song that envisions the enemies of the throne licking the dust (v. 9) is rightly suspect, and so one should ask: What distinguishes this vision of peace from the Pax Romana, the Pax Assyriana, or any imperialistic reign of any period? The answer lies in its canonical

31. Maier, *Daughter Zion, Mother Zion,* 207.

32. Ford, *Self and Salvation,* 130.

33. References to Jerusalem/Zion or the Temple appear in Pss 122, 125, 126, 128, 129, 132, 133, 134, and 135; the superscription of Ps 127 associates it with Solomon, presumably as (co-)builder with God of the "house" that is the theme of the psalm.

context. In fact we know from the Deuteronomistic Historian that Solomon followed standard imperialist policy in subjecting Israelites to forced labor, requiring them to leave their villages and farms one month out of three to work on royal projects or serve in the militia (1 Kgs 5:27–32 [EVV 5:13–18]). Further, his son Rehoboam's intention to perpetuate harsh treatment was the final nail in the coffin of the united monarchy, according to that Historian (1 Kgs 12:3–4). Viewed as background for the psalm, this history gives substance to the prayer that the king should show pity upon the poor and needy and deliver them from violent oppression (vv. 13–14). It is a prayer from those who would gladly give their labor and loyalty to the king or son of a king (Ps 72:1) who would treat them justly. Read thus, Ps 72 is a wake-up call addressed to the "listening heart" for which the young Solomon once prayed (1 Kgs 3:9). Further, the psalmist's vision of the hill country cresting with waves of grain (Ps 72:16) is a reminder that the blessing of food sufficiency is never separable from political arrangements, including those at the highest level of power. Read in full canonical context, in light of the Former and Latter Prophets, this prayer for justice stands within the canon as a supplication largely open to the future, still seeking full manifestation of the divine promise.

4. Psalm 147 is part of the great crescendo of praise in which the Psalter culminates. Notably, it opens with praise for YHWH as

> the Builder of Jerusalem;
> he gathers the outcasts of Israel;
> the Healer of the broken-hearted,
> the One who binds up their sores,
> counts the number of the stars;
> he gives them all their names. . . .
> For he is the One who establishes *shalom* in your territory;
> he satisfies you with rich wheat. (vv. 2–4, 14)

Many of the verbs here and throughout the psalm are participles; this is a recitation of the characteristic actions of God: building Jerusalem (likely here, rebuilding it after disaster), maintaining the stars in their individuality and the seasons in their courses (vv. 16–18), providing food for animals (v. 9), upholding the wounded and the brokenhearted, speaking a revelatory word to Israel alone (vv. 19f). Throughout, God is honored as Creator and Preserver, and no distinction is made between God's actions in the realms that we separate and name Nature, on the one hand, and History, on the other. This beautiful hymn of praise leads to the logical inference that Jerusalem and the people Israel are no less part of the fundamental ordering of the world than are the heavenly bodies or God's statutes and decrees (v. 19). Yet despite its assurance of God's favor for Israel, the tone here is at the furthest remove from militarism, or a nationalism that constitutes a threat to others:

> He does not delight in the horse's might,
> nor take pleasure in a man's strong legs.
> YHWH takes pleasure in those who fear him,
> who are waiting upon his covenant-love. (vv. 10–11)

Beginning to end, the tone here is one of pure gratitude, that supple, patient virtue that endures suffering, rejoices in what is good, and trusts that the One whom Israel is charged to obey and to praise without ceasing will, in God's own time, restore order to a broken world.

As we have seen, the songs of Zion conceive of Jerusalem as an actual city where people live and work and fight and suffer, where kings rule, wisely or not, and at the same time as the place where God's real Presence may be experienced in a way that we might call sacramental.[34] These four psalms develop some morally and ethically significant dimensions of this theological understanding. Thus they provide several different focal points for prayer for the *shalom* of Jerusalem as it might be experienced in this world, and indeed by peoples of different faiths and nations:

- Psalm 87 envisions a radical inclusiveness of the nations within the favor extended to Zion. This is expressed as a fundamental reframing of identity; each is claimed as "native" to Jerusalem.

- Psalm 131 expresses a radical humility before the "great things" that infinitely surpasses my own.

- Psalm 72 looks to the *future* manifestation of God's justice in political systems, joined with a *present* critique of existing political systems.

- Psalm 147 seeks healing for broken hearts and the restoration of order to a broken world, effected through God's (re)building of Jerusalem.

---

34. Richard Lux suggests that Christians may "reimage" the Holy Land thus: "*As Christ is the sacrament of our encounter with God, the Holy Land is a sacrament of our encounter with Christ.*" He adds: "This sacramental experience neither invalidates nor supersedes the Jewish experience and covenantal connection to the land of Israel, but adds a new dimension of experience and meaning specific to Catholic Christians, who, since the Second Vatican Council, are called upon to understand, appreciate, and affirm the reality of the Jewish experience in the twenty-first century—in addition, I would argue, especially the Jewish experience of their connection to the land of Israel" (*The Jewish People, the Holy Land, and the State of Israel*, 60; italics original). My intention in this essay is not to urge, with Lux, that Christians should view Jerusalem (or the land) as a sacrament, but rather to offer sacrament as a metaphor or analog for the way some biblical writers seem to see it.

Highlighting these themes from four psalms is no more than an illustration of how one might listen to the several dozen biblical songs of Zion with a desire to pray toward the peace of that place. It would seem to be an imperative for our generation to incorporate an awareness of global political realities into such prayer in a way that earlier Christian hymnody did not do, to pray from an integrated vision of Jerusalem as both a geopolitical entity and a multivalent religious symbol of a wider, even global, community "whose parts are bound tightly together" (Ps 122:3). Although earlier hymnody may not have attempted such an integration, nonetheless the best Zion hymns written and sung by Christians through the centuries—those of Abelard, Watts, Newman, Blake—do reflect some of the spiritual tone and themes we have seen in these songs of Zion: for example, radical inclusiveness, dependence on God's grace and wisdom, the absence of triumphalism, sober recognition of the distortions inevitably present in human dispositions of power.

I conclude this essay by pointing to an experience that underlies it. About twenty-five years ago, in my first year of teaching, I was fortunate to work on the Psalms with a student who was an accomplished singer. It was her practice to chant each of the psalms we studied, or sing them to some familiar tune. But when we focused on songs of Zion, somewhere near the end of term, she was surprised to find that unlike the others, these psalms would not be confined to an established tone or melody. It seems that each of them produced its own new melody; they sang themselves, as it were, and she was their instrument. Then and ever since I have wondered if her experience suggests something of how the songs of Zion participate in the *numen* of the place they celebrate and how they invite us into the mystery—invite us, perhaps, to be willing instruments of God's peace, instruments of the peace of Jerusalem.

6

Catalyzing Compassion: Jeremiah?

Barbara Green
Dominican School of Philosophy and Theology,
at the Graduate Theological Union Berkeley

1. Introductory Considerations

IN THE BOOK OF Jeremiah, amid all the language of anger and threat, accusation and blame, recrimination and retaliation, is there also language that shows both deity and prophet able to act with effective compassion, such that their love moves other characters fruitfully and effectively, and helps us as readers discern and enact similar love?

I will demonstrate how Jeremiah can be shown to struggle toward a point where he himself foregoes participating in what he has been urging as the one thing needful for survival and flourishing, once some have chosen it, spending the rest of his life-span urging others to such a choice. That he fails to persuade most of those to whom he preaches only highlights the quality of the gift he gives, and it is our challenge to make his compassion additionally fruitful.

An analogy will help us understand the sketch I am urging: think of passengers fleeing a sinking ship, with one of them assisting her immediate neighbors safely to lifeboats, where she could take a place as well. But instead of so doing, she continues to help others find spaces in boats—even when in panic or anger they resist and refuse her efforts. Without perhaps quite knowing when the last moment for her own safety and that of the rest of the group has come and gone, she nonetheless continues to try to assist others to survive. Some of those she tries to save are swept away, while others will survive. Some, recognizing help amid the chaos, can cooperate with her efforts, while others are too frightened. Some witnessing her actions are moved deeply, whether they are saved or not. But even if they do not see it, we do.

2. Biblical Spirituality and the Quest for Compassion

One other discourse that needs introducing before we turn to the presentation of the prophet is that of biblical spirituality, specifically its intersection with biblical studies. I work with the definition of Sandra Schneiders, who has defined Christian spirituality as the "experience of conscious involvement in the project of life-integration through self-transcendence toward the ultimate value one perceives," which for Christians is the triune God revealed in Jesus, approached via the paschal mystery and the church community and lived through the gift of the Holy Spirit.[1] Implicit in the choice to orient my inquiry in such a direction is my sense that apt interpretation of biblical texts will aim to make visible characteristics of God and God's projects with creatures that believers most need to ponder. To adumbrate places in the Bible where God's compassion is mysteriously present shapes my goals here, a choice not thwarted but assisted by engagement with the standard historical- and literary-critical tools of biblical studies. In Christian biblical texts (so in both Testaments, e.g., Exod 34:5–7; Hos 11:8–9; Rom 8:38–39), God's most fundamental nature is compassionate self-disclosure, and compassion is what we humans (perhaps other creatures as well) are called to most basically in our relationships. Karen Armstrong, writing on world religions, maintains that the most consistent insight into and response to God's character is the Golden Rule, where those who love God are moved to love beyond the self, to "dethrone the self from the center of one's world and put another there."[2]

Biblical spirituality, arguably, assists our orienting toward the "biblical God," coextensive with God's self-disclosure across the Bible as Scripture. Biblical spirituality, to be pragmatic and effective, should assist us in dwelling intentionally within the heart of God, inhabiting Scripture and practicing God's compassion. If the book of Jeremiah is to assist such realities, then we need to look for the places where the prophet demonstrates, even enacts, this divine compassion in a way that we can understand and implement ourselves. That is, if Jeremiah ministers effectively with a compassionate God, we need to know about it so as to move with its currents. Coincidentally, we also need to note how much of the discourse of the book can seem to run

1. Schneiders, "Christian Spirituality," 1, 3.
2. Armstrong, *Case for God*, 24.

against the compassion-tide, so we can appreciate how God, Jeremiah, and a few people can sight and catch their wave to ride it into shore.

To offer another productive angle on compassion, I draw on the work of philosopher and ethicist Charles Taylor.[3] He speaks of "flourishing," and asks under what circumstances any of us can renounce what is culturally understood as our own flourishing in order to reach for something less apparently good, even possibly giving up what seems best for ourselves in order to contribute to the flourishing of another. Noting it as paradoxical, he insists that it is not rare in religions and draws on Buddhism for the notion that the renouncer of his or her own flourishing is a source of compassion for those who suffer. Christians will perhaps not think he need have reached so far for such a figure, but that this phenomenon is demonstrated and valued in diverse culture sets is only good.

Finally, since this paper is drawn from a fuller work where basic positions will have been demonstrated at greater length than is available here,[4] let me name some support beams that sustain the portrait offered here. I posit that the main engine of the book of Jeremiah—set against the events of the late seventh and early sixth centuries leading to the defeat and destruction of Judah and Jerusalem at the hands of Babylonian imperialism —is to demonstrate artistically that only one survival-option is viable, that of a group choosing quasi-voluntarily to relocate to Babylon before the final devastation and defeat of Judah/Jerusalem by the Babylonians in 587.[5] Consider another analogy: We may be familiar with the anguish that can arise in the lives of elders when it becomes clear that they can no longer live safely in their homes as they have done in the past but must move into housing where assistance is more readily available. Rarely does this insight and decision come easily, and those faced with the challenges of old age tend to deny that moving is necessary, or they hope it can be delayed. Friends and kin who seek to be helpful have a variety of strategies of threat and persuasion: to name the dire things that could happen at any time (e.g., the elder may fall and become incapacitated, be unable to call for help; the choice to walk into an assisted living complex with some worldly goods is preferable to arriving in an ambulance and being placed in a full-care unit).

---

3. Taylor, *Secular Age*, 17–18.

4. Green, *Plans of Well-Being*. The present essay is based in part on material in that book.

5. I have no doubt that such a viewpoint is exilic or post-exilic, aimed to validate the community that becomes the *golah* group, replanted in the land and surviving to become post-exilic Yehud. But the book, not a-typically, does not focus on that later moment but retrojects its narrative to an earlier time, that of the late seventh and early sixth centuries before the defeat of the "Judah project."

Occasionally, the person needing to move can come to see and accept that, though the decision will never be preferred wholeheartedly, moving may be better than other choices (or non-choices). In time, the move can sometimes come to be seen as good.

The book of Jeremiah, then, struggles to articulate how God can possibly conceive such a counterintuitive plan as desirable, shows how God—filled with anger-language—can move beyond it, so to speak, to conceive and communicate plans of well-being amid all the other outcomes God enunciates. It becomes God's challenge to share the plan with Jeremiah and for them, together, to make it attractive enough to some group that it becomes feasible to do.[6] That is, Jeremiah and God, as characters, need to sell this single option to some group if God's Judah-project is to survive. The language of the book is taken up with this challenge, as deity and prophet address various audiences in Judah and Jerusalem: several kings, the palace elites, prophets and priests, men of Judah and Lady Zion. Few heed; in fact, just one group is represented to do so. For a forty-year effort, it seems a small result. Though including brief reference to Jeremiah's success with the one group that heeds him and finds itself, against likelihood, participating in God's gifts of well-being, we will concentrate primarily on Jeremiah's failures with Judah's last king, Zedekiah, presiding over the siege of Jerusalem and defeat by the Babylonians. The challenge will be to see how the prophet's ostensible failure is undergirded, and even overcome, by a divine and human compassion available to us.

3. Hearts Changed:
Deity (Jer 16:19—17:13) and Prophet (Jer 20:7–13)

We begin with a scene in the long biblical book where we are shown the deity coming to a crucial and compassionate insight. In much of the first "half" of the book (chs. 1–20), the rhetoric of shame and blame, accusation and anger, recrimination and retaliation seems to dominate: hearts angry, paralyzed, predatory. God talks that way, as do Lady Zion and the men of Judah in speech attributed to them before they fall silent. Jeremiah himself

---

6. In order for us to understand and appreciate that this is not "a pro-Babylonian option," please reconsider briefly both analogies offered: no refugee from a sinking ship can be considered "pro-lifeboat," nor a person seeking assisted living "pro-rest home." So here: the relocation to Babylon is not a desirable thing but the best of bad options. It helps us appreciate the difficulty and deep distastefulness and even scandal of the option of God, prophet or people "choosing" to leave the land of promise. The point to consider is how some alternative to our preferences can become imaginable, tolerable, acceptable, eventually chosen, and if we are fortunate, even fruitful.

participates in like manner with a certain enthusiasm. His six laments (often called "confessions"), clustering in chs. 11–20, invest heavily to detail the shortcomings of his opponents and his desire for them to get as good as they gave, to suffer what they laid on him.[7] No compassion in evidence yet! In that same set of chapters, God has eight soliloquies laying bare the divine decision-making process. Sounding hurt and angry, the conclusions God draws list heavily toward the filling full of God's plans for destruction.[8]

But in the seventh rumination, God articulates the mystery of hearts, specifically the human variety, presumably thinking about corporate and individual hearts of Israel and Judah and plausibly of Jeremiah's heart as well, since the prophet's laments intersecting the deity's soliloquies persistently if intermittently call for divine retaliation on those who have caused him to suffer. The divine soliloquy is structured as follows:

A. Introduction: a pair of "invited quotes" (16:19) and then a divine comment on them (16:20–21);

B. Central section of three more extensive divine ruminations (17:1–11):

    1. Claim regarding Judah's condition, YHWH's conclusions, choices (17:1–4);

    2. Alternative trees (17:5–8):

- cursed the man who trusts in mortals//who makes flesh his strength//who turns his heart from YHWH:

  he is a juniper in the wilderness//he will not see good if it comes,

  he dwells in wilderness, salt waste, uninhabited;

- blessed the man who trusts in YHWH//YHWH becomes his trust:

  he is like a tree transplanted by a stream, sending out its roots// it will not fear[9] if heat comes; it will make luxuriant leaves, not worry even in drought, not stop bearing fruit;

---

7. Jeremiah's laments include: 11:18–23 (trusting lamb); 12:1–6 (sheep for slaughter); 15:15–21 (tasty words); 17:14–18 (reluctant shepherd); 18:18/19–23 (the pits); 20:7–18 (enticing deity).

8. God's soliloquies are more complex than Jeremiah's, also less clearly recognized in criticism. I list them as 11:15–17 (fire and the green olive); 12:7–13 (destroyed heritage); 13:15–27 (the flock whisperer); 14:1–10 (wandering feet); 14:17–22 (tears amid drought); 15:5–14 (grieving women, whining sons); 16:19—17:13 (hearts gone off); 18:13–17 (provocative anomalies).

9. For "fear" rather than "see," consult Lundbom, *Jeremiah 1–20*, 779, 782, 785. The Hebrew words are related paronomastically, with the second tree not *fearing* what the

3. The human heart: its condition, consequences for the deity (17:9–11):

- Assertion: twisted the heart . . . more than all . . . desperately sick[10] (v. 9a);

- Question, answer, purpose/outcome: Who can know it? I YHWH probe heart/test kidneys, to give a man according to his ways// . . . to the fruit of his deeds (v. 10);

- Assertion: . . . [someone] nests but does not hatch//one makes riches but not with justice; in half his days he leaves it,[11] ends a fool (v. 11);

C. Conclusion: a pair of "invited quotes" (17:12–13a) and rejoining comment (17:13b)

Our interest is in the central part of the reflection, bounded by issues of human incorrigibility as God has appraised them. In between those matched units, how does God ponder, decide, soliloquize his conundrum to practical gain, and what other clue are we given? In the first rumination (17:1–4), God reflects on the engraved nature of Judah's sinful heart, scored so deeply that Judah and offspring persist in false allegiances, with the consequence that YHWH and Judah together throw away the gifts Judah had been given. Judah kindles and YHWH burns unquenchably. There is nothing hopeful, no alternative to the deep sin that leads to more sin. Destructive agency is shared, collaborative.

The center of the middle portion (17:5–8), midpoint of the whole soliloquy, is a beautifully balanced reflection on the choices, seen as the mysteriously contrasting trees. Neither tree escapes challenge, but the tree trusting in itself is blind to what good comes its way and so compounds its choices until, languishing in the desert, it dries out. The other tree, trusting differently is met differently and produces differently, not seeing or fearing when bad comes, but stretching toward water to make leaves and fruit with the crucial moisture. One tree refuses water/life while the other—transplanted—revels in it, collaborates with what moisture there is.

Finally the last section of rumination comments on the first two: God asserts at 17:9–11 "how twisted[12] is the human heart, more than all, quite desperately sick. Who can know it?" God asks, then responding: "I YHWH

first refused or was unable to *see*.

10. Ibid., 787.

11. McKane, *Critical and Exegetical Commentary*, 402: reads "they leave him." It does not matter for what I am arguing.

12. Lundbom, *Jeremiah 1–20*, 787.

probe heart/test kidneys, to give a man according to his ways// . . . to the fruit of his deeds." God seems to discover, conclude, resolve that, in the case of such hearts, any change must come by divine initiative and not rely upon the human self, which, God concludes, is not a very good chooser of good. All God can do—and only God can do it—is discern hearts, sort them, recompense their investments, meet their yearnings to assist what is so vulnerable. God appears to have given up on "informing them," seems content to go to the sites where hearts are not utterly closed off, to be available there for collaboration.[13] God's assay carried out there will be determinative, in one direction or the other. God wraps up this reflection reinforcing what has just been said: a creature who broods without hatching, one who piles up unjustly, will get precisely the apt return on the investment, notably no offspring and false riches, ultimately the label of "fool." God makes no move to intervene. By the end there is not even the collaborative image of one igniting and the other burning. God says the most that will happen is that the false claim will be laid bare, will be named. The concluding comment replays the imagery of the middle of the rumination: the refusal of water by the "thirstless heart." God seems to be drawing back, to have learned some limits when dealing with human hearts that are incorrigible—which is not quite all of them. The struggling tree, transplanted so as to respond to water, provides hopeful insight, a way forward for the deity. God is shown responsive to new insight, to move beyond futile wishing toward something more helpful.

Jeremiah's heart has a more difficult process. The prophet's laments remain largely steeped in anger at his opponents, and he calls for them to

---

13. A quick review of basic imagery that pervades and unifies these divine ruminations: the deciding and decided heart (alluded to in 16:19–21 and named explicitly in 17:1–2, 5, 7–10), is perhaps re-writable but ultimately made up and committed irrevocably. God's reflection begins with the possibility of changing hearts but drifts toward discerning and classifying them, compounding their choices. The unit bristles with imagery about the making up of hearts: they are made to know (16:21), written, engraved with permanent marks, analogous to the way altars are (apparently) inscribed and thus drawing the children of worshipers into false worship (17:1). Some hearts may claim to be reprogrammed while others are not. Bad-heart parents produce bad-heart children. Hearts remember. The imprinting of hearts from one generation to the next leads to the loss of the heritage-goods, sold off to no gain for any (vv. 3–4), not ransom so much as plunder, heritage let go to no purpose, perhaps unavoidably, surely pointlessly. Hearts go off, often of their own accord, without hope of rescue. Two kinds of hearts are contrasted as trees: those that rely on humans and those that trust in God. Each tree is stuck in a hot, dry, and challenging place (vv. 5–8). One of the trees cannot see good, much less respond. But the other does better, is transplanted near enough to water as to stretch towards it. This second tree does not lose focus when heat and even drought come, as may happen. It sends its roots to water and retains leaves, even bears fruit. The heart is summed up in verses 9–10, inscrutable to all but YHWH, who alone can assay it and will do so.

suffer what they have inflicted upon him. There is scant evidence that Jeremiah learns much from what God is discovering, bearing out precisely what God has ruminated. And yet, by the end of this long unit featuring these soliloquies, Jeremiah nonetheless, without sounding too happy about it, asserts that he throws himself into to God's projects: "'O Lord of hosts, you test the righteous, examine the inner parts, . . . I lay my case before you . . . who rescue the needy'" (20:12–13). 'I'm your man; count me in.'[14] Not a lot, we might appraise, but good enough. God can go there to assist this feeble choice his prophet has made.

Before turning to examine Jeremiah's ministry of compassion in three moments, we can look quickly at God's eighth and last soliloquy of the book, a follow-up to the language about hearts and trees. In God's final brief rumination (18:13–17), the imagery exposes the anomaly of water unthinkably gone from its accustomed places, to the shocked reaction of witnesses. God contemplates unthinkable removal, knowing it will seem like a punishment. But perhaps it will be best in the long run for thirsty hearts, unable to choose their own good decisively or even to recognize it as such until after the creative divine deed is underway. Removal, though anomalous and unthinkable, is urgent.

4. Hearts Changed: Some People, Prophet (ch. 26)

As prophet and deity shape their combined resources to effect the anomalous but urgent transplanting of a small group of hearts from their accustomed dwelling place, we see, in chapter 26, Jeremiah's first, even *only* moment of "success" in his long ministry—the only time a group he addresses seems to consider his words as helpful, if not quite welcome.[15] We need to appreciate this moment, with Jeremiah like Van Gogh: never selling a painting until he finally manages to shift *one*! Such experience may not be the most obvious seedbed for compassion. The occasion here is the prophet's proclamation of words God rehearsed in chapter 7, and now ready for delivery. The main proclamation (26:6) is that Jerusalem is headed toward becoming like Shiloh, a shrine once thriving but now devastated and in ruins. The proclamation is not well received by many of those listening, with Jeremiah seized by priests, prophets, and people and condemned to die (26:8–11). Most scholars see here a sort of vigilante process where Jeremiah is put on trial by palace officials, specifically over the claim that it is *God's word*

14. The sigla '. . .' indicate my paraphrases of the discourse, generally accurate but simplified to stress what I think is the "pitch" of the language.

15. Stulman, *Jeremiah*, 65.

promising to turn Jerusalem to resemble Shiloh. Restating his claim to have been sent by God and ordered to say these words, Jeremiah concedes readily, if not quite graciously, that he is in the hand of his opponents who can put him to death if they so wish, though it is innocent blood they will be shedding (16:12–15). His refusal to lash back at them in counter-blame, his concession of their power over him, possibly even of their benighted sincerity, coupled with a reminder that his prophecy included an escape clause—not too late to mend their ways and act otherwise—all collaborate to generate adequate and respectful space where at least some of those in attendance can find precedent for Jeremiah's behavior (26:16–19). But by scene's end, the prophet has had to be rescued, implying he was not acquitted, leaving marked but available for interpretation this openness on the part of a few. Relying on the anomaly of this single success, I construct this group who heeds as those going early and quasi-willingly to Babylon: the seedbed for first-figs of chapter 24, the community receiving the letter in chapter 29, the recipients of the words of consolation in chapters 30–31.[16] Building on God's insight about a few transplanted hearts thirsting for water and able to flourish near it, Jeremiah's extension of respect and his refusal to rush to his own defense catalyzes a helpful response on the part of some. Note that Jeremiah writes to them but does not join them. No seat in the lifeboat for him while others remain in danger of perishing. Were I Jeremiah, I would volunteer to take the letter myself or myself as letter to that group, the only one with whom he succeeded. But that is not what happens.

5. Hearts Not Changed: King and Elites (38); Prophet? Readers?

Rather, Jeremiah bends his efforts both more intensely and also more fruitlessly toward King Zedekiah and his elites—determined to maintain their position, dug in to beleaguered Judah, and the soon-to-be intermittently besieged Jerusalem (chs. 21–23, 26–28, 34–39). Jeremiah enacts repeatedly for that audience the fate they are blindly and deafly choosing, allowing himself to be placed in and out of stocks and jail cells, down and up in pits, in and almost out of the city.[17] On occasion, Jeremiah models release, though never

16. That chapter 24 pointing out first-ripe figs precedes 26 is one of many reminders that the ordering of this book pays minimal heed to chronology (until chs. 39ff.), organizing by some other criteria.

17. The seven narrative occasions on which king and prophet confer and where Jeremiah enacts the reality he is trying to speak persuasively about, named for easy reference, are 21:1–14 (wistful wish flattened); 27:1–22: (yokes contested); 32:1–44 (land deed needed); 34:1–22 (slave reprieve revoked); 37:3–21 (disputed departure); 38:1–13 (in and out of Malchiah's mud). The seventh of their encounters will be

so adequately as he is begging his hearers to do. His most intense moment of ministry comes, I think, at the last moment before the collapse of the city. I want to zero in on what I think is his most signal moment of failure, except to cast it against the challenge of renouncing one's own thriving for the less obvious and even unlikely good of another.

The main point to explore here is the sketched overlap between prophet and king, the sustained correlation of their positions and speech: Jeremiah's willingness to engage the frightened and frozen heart of the king in the hopes of appealing to him. Ostensibly opponents, they are actually bound together such that one of them cannot move without the willingness of the other. The urgent question is whether Jeremiah can shift the king and his people "into the lifeboat," or alternatively if both will be lost. The scene gives Jeremiah his best—in fact his last—chance with the king. That he fails is less important than how the scene unfolds, in terms of the catalyzing of compassion.

So we meet this pair of characters at 38:14–28.[18] First, we may note the position of the pair as we see them conferring face to face at the third gate of the Temple, to which Jeremiah has been recently released and Zedekiah apparently comes unhampered—or constrained by nothing except the intensifying siege of Jerusalem. Jeremiah arrives, narratively speaking, fresh from his lowest position, sunk in the mud at the Malchiah-house pit, where he had been both placed and freed at Zedekiah's word. Reprieved to the court of the guard, the question of Jeremiah's destination is both asked and answered in this passage. Jeremiah has suffered his worst (the Jonathan-house prison or the Malchiah-house pit) and will not be dropped in there again. Zedekiah, about to learn that his own feet are also trapped in mud, has his worst position ahead of him, a fate inevitable once he no longer engages with Jeremiah. So the two figures blend as we watch. Each needs something from the other and each is vulnerable to what the other might do. As they confer and bargain, their ostensibly uneven captor/captive positions blur so that they resemble each other in their need for reciprocal help. As they part, shortly, each is still trapped and doomed.

---

examined in more detail.

18. Callaway, "Telling the Truth," 256, 259 makes a case for the distinctiveness of this scene, e.g., that the king is unaccompanied here; that his advisors are always narrated negatively and he is without them here is adequate signal of something new on the king's part. Cf. those who want to see the king as more generalizably characterized: e.g., Boyle, "Ruination," 43, who characterizes Zedekiah as "chronically indecisive," "cunning and manipulative." Diamond, "Portraying Prophecy," 105, calls him "weak, acting exclusively out of personal cowardice." For a fuller treatment, consult Roncace, *Jeremiah*, ch. 3, specifically 95–115.

Next we ponder their discourse: The king opens (38:14–15)[19] with a compound request, spoken more plainly by him than we have heard to date: 'I want something/don't refuse me.'[20] The prophet parries also in paired statements: 'If I tell you true you will put me to death, and if I advise you, you won't listen.' The king counters half of this prophetic rejoinder (38:16), sign of his determination here to proceed. He reinforces his request with an oath: 'I swear I will not kill you or hand you over to others.' But he also confirms Jeremiah's assertion by withholding any promise to obey what he may be counseled. The king's oath purports to be a promise of safety for the prophet; but can Zedekiah deliver on this word, since we heard him say in 38:5 that he cannot count on landing a word effectively? We have seen the king break his words to freed slaves, have witnessed royal indecision on the handing over of Jeremiah, when pressed. Is the royal promissory word different on this occasion?

But still, having grounded his own position and offered assurance to his interlocutor, Zedekiah does not, in our hearing, actually make a specific request—a provocative omission. The topic raging is how to escape the tightening fate, precisely what the king just promised the prophet under oath. We can fill in the king's question only from what the pair discuss and from earlier requests: 'How do I get out of here safely?' It is, of course, the question for both, for each: 'How to get out of here?' It is what the king needs and wants to know, wants help with. It is also what the king will shortly remind the prophet that *he* ought to be concerned with. Previously the king has consulted the prophet on other topics, but now he seems to sense that events have moved beyond those matters to something more urgent for himself. We can glean verbal evidence that he has in fact listened to Jeremiah's words—both a good and a bad sign. The king's capacity to have heard what the prophet is saying might have helped him but ultimately renders him more culpable when he refuses to heed it. The prophet offers the same choice as before (38:17–18): "Submit and survive," save yourself, your house, the city; or "dig in and die," causing defeat, destruction of the city by fire, and capture of the king and heirs. Is Jeremiah's language reliable? Is this proffered option still viable? Historically it is impossible to say. Literarily, we have hints: Jeremiah has already enacted a departure from Jerusalem (his *disputed departure* of 37:3–21), which was thwarted, misrepresented and distorted, resulting in accusation, arrest, imprisonment. We

19. Brueggemann, *Commentary*, 365, lays out a structure of this encounter.

20. Roncace, *Jeremiah*, 104–7, and others make the case that Jeremiah's offers are more variable than I think really matters. There are details that change, but I cannot hear the basic choices as other than consistent, at least at a fairly general level of abstraction. See also Diamond, "Portraying Prophecy," 99.

have seen the king rescue the prophet several times by his word, though we have also seen him claim to be unable to manage his own men by words. We have not yet seen the prophet able to save the king. Who can assist the other effectively? Neither, it will turn out.

But in any case and in a moment of great apparent candor, Zedekiah explains why he cannot do what Jeremiah counsels (38:19). First we hear that he has in fact considered it, even if to reject it. This is an amazing moment in the long Jeremiah book, with the king in effect reducing the whole matter of Babylon vs. Judah and Jerusalem to his own fear of what might happen to him at the hands of others. Zedekiah will pull down the venerable Davidic enterprise because he dreads a hypothetical outcome, though one easily imaginable. He says he fears the people of Judah who have done already the very thing Jeremiah has been urging: "Submit and survive." This is a complex moment for all participating: The king cannot act because he fears abuse at the hands of those who have done what Jeremiah says *he* must do—go toward resettlement in Babylon. Enacted speech: The prophet stands before the king, abused for his own controversial actions, witness the present scene and those preceding. Once again, the pair overlap substantially. The ethical/moral/spiritual question posed, ultimately, is whether dreadful fear will deter integrity or not. Jeremiah has made one response in his life, and the king stands poised at his own defining moment. For an instant, again, they nearly coincide. But the king backs off (and some feel the prophet does too!). That is, Zedekiah looks in the mirror at Jeremiah, sees a man abused by his enemies, and declines to risk inviting what Jeremiah's life embodies. We may construct language for the king: 'How can I do what you say when in fact you are making visible for me how it will fulfill my worst expectations?' That is, again in literary terms, the main disincentive for this whole catastrophe is the king's fear of the trap he has put himself in, specifically in his relations with Babylon and Egypt which have made what he fears inevitable.

Jeremiah then (38:20) fatefully pushes this candidly poignant utterance aside—as has often been done to his own words—and replies, again with his best advice: 'That won't happen. Obey and live.' But the dis/incentive now *enacted* is fresh and distinctive (38:21–23): The prophet paints for the king a scenario given him by God, he says, a proleptic vision of what has not yet happened to the king but, presumably, is about to happen (though we will not witness it in this form).[21] Jeremiah says: 'If you dig in—refuse my advice—I see women led out to the Babylonians and they are blaming you. Listen to their *quoted speech* here: "You are sunk in the mud, placed

---

21. Lundbom, *Jeremiah 37–52*, 77, calls it a vision; Brueggemann, *Commentary*, 290, wonders whether it is a lament or a taunt song.

there by untrustworthy friends who, in any case, are deserting you." You and your women and children will be captured and the false allies will escape.' Prophet and king face off at what is, arguably, both climax and nadir of their relationship. The wifeless and childless prophet calls forth the reproach of the king's family to taunt or upbraid him for failing to do what Jeremiah wants him to do. But, as before and perhaps not surprisingly, the prophet is ineffective at this crucial moment and distinctive opportunity.

Abruptly, this intense and honest exchange breaks off to wind down quickly. Zedekiah makes no response to what Jeremiah has shown him except to insist that it not be made public. That is, without engaging the content of the scenario the prophet has just shown him or making any verbal response to it, the king moves to disaster containment (38:24): 'No one must know what we have talked about.' We have yet another remarkable gap or silence on the part of the king, inviting our interpretation. Perhaps we read the king as so shocked by what he is shown that he must suppress it from others' hearing and his own consciousness. Jeremiah, I suggest, has used language so powerful that instead of providing the king an incentive, frightens him into the very corner he was emerging from. Each, having been vulnerable, is exposed. Each retreats. The king takes the initiative to seek cover for both, opens an escape hatch they can both take back into their prison. Zedekiah says (38:25–26): 'They'll ask you what was said and even threaten you, but don't tell.' The king quotes his officials, apparently knows just what they'll say, and he tells Jeremiah what to say, quoting him as well from a previous narrative moment (37:20): 'Say you were begging not to go back to the Jonathan house.' Do we, does the Jeremiah of our constructing, hear that as a threat as well as a promise? Is Zedekiah's 'Do this' also a 'Better not do that,' his 'If you don't do this' a veiled 'Else I'll do that'?[22] Does Jeremiah lose integrity here, as a number of commentators say?[23] I think not inevitably so, given the ambiguity of reused speech. Jeremiah now falls silent, rare moment in this

22. Roncace, *Jeremiah*, 98–100, shows how deceiver and deceived roles toggle in the person of the king. Lundbom, *Jeremiah 1–20*, 78, explains how it is a veiled threat.

23. Roncace, *Jeremiah*, so charges: see one sort of argument on 55, another developing on 111–13. But the very Bakhtinian strategies he cites suggest otherwise. The king crafts an utterance, which quotes Jeremiah on an earlier occasion; the king anticipates the participation of his officers in the conversation between himself and the prophet. The king also intonates the complex utterance as a promise and threat and hands it to Jeremiah, who does not, in our hearing, take it up. His silence may be his own potent rejoinder. The narrator summarizes, but very generally. There is not sufficient clarity to say Jeremiah dissimulated. Jeremiah's utterance of what the king told him to say is ultimately unverifiable. See also Callaway, "Telling the Truth," 257, who thinks the prophet at least complicit with a misrepresentation of truth; but also by the reading strategies which introduce her article, it is not so simple.

long book. He makes no reply to this royal offer, perhaps circling back to his opening remark at 38:15: 'Our chatting never comes to anything.' Perhaps we sense that he has nothing helpful to offer, but we must also appreciate that he finds nothing scathing and blaming to say either. His discourse shuts down, and so far as we can see, he falls into the plan that Zedekiah makes for his own royal protection, for their mutual protection. And the narrator lets us infer (38:27–28) that Jeremiah complied, since he was given the favor Zedekiah told him to say they had been discussing: no return to his worst pit, though no real reprieve, either. But remarkably at such a devastating moment, there is no blame, no retaliation, no recrimination, no defiance. Jeremiah's heart looks good here, even in this abject moment of incapacity to reach the king and persuade him to avoid his worst fate. His earlier righteousness, sampled in his laments, appears to have been smoothed away. Hard learning bears fruit.

This is, arguably, a diagnostic moment for ourselves, reading. If, as I argue, the prophet has long deferred his own flourishing for the sake of his ministry but has just stumbled badly and failed to act with effective compassion when it was most needed, what's in it for us? How do we appraise his portrait, construe his failure, supposing we are able to name it that? I have found no other interpreter who reads this scene as I do, and so my construction may be too ambitious. But I challenge readers to pause and reflect: Is Jeremiah a failure here, and in what ways? Does his intervention with the king scuttle their mutual escape? If, as appears to be the case, the king's last opportunity for safety vanishes here—perhaps the prophet's as well—it is simply a waste, an error, grounds for frustration and anger at them, perhaps at God as well? Or is it salutary in some way? When the prophet falls silent and seems, in fact, not prompted by God to say more, are we relieved? chagrined? disappointed? angry? If the prophet has acted with compassion, does our witnessing it help us?

6. Hearts Not Changed:
King and People (39–44); Prophet?

Shortly after this painful moment, the siege breaks through the city walls with much ensuing death and destruction (ch. 39). The king attempts to steal away virtually alone, leaving the city and its people in death throes behind him, resembling compassion and the generous deferral of one's own good not at all. Many die, a few are rounded up and forced to Babylon.[24] Jeremiah is given a choice, in fact pressured to make one when he seems to have fallen inexplicably silent (39:11–18; 40:1–5). Why would he not select to go where he has

---

24. Note that eventual forced exile is not the same as preliminary chosen resettlement.

been urging others? But once again he does not do so, remaining with a group given permission to continue in Judah with a Babylonian-appointed leader, one of Jeremiah's scribal friends (40:5). Inferrably there is some possibility of survival for this group, and our prophet is willing—resigned?—to do it.[25] And yet when that Babylonian-appointed leader is assassinated by a David-kin and the survivors beg Jeremiah to inquire of God as to what they should do, and when Jeremiah takes several days to do so, finally returning with the answer, "Not Egypt," the people go anyway and take the prophet with them, protesting that it is precisely the wrong venue.[26] Thus Jeremiah disappears from sight and hearing, lamenting the bad choice and yet enduring it with the people. Perhaps there remains hope, but of course the book of Jeremiah gives us no reason to suppose that the Egypt choice is viable; quite the opposite.

7. Our Insight?

So back to our entry question: Does Jeremiah work with God in such a way as to catalyze compassion? Where? How? What is offered to us? As we see even God, shown to struggle to transform a long-running anger into a more gracious resolve, and note the prophet commit to that project even while still trapped in his self-concern and anger at opponents, what is offered to us? Happy with his single success, what do we make of his inability to speak well to the king at the moment of greatest opportunity? Do we hear compunction and compassion in the prophet's silence? Even if we can spot his compassion, how can we claim that it helped his peers and can assist us?

It's great to claim that Jeremiah succeeded with one small group which becomes, in many ways, the hero of the book: those able to respond to transplanting, to reach their roots toward water, to choose life rather than death, survival rather than destruction. But we cannot readily ignore that the deity-prophet team does not persuade any other opposing hearts, nor does Jeremiah appear to save himself in the manner of the Isaian servant (Isa 40–55). To have his final words be a rant is a disappointment to me![27] But perhaps I

25. We may be distracted by knowing that, in fact, this prophetic book demonstrates quickly how futile was any small hope of fruitful dwelling in the land and that, in its view, none survived in the land of Judah. But from the view of the character Jeremiah, that at the time of the 587 surrender some were allowed to remain suggests that Jeremiah's character may be drawn to show he had a ministry to them. It is only the more poignant that he proves wrong to think he has any more good to do, and more generous.

26. This extended narrative unfolds in chapters 40–43, followed by what even I must see as more harsh language in chapter 44, as the prophet hears his and God's word vehemently and definitively rejected.

27. He speaks to his Egypt-determined companions in 44 and is shown to speak

am asking too much of an individual and underappreciating the corporate nature of the project. The question for us this: Is Jeremiah's failure to save more people of Judah and Jerusalem from destruction, his persistent refusal to climb into a lifeboat when he might have done so, his determination to stay and continue to minister among the drowning—even working with those who seem determined to perish—salutary for us in a way it does not appear to have been for them?

Compassion is more a commitment than a prompt, more like a muscle than a secretion. We read to grow, to be transformed. "Narrative, in short, is more than literature, it is the way we understand our lives. . . . Great literature speaks to the deepest level of our humanity; it helps us better understand who we are."[28] Speaking for myself, I can say that to see others able to act for the possible flourishing of others at the immediate price of their own helps me, especially as I see it the fruit of a long struggle. To witness a crucial moment of inability is a privilege and a gift. That is, I trust more deeply as I see compassion learned through suffering. To have experienced and hence somewhat understood the process by which someone can love thus helps me see one way of reading Jeremiah. He is not a model so much as a blueprint, or perhaps one of several sets of blueprints available to help me read him and other nearby hearts as well. The force of God's anger throughout this long book can be a stumbling block, except insofar as we see it as the deep effort of a people to understand how nigh-inexplicable things can happen to them. Jeremiah's lapsing back into harsh language at an intense moment, also arguably a failure, actually shows us something valuable if in negative space: Violent language persuades no hearts. To draw—or to construct—God able to go beyond such language and feeling and resolve to help rather than blame and write off the human condition helps me. The Bible, specifically as Scripture, is as able to run as far with love and compassion as we, its readers, are. For Christians, Jeremiah and the God whose prints are in this book is not likely the most fruitful biblical text to consult for compassion. And yet, having found, read, engaged, and struggled to be taken over by such love elsewhere in Scripture and in life illumines the deity-prophet-king-people team so that, in fact, they do catalyze compassion in me. Or if they fail, the problem may not be theirs!

words of encouragement to Baruch at 45 and to Baruch's brother Seraiah at 51:59–64, though compassionate is not the first adjective that comes to mind.

28. Bellah, *Religion in Human Evolution*, 280.

7

"I Perceived in the Books"

*The Portrait of Daniel
as a Spiritual Student of Scripture*

Richard S. Briggs
University of Durham

THERE ARE MANY WAYS to imagine the interactions between the Bible and spirituality. The angle of approach I wish to take here looks at what sort of reader the Bible imagines is best placed to attain to spiritual insight. Such a reader is presented by implication in biblical narratives that assume certain virtues and dispositions in the character of the reader. Such a reader may also, on occasion, be presented more or less directly where biblical texts describe spiritual readers. There are not many narratives where the character of a reader is the direct focus of attention, but there are biblical texts that could be said to illuminate our topic from both these angles, the implicit and the explicit. The book of Daniel is such a text.

Like all serious and frequently reread texts, the book of Daniel has many concerns, agendas, implications, and intentions. One of them is to portray the man Daniel as a virtuous or wise character from whom the reader can learn. In Daniel chapter 9, Daniel reads Scripture, and as a result discerns the Lord's will with regard to the exile as it affects Jerusalem. This is actually a relatively rare hermeneutical dynamic in the Old Testament. We have texts that are occupied in various ways with the role of other texts in the life of faith—one thinks of Josh 1:8, or the images of Ps 1 or 119—but arguably only here, in Daniel, do we have an extended narrative portrait of a reader of Scripture, and indeed such a portrait is only occasionally in view in the New Testament too (with Acts 8:26–39 being an obvious example). Scriptural texts that deal with the reading of Scripture are excellent material for reflecting on various aspects of the hermeneutical enterprise.[1] In this paper I wish to explore the portrait of Daniel as a spiritual student of Scripture: explicitly as he is portrayed in Dan 9 and the rest of the book; and implicitly as the book works to shape the character of an implied reader who can in turn perceive in the book what the God of Daniel would like them to see.

There is a virtuous circularity to such an approach: how one reads the text feeds into what one sees in the text; and vice versa. Nevertheless, for the sake of exposition I shall take in turn four key areas: the relevant aspects of a hermeneutical framework for reading the book of Daniel as a realistic, ascriptive narrative; the portrait of Daniel as it emerges from such a reading; a reading of Dan 9 as an episode of hermeneutical adventure; and then an attempt to draw together an analysis of the key virtues of the spiritual student of Scripture as they are illuminated by this text.

Obviously, the delineation of Daniel's portrait falls short of offering a full scriptural account of spiritual reading (or indeed a full spiritual account of scriptural reading); but given the striking and particular focus of this text we may at least say that any such full account will not require less of the reader than what we find here. The present paper, therefore, offers one constructive step along the way to building up the portrait of the character of Scripture's implied reader.[2]

1. Reading the Book of Daniel

It should not be controversial to take the book of Daniel to be, in its final form, a theologically constructive work located in the second century BCE, specifically around 167–64 BCE, and drawing upon oral traditions that by that time go back several centuries. This "book of two halves" draws strong (and in their own way, typological) parallels between the figure of Daniel— and his friends—as faithful resistors in the midst of the Babylonian exile, and the community of the faithful in the run up to 164 BCE in the midst of

---

1. It is an unexplained oddity of the generally illuminating study of Venema, *Reading Scripture*, that he does not consider this text in Daniel, even in passing.

2. It thus builds on, and is entirely congruent with, the earlier portrait of Scripture's implied "virtuous reader" in my *Virtuous Reader*, where Daniel was offered as a potential example of what was being discussed (211–12). The present paper seeks to demonstrate that potential.

the crisis in and around Jerusalem precipitated by Antiochus Epiphanes IV, the Seleucid troubler of Israel.[3]

What is noteworthy here is the inherent hermeneutical stretch—the dual-focus that is woven into the fabric of the book. As a result, this is a book that confronts even its earliest readers with a certain inbuilt theological momentum, carrying one forward well beyond the historical confines of the narrative it relates. In short: an imaginative reading of the scope (*skopos*) of the text—that is, as traditionally understood, its aims, intents, and envisaged frames of reference—is more or less handed to the reader who is situated in subsequent centuries. Thus did Childs, in his famous *Introduction*, urge that the book's notoriously tricky calculations of time frames and prophecies were not unfortunate obstacles, which critics had to learn to circumnavigate, but were rather indicators of a different—canonical—dynamic whereby later readers were being asked to reconsider their own times within the framework of God's action as laid out in the book.[4]

To offer a Danielic spin on Barth's famous dictum: We are not walkers in the furnace or residents in the lions' den, but we are to ask what one may say of God building upon the foundation of those who walked in the furnace or survived the lions' den.[5] And that lions' den or furnace may be Egypt (cf. Deut 4:20), exile (as per Isa 48:10's "furnace of adversity"), or any subsequent overwhelming experience of trouble.

The book of Daniel is thus a relatively straightforward candidate for that category of narrative that Hans Frei labeled as realistic and ascriptive. That is, rather than fundamentally *describing* the world as it was, it *ascribes* to a secondary world the key qualities, characteristics, and evaluations that are urged upon the reader, even while the secondary world looks like and functions as the one in which we live.[6] The book of Daniel thus invites

---

3. Antiochus desecrated the Temple in 169 BCE, besieged Jerusalem in 167 BCE, and died of consumption in 164 BCE. The finished book of Daniel makes sense as deriving from between these dates. For standard critical discussion of these (and many other) issues, see Collins, *Daniel*, esp. 24–38.

4. Childs' chapter on Daniel (Childs, *Introduction*, 608–23) seems to me to have been largely ignored in subsequent work on Daniel, but represents his typical canonical vision still at its thought-provoking best, even at the end of his lengthy book. It is taken up in a technical and slightly inconclusive way in Scheetz, *Canonical Intertextuality*. A real oddity is Goldingay's juxtaposed comments (Goldingay, *Daniel*, 322) that (*a*) there is no merit in Childs' claim to canonical shaping here, followed by (*b*) an example of how the end of the book does indeed point to a significant canonizing reading.

5. Barth spoke rather of prophets and apostles in his search for a way to characterize theological engagement with Scripture, as an aspect of "dogmatics." Barth, *CD* I/1, 16.

6. The key framework for Frei's argument is found in Frei, *Eclipse*, 1–16; but the terminology of "ascriptive" over against "descriptive" narrative is elsewhere, notably in his essay "Literal Reading," 122–23, and perhaps most clearly contrasted in his *Types*

readers with historically attuned imaginations to see its narratives as pointing both backwards and forwards. On the one hand, it points back to the world as it was being experienced by the narrative's protagonists in 605 BCE or 164 BCE or whenever the narratives situate themselves. On the other hand, it conjures up the world as the narrative's readers might imagine it differently. Furthermore, for all readers, the book points to the real world as a theatre of divine action, both then and now. Read this way, most of the so-called critical issues that all but submerged discussion of the book in the nineteenth and twentieth centuries turn out not to be so critical after all. Indeed, as John Goldingay noted some time ago, one's conclusions on a whole range of such critical issues make "surprisingly little difference to the book's exegesis."[7]

That the book is patient of a whole range of readings, from the historically credulous to the ideologically suspicious, is neither surprising, nor needing to be denied, in order to create the space for a reading that takes its theological bearings straightforwardly in realistic and ascriptive terms. What the reader can learn from the portrait of Daniel is just one feature of the book that re-emerges into the light after the eclipse of its narrative is set aside.

As John Gammie once rather wistfully noted, "Seeing the way Daniel has been interpreted in other times calls attention to the impoverishment critical studies have imposed upon the contemporary preacher who seeks in Daniel a word for our time."[8] And not just preachers, I would suggest, but all students of the book, and especially those interested in Daniel's contribution to our understanding of spirituality. It is therefore this more traditional angle of approach that we shall follow here.

2. The Book's Portrait of Daniel: Character and Ethics

According to 1 Macc 2:60 Daniel was delivered from the mouth of the lions "because of his innocence" (*en tē haplotēti*), while in 4 Macc 16:21 Daniel was "Daniel the righteous" (*Daniēl ho dikaios*). The Daniel/Danel referred to in Ezekiel is not the same man, since he seems to be listed as a contemporary of Noah and Job in Ezek 14:14, 20, before being described in Ezek 28:3 as wise. This character is sometimes linked to one of the same name in the

---

of Christian Theology, 125 (cf. also 84). The language of "secondary world" is J. R. R. Tolkien's, and has perhaps not been explored as much as it might be in biblical studies.

7. Goldingay, *Daniel*, xl. On another occasion I hope to explore the extent to which the above account of realistic and ascriptive reading matches what we find in the history of interpretation.

8. Gammie, "Journey through Danielic Spaces," 144 (and see also 156 especially).

second-millennium BCE Ugaritic Aqhat myth: an esteemed judge, a protec-
tor of widows and orphans. Even so, our early evidence of the reception of
Daniel the character, in 1 and 4 Maccabees, points us to an innocent and
righteous man.[9]

In general, the narratives of the book itself require the reader to dig a
little more deeply to work out what sorts of character notes one might apply
to Daniel, since like so much Old Testament narrative, no moral evaluations
are appended to the descriptions of words and deeds in the stories themselves. A notable exception is when Daniel and his friends are introduced as
"young men" in 1:4; they are ascribed the qualities of being

> without physical defect and handsome,
> versed in every branch of wisdom,
> endowed with knowledge and insight. (1:4 NRSV)

The physical description is clearly intended as part of the character
analysis, and the technical capacities listed are not unrelated to character.
Subsequent character notes for Daniel, implicit and explicit, might be
deduced from the narrative as follows, with attention paid to anything that
might give us insight into what is motivating him, or what convictions he
holds:

- he acts with conviction (1:11ff.) with respect to imperial food, though
  on what basis, exactly, is notoriously difficult to say;
- he is given "knowledge and skill" in literature and wisdom, from God
  (1:17);
- he is portrayed as exceptionally wise and understanding (1:20);
- he responds to Arioch with "prudence and discretion" (2:14);
- he turns to God when confronted with difficulty (2:18);
- (though note that he does not attribute to wisdom the receipt of
  revelation [2:30]);
- he is described in Nebuchadnezzar's letter as "endowed with a spirit of
  the holy, divine gods" (4:8, 18 [=4:5, 15 MT]);[10]

9. It is not within the scope of this study to consider the reception of Daniel in other
ancient literature. Although much has been written on this it is in general more focused
on questions of literary dependence and evidence of canonical status, rather than the
character of Daniel as portrayed in the book. See, for example, several of the essays collected in Collins and Flint, *Book of Daniel*, noting Michael Knibb's conclusion that after
surveying the book of Daniel in its context, it is best understood as *"sui generis"* (34).

10. At least according to the NRSV, which offers a marginal reading of "a holy, divine spirit," based on taking the significance of the plural Aramaic (*ĕlāhîn qaddîšîn*,

- he is willing to speak truth to power, as the phrase goes, even when the prospect distresses and terrifies him (4:19 and ff. [=4:16ff. MT]);

- he counsels Nebuchadnezzar to atone for his sins with righteousness (Aramaic ṣidqâ, which in later Hebrew meant "almsgiving," as attested by the Greek versions' eleēmosunē; 4:27 [=4:24 MT]);[11]

- he is possessed of "an excellent spirit" (5:12)—according to the "Queen" (possibly Belshazzar's mother);

- the report about Daniel, at this time, is that "enlightenment, understanding, and excellent wisdom are found in you" (5:14);

- he refuses to accept reward from the king for his interpretive work (5:17);

- he is distinguished in his work in Darius' government because "an excellent spirit" was in him (6:3);

- he is beyond reproach in terms of his work: neither negligent nor corrupt, such that he can only be caught out by a trap (6:4ff.);

- he values prayer more highly than obedience to the (civil) law (6:10);

- he trusts in God (6:23)—though it is notable how little of Daniel's interior disposition is revealed or discussed in this particular narrative;

- the second half of the book offers less material except by way of implication from the nature of the visions received, but one might note: 7:15, 28—great terror as a result of the visions received; 8:15— the need for angelic interpretation of the vision; 8:27—sickness and dismay as a result of the vision; the study, perception and prayer of chapter 9, which we shall consider below; 10:2–3—his mourning (for Jerusalem?); 10:12—his willingness to humble himself before God; and, in general, his quest for understanding of the vision.

This need not be a complete list, but it is at least an initial attempt to locate more or less direct points of reference for Daniel's character in the book (and, to note, the additions—Susanna and Bel and the Dragon—do not add substantively to the qualities included on this list). If one were to attempt to construct a composite character picture from all these points,

---

"holy gods") as a singular, such as is defended by Collins, *Daniel*, 222. Goldingay suggests "the spirit of holy deity" (*Daniel*, 78).

11. On the delights that await the interpreter of this verse, see Anderson, "Redeem Your Sins," which includes an enthusiastic treatment of how to read this topic in the wake of the Reformation (66–69). More widely, see his *Sin: A History*.

some of which are a good deal less direct than others, what might the resultant portrait look like?

We could organize these characteristics by relating Daniel, in his character, to a range of significant "others." With respect to God, Daniel is committed to serving him, reliant upon him, completely trusting in him, very much susceptible to fear and trembling in response to divine visions, and convinced that it is to God that he owes his abilities to interpret and understand, especially with respect to dreams and visions. He believes in the value of prayer, and he (probably) thinks almsgiving can compensate for sin, at least in Nebuchadnezzar's case. Some of these are convictions and practices, rather than direct character notes. Perhaps if one were to sum up this character in an adjective it could be "devout," although a combination of wise and trusting perhaps reflects the conceptuality of the text more closely.

With respect to those in power, he is willing to speak boldly, but his attitude varies from king to king. As has sometimes been noted, it is possible that in the book as a whole Nebuchadnezzar, Belshazzar, and Darius play the roles of three different paradigms of authority in terms of faithfulness to God in the midst of foreign politics. Daniel is respectful but willing to confront Nebuchadnezzar; he lacks respect for Belshazzar, who himself seems to despise the Judeans subject to him; and then he seems completely at home in Darius' government. Whatever the merits of seeing this schema as the book's attempt to map out the different possibilities, one result in terms of the portrait of Daniel is that his character is that of someone who prioritizes service to God first and then accepts the consequences in terms of dealing with kings. This is therefore a man of sincere conviction and integrity.

Finally, with respect to other people, the most interesting note is his "prudence and discretion" in 2:14, along with the absence of negligence or corruption in 6:4. The direct implication of 6:5 ("The men said, 'We shall not find any ground for complaint against this Daniel unless we find it in connection with the law of his God'") is that even in Persian terms his character is beyond reproach.

It is obvious, I think, that this overall portrait reflects an idealized person. He never grows faint or weary, nor falls exhausted, but is lifted up on the second-century BCE equivalent of eagles' wings. The nearest he gets to frustration is his aggressive confrontation with Belshazzar in chapter 5, but even this is couched in terms of the king's willful disregard of the lessons that should have been learned from Nebuchadnezzar. The overall portrait is all very reasonable, carefully thought out, wise, and spirit filled. Of course, one will not be surprised at this, given the plausibility of reading Daniel in ascriptive terms. The goal of the text, one suspects, is at least in part to provide an exemplar of wisdom in a foreign setting: a "lifestyle for diaspora," as Humphreys once called it.[12] That any historical Daniel would doubtless have struggled to live up to such a character portfolio on a day-to-day basis is, we note, irrelevant to our hermeneutical concerns—just one advantage of the ascriptive reading strategy deployed.

The character of Daniel, in these broad literary-critical terms, has not received all that much attention in the modern era, hampered as Daniel scholarship has been during that time by its preoccupation with the quest of the historical Daniel. One of the most sustained literary readings of the book, or at least its first half, is Danna Nolan Fewell's *Circle of Sovereignty*.[13] Although she is interested in, among other things, characterization, she does note the lack of any significant interior dimension to the profile of Daniel: "We do not even know if [Daniel] has second thoughts about anything because we are rarely ever told what he thinks."[14] Interestingly, despite her many keen observations of the literary dynamics of the text (albeit somewhat beholden to a penchant for deconstruction), Fewell concludes that Daniel is "a somewhat synthetic character, a character too wise, too knowledgeable, too faithful to be true."[15] It is intriguing that even her keen literary sensibilities seem to miss the ascriptive function of the text.

The nearest I have found to a studied account of Daniel's character is the psychologically orientated reading of Barbara Leung Lai, whose methodological concerns lie with the notion of a character's inner life in the Hebrew Bible.[16] She too notes the paucity of direct evidence of interiority in Daniel's case, with the exception of what we might call the "fear and trembling" theme (which is most apparent in chapter 4 and then in the second half of the book). She posits two discrete "characters": a public self who is the epitome of self-confidence in chapters 1–6, while chapters 7–12 offer "the portrait of a weak, frightened, helpless, speechless, strength-less and dysfunctional seer."[17] This seems unnecessarily emphatic in its disjunction—as the evidence of 4:19 attests. Leung Lai is interested in the inner self as psyche, with a view to offering a psychologically thick description of the reading of Scripture in turn, but it is interesting to ask whether her insights can equally well be transposed to our consideration of character.

12. Humphreys, "Life-Style for Diaspora."

13. Nolan Fewell, *Circle of Sovereignty (Story)*, revised and briefly extended to include chapters 7–12 as *Circle of Sovereignty (Plotting)*.

14. Nolan Fewell, *Circle of Sovereignty (Plotting)*, 125.

15. Ibid.

16. As the subtitle of her book *Through the "I"-Window* has it: *The Inner Life of Characters in the Hebrew Bible*. Pages 43–77 are on Daniel.

17. Ibid., 75.

Indeed, what Leung Lai presents as two discrete voices (albeit in a kind of Bakhtinian dialogue) seems more profitably explored as a potential key to the single portrait of Daniel as the whole book presents it. It is certainly imaginable that the heart of the portrait lies here. Daniel is able to maintain a public political presence as calm and wise alongside experiencing inner turmoil in the face of the private divine revelations of the second half of the book. Further, as is well known, the way in which the various elements of the narrative are ascribed to different reigns creates a chronological overlap between the two halves of the book: these two halves are not imagined as a series of public stories followed subsequently by a series of private visions, but they interrelate:

Chapters		Reign of King
1–4		Nebuchadnezzar
5	7, 8	Belshazzar
6	9	Darius
	10–12	Cyrus

It is irrelevant to this ascriptive reading that no such Darius reigned between Belshazzar and Cyrus, and equally it matters little if the intention was that Darius was a later king: the point is still that the two cycles of chapters (1–6; 7–12) overlap. So what we see here is not a confident sage becoming a troubled seer, but a juxtaposition of these two themes, and it is in the juxtaposition that something profound is being said about what makes Daniel the man he is.

Wisdom, I have argued elsewhere, is the ability to hold together the confusions of the past and the present with a clarity of vision and purpose for moving ahead into the future.[18] Daniel is particularly uncertain as to how this future will play out, but the book as a whole clearly intends to offer hope to the beleaguered readers in the time of Antiochus, in a way that was deemed by the compilers of the book to transcend its lead character's evident failure to predict accurately what would happen to Antiochus, in the notorious "failed prophecy" section of 11:40–45. The result is a portrait of Daniel the wise man, seer, apocalyptic prophet, and powerful member of a foreign government, who *does not know how God will sort out the problems of his time.* But he does know that holiness, faithfulness, prayer, and study are the appropriate next steps to take, along with the continued embodiment of his public calling to serve the king—whether by way of confronting the Babylonian king or governing on behalf of the Persian king.

18. I draw my account of wisdom from 1 Kgs 3, in *The Virtuous Reader*, 71–101.

If our interests in character are more ethical and less psychological, how might one draw out the nuances of this portrait? There is no space here to survey all the issues raised in ethically orientated discussions of the book, but one or two key points are worth noting. In his clear survey of the issues in Daniel's "theological ethics," John Barton argues that "there is a general ethical attitude that pervades the book of Daniel, that of intense loyalty to the God of Israel," which he goes on to characterize as "an idea of *submission* to God: that is its theological ethic."[19] This is possibly one way of picking up on the theme of devotion—of being devout—which we noted above, but Barton links it more to a kind of fatalism.

Now it is indeed often said that apocalyptic texts tend in this direction, and thus Barton urges: "it is probably fair to describe Daniel as deterministic in its attitude to history."[20] He suggests Dan 3:17–18 as a parade example of this approach, and although of course that is not about the character of Daniel as such (and indeed might be taken in other ways than "deterministic"), it is doubtless fair to suggest that the portrait of Shadrach, Meshach, and Abednego —who form a composite character of their own in many ways—fulfils largely the same functions as that of Daniel. So Barton is perhaps right to suggest that the general view of Daniel's ethical engagement *can* lead to a form of political quietism, with one result being that Daniel's moral character ends up being seen as a matter of personal spirituality, to be practiced quietly in private spaces while persisting in playing a part in government.

But I wonder whether one needs to draw these conclusions? It is arguably significant that Barton's brief discussion contains no real consideration of prayer as a significant component of the book's ethical or moral vision. The warfare toward the end of the book may be couched in spiritual, or angelic, terms, but, whatever else it is, it is beholden neither to determinism nor fatalism.

Thus by way of contrast, Daniel Smith-Christopher argues that the book of Daniel represents a subversive account of life in the Persian period—a period he reconstrues to be a hostile environment in which Israel is called to practice its faith.[21] His account plays up the forms of passive resistance and willingness to subvert that one finds in, for example, Dan 6. He is also critical of those who follow Collins for arguing that Daniel offers a kind of pacifist account of life in the diaspora. Such accounts hang quite considerable significance on 11:34, where "they shall receive a little help" is

19. Barton, "Theological Ethics," 155 and 159.

20. Ibid., 159.

21. In addition to his striking commentary, "Daniel," note especially his article "The Quiet Words of the Wise." More broadly, see his *Biblical Theology of Exile*.

read as contrasting with, for example, the more gung-ho accounts of armed insurrection found in 1 Maccabees.[22]

It is arguably Dan 9 that offers the strongest indication that "quietism" or "pacifism," let alone determinism, are not quite the right labels with which to try to capture Daniel's ethical stance, and it is to this chapter that we now turn.

3. Daniel 9 as Hermeneutical Adventure

Scholarship on Dan 9 finds it hard to resist the gravitational pull of historical reconstruction: whether of the so-called dismal swamp of Old Testament criticism constituted by the passage's complex attempt to recalculate the end of exile in Gabriel's account of the seventy weeks (9:24–27), or by relating Daniel's central prayer (9:4b–19) sideways to other post-exilic prayers in order to pursue a taxonomy of penitential prayer for this period.[23] The surface-level feature of the book that surely most strikes the careful reader is the strong Yahwistic frame of reference of chapter 9: all the book's eight uses of the divine name (YHWH) are found here (9:2, 4, 8, 10, 13, 14 [2x], 20), either in or immediately framing the prayer (which occupies vv. 4b–19). Of course, we are not short of proposals that suggest that therefore Dan 9's prayer is a later insertion, either because of this feature or the nature of the Hebrew compared to the surrounding passage. The more significant argument along these lines, however, concerns the passage's subject matter: "it is clear that the prayer exhibits a deuteronomistic view of history that is drastically at variance with the deterministic view characteristic of Daniel outside this prayer."[24]

We need not attempt to catalogue the crowds of witnesses who have argued for and against the view that the prayer in chapter 9 is an insertion, or have pursued some mediating position with regard to its being from a different tradition but incorporated here by the author. All we need to note is that the canonical book incorporates this view of divine and human action standing against any fatalism of the day. Providence and petition are brought into conscious juxtaposition, at a time of intense need. In the context of

22. For Collins' original account see his *Apocalyptic Visions*; see also Collins, *Daniel*, 66. For a bracing presentation with respect to Daniel over against 1 Maccabees see Howard-Brook and Gwyther, *Unveiling Empire*, 46–53, and more generally, Howard-Brook, *"Come Out, My People!"* 323–54.

23. On this see the studies collected in the three volumes of Boda et al., *Seeking the Favor of God*, on, respectively, the origin, development, and impact of penitential prayer in Second Temple Judaism. A helpful overview comparison chart of some different prayers is provided by Smith-Christopher, "Daniel," 127.

24. Wilson, "Prayer of Daniel 9," 91.

the book, it seems fair to say that Daniel's prayer is designed to show an appropriate way of responding to the trials of empire, or at least of foreign government. Thus, as Boda summarizes, "chap. 9 presents the posture of those who will comprise the holy and wise remnant" in contrast to those who think that the determinism rules out human activity.[25]

It is also important to note that, according to the logic of the finished chapter, Gabriel's angelic visitation (9:21ff.) occurs in response to the prayer, and all that it exemplifies, rather than directly as a response to the "perceiving in the books" of 9:2. Those who tend towards seeing verses 3–20 as an insertion by a later hand can sometimes present the angelic visitation as a response to a request for knowledge with regard to the details of the prophecy that Daniel is reading (thus: "I perceived it was seventy years, but needed help discerning what that meant, and the help came from the angel"). Evidently such a reading could lead us towards the conclusion that the wise reader of Scripture is one who is enlightened by angels. While I am sure that is not untrue as far as it goes, it would leave the unvisited reader a little in the dark. And in any case, the content of the prayer, with its confession and desire for divine action, seems to be the response to a reading of a prophecy that *has* been understood, rather than the pursuit of a revelation not yet grasped.[26]

In the light of these remarks, then, the key passage for our purposes is this:

> 1 In the first year of Darius son of Ahasuerus, by birth a Mede, who became king over the realm of the Chaldeans—2 in the first year of his reign, I, Daniel, perceived in the books the number of years that, according to the word of YHWH to the prophet Jeremiah, must be fulfilled for the devastation of Jerusalem, namely, seventy years. 3 Then I turned to the Lord God, to seek an answer by prayer and supplication with fasting and sackcloth and ashes. 4 I prayed to YHWH my God and made confession. (9:1–4a)

What aspects of the portrait of Daniel here are most relevant to our inquiry?

First, he is reading Scripture. The plural "books" (*sĕpārîm*) is generally thought to refer to a collection of scrolls, probably a nascent canonical collection of some sort, although it is impossible to know what collection.

---

25. Boda, *Severe Mercy*, 470. He is summarizing here some of the contributions to Boda et al., *Seeking the Favor of God*, especially that of Venter, "Daniel 9."

26. For a brief review of various voices across the spectrum of views regarding vv. 3–21 as an insertion and the difference it makes to read it as integral to the chapter, see Smith-Christopher, "Daniel," 122.

Further, the fact that this collection could not plausibly be a fixed canon is not the same as saying that it is not functioning in ways congruent with the later notions of canon. In fact it is arguable that not a great deal hangs on whether we can be particularly clear about notions of "canon" or "Scripture" in Dan 9: the dynamic of Daniel reading Jeremiah offers itself for the reader's reflection in any case, and in terms of how later readers might appropriate any lessons from the text, they will in their turn perhaps naturally apply such lessons to the reading of Scripture (as canon) that suits a later age. But it is right to see Daniel reading authoritative Scripture here, with the relevant attendant ideas of canon that follow from such a claim (i.e., in the sense of canon as a norm, rather than as a fixed collection).

Wilson makes the suggestion that the plurality of "books" indicated might actually be various sections of the scroll(s) of Jeremiah—in particular chapters 27–29 as a distinct literary unit.[27] While many interpreters pinpoint Jer 25:11–14 as the key passage, Wilson makes a good case for suggesting that Jer 29 is particularly in view, especially the promise of 29:10: "Only when Babylon's seventy years are completed will I visit you, and I will fulfill to you my promise and bring you back to this place." Several specific vocabulary and contextual markers might indicate that the prayer of Dan 9 is triggered by precisely the concerns raised in Jer 29: "The prayer is best understood as an attempt to have Daniel fulfill the conditions for restoration set out in Jer 29.12–14."[28]

For our purposes, all that matters is that the passage propels Daniel to spiritual engagement with God as a result of reading Scripture. Thus, secondly, Daniel "perceives in the books" the significance of what he reads. This is not the deployment of a particular hermeneutic, so much as the perception of how the words in the scroll relate to the situation in which he finds himself. The relevant verb is *bînōtî* ("I perceived"), a not uncommon term, particularly in wisdom literature, for which some interpreters have suggested "I considered" as a more appropriate translation in this instance. The word is used quite frequently in Daniel, though mainly in the sense of understanding visions, so perhaps one point here is that the kind of understanding in view is appropriate to "texts" of various kinds, whether written words or dreams.[29]

Thirdly, the reading and the discernment lead to repentance and prayer. What is Daniel repenting for? Clearly the import of the passage is that his reading about the exile drives him to recognize the sin of God's people, hence

27. Wilson, "Prayer of Daniel 9," 93–94.

28. Ibid., 97.

29. *bînōtî* is an unusual Qal form of *bn*, which occurs twenty-two times in Daniel. For "considered" as a translation option, see BDB, 106. On the term becoming "a technical word for understanding visions" in Daniel's vision accounts, note Fretheim, "*byn*."

the penitential prayer, and the recourse to the hope derived from angelic intervention. It is the reading of the text that triggers this whole response and longing for divine action. But it is clear that there is no hermeneutical method at work here that is laid out for us to follow. Indeed, whatever hermeneutical processes may have been at work in Daniel's mind are bundled together under the verb of discernment or apprehension. The reader is not to learn from this, I suggest, that we must (a) read, (b) perceive, and (c) repent and pray, as if this were some form of hermeneutical prescription. Rather, the point is that the reader is drawn to see that a reader of Daniel's character does in fact see Scripture this way, and allows it to shape his understanding of God, of his people, and of the appropriate way of responding—which is indeed then (at least in this case) in prayer and repentance.

Stated another way, to become the kind of person open to repentance and prayer in the manner of Daniel in chapter 9 is to become the kind of person well suited to "perceiving in the books" what is significant or pertinent to the life of faith. My thesis is thus that the implied reader of Daniel is offered a portrait of the spiritual student of Scripture, rather than any particular hermeneutic. And further, if one should ask, "How then may I become a better/wiser/more perceptive reader of Scripture?" one line of approach open is to seek to model oneself on Daniel. Wise reading, on this understanding, comes as much from pursuing the character trait of wisdom as from pursuing better practices of reading, although of course such a way of putting the matter risks being unnecessarily disjunctive.

In any case, one reason why the process described in 9:1–4 is brief on hermeneutical details is not because the book is unwilling to give up any supposed hermeneutical secrets, but because in fact the manner in which it pursues the question of good reading is by way of its overall portrait of Daniel, on which, as we have seen, it is not so brief after all.[30]

---

30. I should offer a comment here about the stimulating work of Hebbard, *Reading Daniel*, which does indeed emphasize the importance of Daniel's character as a model for any aspiring hermeneut. In broad terms Hebbard's book and the present piece are complementary, although it does seem to me that his actual discussion of character is rather briefer than his (correct) insistence on its importance. He also goes on to make the further and perhaps rather speculative claim that the book of Daniel is intended in some sense as a textbook for hermeneutics, at which I point I do wonder if a thought-provoking interpretive idea has been stretched beyond its natural usefulness. Nevertheless there is real value in Hebbard's angle of approach.

4. The Spiritual Student of Scripture

It is all too easy to overemphasize one way or the other the issues involved in taking the Bible seriously in spiritual terms. On the one hand, such spiritual reading can be conceptualized as a withdrawal from critical engagement, or the bypassing of critical issues, to seek some sort of unmediated spiritual access to the subject matter of the text other than in and through careful engagement with the text itself. On the other hand, such spiritual reading can be conceptualized as an optional add-on to the rigors of critical reading, to be deployed according to one's taste, theology, or general interpretive concerns. Both errors in fact fail to interrogate sufficiently the notion of "critical reading," and take it as a given, around which one must navigate or to which one must defer.

My argument here is that spiritual seriousness in hermeneutical terms must trouble the category of critical reading, and indeed vice versa. The primary mechanism, if that is the right word, through which such troubling occurs is in reconceptualizing the category of the reader. All readings occur in and through particular readers: particular eyes see things in the text; particular ears catch the words of Scripture; particular minds grasp or construe the ideas in particular ways. The usefulness of the category of "implied reader" is simply that it offers a set of prospective construals, understandings and graspings against which one can compare actual readings of the text.

Most of all, the question of who the reader is is one that still requires more serious consideration, even after all these years of recognizing that the reader plays a role in the hermeneutical dynamic. It is appropriate that such reflection as there has been on readers has included serious and persistent attention to questions of gender, race, social location, and so on—even indeed that it has raised questions about the relative merits in hermeneutical terms of faith commitments as against various forms of secular self-identification. But the question of *character* remains in need of careful analysis from a range of hermeneutical angles, which one might suggest are theological (as in recent discussions about "theological interpretation"), but that one might equally suggest are just as helpfully explored as spiritual.

What makes a spiritual reader of Scripture? Again it is not hard to see unhelpful options. Certain types of piety might well advocate that one already knows what counts as spiritual maturity, and that it is such a person who should be trusted to interpret the Bible most wisely (though often the phrase that would be used at this point is "interpret it correctly"). Or certain kinds of hermeneutical commitments lead one to the argument that the spiritual reader is one who makes helpfully spiritual points of practical application from the text. The resource that both such approaches overlook in formulating their ideal is, ironically, Scripture itself. I suggest that the most beneficial way of conceptualizing the spiritual reading of Scripture is in light of how Scripture itself conceptualizes spiritual reading.

Hence the study of the character of Daniel makes its direct contribution to the notion of who Scripture understands to be the kind of reader best placed to read well. Devotion, integrity, long-term commitment, even fear and trembling before God, are all qualities of the spiritual reader, helping to shape the eyes and ears that attend to the text, and that therefore play their part in how Scripture is understood before God. And the spiritual reader, as we saw, can hold together profound trust in God with a keen awareness of not knowing how God might resolve any particular presenting concern.

There are many further aspects of the portrait of Daniel that raise interesting questions about spiritual reading, which not only can I not adjudicate here, but which may not be susceptible at all to a clear evaluation. Let me state just three. First, for example, does Daniel's interpretation of dreams represent an endorsement of studying whatever passes for spiritual enlightenment in one's culture? In other words, is the spiritual reader of Scripture also well placed to read the popular spiritual trends of one's day, or indeed is their Scripture reading facilitated by such a wider awareness? Or again, secondly, is it significant that Daniel is an individual, marked out (sometimes but not always along with his three friends) as particularly wise and discerning? Fashionable as it is in the twenty-first century for theologians to suggest that Scripture is best read by the church in community, Daniel operates more in the mold of the lone scholar, the detached wise man. In what sorts of ways might one draw any conclusions from that? And thirdly, what significance is there in locating Daniel the wise man in the spectrum of significant individuals in the Old Testament? Are there conclusions to be drawn from Daniel's role in foreign government, or the point that he is not a priest, nor professionally a prophet (Jesus' later evaluation notwithstanding in Matt 24:15)? Is the book of Daniel urging that wise readers may be found anywhere, or is that to over-read an incidental angle on the narrative, which should not be pressed? It is perhaps worth saying that these three points move us away from direct questions of character, towards ways of reading the book for insight into hermeneutics that are, shall we say, somewhat more fraught with hermeneutical background. My own view is that there are problems with these kinds of observations, whereas with the question of character we are on firmer ground. But doubtless a case could be made the other way.

We might note, finally, that when one tries to hold together the various ways in which the person of Daniel is portrayed, ascriptively, in the overall book, one ends up with the image of a busy man of government who persists in practices of prayer and study alongside his other duties. Daniel 9 focuses on him in one of the private moments of a busy life. One never knows when significant spiritual insights will result from the study of Scripture—another reason to be cautious about the importance of method in thinking about spiritual reading. What one can do, though, is to prepare for such reading in the way in which Scripture itself suggests we might: through the cultivation of character, with exemplars such as Daniel to give us indications of what the spiritual life might look like.

"If you want to become a better exegete, become a deeper person," as Brevard Childs is reported to have said "in his Introduction to Old Testament class at Yale Divinity School."[31] Correspondingly, to practice spiritual reading, pursue spiritual practices, as those practices are shaped for us in and through Scripture. And thus in hermeneutics, as in certain other contexts: dare to be a Daniel!

31. As cited by Mathews McGinnis in "Swimming with the Divine Tide," 244.

8

Biblical Spirituality

Text and Transformation

Sandra M. Schneiders, IHM
Jesuit School of Theology, Berkeley

1. Introduction

1.1 Clarifying the Substantive: What Is Spirituality?

WHILE THERE IS GROWING interest among biblical scholars on the one hand and spirituality scholars on the other in something referred to as "biblical spirituality," I think we must admit that there is no standard or generally accepted definition of this term. This reflects the fact that even among specialists in the field of spirituality there is no universally accepted definition of "spirituality," the substantive that "biblical" specifies. Hence the need to specify how one is using the term spirituality —what it means and what it covers, as well as what it excludes—if the discussion of the modifier "biblical" and how it specifies spirituality is to be clear and productive.[1]

By (Christian) "spirituality" I mean primarily "the *lived experience* of Christian faith," that is, the subjective appropriation of faith and resultant living of discipleship in its individual and corporate actualization(s), and

1. I attempted to collect most of the going definitions and understandings of the terms *spirituality* and *Christian spirituality* as well as supplying a bibliography of the most current discussions in the field in Schneiders, "Approaches," 15–33, and "Christian Spirituality," 1–6.

secondarily the *academic discipline* which studies this existential phenomenon *as* religious and *as* experience. However, such "living of the faith" can be orthodox or idiosyncratic, fervent or tepid, constant or spasmodic, private or communal, etc. Therefore, I would offer a more specific definition: spirituality is the actualization of the basic human capacity for transcendence in and through the experience of conscious involvement in the project of life-integration through self-transcendence toward the horizon of ultimate value one perceives. Peter Van Ness, in his introduction to the volume on secular spiritualities in the Crossroad series, caught somewhat the same sense of the generic or purely formal meaning of spirituality by defining it as the relation of the whole of oneself to which one has access to the whole of reality to which one has access.[2]

Obviously, this generic or formal definition can embrace Christian and non-Christian, religious and secular, theistic and non-theistic spiritualities. So, a further specification is required in which each formal aspect of this definition is "filled in" or actualized with materially Christian content, for example, that the ultimate value that is the horizon of the life project for the Christian is union with the triune God revealed in Jesus Christ, encountered in the faith community of the baptized who participate in his paschal mystery by the gift of Holy Spirit. In this process of specification "participation in the paschal mystery" is understood to include such things as Scripture, sacraments, prayer, the practice of virtue, and so on. And, of course, as soon as these elements and aspects are introduced theology becomes a methodologically necessary and important feature of the study of spirituality.

But even within the Christian framework spirituality is subdivided and organized by a plethora of principles of division such as tradition or denomination (e.g., Protestant, Catholic, Orthodox), spiritual family (e.g., Reformed, Benedictine), sexuality/gender (e.g., feminine, masculine, gay, queer), vocation or state in life (e.g., clerical, Religious, lay, married, single), emphasis in spiritual practice (e.g., contemplative/mystical, eremitical, ascetical, ministerial), and so on. Furthermore, there are many overlaps and intersections among these distinctions yielding particular individual or communal spiritualities, e.g., a Catholic contemplative Benedictine celibate feminine spirituality or an Evangelical charismatic married masculine spirituality.

Despite this enormous variety among Christian spiritualities, they share certain features that should be characteristic, although to different degrees and with different emphases, of all integral and healthy Christian spiritualities; namely, that they should be trinitarian, incarnational, biblical, liturgical,

2. Van Ness, "Introduction," 1–17.

communitarian, moral, ministerial precisely because they are situated in the church, the Body of Christ, which is one, holy, catholic, and apostolic.

1.2 The Valence of the Modifier: What Is Biblical Spirituality?

For more than thirty years I have been listening to the way people talk about spirituality, trying to discern what they mean by categorizing a particular experience of lived Christian faith or a particular study in the field as *biblical* spirituality when, in fact, all authentic Christian spirituality is or should be, in some sense, biblical and all work in the field must be in some way related to Scripture. There seem to be at least three ways the term *biblical* is used to specify Christian spirituality when the speaker intends to emphasize more than a general relationship to the canonical texts of the believing community.

1.2.1 The Spirituality that Produced the Text
(Discerned by Exegesis and Criticism)

One meaning emphasizes the spirituality that *produced* the biblical text. This is a facet of various exegetical and critical approaches to the text which ask not simply what happened, who wrote what, why, when, and how, but what kind of religious experience was involved in what happened and/or in the composition of the text. What was/is the God-experience revealed in the biblical texts (e.g., the exodus, the Psalms, the Last Supper), or that seems to characterize the writer or the community (e.g., the Deuteronomist or the Matthean community) that produced these texts? Why were the events narrated in the way they were (e.g., doxologically, historically)? These types of questions give rise, for example, to studies on Anawim spirituality in the post-exilic context; Jeremiah's spirituality vs. the royal consciousness in the face of the impending exile; Job's spirituality in contrast to that of his interlocutors; Pauline or Synoptic or Johannine spirituality of Christian community.

1.2.2 The Spirituality in the Text
(the Subject of Biblical Theology/Spirituality)

The foregoing type of study easily shades into (and is often barely distinguishable from) a second meaning that is closely related to the first but broader, more systematic and categorical, and probably less hypothetical and more readily controlled than the former, namely, the spirituality we find *expressed in* the biblical texts regardless of who wrote them or why. In the text as it now stands there are certain relatively coherent and integrated patterns of religious experience, which seem to have certain characteristic features. These may be associated with a particular author (real or attributed), book, tradition (e.g., Pauline, Deuteronomistic, prophetic, or apocalyptic spirituality), or with themes or motifs that seem to represent a characteristic way of relating to God, such as wisdom, covenant, creation, atonement, or kenotic spirituality. These types of biblical spirituality overlap and flow in and out of one another but someone deeply familiar with Scripture will easily distinguish apocalyptic from covenantal spirituality and probably find more resonance between prophetic and covenantal spirituality than between either of these and sapiential spirituality. There is a significant difference between Synoptic and Johannine spirituality even though both deal with all the major categories and themes of Christian spirituality. For our purposes, we can probably agree that all of these spiritualities are found in Scripture, that is, they are *biblical spiritualities,* whereas, by contrast, a spirituality of realization in the non-personal void of nirvana or of reductively intra-historical flourishing in secular humanism or of purely natural environmentalism (to say nothing of such negative foci of life-organization as substance addiction or world domination through violence) would not.

Another concern of those studying biblical spirituality in this second sense—that is, the spirituality(ies) in the Bible regardless of who or what is responsible for its being there—centers on certain patterns of thought and living that have developed in the history of Christianity and whether or how they are related to what we discern in Scripture. Do these developments cohere closely with, or find their roots in, the presentation of these or related features in the Bible? So people will ask whether a certain form of prayer, a certain understanding of discernment, a certain approach to the body or sexuality, a certain theology of obedience or forgiveness, of sacrifice or self-fulfillment is authentically biblical, implying that there are non-biblical or even anti-biblical approaches to these understandings and practices. The concern with these thematic issues is often establishing a foundation for examining, criticizing, promoting, or discouraging contemporary ways of understanding or enacting these elements or dimensions within the spirituality of contemporary Christian churches or individual Christians. The question might be, for example, is twelve-step or recovery spirituality genuinely biblical? Can feminist or ecological spirituality be biblical? How biblical is charismatic spirituality?

1.2.3 The Spirituality the Text Produces (Hermeneutical Engagement)

A third meaning of biblical spirituality, which comes closer to the concerns of this paper, is not the spirituality(ies) that produced the Bible insofar as historical and literary critical methods can establish that, nor the spirituality(ies) we find in the Bible, but the spirituality that the Bible *produces* in readers by their contact/interaction with it. Scholars like Walter Brueggemann[3] or Barbara Green[4] in relation to the Old Testament and Marcus Borg[5] or Mary Coloe[6] or Walter Wink[7] in relation to the New Testament model a way of reading or interpreting Scripture in relationship to the contemporary or perennial human situation that is not the kind of extrinsic "application" of biblical material to contemporary life that often characterizes preaching but which somehow illuminates from within the situation of the reader so that it becomes a site of divine revelation.

These scholars are facilitating in the believing community an appropriation of the biblical text as Paul Ricoeur describes this process in relation to texts in general.[8] The reader does not simply acquire informational knowledge, either of the ancient biblical world or of theological topics, from study of the text but comes to incorporate into his or her life the dynamics, concerns, attitudes, worldview that structure the biblical view of God, humanity, the world, and human participation in it. The spirituality of such readers is not merely virtuous in some vaguely religious sense that acknowledges a supreme being of some sort, nor is it the spirituality of a secular humanist, an agnostic, a Buddhist, an atheist, or a simple "golden rule" garden variety civil religion version of Christian. It is a distinctively biblical spirituality. In Pauline terms it is a progressive "putting on of the mind of Christ" (cf. Phil 2:4) through engagement with the Bible not simply as history, literature, or source of theological information, but specifically as Scripture, as Word of God.

(Of course, we have to acknowledge that the term *biblical spirituality* [a life organization and mentality precipitated by one's engagement with Scripture] used in this sense—that is, "what the Bible produces" rather than simply "what the Bible contains or communicates"—can run the gamut from the deeply biblical commitment to freedom of a Martin Luther King,

---

3. Brueggemann, *Finally Comes the Poet*; Brueggemann, *Prophetic Imagination*, among many others.

4. Green, *Jonah's Journeys*.

5. Borg, *Meeting Jesus Again*.

6. Coloe, *Dwelling in the Household of God*.

7. Wink, *Bible in Human Transformation*; Wink, *Naming the Powers*; Wink, *Unmasking the Powers*; Wink, *Engaging the Powers*.

8. Ricoeur, *Interpretation Theory*.

Jr. to the biblically inspired justifications of American slavery or South African apartheid or gay bashing. But that kind of aberration, while necessarily noted, acknowledged, and repudiated, is not our concern here.)

This understanding of biblical spirituality as transformative experience mediated by the Bible as Scripture is not a new development arising without precedent in contemporary biblical scholarship. In fact, it is probably the oldest meaning of the term. It is what Paul urged in Col 3:16–17: "Let the word of Christ dwell in you richly [so that] . . . whatever you do, in word or deed, [you] do everything in the name of the Lord Jesus, giving thanks to God the Father through him." It was the constant occupation of the first desert hermits in their "rumination on the Word," which was usually encountered in or derived from a biblical text,[9] and what medieval monastics were doing in their prolonged *lectio divina* and their daily round of chanting the psalms in the Divine Office. It is a kind of reading scholars tend to associate with so-called precritical biblical scholarship, which, during the rise and rule of the "scientific" historical critical paradigm, was dismissed or even despised as ungrounded, fanciful, or even fantastic. In our own day, however, it has risen from its grave of irrelevance in contemporary forms of centering prayer and Bible study in base communities, as well as in narrative critical work with parables, feminist and post-colonial criticism, and other practices developed to facilitate a fruitful and effectively transformative encounter of readers with the Word of God in and through Scripture.

The question with which I am wrestling in this paper, trying to formulate it clearly and find a rigorous way to think about it, is what is the nature of this biblical spirituality, this experience of empowering Christian faith that emerges in the encounter itself with the biblical text, not as imitation of some first-century (or earlier) model reflected in the text, or the application to life of theological knowledge extracted from the text, but as personal transformation in and through the reading itself. How is the text-as-read itself revelatory, and is (or how is) textually mediated revelatory experience transformative? What is the nature of the text itself that grounds this possibility; what are the necessary and sufficient conditions in the reader for this kind of reading; what kind of reading process can allow the encounter of reader with text to be transformative? This is somewhat analogous to asking what it is about a conversation as interpersonal encounter that is transformative in a way that simply reading or hearing an objective scholarly presentation on the same subject matter is not? What is it that makes contemplating a great work of art life-changing in a way that studying the

9. For an authoritative full-length treatment of biblical spirituality in the desert, see Burton-Christie, *Word in the Desert*.

same work in an art class is not? What makes genuine liturgical celebration spiritually transformative in a way that studying even a great sermon is not? Obviously, I am raising the question of the aesthetic as opposed to the rational or discursive engagement of the biblical text.

2. The First Task: Delineating the "Topics" that Must Be Addressed

The first task of this project, as I see it, is to try to situate the topic of "biblical spirituality" as transformative textual interpretation within the overall project of Resurrection-rooted Christian spirituality.[10] (I will put off the critical issue of the Resurrection until the end of this essay in order to concentrate on the issue of biblical interpretation. At the end I will indicate why and how the two areas of inquiry are mutually implicating.) What are the topics or loci that must be delineated, unpacked, and then interrelated in order to understand and place biblical spirituality—that is, the transformative reading of Scripture—within the whole Christian enterprise understood as life-giving or salvific encounter/relationship with God in the Risen Jesus by the power of the Holy Spirit?

2.1 Perception

Salvation understood in Christian terms is revelation, that is, God's self-gift as received by humans in responding self-gift. Contrary to the spontaneous understanding of revelation in ordinary language as simply God's self-communication to humans, all communication—whether textual or otherwise—is only communication if it is mutual and reciprocated. God's self-gift is only gift if it is accepted, received, responded to in reciprocal self-gift. Reception, therefore, is integral to and determinative of revelation.[11] Thus *perception*, the process of receiving God's self-gift, becomes a critical category for understanding the whole Christian mystery of union with God in and through revelation. The perception[12] with which we are particularly

10. For the time being I am using the orthographic tactic of capitalizing "Resurrection" when referring to the Resurrection of Jesus and leaving it lowercase in relation to that of believers, the theology of resurrection, and so on.

11. The best contemporary treatment of the constitutive role of reception in the dynamic of revelation is Rush, *Eyes of Faith*, especially Part II, which is a comprehensive investigation of the issue.

12. I am using the term *perception* rather than the broader term *reception* to forestall the inclination to understand the human participation in revelation as passive.

concerned is that which occurs "textually," that is, in our reading of the Bible as Scripture. How does revelation through Scripture take place? Our concern is not how God "speaks" but how we grasp, understand, participate in, integrate, respond to what God offers us in Scripture, namely, divine life. What do we contribute to the very content and constitution of revelation by the process of reception through perception? And what are the ramifications of the answers to these questions for the issues of concern here, namely, how God is experienced in and through the encounter with the biblical text?

The whole discursive field of perception has broadened and deepened in recent years and large swaths of current research in this field are concerned in some way with the question of "spiritual perception": whether, if, or how finite human beings come to know God. We are, in some senses, well beyond Platonic and Aristotelian, Cartesian, empiricist, Kantian, or purely linguistic conceptions of what it means to perceive, to come to know, even though "going beyond" in this area does not mean jettisoning the insights of earlier epistemologies but carrying them forward in partial ways to the extent that they are helpful. Furthermore, my discussion of this matter (because my competence) is limited to what is developing in a Western, Christian context, which leaves out of consideration developments in other cultural, religious, philosophical, and anthropological areas. So, this is not an attempt to arrive at a definitive "answer" to *the* question but to elaborate one way of thinking about the subject of experience of God through Scripture within the religious and academic parameters within which I function.

I want to take up three topics which I think are both necessary and sufficient for suggesting an approach to the issue of biblical spirituality as textually mediated encounter with God without claiming that they are the only relevant topics. First is the question of the nature of the organon or instrumental system for perceiving, that is, coming to know God. Here I will discuss briefly the theory of the "spiritual senses" and the theology of the *sensus fidei fidelium*. Second is the role of the imagination in mediating the relation between corporeality, in which all human experience is rooted, and religious experience generated through the functioning of this organon of perception. And third is the nature of biblical texts (and especially the Resurrection narrative) as the mediational locus of the particular experience of revelation that I am calling biblical spirituality or the experience of God in and through the engagement with Scripture.

2.1.1 The "Spiritual Senses"

The theory of the "spiritual senses"[13] goes back at least to Origen (c. 185–c. 254) and is rooted in many allusions in Scripture itself, such as, seeing with the eyes of the heart, hearing the word of God, tasting the goodness of the Lord, smelling the sweet odor of Christ, handling the word of life, or embracing or being embraced by God. The question that is pursued and debated throughout the long history of treatments of the spiritual senses is how the notion of "senses" is used. Are spiritual sight, hearing, taste, touch, smell functions of a *real spiritual organon* parallel to the physical or corporeal organon of the senses (eyes, ears, etc.)? Or is the term "spiritual sense" *figurative language*? And if the latter (which seems preferable), is the term a metaphor, analogy, or symbol derived from the corporeal senses suggesting how we experience different spiritual realities?

Those who see the term "spiritual sense" as a *metaphor* raise the question of whether the spiritual senses' likeness to the physical senses suggests that the perceiver has a variety of capacities for perception (comparable to eyes, ears, etc.) or suggests that the spiritual objects perceived are diverse (comparable to light, sound, etc.). In other words, does the metaphor derive from the differentiation of the experiencing or the diversity of the objects experienced?

Others see the spiritual senses, whatever they are, as *analogous* to the corporeal senses, that is, they are real capacities for perception that are somewhat like, but actually different from, the organs of physical perception such as eyes or ears. As we perceive visually by seeing colors with the physical eyes, so we perceive spiritually by understanding with the mind; as we hear sounds that convey meaning with the physical ears, so we grasp meaningful spiritual communication, and so on.

Or, again, are the spiritual senses the capacity we have to grasp the transcendent in and through the *symbolic*? Do we, in and through actual corporeal realities (eucharistic *bread*, the *words* of Scripture, relationships with fellow *Christians*) actually encounter and experience spiritual reality (the glorified Christ, biblical revelation, being "Christ's body"), which, of course, raises the question of the meaning of "real presence."

All of these positions and variant versions of each have been espoused and expounded by major figures in the history of Christianity. For our

---

13. An important resource for initiating oneself into this subject and its history, which is virtually coterminous with Christian history itself, is Gavrilyuk and Coakley, *Spiritual Senses,* in which specialists in each of the major thinkers on this topic from Origen in the second century to Karl Rahner, Hans Urs von Balthasar, and the analytic philosophers of religion in the twentieth century supply succinct scholarly introductions to the relevant theories of spiritual perception.

purposes, however, no matter how one understands the nature and/or functioning of the spiritual senses there seems to be a wide consensus that humans are capable of perception that is not reducible to sense knowledge but also not pure infused knowledge or the immediate, direct knowledge usually referred to as mystical experience. It is mediated in some way. In other words, we are susceptible to the kind of revelation of which the incarnation of the Word in Jesus is the paradigm.

2.1.2 *The Sensus Fidei*

The "sense of the faith" as the term has been used in the history of theology is the Spirit-given capacity of the believer to experience revelation not as discrete propositions or information but as a "whole," which constitutes a horizon of meaning as well as being constituted by its specific content.[14] Claiming that baptism "illumines the eyes of faith" or "opens the ears of the heart" is a way of saying that a whole new receptive capacity for participation in revelation through perception, which is not reducible to the intellectual capacity to understand the propositions of the creed or tenets of doctrine, is made operative in the baptized. In other words, just as rationality is the basis for the knowing based in sensible experience, so there is a "sense of the faith" that is the basis for the knowing based in spiritual experience. John 9, the story of the cure of the man born blind, is a narrative symbolic presentation of this reality. The man born blind, through the anointing of his eyes by Jesus and his washing in the "Sent One," which is, according to Christian faith, what happens in baptism, becomes able progressively to perceive in the man Jesus of Nazareth a wonder-worker, a prophet, and finally the Son of Man.

While the content of faith—for example, the creed—can be thought of as common to all believers, the "sense of the faith" is unique to each person somewhat analogously to the way that all the members of a family have a unique and individual "sense of the family" that relates them both to the family and to each other. Each believer's unique "sense of the faith," if it is adequate, relates the person not only to the content of faith but to the whole *fidelium* or community of believers in its life, tradition, sacramental experience, etc.[15]

14. See Rush, *Eyes of Faith*, esp. chapters 1–3 and 8.
15. See ibid., 238–40.

2.2 Imagination Rooted in Corporeality

The relationship between the spiritual senses by which we perceive non-sensible but mediated data and the *sensus fidei*, which synthesizes and integrates the data of spiritual perception, reflects the relationship between imagination and corporeality. The Aristotelian dictum that nothing is in the mind that is not first in the senses is an affirmation that all knowledge begins as sense experience but that it does not terminate there. In the past half century increasing attention has been focused on the role of the imagination in the synthesizing and integrating of sense experience in the holistic encounter with reality in general, including religious encounter with and experience of God. This reflection tends to be situated in the discourse on theological aesthetics. Theologians have become increasingly interested in the role of the imagination in this whole process. So, one area that requires further exploration in the effort to construct an adequate understanding of the experience of God that we call spirituality is the relationship between sense experience, the spiritual senses, and the *sensus fidei*. Imagination is the key category for this reflection.

2.2.1 *Imagination*

Imagination is not simply the capacity for fantasy (e.g., "dreaming up" a purple giraffe) or even for memory or reconstruction (e.g., mentally conjuring up my office when I am at home). Much more importantly, imagination is the synthetic activity that constructs reality in its "wholeness" so that we do not experience discrete sense perceptions (red as distinct from round as distinct from sweet), which we then combine into composites (apple), or psychological or mental states (fear, joy, danger) but "wholes."[16] Ormond Rush, as we have already noted, in talking about the way the imagination functions in the development and operation of the *sensus fidei*, says that each Christian develops a kind of "personal catechism" or holistic understanding of the faith within which are integrated all the aspects of one's religious experience including what one believes, how one prays, one's ecclesial sense, and so on. This is the context or horizon within which the person receives, thinks about, integrates, discerns, and appreciates all that pertains to their faith.[17]

16. I have dealt with the issue of the "paschal imagination" in *Revelatory Text*, 102–8.
17. See Rush, *Eyes of Faith*, ch. 8, esp. 215–38.

2.2.2 *Corporeality*

As Ray Hart, a theologian and philosopher of religion, so insightfully put it many years ago, imagination is "the cognitive mode of the will" that integrates the whole range of interior faculties and functions.[18] But the starting point of this imaginative activity is corporeality. It is our interaction with the whole of reality through our bodily presence and action in the world that is the source of all experience, whether sensory, intellectual, emotional, psychological, spiritual, or the integration of any or all of these.

An immense amount of theoretical work is being done today on the issue of "the body." We are increasingly aware that the body is not so much something that we *have* as something that we *are*. And it is not simply a composite of atoms, cells, organs, systems, and so on. It is our complex, multifaceted, symbolic (material-spiritual) presence in the world within which we integrate all reality as we participate in it. The body does not end with our skin. In a certain sense it starts there.

The importance and complexity of the idea (and the reality) of body is the reason why the bodily Resurrection of Jesus is crucially important for Christian spiritual experience in the present. The Resurrection of the body establishes the continuity between the pre-Easter Jesus experienced by his historical contemporaries in first-century Palestine and the post-Easter Jesus universally but personally present and active since Easter. The bodily Resurrection is the ground of the permanence of the Incarnation in the cosmos, especially in human history, and in the personal and corporate experience of believers. (This is part of the reason why I want to bring these reflections to bear in a particular way on the Resurrection narrative even though the theory I am developing is, I hope, relevant to many other biblical texts, especially narrative ones.)

The bodily based imagination is the natural substrate of the organon of spiritual experience, the human subjective pole of the revelatory experience, while the biblical text is the objective pole. It is important to note that we are not discussing a "subject" (the reader) over against an "object" (the text) but a textually mediated interrelationship between God and the human subject.

18. Hart, *Unfinished Man.*

2.3 Texts

2.3.1 *What Is a Text?*

As we are all well aware, the seemingly self-evident meaning of "text" as an objective, freestanding, material reality that contains and delivers a single stable meaning implanted in it by an author(s) and retrievable by the appropriate methods has been virtually totally subverted within the last three or four decades. And these developments bear directly on how we can conceive of the biblical text participating in the spiritual transformation of a reader, that is, being the locus and even the mediator of biblical spirituality. Are texts the inscriptions of performance (as those studying texts as media believe) or the literary residue of cultural interactions (as new historicists would claim) or analyzable closed systems of signification (as structuralists see it) or tissues of never-ending plays of difference (as deconstructionists would have it) or relatively reliable records of past persons or events (as more traditional historical critics would claim) or artistic creations more akin to music or painting (as those in theological aesthetics or literary studies see it) or language as discourse under the conditions of fixation (as hermeneutical philosophers following Ricoeur would suggest)? Or indeed one of a number of other possibilities or some combination of these?

2.3.2 *The Resurrection Narrative(s) as Text*

Because it is a vast topic and would take us too far afield I am not going to attempt in this essay to interpret the Resurrection narrative as an exercise in biblical spirituality. But, for two reasons, which I want to mention here, these texts are in the background of my considerations and where I eventually want to "land" in the larger work to which this essay is a preamble. The first reason is methodological. The second, and more important, reason is substantive.

2.3.2.1 THE METHODOLOGICAL REASON

Many years ago, in a small book titled *The Virginal Conception and Bodily Resurrection of Jesus*, Raymond Brown pointed out that at the beginning and at the end of the quasi-biographical accounts of the life and career of Jesus from his birth as a human being to his death and burial were two "accounts" of extra-historical (or I would say transhistorical) "events." The character and status of these texts is important for the suggestion I will make that it is not as historical records or theological treatises that biblical texts function in biblical spirituality.

Neither the conception of Jesus (presented as not occurring through human sexual intercourse but by divine intervention) nor the Resurrection (presented as somehow not available to all potential observers but only by revelation to specially chosen witnesses) was an "historical event" in the normal sense of the word, as were, for example, Jesus' healings, his trial, his crucifixion, or burial. The conception of Jesus and his Resurrection were not, even according to the texts, events taking place in time and space and subject to the intra-historical laws of causality, which is what we normally mean by an "historical" event. Neither of them could be investigated by "historical methods" as these are practiced by historians (although both have been the object of extensive historical critical exegesis).

However, these transhistorical realities are presented as the beginning and end of, that is, in natural continuity with, a historical narrative that runs from Jesus' physical birth to his physical burial. These two transhistorical events integrate some historical features (e.g., Mary was physically pregnant, Jesus was born at a particular time and in a particular place, the body of Jesus was not in the tomb on Easter Sunday morning). The conception and Resurrection are themselves narrated as if occurring in time and space because the participants in the events (the Mother of Jesus, Mary Magdalene, the Beloved Disciple, Thomas the Twin, the disciples) are presented as experiencing them in "ordinary waking time" rather than in a dream, trance, vision, or some extra-historical context. So the reader can easily mistake the literary genre of the Resurrection narrative as whatever kind of history the rest of the Gospels are thought to be.

We are further ahead methodologically in regard to the beginning of the Gospel than the end. Recognition that the *theologoumenon* of the virginal conception is followed by the infancy narratives, which are clearly midrashic, helps the biblical interpreter see that, until the public appearance of Jesus and his baptism by John in the Jordan the Gospel is not dealing with strictly historical events but with theological constructions cast in narrative form which, in some instances, are related to historical events such as the census of Caesar Augustus but in other cases, such as the coming of the Magi, may not be. That means that exegesis and interpretation of what precedes the baptism cannot be historical critical in any ordinary and certainly not exclusive sense. Furthermore, we know enough about how midrash works to have a fairly reliable alternative method for approaching the first two chapters of Matthew and Luke.

The history of work with the Resurrection Narratives, however, has not made as much progress.[19] The questions and discussions are still dominated by the kinds of concerns characteristic of classical historical criticism: what "really happened" on Easter morning, meaning who saw (or could see) what. Was the tomb really empty (or, for that matter, was Jesus ever buried)? Was Jesus physically alive? Was he ascended or not yet ascended when Mary Magdalene saw him? How did he get into the locked room? Did Thomas actually touch his wounds? Et cetera.[20] The arguments about the Resurrection are still, for the most part (and however disguised by the introduction of new methodological concerns), about physical resuscitation vs. some kind of non-bodily revivification—both, in my opinion, serious mistakes.

My methodological interest in the Resurrection Narrative is based on the "in-between" character of the narratives themselves. They are not clearly "non-historical" as is midrash or a parable, nor are they clearly "historical" in the sense of recounting singular events taking place in a particular time and place and subject to the laws of natural causality. So the Resurrection Narrative texts supply a "pure" type of text that can be discussed in relation to my substantive concern, biblical spirituality, that is, the issue of how *texts as texts* (not as factual historical records or sources of theological affirmations, etc.) function as locus and mediation of *spirituality* as lived faith experience.

2.3.2.2 THE SUBSTANTIVE REASON

My substantive reason for selecting the Resurrection narrative for this purpose is that the bodily Resurrection of Jesus (which alone allows him to be alive after his death in the full integrity of his personal humanity) is the *conditio sine qua non* for his real contemporary presence and action (as opposed to simply "influence," which might be due to memory, idealization, etc.) in the life of the believer. I strongly suspect, precisely because so many Christians seem to live their religious lives without particular reference to the Resurrection, that the Resurrection does not actually play this role. The Resurrection is something that "took place" (like other historical events) some time in the past, winding up the life of Jesus by proving that he was

19. An excellent collection of specialist essays bringing research on the Resurrection up to the twenty-first century is Davis, Kendall, and O'Collins, *Resurrection*. The most original recent work, which marks a genuine advance over previous studies, is Kelly, *Resurrection Effect*.

20. A major step beyond these concerns is represented by O'Collins, *Believing*, which presents a good critical overview of the most recent work as well as charting new territory.

really God and giving him the last word in relation to his persecutors. With these matters taken care of, Christian life can go on as an essentially ethical project of living in conformity with the life and teaching of Jesus.

Jesus himself, most people probably believe, is somehow existent, with God, somewhere outside this cosmos ("in heaven"). He is able to affect living humans in some spiritual way (through grace, inspiration, etc.) and after death we, similarly "spiritualized," will "see" him or "join" him, wherever he is. More literal imaginations may entertain the possibility of huge crowds of post-death people in some less than earthly realm. But the real content and motivation of Christian life is not the Resurrected Jesus here and now present and active but the *memory* of his pre-paschal life and teaching and *theological beliefs* about him which one must hold to be saved. In sacramental traditions he is present mysteriously in the eucharist and in more word-oriented traditions, in preaching, but these tend to be intensified instances of memory and theology. In other words, my suspicion is that, for most people, Jesus himself is much like other significant people who have died, only more so.

In contrast to this relative non-functioning of the Resurrected Jesus in the life of the ordinary believer we have numerous accounts from Christian mystics and contemplatives (that is, people of highly developed spirituality) throughout history of an intense and continuous experience of Jesus himself, bodily (though I would argue not physically) and personally present to them, in and through Scripture, sacraments, personal prayer, service of neighbor. But this is not vicarious experience of someone who is, in fact, absent. Like Paul on the road to Damascus, they experience the person who says, "I am Jesus."

My substantive concern is the subject of a larger project on the Resurrection of Jesus as the condition of possibility of such Jesus spirituality/mysticism, the real and experienced presence of Jesus, in the full integrity of his personal glorified humanity in the experience (not just the faith conviction) of the believer. But part of that project, which is the subject of this essay, is to understand the role of Scripture in that experience, that is, the biblical spirituality of the Resurrection.

If the Resurrection narratives as they bear on the post-paschal Jesus are not accounts of historical events in the same sense as his healing of the blind man or his trial before Pilate, nor theological texts in the discursive sense of that term such as Paul's treatment of the Resurrection in 1 Cor 15, but witnesses to something altogether different, what I am calling "transhistorical" reality experienced by real people who are themselves historical in their historical contexts, we have to decide what kind (genre) of text we are dealing with. I want to suggest that these texts, and in a particular sense John 20–21 (and the Emmaus event in Luke 24:13–35), because of their distinctively constructed narrative character, are exercises in *theopoetics* rather than in any kind of history or theology in the normal sense of these words. They are constructed artistic compositions, narrative analogues of Paul's conversion experience as recounted in Acts 9:1-7. They are a "narratizing" of transhistorical reality as experienced and interpreted by historical agents.

Like all human experience, including faith experience, the experience of the Risen Jesus is rooted in corporeality and constructed and elaborated imaginatively. The Resurrection is quite real, indeed bodily, and the experiences of the Risen Jesus—like musical appreciation of a Beethoven sonata, being in love, or religious conversion—are real. Not only is the experience real but also that which is experienced is real. But they are not the same kind of experience, nor of the same kind of reality, as eating an apple or having a conversation or writing an article.

It is in our engagement with, through our reading of, these texts that we readers of the Gospel are integrated into a real, alternate, though not physical "world" within which, through the functioning of the spiritual senses informing and activating the *sensus fidei*, we perceive and participate in the reality and life of the Risen Jesus. (This textual mediation is paralleled by other forms of participation in his life such as sacraments, prayer, life in and service of the ecclesial community as his body, but our concern here is with the biblical form). In other words, *the organon of perception of the Risen Jesus is the whole person*, not the physical eyes or ears, the emotions, or the reasoning of the discursive intellect, even though all of these forms and operations of human perception are involved in the actual relation to the real Risen Jesus because all human experience is rooted in corporeality and integrated by the imagination. It is this participation that transforms the reader who "puts on the mind of Christ," or "dies and rises with Christ," or is "hidden with Christ in God," or becomes the "body of Christ" in the world.

3. Theopoiesis

This brings me, finally, to the issue with which I am really concerned in relation to biblical spirituality, namely, theopoiesis or the shaping of religious experience by aesthetic engagement with the biblical text. The thesis I am exploring (and proposing) is that *biblical spirituality is the transformative experience of God mediated by engagement with the theopoetic text* or the biblical text approached as theopoetic. Exegesis of the text approached as a source of historical or other kinds of data may supply information about the past or the production of the text (the world behind the text). Criticism of the text approached as literature may illuminate the theological, psychological,

literary, or other content of the text itself (the world of the text). But hermeneutics or interpretation of the text as theopoetic opens the reader to, or
plunges the reader into, a new "world," a new construction of reality (the
world before the text) which one can enter only by participation and at the
price of personal transformation.[21] The three primary features of aesthetic
experience—that it is revelatory, transformative, and participative—are
verified in the process of interpretation of the text that is not historico-
critical or rationally analytical but aesthetic.[22]

To begin with, we need to recognize that the discourse about "theopoetics" in general and particularly in relation to the interpretation
of Scripture is a quite recent development arising at the intersection of
theology and literary studies much like "biblical spirituality," which arises
at the intersection of biblical studies and spirituality. The interactive
meeting ground of literary biblical studies, theology, and spirituality is
precisely theopoetics or a theory of the spiritually transformative power
of biblical texts as texts, actualized through a certain kind of reading or
interpretation which these scholars are calling "theopoiesis."

Theopoetics as a theological discourse is usually traced to the work of
the theologian and literary scholar Stanley Romaine Hopper, who seems to
have introduced the term in a 1971 lecture titled "The Literary Imagination
and the Doing of Theology,"[23] and Amos Niven Wilder, the literary biblical
critic, who developed the theme in his 1976 volume *Theopoetic: Theology
and the Religious Imagination*.[24] It would probably be accurate to say that
theopoetics is the literary or textual face of the wider concern with theological aesthetics as an approach to spirituality.

Without getting into the discussion of the field as a whole, I will
explain how I understand the terms *theopoiesis* (a process) and *theopoetic*
(a product) as giving rise to a praxis that is often called *theopoetics*. Theopoiesis means, literally, "making God" but "making" in this context does
not refer to bringing into existence or fashioning. It refers to "shaping" out

21. A good brief summary of this subject can be found in Rush, *Eyes of Faith*,
234–38. Here he makes the connection between the *sensus fidei* and transformative
interpretation of Scripture.

22. For a good introduction to the current situation of theological aesthetics as a field
of study, of which theopoetics should be seen as a subdivision or form, is the "Introduction" to Bychkov and Fodor, *Theological Aesthetics*, i–viii. Other informative articles specifically concerned with theopoetics include Holland, "Theology"; Guyn, "Theopoetics";
Caputo and Keller, "Theopoetic/Theopolitic"; May, *Body Knows*; Alves, *Poet*.

23. Hopper, "Literary Imagination," 207–29. All ten of the essays by Hopper himself
in *Way of Transfiguration* are important. See the lengthy and important essay by Keefe-
Perry, "Theopoetics," for a history and analysis of the development of the field.

24. Wilder, *Theopoetic*.

of pre-existing materials. And it is not God that requires shaping but the human experience of God. Theopoiesis is the kind of writing (whether in prose or in poetry, in narrative or drama, in prayer or song, or other form) through which the writer creates a theopoetic text. In other words, theopoiesis is not a way of rationally "constructing God" as are various kinds of systematic theology; it is a way of imaginatively shaping the human experience of God through the creation of texts just as poetry shapes our experience by the words, the images, the dynamics of the poem. (There are other ways of imaginatively shaping our God-experience—as in visual art, architecture, drama, dance, music—but the emphasis in theopoetics is on aesthetic texts or the aesthetic dimension of texts which might, themselves, be primarily historical, theological, or even philosophical.)

One might say that theopoetics is parallel to rational discourse in that both are ways of knowing. But rather than being primarily analytic, logical, and linear, as is discursive thinking which moves from data to conclusions, theopoetics is primarily synthetic, aesthetic, and holistic, moving from experience to participation, that is, to a depth engagement or an engagement of the depths in which truth and beauty coincide, in which God is experienced not as knowable and ever more accurately and adequately known, but as hidden, unknown, attractive, self-giving, luminous, transforming, enticing, mysterious, paradoxical, challenging. One does not progress in knowledge through theopoetics so much as one deepens in relationship which, as even the Hebrew term for enfleshed love testifies, is, in fact, to "know."

A well-known and illuminating example of the distinction and the relation between theopoetics and theology is John of the Cross' sublime eight-stanza poem "The Dark Night" or "One Dark Night," which is a theopoetic analogue of his systematic spiritual-theological treatise *The Dark Night of the Soul*.[25] John speaks of the treatise as a "commentary" on the poem but in fact the two works are not mutually replaceable texts or even, strictly speaking, corresponding texts. The treatise is not so much a commentary as another text offering a parallel treatment of the same topic. The poem and the treatise are two ways of understanding the same spiritual itinerary. The poem plunges one into the experience of union with God, uses mysterious words to shape that experience, while the treatise constructs and explains the itinerary toward union with God using the clearest theological language available. The treatise clearly explains the stages, signs of development or regress, obstacles and challenges, sources of assistance, byways and successes of the spiritual journey. The reader can literally "look up" various "topics" such as prayer, spiritual direction, temptation, distraction, and so on. One

25. Both works are available in critical English translation in *The Collected Works of St. John of the Cross*, 358–457.

can study the treatise until one grasps, at least theoretically, the concepts and dynamics even if one has not had the experience being analyzed.

But the poem does not, because it cannot, really "tell the reader" anything that one does not already know, even though one might not know, until one has read the poem, that one knows it. It involves the reader in a deep appropriation of her or his own experience of this itinerary and one understands to the extent that one has "been there." The enlightenment is not by way of increased knowledge or expanded information but by way of illumination of experience. The reader does not say, "Now I finally get it" or "Now that aspect of prayer is clear," but simply, "Yes." The resulting silence is that of a person who has read a deeply moving poem.

Whereas the treatise is clear and all competent readers will end up knowing roughly the same content, the poem will be personalized in the reading of each reader depending on her or his own spiritual experience. There will be a family resemblance among competent engagements with the poem but nothing like the discursive clarity and communicability of various readings of the treatise, which can be exegeted, debated, and clarified by discussion. One can teach the treatise but not the poem. Students can argue over the interpretations of the treatise and one reading may be superior to another. But one's reading of the poem will deepen, expand, even change direction as one's experience of the spiritual life changes and a variety of interpretations is not a contest but an enrichment.

The theopoetic experience is like what one experiences in seeing *Hamlet* in contrast to what one learns about *Hamlet* by reading a literary critical study of the play. Contrasting the poem and the treatise, or the play and the critique of it, one is reminded of the saying about the Gospel of John that in it the child can wade and the elephant can swim. Or of Barnabas Lindars' wonderful image of the Gospel as a kind of spiral staircase around Jesus who is seen ever anew as the contemplative reader ascends and descends, not straight up and down as in an elevator, but ever circling what does not "move" but is ever ancient and ever new. John's Gospel is not only a theological treatise and a historical record; it is most adequately described as a theopoetic text, which is precisely, in my opinion, what Clement meant in calling it "the spiritual Gospel." It is not so much what the Gospel is "about," or even the sublimity of its theology, that makes it "spiritual," but the way the Gospel is written, its capacity to reveal the reader to him or herself in and through the person's relationship with Jesus to the extent that one surrenders contemplatively to its dynamics that makes it the primary New Testament locus of mystical or spiritual experience.

To return now to the thesis in the first paragraph of this section, the Gospel text is a theopoetic of the experience of God in the Risen Jesus. (I am drawing my examples from the Gospel of John in this essay but the same issues would need to be raised about the Synoptics, which are also theopoetic texts.) Whoever "John" is, he or she was a spiritual genius who produced a text that functions primarily neither as a systematic theological treatise nor as a history or biography (though it has both characteristics). It functions as art. It shapes the reader's experience of God through the poetic/dramatic narrative into which it invites the reader. It works not by communicating information, even theological information, but by transforming the person. And that transformation is not primarily a change of mind but a change of person. The reader does not primarily *know* more; one *is* more.

This is true not only of certain parts of the Gospel but of the Gospel as a whole. It has been suggested that John is a long, dramatic judicial trial in which it seems that Jesus is being interrogated, judged, accepted or rejected but in which, in reality, it is the reader who is placed in crisis and must situate him- or herself in relation to the one who is the Truth, the "Light of the World." And that self-situation actually changes the person, makes her or him other than she or he was prior to the engagement with the text. It has also been suggested that the Gospel is a narrative of a "new creation," seven "days" during which a new reality, a new "world," is imagined into existence and which the reader must choose to enter and become part of by leaving behind the reality construction of the Prince of this World and becoming the new person who is a disciple of Jesus. Others have seen the Gospel as a series of "make or break" encounters with Jesus to whom one must come or from whom one turns away but to whom one can no more remain neutral than one can to a person whom one meets. These are not, from a theopoetic point of view, alternative critical theses among which a reader may or must choose, as is suggested by many commentaries, which attempt to establish the priority or relative superiority of a particular thesis over "competitors."

All of these and other holistic "takes" on the Gospel are really identifying it as a theopoetic of salvation into whose dynamics one enters in terms of one's own experience of God in Jesus. To participate in this text is to undergo theopoiesis, an imaginative reconstruction of self and reality. But what is crucial is that if the text functions this way for a given reader, the person "cannot go home again." Like the experience of being in love, one cannot extricate oneself from the definitive change in one's being that has taken place. One can break off a relationship but one will not be, cannot be, what one was before that relationship was lived. One cannot return to the "place" where one was, the "person" one was prior to the experience. That is as true of Judas who repudiates Jesus as of Mary Magdalene who becomes the first apostle of the Resurrection.

4. Conclusion: Theopoetics and the Resurrection

My thesis is both ancient in the church and something of a novelty in the modern biblical academy. The purpose of Scripture is not primarily to recount history or even to develop a theology. Its purpose is first of all revelation, the salvific interaction between God and the believer in Jesus Christ through the power of the Spirit. The text mediates that relationship not by conveying information or by presenting a convincing rational discourse (though it may do both of these) but in the way an art object, when engaged by contemplative reading, performance, etc., draws the person into a personal, transformative participation in that which is mediated by the work of art. In other words, while it may not be wrong to say that in the Gospel we are dealing with historical or theological material, it is wrong to reductively identify the biblical text as such. As we have recognized, for example, the genres of midrash or parable or drama or poetry (all forms of art, i.e., revelational theopoetics, not rational discourse) in the Bible, it is perhaps time to recognize that much, maybe all, of the biblical text, insofar as it is Scripture, is theopoetic.

My particular concern is with the Resurrection Narrative(s), which scholars as well as ordinary believers have tended, for centuries, to treat as either a primarily historical or primarily theological text. (It was not treated as such at the beginning when it was primarily a baptismal and/or Eucharistic text.) This is no doubt due to the apologetic function that has been assigned to the Resurrection in post-medieval times. But my thesis is that this is a "category mistake." Or at the very least a "genre mistake." However, this mistake in relation to the Resurrection texts is more serious than it would be in relation to any other part of the New Testament.

If the contemporary, post-paschal believer is to be in a salvific relationship with Jesus, then Jesus must, indeed, be alive and present. Since Jesus really died and was buried, only resurrection can ground that relationship. If, as Paul says, Christ is not risen, our faith is in vain (see 1 Cor 15:14). It is faith in a dead man whose inspirational life can be imitated and whose sublime teaching can be followed. But it is not a relationship with a living person now present and active in one's life. If it is to be a relationship with the real Jesus, numerically identical with the person who lived in Palestine in the first century and died under Pontius Pilate, then it must be grounded in the Resurrection of the whole person, the incarnate Word who was and is and remains Jesus, yesterday, today, and forever. This is the theological freight of the confession of the "bodily Resurrection."

The Resurrection narrative is a theopoetic text, an aesthetic mediation of participative and transformative meaning. But it is not, like *Hamlet* or *Moby Dick*, the mediation of meaning through a fictional character, story, or setting. It is the mediation of the meaning of a real, living, present person. If this is the case, another set of questions eventually must be engaged: historical issues of the identity, credibility, etc., of the witnesses, the competence and validity of their witness, the meaning of their discourse, and so on; philosophical issues about the meaning and continuity of bodiliness in earthly life and through death; theological issues concerning the intersection of the mysteries of creation, incarnation, Trinity, and eschatology. But these questions, and others like them, are only meaningful and urgent if, in fact, Jesus is truly risen and the reader is actually in relationship with him. In other words, the theopoetically mediated revelatory experience precedes and grounds all other inquiry the way an actual love relationship makes questions about the lover's personality, character, integrity, family, education, work, faith, intentions, etc., meaningful and important. The relationship is not based on these questions or their answers; the questions are meaningful because of the relationship. We do not reason our way *to* relationships, even though prudent persons reason *about* their relationships.

I suspect the reason that the Resurrection has so little valence in the spiritual lives of so many believers is that these contextual or subsidiary questions have held center stage in believers' ordinary engagement with the Resurrection texts. It is easier to "relate" to Jesus in his earthly ministry or in his passion and death, which have close analogues in our own experience and which are historical events analogous to those of other historical heroes and models. We have no historical analogues for the Resurrection. It is a singular event whose imaginative engagement is unique. As Rubem Alves so provocatively says:

> explanations destroy the magical power of words[;] . . . the story is always happening in the present because it never happened in the past. . . . Stories are like music. One does not ask of Brahms' First Symphony: "Did it ever happen?" No, it did not. The symphony is not a portrait of something which happened "apax," once and for all. That which happened once and for all is forever lost. The symphony: every time it is played its magic happens again. The beautiful wants to return. . . . Its time is sacred; it is reborn every morning; it is the time of the resurrection. . . . "Once upon a time, in a far distant land . . .": a cloud of mist covers the narrative to conceal its real time and space which are "now" and "here."[26]

26. Alves, *Poet,* 40–41.

9

The This-Worldliness of the New Testament's Otherworldly Spirituality

Michael J. Gorman
St. Mary's Seminary & University, Baltimore

FOR MANY PEOPLE, INCLUDING Christians of various kinds, the word *spirituality* connotes an experience of the transcendent, even specifically of God or Jesus, that is not connected to life in the world. Its purpose, so to speak, is to transport people out of the trials and tribulations of this world through mystical experience(s), an interiority focused on the self or the god/God within, or an eschatological orientation that pays scant if any attention to social ills. Although recent scholarly interpretation of Christian existence has opposed such approaches to spirituality, much popular spiritual writing and some Christian music (both traditional and contemporary) reinforce such sentiments. The resulting spirituality is often otherworldly, escapist, and even narcissistic.

In this essay I argue for the "this-worldliness" of New Testament spirituality. I do so by tracing the relationship between certain mystical or quasi-mystical experiences narrated in the New Testament and actual life in the world as it is depicted in the larger biblical texts within which the experiences are narrated.[1] We will consider four such experiences in context: (1) the transfiguration accounts in the Synoptic Gospels; (2) Paul's trip to the third heaven

---

1. My approach is largely literary-theological, rather than social-historical, though the two approaches are complementary.

in 2 Cor 12; (3) resurrection and ascension with Christ in Col 3; and (4) John the Seer's trip to (or vision of) the heavenly throne room in Rev 4–5.

In each case, the mystical encounter—a moment of intensity in the relationship with God—issues in a particular way of being in the world that is derived from the experience itself, though often in unexpected ways. Ironically, moreover, although the New Testament's basic narrative pattern about Jesus, and therefore the normative narrative pattern for Christians, is suffering and death followed by glory, these passages indicate another normative pattern at work in Christian existence: the *reverse* pattern of glory (broadly construed) followed by suffering and death (also broadly construed; we will use the term *cruciformity*). In these passages that narrate intense encounters with the glory of God and/or Christ, glory is the prequel to, and perhaps even the prerequisite for, cruciform existence. Life in this world is made possible not only by the *hope* of future glory, but also by the *experience* of past or present glory.[2] Paul's words in 2 Cor 3:18, spoken in the context of describing this-worldly, cruciform ministry, are thus arguably the quintessential expression of a Christian spirituality grounded in the New Testament (which in turn is rooted in the Old Testament): "And all of us, with unveiled faces, seeing the glory of the Lord as though reflected in a mirror, are being transformed into the same image from one degree of glory to another; for this comes from the Lord, the Spirit."

We begin with some working definitions—of *spirituality*, *mystical experience*, and *this-worldly*.

1. Defining Key Terms

In this context I use *spirituality* to mean Christian spirituality, assuming it will be grounded in and shaped by the Bible, with particular emphasis on the New Testament.[3] By "New Testament spirituality" (in the essay title) I mean both the spiritualities found in the New Testament texts and the spiritualities shaped and nourished by those texts.[4] Yet the definition of *spiri-*

---

2. In fact, the full pattern will be described as tripartite: glory/cruciformity/glory.

3. See also Kourie, "Reading Scripture," 136.

4. The mingling of singular ("spirituality") and plural ("spiritualities") is deliberate, for there is both similarity and difference in the spiritualities found in and shaped by the New Testament texts. Furthermore, since the study of spirituality is recognized as inherently "self-implicating" ("self-involving," "participatory"), holding these two aspects of biblical spirituality close together seems appropriate. Although the distinctions made by Sandra Schneiders (in this volume and elsewhere) among (1) the spirituality that produced the text (exegesis), (2) the spirituality in the text (biblical theology), and (3) the spirituality the text produces (hermeneutics) are useful heuristically, in theological interpretation they finally constitute a unified whole.

tuality is debated among Christians. One standard definition is "the lived experience of Christian belief"[5] or "of Christian faith and discipleship."[6] This definition, though useful, may be too general. Another option is "a transformative relationship with God," with emphasis less on experience and more on transformation.[7]

A more comprehensive definition may prove beneficial. I propose the following:

> An ongoing relationship of joyful communion and union with the Triune God, focused on Jesus Christ and shaped by his story, enabled by the Spirit, punctuated by moments of intensity, expressed in daily life, and transformative of the individuals and communities in the relationship.[8]

The phrase "shaped by his story" points to the nature of New Testament and thus Christian spirituality, informed by the story of Jesus within the "meta-narrative" of creation to re-creation, as itself having a narrative character.[9]

One phrase in this working definition of spirituality is especially important for our subject: *moments of intensity*. The witness of the New Testament and of the Christian tradition is that (some) Christians have occasional unusual encounters with God, in which God's presence, holiness, power, and/or love are felt in an overpowering and even transformative way. Frequently such "mystical experiences,"[10] often described also as "breakthrough experiences," cannot be fully articulated in normal human language. The term *mystical experience*, however, can unfortunately be used to reinforce a totally otherworldly, escapist spirituality. I therefore prefer the term *moment of intensity* for various experiences in which Christians sense God's presence in unusually palpable ways (whether in private prayer

5. The substance of the "working definition" used in the preparation of McGinn and Meyendorff, *Christian Spirituality*, xv.

6. The operative definition in Holder, *Blackwell Companion*, 1, 5.

7. See especially Waaijman, *Spirituality*, 305–591.

8. For a compatible definition, see Schneiders, "Christian Spirituality," 1: "the living of the paschal mystery within the context of the church community . . . [involving] the person with God, others, and all reality according to the understanding of these realities that is characteristic of Christian faith." Joy is not antithetical to participation in the paschal mystery: "[T]he most illuminating interpretations of Christian identity are found in particular lives marked by joy and sacrificial responsibility" (Ford, *Self and Salvation*, 2). See also the essay by Stephen Barton in this volume.

9. That is, Christian spirituality reflects and tells a story. See my *Cruciformity*.

10. See, e.g., Perrin, "Mysticism," with emphasis on divine love as the core of mysticism.

or corporate worship, on a pilgrimage, at the bedside of a dying family member, etc.), and are (often) changed by the encounter.

This is not to deny the reality or importance of these moments of intensity, or their otherworldly (i.e., transcendent) character. But, as the extended definition suggests, Christian spirituality is expressed in daily life; the moments of intensity must be translated into life in this world. The love of God encountered in such experiences, says the Christian mystical tradition, "is not to be locked up within the confines of a monastic cell," for mysticism "expresses the truth about the way in which God is alive in the world."[11] New Testament spirituality has an inherent dynamic that is *centrifugal* rather than *centripetal*—propelling us outward.[12] The texts we will consider support and give shape to this contention; it is what the phrase "this-worldliness" refers to.[13]

To speak of Christian spirituality as "this-worldly" is first of all to make a theological claim about the Christian faith itself. In his (now published) 1979 inaugural lecture at Princeton Theological Seminary, "The This-Worldliness of the New Testament," Paul W. Meyer acknowledges that the term *this-worldliness* is awkward.[14] He insists on its use, however, in deliberate opposition to the term *otherworldliness* and all attempts to understand Christian faith as flight from this world. Meyer contends that for the earliest Christian communities, and for us, the very this-worldly crucifixion of Jesus—as historical fact, as God's means of redemption, as hermeneutical key—renders Christian faith inevitably this-worldly. For the New Testament writers, everything they know about God and life, Meyer contends, "has been stamped with the branding iron of the crucifixion."[15] He continues:

---

11. Ibid., 444.

12. Ellen Davis wondered at the symposium whether this metaphor was problematic because "centrifugal" erroneously suggests leaving the center (God) behind. But my point is the contrast between inward and outward movement from the self (i.e., the self-in-its-encounter-with-God) as the metaphorical center. (Professor Davis also insightfully suggested another creative metaphor for the ongoing spiritual life punctuated by moments of intensity: the Richter scale of seismic activity.)

13. Even biblical scholarship can inadvertently promote a centripetal spirituality, as in the usage of terms like "Christ-mysticism" (Deissmann, etc.) or even the more recent "participation" (Sanders, etc.) to refer to the core of Pauline "religion," terms that can be misleading or even vacuous if not explained carefully. Recent attempts to connect participation in Christ with narrative (see my own *Cruciformity*) and with concrete practices (see Hays, "What Is 'Real Participation in Christ'?" as well as my *Inhabiting the Cruciform God*) interpret the language of participation in a concrete, this-worldly fashion without denying its transcendent reality.

14. Meyer, "This-Worldliness," 7.

15. Ibid., 14.

All has become irreversibly this-worldly, because the transcendence and authority of God himself now underscore and authorize that this-worldliness. And there is something on the stage of history that was not there before: a community that calls itself by the name of the crucified Messiah. It is one that can say now with integrity that it has been brought into being not by a flight into another world or by visions of things yet to be, but by its experience of life and by God's confirmation of the same.[16]

In a very different context, Dietrich Bonhoeffer foreshadowed Meyer's claims. In his *Ethics*, and in his letters and papers from prison, Bonhoeffer developed the notion of *Wirklichkeit*, meaning "reality" or "this-worldliness." Writing to Eberhard Bethge one day following the failure of the July 20, 1944, attempt to kill Hitler, Bonhoeffer referred to the incident in the following way:

Later on I discovered, and am still discovering to this day, that one only learns to have faith by living in the full this-worldliness [*Wirklichkeit*] of life. . . . [A]nd this is what I call this-worldliness: living fully in the midst of life's tasks, questions, successes and failures, experiences and perplexities—then one takes seriously no longer one's own sufferings but rather the sufferings of God in the world. Then one stays awake with Christ in Gethsemane. And I think this is faith; this is *metanoia*. And this is how one becomes a human being, a Christian.[17]

My point is not to condemn or condone Bonhoeffer's involvement in the plot, but simply to highlight what he says he had discovered: Christian spirituality must be expressed in the realities of this life. Or, more theologically: Christ's lordship cannot be relegated to the private realm and kept out of the public realm, for "Christ is the place in which the reality of God meets the reality of the world."[18]

With these definitions in place, we turn now to consider our New Testament texts.

16. Ibid. Meyer also rightly stresses that only with the resurrection does the crucifixion have any theological or existential import (ibid., 11–14, 17–18).

17. Bonhoeffer, *Letters and Papers from Prison*, 486.

18. I am indebted to my student Frank (Trey) Palmisano for this reference and for reflections on its context in Bonhoeffer's struggle with the Nazis. The quotation is from personal correspondence from him dated March 24, 2012. Regarding Bonhoeffer's involvement in the plot, see Fowl and Jones, *Reading in Communion*, 135–64.

2. Encounters with the Glorified Christ

The texts we will consider narrate or describe mystical or quasi-mystical experiences—moments of intensity—that are human encounters with the glorified Messiah in heaven itself or in a heaven-like space. These encounters can take the form of brief experiences or of continuous states that result from such moments of intensity.

At least some of the encounters with the glorified Messiah are probably best understood as examples of Jewish merkabah mysticism reworked, so to speak, around the early Christian experience of Jesus as the crucified and resurrected/glorified Messiah. Space precludes a discussion of this phenomenon or an analysis of our texts in relation to other accounts of it.[19] Rather, in what follows I will consider the nature of each experience as it is narrated or described in the text, focusing on the implications of the experience for this-worldly existence as those implications emerge from the text itself or from its co-text. These texts will both illustrate and underscore the contention I am making about the this-worldliness of New Testament spirituality.

We will begin with a brief consideration of the Transfiguration, followed by longer analyses of the accounts in 2 Corinthians, Colossians, and Revelation.

2.1 The Transfiguration (Matt 17:1–8; Mark 9:2–8; Luke 9:28–36)

The synoptic account of Jesus' Transfiguration, or metamorphosis (Gk. *metemorphōthē* in Matt 17:2; Mark 9:2), has received a variety of interpretations over the centuries. Christologically, for instance, it has been seen, in connection with Jesus' baptism, as evidence for his divinity and as a foreshadowing of his post-resurrection glory. Spiritually, it has been viewed both as a unique experience for the disciples present and as a summons for all to contemplate Christ and be transformed into his likeness. Theologically, therefore, it has also been interpreted as a sign of the eschatological reality the faithful will one day experience.

All of these interpretations go back to the patristic period.[20] Yet another significant approach to the Transfiguration dates to the patristic era, too. This approach stresses the close literary and theological connections

---

19. For a brief overview and suggested readings, see Rowland, "Revelation," 596–99.

20. See Simonetti, *Matthew 14–28*, 52–58; Oden and Hall, *Mark*, 109–14; Just, *Luke*, 157–61.

between the Transfiguration and the cross,[21] and therefore discourages Christians from overemphasizing mystical experiences of Christ's glory.

Commenting on Peter's statement, "Lord, it is good for us to be here . . ." (Matt 17:4), Leo the Great in the fifth century called it "inappropriate" for both christological and spiritual reasons. For one thing, "the world could not be saved except by Christ's death." For another, Peter was

> [e]xcited . . . by these revelations of secret realities . . . spurning the mundane and loathing earthly things . . . seized by a certain excess of passion toward a yearning for eternal things. Filled up with the joy of the whole vision, he wished to dwell there with Jesus where he was delighting in Christ's manifested glory.

After noting the necessity of Jesus' death, Leo continues: "Among the temptations of this life we should understand that we are to ask for endurance before glory. Good fortune in [eschatological] ruling cannot come before a time of enduring."[22] Much more recently, Joel Marcus has noted that some early Jewish and Christian traditions conceive of paradise on a mountaintop. "Understandably enough," writes Marcus, "Peter wants to prolong his sojourn in this re-creation of paradise."[23]

Modern commentators also point to the narrative of ministry to human need following each Transfiguration account as an appropriate "counterpoint" to the Transfiguration.[24] Jesus and the disciples have moved from the mountaintop of divine glory to the valley of human need—a boy with a demon/unclean spirit (Mark 9:14–29 par.). After that, both Jesus and the disciples will move toward the cross. The moment of intensity we call the Transfiguration prepares them for this journey, providing hope and sustenance for what lies ahead. The Transfiguration narrative does not allow disciples of Jesus to stay in a state of mystical experience. The divine summons to listen to Jesus (Mark 9:7 par.) means "hearkening" to his call to take up one's cross and "descending with Jesus from the Mount of Transfiguration into the valley of human weakness, need, and pain."[25]

---

21. In each of the Synoptics, the Transfiguration follows immediately after Jesus' first passion prediction and its corollary call for the disciples to take up their own cross.

22. Sermon 38.5, cited in Simonetti, *Matthew 14–28*, 55.

23. Marcus, *Mark 8–16*, 638. Marcus here also indicates parallels between the Transfiguration story and the heavenly vision in *1 Enoch* 39:4–8.

24. So, e.g., Boring, "Matthew," 367, and Culpepper, "Luke," 208. Boring notes Raphael's painting in which the transfigured Christ's glory and the human misery at the foot of the mountain are both depicted.

25. Marcus, *Mark 8–16*, 639; cf. 656.

The Transfiguration confirms Jesus' status as the Son of God who shares in the divine glory and desires to share that glory with his disciples. For the disciples, it is "a foretaste of Jesus' resurrection glory."[26] But the Transfiguration also confirms the *way* in which Jesus would be the Son of God: in and through his paradigmatic suffering and death, and in ministry to the suffering. This moment of intensity, of glory (for Jesus, the disciples, and all who read the Gospel narratives) is not the final or ultimate spiritual experience. We cannot stay on the mountain. Already the gospel tradition assumes that those who share in Jesus' glory do so in a this-worldly, centrifugal, cruciform way. A mystical encounter with Christ must lead to encounters with others in their need.

We find this same sort of spirituality throughout the New Testament. Three passages outside the Gospels will support this claim.

2.2 Paul's Journey to the Third Heaven/Paradise (2 Cor 12:1–10)

The account of "a person in Christ who fourteen years ago was caught up to the third heaven . . . was caught up into Paradise and heard things that are not to be told, that no mortal is permitted to repeat" (2 Cor 12:2–4) is almost universally understood as Paul's third-person reference to his own experience. The precise nature of that experience is unclear even to Paul—he twice says "whether in the body or out of the body I do not know" (vv. 2, 3)—though it is usually described as a specimen of ancient heavenly ascents and is perhaps an early example of Jewish merkabah mysticism.[27] Most commentators agree that Paul narrates a single trip to the third heaven/Paradise, the latter referring to the place of the deceased righteous, the former probably referring to the highest (level of) heaven and thus also to Paradise itself.[28] For Paul, of course, heaven is also the place where God and Christ dwell.

Paul says that he has heard (and, implicitly, seen [v. 1]) "things that are not to be told, that no mortal is permitted to repeat" (v. 4). The apostle demonstrates this assessment of the experience by telling us precisely nothing explicitly about the revelation/vision/audition itself except its "location"—the third heaven/Paradise—and its subject (or, less likely, source)—"the Lord" (v. 1), meaning almost certainly Jesus.

26. Ibid., 637.

27. See Morray-Jones, "Paradise Revisited (2 Cor 12:1–2)." Lincoln (*Paradise Now and Not Yet*, 84), however, rightly stresses as well the distinctively Christian character of Paul's vision.

28. See the discussion in Lincoln, *Paradise Now and Not Yet*, 77–81.

The account, therefore, "can only be considered an 'anti-apocalypse.'"[29] In contrast to typical records of apocalyptic visions, it "presents a teasing 'form' of an apocalypse, without any recorded revelation of secret things."[30] The inexpressible character of the experience (v. 4) is, as we have noted, a common component of moments of intensity. Paul does, however, speak clearly about the *aftermath* of his "mountaintop experience," and from his account of the consequences, we learn about the experience and its significance.

Paul says that he received both an unexpected, undesired gift and a word from the Lord interpreting the gift. The gift, of course, was his famous "thorn . . . in the flesh," or perhaps "against the flesh" (v. 7). The interpretive word is no less famous: "My grace is sufficient for you, for power is made perfect in weakness" (v. 9). It is *this* revelation that really matters, Paul says, while revelations of the other sort do not. This interpretation of mystical experiences is in direct contrast to that of the super-apostles (v. 11) and is designed to teach Paul, the Corinthians, and us about Christlike humility and dependence on the Lord, and not to glory in esoteric experiences.[31]

But there is more going on here than simply pedagogy in humility and a critique of hyper-charismatic or otherworldly spirituality. As Humphrey puts it, the "ultimate revelation, or apocalypse, is Jesus Christ himself, and what God has done in his Son."[32] If Paul has truly, in some real but inexpressible sense, seen the Lord Jesus in this trip to heaven, he has seen the *glorified* Jesus, for this is by definition the nature of the post-resurrection, exalted Jesus. At the same time—and I would suggest that this is at the heart of the unspeakable mystery Paul has encountered—it is almost certainly the case that for Paul the exalted Lord Jesus retains the identity of the crucified Jesus.[33] This conviction is precisely what separates Paul from the super-apostles: they know only an exalted Jesus who presently shares his glory with his apostles, whereas Paul knows a *crucified* exalted Jesus, who presently shares his crucified and cruciform identity with his apostles. Paradoxically, for Paul this *koinōnia* with the crucified Messiah is a form of power and glory, but not in the way the super-apostles contend; it is the power of

29. Humphrey, *Ecstasy and Intimacy*, 69.

30. Ibid., 70.

31. Ibid.

32. Ibid.

33. Although I cannot prove this claim, it seems to be a common experience and conviction among NT writers, including John the seer of the slaughtered but resurrected Lamb of God (Rev 5); Luke, who narrates Jesus' self-revelation in breaking bread (24:13–49); and John the evangelist, who tells of Jesus appearing with visible wounds (20:19–31). See also Gal 2:19–20, where in the same breath Paul describes the indwelling Christ explicitly as the crucified Christ and implicitly as the resurrected Christ.

weakness, a testimony to divine glory via human frailty (12:9–10).[34] Paul is deconstructing and reconstructing his culture's, and the Corinthians', understanding of *doxa* (honor).[35]

In addition to humility, therefore, Paul has learned or relearned something critical about the relationship between Jesus' identity and apostolic identity (and we could say Christian identity more generally), and something equally critical about the nature of glory and honor. If Jesus remains the crucified as well as the exalted Lord, then encounters with him will necessarily be encounters with the paradox of glory that is connected to suffering and death. Such encounters will lead, not to a spirituality of glory *apart from* suffering and death, but to a spirituality of glory either *in the midst of* suffering and death or *following* suffering and death—or perhaps both. We may refer to these as the patterns of *simultaneous* and of *sequential* suffering and glory.

Throughout 2 Corinthians, and the Pauline corpus more generally, we see these two patterns of suffering and glory at work. We are most familiar with the pattern of sequential suffering and glory, in which glory is a future reality.[36] To be sure, the glory of God and Christ Paul saw in the third heaven gives testimony to the glory to be revealed. This certainty of future glory, eternal and weighty rather than momentary and light (2 Cor 4:17), sustains the apostle and all Christians in the difficulties of life in this world, especially in cruciform ministry.

At the same time, the hope of that future glory, or the foretaste of it in ecstatic experiences, does not invite us to focus or dwell on itself. It does not permit Paul to remain "there," aloof from the world. Rather, he is now prepared and expected to re-enter the world of persecution and of anxiety for his churches (2 Cor 12:10; cf. 11:22–33)—in a word, the world of weakness, not glory. Interestingly, the interpretive word Paul receives after the vision is first of all about grace, not glory: "My grace is sufficient for you" (2 Cor 12:9). Its focus is neither his recent moment of intensity nor his future state of glory; it is grace in the present. This word of grace compels him back into the world, with all its trials and tribulations, and at the same time sustains him in it.

This is not to say that Paul never experienced glory; he did, not least in the trip to the third heaven. He was transformed by beholding the glory of God (2 Cor 3:18), further transformed into the likeness of Christ the image of God in order to share in his identity through cruciform apostolic

34. Although the word *glory* does not appear in 2 Cor 10–13, it is self-evident that the vision of heaven would involve the heavenly glory of God and Christ.

35. This was stressed by Stephen Barton at the symposium.

36. E.g., Rom 5:1–5; 8:17–18, 21; 1 Cor 15:43; Phil 3:21.

ministry, which, like the cross itself, is paradoxically life-giving (2 Cor 4:8–12). Paul may have learned a lesson about suffering, death, and weakness, but this weakness is itself the way in which power—Christ's distinctive form of power—is manifested (2 Cor 12:9).

This is an experience of present glory inasmuch as it is transformative into the image of Christ, and thus the image and glory of God, *now*. It is why Paul can speak of glorification as a past reality (Rom 8:30) and an ongoing reality (2 Cor 3:18), not just a future reality. In this sense, Paul has an ongoing, daily experience of the power and glory of God/Christ.

Thus 2 Cor 12 inevitably points us back to 2 Cor 3–4, where present glory is explicitly predicated of Christian life and ministry (2 Cor 3:7–18). In 2 Cor 10–13 Paul refutes the understanding of power and glory advocated by the super-apostles—and all the possible existential implications thereof for the church, ministry, and daily life in Christ. He also refutes their corollary means of allegedly attaining and/or demonstrating this (false) power and glory/honor, namely, dreams and revelations. In both parts of the letter Paul offers an alternative understanding of power and glory as weakness, and he provides concrete examples of how this understanding is manifested in the daily life of a true apostle (and implicitly also the daily life of all in Christ). In chapter 3 he names the alternative avenue to attaining this cruciform power and glory—contemplation of Christ: "all of us, with unveiled faces, seeing the glory of the Lord as though reflected in a mirror, are being transformed into the same image from one degree of glory to another [lit. "from glory to glory"]; for this comes from the Lord, the Spirit" (2 Cor 3:18).[37]

In antiquity, beholding a deity was generally understood to be transformative.[38] But how does Paul understand contemplation of God/Christ, since there is no image per se, no statue or other representation? Is it merely a matter of imagination? No—contemplation of the Lord is made possible by the apostolic ministry of proclaiming and embodying the "gospel of the glory of Christ," which gives us "the knowledge of the glory of God in the face of Jesus Christ" (2 Cor 4:4–7).[39]

We see, or contemplate, the Lord Jesus first, says Paul, when we hear the gospel narrative preached, interpreted, and embodied—that is, the gospel of Christ crucified as the power (and thus glory) of God (1 Cor 1:18–25). The language of light and glory in 2 Cor 4:4–7 must not be read

37. The verb translated "transformed" is from the Greek *metamorphoō*, used in the NT only here, in Rom 12:2, and in the Markan and Matthean accounts of the Transfiguration. Paul is reinterpreting the experience of Moses (Exod 34:29–35).

38. See, e.g., Furnish, *II Corinthians*, 420, and the literature cited there. For more extensive discussion, see Litwa, *We Are Being Transformed*.

39. See especially Knowles, *We Preach Not Ourselves*, 112–46.

as if it were a separate gospel of resurrection power divorced from Christ crucified; that would negate all that Paul has said in 1 Cor 1:18–25, all that he will say in 2 Cor 10–13, and all that he implies in the immediate context, where Christlike ministry is described in highly cruciform terms (2 Cor 4:8–12). Jesus the Lord who gives his resurrection life to people remains the crucified one.

We contemplate the Lord Jesus as well in seeing the story of Jesus embodied in the lives of those who proclaim him, those who are: "always carrying in the body the death of Jesus, so that the life of Jesus may also be made visible in our bodies. . . . So death is at work in us, but life in you" (2 Cor 4:10–12; cf. Gal 3:1; 1 Thess 2:7–12). We may speak of this Jesus, proclaimed and embodied, as the *narrated* Jesus.

Paul is able to claim that contemplation of Jesus, and therefore of God, is possible through the apostolic narration of Jesus in speech and life because he is persuaded that the *narrative identity* of Jesus in this proclamation corresponds precisely to the *ontological identity* of Jesus, the real Jesus who is in heaven and whom Paul has seen. Because of this correspondence between the narrated Jesus and the real Jesus—a correspondence that does not obtain in the case of the super-apostles—two things follow. First, it is unnecessary to have visions, revelations, or heavenly trips to contemplate Jesus. Second, whenever someone does claim to have had such a mystical experience, its legitimacy as an encounter with the real Christ depends on two things: its being narrated as an encounter with the exalted *crucified* Christ, and its being translated into a life-narrative that corresponds to the reality encountered. Transformation into the image of God in Christ, which means into a cruciform existence, reveals to all whether one has truly encountered the glorified Christ. This holds true as well for those who claim to have seen the Lord in non-mystical ways, through hearing or observing apostolic ministry. Once again, the proof is in the pudding: transformation into the image of God revealed in Christ.[40]

To summarize: Paul's heavenly encounter with the glorified Christ propelled him back into the real world of his churches, and into cruciform ministry on their behalf. Encountering the exalted Christ as the crucified Christ—whether in a vision or through preaching or by observation—transforms the participant into a person of power-in-weakness, and this is itself a form of present glory. Thus those who are in Christ and who behold him day by day are summoned to ongoing transformation into the image

40. At the symposium Walter Moberly observed the parallel between Paul's perspective on visions and his view of glossolalia in the assembly: their ultimate value is Christlike edification of others.

of the exalted crucified Lord, embodying cruciform glory in the present in anticipation of the fullness of divine glory in the age to come.

5. Being Seated with Christ in the Heavenly Places (Col 3:1–4)

Colossians 3:1–4, which speaks of being "raised with Christ" and of "[s]et[ting] your mind on things that are above, not on things that are on earth," relates to the subject of this essay in a particularly poignant way. This part of Colossians "inevitably raises questions about the relationship of otherworldliness and this-worldliness in Christian existence."[41] As we will see, however, the spirituality of this text is not ultimately otherworldly. Rather, the heart of Col 3 is "the integral connection between participation in Christ and the life of discipleship."[42]

To be sure, however, this text can be heard as promoting a very otherworldly, and therefore very un-Pauline, spirituality. Colossians 3 is, in fact, one of the key texts in the letter that convince some people that Paul is not the author, since (they argue) Paul believed that resurrection/glorification was only a future reality for believers, whereas this text claims that resurrection/glorification is a present reality; the genuine Paul's "reserved" eschatology and Colossians' realized eschatology are theologically incompatible.[43] Furthermore, it is sometimes argued, the view of Christian existence offered by Colossians, or at least implied by 3:1–4, is at odds with that of the genuine Paul. As we have seen, the super-apostles at Corinth (and possibly other Corinthians as well) probably believed in present exaltation, leading them to overvalue ecstatic experience and undervalue life in the real world, especially cruciform existence. A view of present resurrection/glory could imply that the writer of Colossians does not share Paul's concern about life in this world.

I think this interpretation of Colossians is wrong, though space permits only a brief response. First, Paul did indeed believe in a form of present glory (as we have seen), and he also uses the metaphorical language of present resurrection (to newness of life—Rom 6), though this lived experience has a cruciform narrative shape. Life in Christ is a partial, proleptic experience of future resurrection and glorification. Thus on this topic, Colossians does not differ significantly from the undisputed letters of Paul.[44] Second, the present

41. Lincoln, "Colossians," 640.

42. Thompson, *Colossians & Philemon*, 69, referring specifically to 3:1–4 but alluding also to the larger passage.

43. See, e.g., Martin, "Paul's Disciples."

44. On present resurrection in Rom 6, see Kirk, *Romans*, 107–23; Gorman,

resurrection/glory described in Colossians is not an escapist spirituality but is, in fact, a this-worldly and even cruciform spirituality, as we will see presently. Thus the undisputed Pauline letters and Colossians are in essential agreement about the nature of Christian existence in the world.[45]

The chief theological and spiritual issue raised in Colossians is the question of the sufficiency of Christ for obtaining divine wisdom and access into the presence and glory of God. It appears that a person or group, sometimes called the errorist(s), has questioned the sufficiency of Christ, averring that Jewish symbols of covenant membership, extreme asceticism, angel veneration (or something similar), and visions are necessary for true wisdom and piety. While there is considerable debate about the errorists' precise teachings and practices, considering them Jewish but syncretistic, mystical ascetics seems a fair, if basic, reading of the evidence.[46] It is possible, as many scholars have suggested, that this mystical asceticism was a form of Jewish merkabah mysticism.[47]

The verbs in Col 3:1–4 indicate that the resurrection/glorification of Christians is both a present reality connected to an initial event in the past (vv. 1–3: "you have been raised with Christ . . . you have died . . . your life is hidden with Christ in God") and a future hope (v. 4: "you also will be revealed with him [Christ] in glory"). The accent, however, clearly falls on the present reality. Why? The Colossian "teachers" whom the author excoriates in the letter seem to have combined asceticism (especially fasting) and a form of mysticism involving angels and visionary experiences to try to find their way to God and the heavenly realm of divine glory apart from, or in addition to, Christ (Col 2:18).[48] Colossians, to be sure, rejects the pursuit of mystical experiences of God—and thus of the divine glory—in the form of venerating angels, invoking angels for magical or protective purposes, or worshipping with angels because these are intended to supplement or even supplant worship focused on Christ. But Colossians does not denigrate mystical experience per se. Rather, it redescribes it. Through participation in the death and resurrection of Jesus, people have the ultimate mystical experience, the most

"Romans: The First Christian Treatise on Theosis," where connections to glory are made; and Lincoln, "Colossians," 624–25 (arguing that the issue should not be decisive in discussions of authorship).

45. All that said, because there are other issues involved in the authorship question, I will refer to "Colossians" rather than "Paul" as the voice we hear, though decisions about authorship do not greatly affect interpretation of the text.

46. See Gorman, *Apostle of the Crucified Lord*, 471–77.

47. See, e.g., Bird, *Colossians and Philemon*, 20–26, and his list of others who concur (20 n.72).

48. See, e.g., Lincoln, "Colossians," 562–68.

complete encounter with the divine reality possible in this life. This experience begins in baptism (Col 2:12–13) and then continues in daily life.

It is therefore both paradoxical and appropriate that such a mystical life is actualized in the daily practices of God-like, Christlike compassion, humility, forgiveness, peacemaking, and so on (Col 3:5ff.).[49] It is also appropriate that these practices be described in the language of death and of renewal/resurrection/exaltation: "Put to death, therefore . . ." (3:5) the former practices, "seeing that you have stripped off the old self with its practices and have clothed yourselves with the new self, which is being renewed in knowledge according to the image of its creator" (Col 3:9b–10), and "clothe yourselves" (3:12, 14 [v. 14 implied in the Greek]) with new practices. The reality of death and resurrection/exaltation in Christ works itself out in the nitty-gritty of everyday life. Those who are with Christ in God put to death the old ways and clothe themselves—perhaps an allusion to baptismal garments—with practices that demonstrate their resurrection with this particular Lord.

Thus the "therefore" (*oun*) in Col 3:5 is not simply a rhetorical transitional device but a bearer of significant semantic weight.[50] Although the exhortations in 3:5ff are more general than those in 2:16ff, they are still closely connected to the specific Colossian situation and to the spiritual reality of death and resurrection/exaltation that is the fundamental reason for not seeking other mystical experiences. Indeed, it is precisely these generic, even mundane, Christian practices of death and resurrection that achieve and embody that which the Colossians are being encouraged to seek elsewhere.

Essentially, then, in Colossians daily life is the ultimate mystical experience. In daily life believers experience the divine mysteries and knowledge that are both fully *embodied* in Christ as the fullness of God, and fully *experienced* in Christ, as the one who conveys that fullness to those who live in him (2:9–10; cf. 1:19). This is an understanding of mysticism and of experiencing the glory of God that is, once again, inseparable from the reality of Christ crucified. Paradoxically but appropriately, it is the power of the divine glory and the reality of present participation in it that enable (joyful!) cruciform existence in this world (Col 1:11):

> May you be made strong with all the strength that comes from
> his glorious power [lit. "the power of his glory," *to kratos tēs*

49. The grounding of Christian existence in the action of God and Christ on the cross is clearest in the calls to forgiveness (3:13, "just as the Lord has forgiven you") and peace (the "peace of Christ" in 3:15; cf. 1:20), but it is implicit throughout this passage, especially in the presence of words like *humility* and *love*, which are associated with the cross in the Pauline correspondence. Cf. the similar passage in Eph 4:31—5:2.

50. On 3:5, cf. Bird, *Colossians and Philemon*, 99–100.

doxēs autou], and may you be prepared to endure everything with patience, while joyfully giving thanks to the Father, who has enabled you to share in the inheritance of the saints in the light. (Col 1:11–12)[51]

This prayer-wish, early in the letter, undergirds and informs the argument *against* the new, otherworldly mysticism of the Colossian teachers and the argument *for* the this-worldly Christ-mysticism proposed in the letter. Although the hope of full, eschatological glory remains just that—a hope (1:5, 23, 27; 3:4)—believers participate now, really if not fully, in the light-filled glory that is the inheritance of God's holy ones.

Marianne Meye Thompson, echoing Leander Keck, suggests that Paul's understanding of salvation (and what we call spirituality) is captured in two words, participation and anticipation.[52] Both of these realities appear in Col 3.[53] Seeking the things that are above is not a call for seeking what the Colossians hoped to attain through or with angels; rather, it is an allusion to Christ's sovereignty (cf. 2:10) and thus an injunction to "pursue a complete reorientation of their lives . . . , which will entail bringing all of life into the sovereign Lordship of Christ."[54] Such a life is not a denial of the importance of life in this world; instead, the text "brings to bear upon earthly realities the 'pressure' of the heavenly realm."[55] Thompson aptly quotes Andrew Lincoln: what Colossians has in mind is "the sort of heavenly mindedness that transforms every part of life by seeing it in relation to the lordship of the exalted Christ."[56]

Thus the exhortation to "[s]et your minds on things that are above, not on things that are on earth" (3:2) is not an invitation to withdraw from the world but to engage the world appropriately. The earthly, fleshly things to be left behind are the practices of the former way of life (2:11–14; 3:5–10) and the vacuous mystical practices that promise human liberation and access to divine glory but fail to deliver (2:22–23).

Honest and healing speech, compassion, humility, forbearance, forgiveness, peace, and love may not have generated in Colossae the excitement associated with visionary experience; cruciform living seldom does. But from the perspective of Colossians, human beings enter most fully into the glorious

51. That Col 1:11–12 is explicitly connected to the exhortations in chapter 3 is indicated by the presence of the noun *makrothymia* ("patience") in both 1:11 and 3:12.

52. Thompson, *Colossians & Philemon*, 69.

53. See, e.g., Knowles, "Christ in You," 183.

54. Thompson, *Colossians & Philemon*, 70.

55. Ibid.

56. Ibid., 72, quoting Lincoln, "Colossians," 640.

presence of God in heaven when they embody the character of God in Christ in their daily lives—right here on earth. This constitutes the this-worldliness of the otherworldly spirituality of the letter to the Colossians.

2.4 John the Seer's Trip to the Heavenly Throne Room (Revelation 4–5)

We turn finally to John the Seer's trip to and vision of the heavenly throne room. Elsewhere I have referred to Rev 4–5 as the "central and centering vision" of the book of Revelation.[57] The word *vision* is only partially accurate, however, as John is called up by Christ himself (Rev 4:1 in light of 1:10–15) into the heavenly throne room. This vision, then, is part of a trip to heaven. In that journey, John sees God the emperor-like sovereign, as well as Christ the slaughtered-but-resurrected Lamb of God, in their heavenly glory, worshipped and hymned by creatures, elders, myriads of myriads, and indeed all creation. Here, in contrast to 2 Cor 12, we have a legitimate apocalypse, "a drawing back of the curtain which normally restricts humanity's view of the heavenly realm, enabling [us] . . . to see the world in a radically new light."[58]

This text raises numerous questions of various sorts. What concerns us at the moment is the rhetorical and spiritual function of the passage in its context. The vision of chapters 4–5 follows, of course, the messages to the seven churches in chapters 2–3, which in turn follow the opening vision of the glorious, heavenly Christ in 1:9–20. Thus these two visions of heavenly glory surround the seven messages like bookends.

In each case, John prefaces the account of the vision by telling us that he was "in the Spirit" (1:10; 4:2).[59] These two moments of intensity in the Spirit allow John, and all those with whom he shares his account, to see that the faithful witness Jesus (Rev 1:5) now shares in the glory of God and thus in the worship due God alone. It is this slaughtered but victorious and vindicated Jesus who walks among the churches (2:1; cf. 1:13), who speaks to them corporately and individually (1:11; 2:1, 7; 2:8, 11; 2:12, 17; etc.), who is worthy of their worship and allegiance (4:12–14), and who assures them that they too can be victorious (2:7, 11, 17, etc.; NRSV "conquer"). Their victory, like that of Jesus, will be through cruciform faithful witness, or "Lamb power"—power in weakness, as Paul would say.[60] Additional visions in Revelation, additional

57. Gorman, *Reading Revelation Responsibly*, 102–15.

58. Boxall, *Revelation of Saint John*, 79.

59. So, e.g., NIV, TNIV. NRSV's "in the spirit" (cf. NAB "in spirit") misses the clear reference to the Spirit of God. CEB has "I was in a Spirit-inspired trance."

60. Speaking of Christ's victory as the slaughtered Lamb (and implicitly also that

moments of intensity, reinforce these visions of Jesus, together with the hope they offer and the call to faithfulness they extend. These include the visions of hope in the eschatological scenarios of chapters 21 and 22, and also the visions of the saints who have been victorious and who now stand before the Lamb, robed in victory-white, faithful witnesses worshiping God and the Faithful Witness, the Lamb (7:9–14; 14:1–5).

Interestingly, we find a similar phenomenon in the letter to the Hebrews. The writer speaks of God's people in this world being "surrounded by so great a cloud of witnesses" (Heb 12:1), who are now in their heavenly rest. Yet the exhortation to faithfulness and perseverance focuses also, and especially, on Jesus, "the pioneer and perfecter of our faith, who for the sake of the joy that was set before him endured the cross, disregarding its shame, and has taken his seat at the right hand of the throne of God" (Heb 12:2). John has similarly surrounded the churches in his care with the one great Faithful Witness, Jesus Christ, the Lamb of God, and with additional faithful witnesses who have become victorious. Just as the writer of Hebrews deploys both Jesus and the cloud of witnesses to encourage the suffering to endure their trials with covenant faithfulness and faithful resistance, so too John recounts his visions of Jesus and of the faithful saints in heaven to encourage the churches still on earth to resist the idolatrous temptations around them, and to be faithful during the present (and/or imminent) persecution.

That is to say, these moments of intensity, in which John directly, and we vicariously, encounter the glorified Christ, motivate and prepare him and us for the difficult task of faithful living in the challenging environs of places like Ephesus and Pergamum and Laodicea, where idolatries and immoralities aim to seduce the people of God. The experience of being in the Spirit, and therein seeing the Lamb, God, and the victorious saints in heaven, is not an end in itself; its purpose is to make it possible to "follow the Lamb wherever he goes" (Rev 14:4). The exalted Lamb, in an important sense, is thus not confined to heaven; he still leads the church into the world and thus into faithful witness and mission. Those who have already followed Jesus anywhere and everywhere are to be the first fruits (14:5) of an entire harvest of faithful followers inspired by the visions John recounts.[61]

Therefore, despite this book's admonition to come out of Babylon (18:4), the faithful living to which the Spirit calls the church via these visionary moments of intensity is not an escapist spirituality. Rather, it is an active prophetic and missional witness inspired by that very Spirit. As I have written elsewhere about Revelation's missional spirituality:

---

of Christians), Frank Matera says, "To use Pauline language, it is a victory won through the weakness and folly of the cross" (*New Testament Theology*, 416).

61. On discipleship in Revelation, see, e.g., Aune, "Following the Lamb."

> The notion of a *missional* spirituality may seem odd at first, especially in light of Revelation's summons to "Come out of her [Babylon], my people" (18:4). This would seem to curtail any conversation about mission before it even begins. However, . . . [t]he withdrawal is not so much a physical exodus as a theo-political one, an escape from civil religion and the idolatry of power-worship. . . . It is a creative, self-imposed but Spirit-enabled departure from certain values and practices. This is the necessary prerequisite to faithful living *in* the very Babylon from which one has escaped. That is, the church cannot be the church *in* Babylon until it is the church *out of* Babylon.
>
> Revelation says "yes" as well as "no" to the world. The church that is both in and out of Babylon will not be able to sit still.[62]

This missional identity of the church is also embodied in the cryptic two witnesses of Rev 11:1–13. Whatever their intertextual identity (Moses and Elijah?), their narrative identity in Revelation includes the church as a whole.[63] Their faithful witness that leads to suffering and death (11:7–8) will be rewarded by resurrection (11:11) and ascension, as they are invited to the heavenly throne room just like John in his vision/trip: "Then they heard a loud voice from heaven saying to them, 'Come up here!' And they went up to heaven in a cloud while their enemies watched them" (11:12). The heavenly vision is a reality, the divine reward for faithful witness. It is meant to inspire and sustain a similar life of faithful witness among the churches. (See also the vision in 11:14–19).

For John and his audience, then, the pattern of a faithful life will be like that of Jesus and the two witnesses: present faithfulness even to suffering and death followed by future resurrection to glory in the presence of God— the pattern of *sequential* glory noted above. But that pattern is enabled and sustained by the vision and the partial, proleptic experience of the glory that is to come *now*, during the period of suffering and death. This occasional glory—being in the Spirit and thus in the heavenly presence of God and the Lamb—may be known in ecstatic experiences or, perhaps more commonly, simply in worship that is rightly understood as participating in that heavenly worship. It would be more accurate, then, to describe the pattern of a faithful life as tripartite: vision of glory/faithfulness even to suffering and death/fullness of glory. Indeed, since the vision of glory is not a mirage, but rather a foretaste of the reality, we might more concisely and more accurately describe the pattern as (preliminary) glory/suffering/(final) glory.

62. Gorman, *Reading Revelation Responsibly*, 185.

63. See, e.g., Blount, *Revelation*, 201: "The story of the two witnesses is meant to be their [John's "hearers and readers"] story, too."

For John's communities, the present, or preliminary, glory was what they could share with John, in the Spirit, particularly in worship. In so doing, they were not preparing to leave the world, but to re-enter it, for "true worship is presented here not as some naïve flight from the world, but that which enables its participants to confront the realities of the world with renewed vision and insight."[64] Indeed, when we read Revelation properly as a theopolitical text, this vision "is a powerful example of the way in which an otherworldly religious experience can have a decidedly this-worldly social and political impact."[65]

3. Conclusion

Charles Taylor and some of his interpreters (especially Andrew Lincoln) have focused our attention on the importance of the "social imaginary," or symbolic universe (as others might call it), for the study and practice of spirituality.[66] What kind of universe do the authors of our four texts imagine for themselves and their hearers/readers?

It is first of all a universe in which God and Christ reside in heaven but allow occasional intense encounters, as well as ongoing less intense encounters, with their glorious presence. These encounters may take the form of mystical experiences, such as visions, or the form of earthly worship that is, in fact, also participation in the heavenly worship. This universe is, secondly, one in which Jesus the crucified Jewish Messiah has been vindicated by God and installed in heaven as the Lord of all, while permanently maintaining his identity as the crucified one. And it is, finally, a universe in which the experience of God's glory in the exalted crucified Jesus compels those who experience it to return to their world to engage in cruciform life and ministry within that world. Such a life is, indeed, the ultimate spiritual experience.

We may describe the life-pattern that emerges from this "social imaginary," or symbolic universe, as one of glory/cruciformity/glory. Despite the differences among our various texts, this pattern is an appropriate summary of the this-worldly, otherworldly, centrifugal spirituality we have discovered in the New Testament. It is also an appropriate pattern for the life of contemporary Christians.[67]

64. Boxall, *Revelation of Saint John*, 93–94.

65. Blount, *Revelation*, 85.

66. See Lincoln, "Spirituality in a Secular Age."

67. I am grateful to Andy Johnson for his comments on a draft of this essay, and to my colleagues at the symposium for their feedback.

10

Spirituality and the Emotions in Early Christianity

The Case of Joy

Stephen C. Barton
University of Durham

1. Introduction

1.1 Defining *Spirituality*

Spirituality is a slippery word, so I begin with a definition:

> Spirituality as lived experience can be defined as conscious involvement in the project of life integration through self-transcendence toward the ultimate value one perceives. . . . The ultimate value which generates the horizon of any spirituality relates the one who lives that spirituality to the whole of reality in some particular way. When the horizon of ultimate value is the triune God revealed in Jesus Christ and communicated through the Holy Spirit, and the project of self-transcendence is the living of the paschal mystery within the context of the church community, the spirituality is specifically Christian and involves the person with God, others, and all reality according to the understanding of these realities that is characteristic of Christian faith.[1]

1. Schneiders, "Christian Spirituality," 1.

This is a helpful definition. It captures well the general characteristics of an area of intense human interest and investment that has become characteristic of late modernity. It also captures in a comprehensive yet succinct way the specific features of *Christian* spirituality.

In expanding on the latter, Schneiders draws particular attention to the emphasis nowadays on "the *holistic* involvement of the person in the spiritual quest," and says, "Thus the body as well as the spirit, gender and social location as well as human nature, emotion as well as mind and will, relationships with others as well as with God, socio-political commitment as well as prayer and spiritual practices, are involved in the spiritual project."[2] The inclusion of *emotion* in this characterization offers a point of entry for the subject matter of this essay: for what I offer is a study of the emotion of "joy" as a remarkably pervasive feature of what we may call the spirituality of the early Christian movement.

1.2 Emotions as Cultural Constructs

Now, in enquiring after the significance of an emotion like joy, it is tempting to assume that joy is something natural and spontaneous, a universal given of psychosomatic, effervescent being in the world. However, philosophical, literary, and social-scientific studies on the emotions generally have begun to point in a different direction: from emotions as natural phenomena to emotions as *cultural constructs*.

First: a philosopher. In a recent essay on Kierkegaard on the emotions, David Kangas emphasizes the importance of "close attention to the *metaphysical horizons* in which emotions acquire significance as emotions. . . . Emotions are not natural, but rather encode and manifest certain fundamental organizing principles, that is, the fundamental metaphors and distinctions, or fundamental ontologies, that inform a culture's engagement with the world."[3] This is an acute account along constructivist lines. Importantly, emotions are said both to *encode* and *manifest* the principles, the distinctions, and the ontologies that shape human activity and interrelation.

Second: a literary critic. In *The Story of Joy* (2007), Adam Potkay introduces his work with these observations:

> Emotion terms are themselves culturally freighted. As the linguist Anna Wierzbicka writes, they "reflect and pass on values, preoccupations, and frames of reference of the society (or

2. Ibid., 1–2.
3. Kangas, "Kierkegaard," 399, n.1. Emphasis in original.

speech community) within which they evolved." Emotions or passions are not simply constant components of human psychology and physiology, the hard wiring of who we are. They are shaped, as well, by histories: the case history of each individual, and the cultural history of each emotion term.[4]

Third: the social-sciences. The recent sociological study by Woodhead and Riis[5] follows a similar constructivist trajectory. Starting from the premise that emotions are "psycho-physical orientations and adjustments within relational contexts,"[6] Woodhead and Riis offer a multidimensional account that contextualizes emotions in relations between individual agents, social groups, and material and symbolic objects:

> Emotions are essential to our constant, active bodily interventions and responses. In Latin they are called *motus animi*—movements of the soul—and in English we say we are "moved" when we feel deeply. Thus we can liken emotions to a field of forces that attract or repel and that lead to harmonies, tensions, or eruptions. On this analogy, social life is a force-field of emotional energies. Emotions are not confined to the heart, or even the brain, of the individual agent, but are integral to the flux of social and symbolic life. As we negotiate through life, so we range through different emotional fields, shaping and being shaped by them in the process.[7]

Against the background of these multidisciplinary approaches, with their convergence on the interpretation of the emotions as cultural constructs, I turn to the meaning(s) of joy in the period of Christian origins. Before that, however, a word about the study of joy itself.

1.3 The Study of "Joy"

To my knowledge, not many modern philosophers or social-scientists have made a study of joy. Suggestive, however, are some comments of social anthropologist Mary Douglas. In an essay on the nature of anthropological inquiry into religion—the religion of Judaism in particular—titled "The Cosmic Joke," she says this:

4. Potkay, *Story of Joy*, vii. The citation is from Wierzbicka, *Emotions*, 32.
5. Woodhead and Riis, *Religious Emotion*.
6. Ibid., 21.
7. Ibid., 22.

> If I try to explain how the anthropologists work, and claim that their results are not a threat to belief, in return perhaps believers will be able to tell me something about religion that the outside professionals cannot explain. What is it about religion that makes a person ready to die for it? People seem ready to kill each other for quite trivial reasons, so why they kill for religion is not very mysterious. But why do they die for it? *I suggest it is something to do with rejoicing. The inexplicable, irreducible thing that mystifies outsiders is that the Jews rejoice in the law.*[8]

Having drawn attention to the mystifying fact that "Jews rejoice in the law," she proceeds, in the main body of the essay, to offer an interpretation of the biblical laws of purity, demonstrating in the process their profound cogency and coherence at a symbolic level. She concludes as follows:

> Part of my argument has been to insist that each religion has its own "physics," its ontological theory which gives the principles of time, space and all existence. This, I suspect, points to why believers may be ready to die for their religion. The outsider wonders, whence is their joy, and why all this rejoicing? The Bible gives the answer: like the dumb beasts, *the people rejoice in living the sacred order.* Like the worms and snakes, like the camel and the pig, the lizard and the spider, *the law fulfils their own being.* Refusing to see boiled lobster or crab on their festive table, the Jews honour the cosmic joke: the mighty are bowed down and the lowly are lifted up.[9]

I think that Douglas is on to something. "[T]he people rejoice in living the sacred order"; and this is evident even and most especially when the existential stakes for individual and community are highest, as in matters considered worth living and dying for. Here, we are not at all far from the view of David Kangas that emotions (like joy) express a people's metaphysical horizons—"the fundamental metaphors and distinctions . . . that inform a culture's engagement with the world."

The case study Douglas takes is from Jewish religion. Her perception as an anthropologist about the significance of rejoicing in the law finds strong support in the work of Professor of Jewish Studies Michael Fishbane in his 1998 essay "Joy and Jewish Spirituality."[10] For their evident sympathy with the scholarly views cited already, his opening words are noteworthy:

8. Douglas, "Cosmic Joke," 193–94. My emphasis.
9. Ibid., 211–12. My emphasis.
10. Fishbane, *Exegetical Imagination*, 151–72.

Comprehensive religions give direction to the behaviour and inner life of their adherents, marking off proper and improper actions and emotions. Judaism is such a religion, and *a vast number of its instructions attempt to guide and even regulate states of delight or sorrow for religious practice and celebration.* In the process, various ideals and dangers are formulated. There is thus no purely natural state for humankind in Judaism, or any other religious culture for that matter, since the natural self is transformed from birth into a cultural self—heir through training and tradition to the wisdom and practices of the past. In a tradition as complex as Judaism, the whole range of accumulated values is constantly sifted and reformulated by its teachers in each generation. This is particularly the case with respect to the emotion of joy and its transformations. Over time, some of the deepest dialectics of Judaism are called into play.[11]

The focus of Fishbane's essay is on the generation, refinement, and regulation of joy over time in the traditions of the rabbis—on how biblical traditions about joy come to be "exegetically inflected in light of the sages' concerns with the commandments, religious sobriety, and the study of Torah."[12]

The aim of this essay is to consider the neighboring case of early Christianity. Are joy and rejoicing as characteristic of the emotional culture(s) of early Christianity as they are for biblical and Jewish religion? If so, what do they express about the first Christians' spirituality—that is, their metaphysical horizons, their fundamental organizing principles, metaphors, and distinctions, their self-understanding and behavior in their (practical and symbolic) engagement in space and over time with God and the world? Is there evidence in Christianity of a pedagogy in joy of the kind Fishbane discovers in rabbinic Judaism? But first, a sketch must be offered of some of the traditions, regimes, and resources that are likely to have informed early Christian joy in one way or another.

2. Joy and Rejoicing in the Bible

There can be no doubt that joy (*śimḥâ*) and its corollaries are prominent aspects of the biblical and early Jewish traditions that form a significant part of the backdrop of the emotional culture of early Christianity. As a wide

11. Ibid., 151. My emphasis.
12. Ibid., 153.

range of texts and traditions shows, the occasions for joy and rejoicing are manifold and have strong behavioral corollaries.[13]

First and foremost, there is *joy in God*. The Old Testament is replete with words and images of affect that ascribe joy to God.[14] In general, God's joy is a manifestation of who God is. It springs especially out of God's relationship with what God has made, with the people he has chosen, and with the good that follows, a good that is itself an expression of the divine nature. For example, Ps 104 makes the remarkable suggestion that creation is sustained by God's joy and would dissolve in its absence: "May the glory of the Lord endure forever; may the Lord rejoice in his works—who looks on the earth and it trembles, who touches the mountains and they smoke" (vv. 31–32). Proverbs 8 speaks of the reciprocal delight shared between Wisdom and God in the act of creation: "I was daily his delight, rejoicing before him always, rejoicing in his inhabited world and delighting in the human race" (8:30–31). And in Isaiah, God's joy over his people is expressed in exuberant marital imagery: "[Y]ou shall be called My Delight Is in Her, and your land Married . . . and as the bridegroom rejoices over the bride, so shall your God rejoice over you" (Isa 62:4–5).

Second, there is *joy in the salvation—past, present, and future—that comes from God*. The Psalms in particular contain many expressions of such joy, giving voice to what, as the gift of God, *constitutes* the people: "But let all who take refuge in you rejoice, let them ever sing for joy. Spread your protection over them, so that those who love your name may exult in you" (Ps 5:11). And again: "Many are the torments of the wicked, but steadfast love surrounds those who trust in the Lord. Be glad in the Lord and rejoice, O righteous, and shout for joy, all you upright in heart" (Ps 32:10–11). Note that rejoicing is made an *imperative*: the practices of joy are how salvation is encoded, embodied and made manifest in the life of the people. Significantly also, it is made manifest in a variety of quite demonstrative ways—here, in singing and shouting; elsewhere in dancing and feasting.

Third, and in line with the observations of Douglas and Fishbane mentioned earlier, *the law of God* is an occasion for joy, and joy springs from faithful law observance. A classic expression of this comes in Ps 119:14–16: "I delight in the way of your decrees as much as in all riches. I will meditate on your precepts, and fix my eyes on your ways. I will delight in your statutes; I will not forget your word." Here we may say that joy expresses a deep sense of *alignment*, both individual and corporate, with

13. See in general, Conzelmann and Zimmerli, χαίρω κτλ.; Beyreuther and Finkenrath, "Joy, Rejoice"; Strawn, *Happiness*, Part One.

14. See further Fretheim, "Pursuit of Happiness."

the will and ways of God. The sense of alignment with the ways of God is fundamental. Joy is the sense of existential fulfilment (both individual and societal) arising in and out of participation in the divine life. Put another way, joy and holiness go hand in hand.

Fourth, joy consists in practices associated with *the cult and the festivals*. This is exemplified in Ps 95:1–3: "O come, let us sing to the Lord; let us make a joyful noise to the rock of our salvation! Let us come into his presence with thanksgiving; let us make a joyful noise to him with songs of praise! For the Lord is a great God, and a great King above all gods." More specifically, joy is associated with the sacrificial feast, with eating and drinking the sacrificial meal. The meal is a corporate, ritual repository of celebration, performance of which is linked to appropriate points in Israel's festal calendar. Commenting on the evidence of Deuteronomy, Anderson observes: "[T]he link between eating sacrificial food and rejoicing before the Lord is unmistakable. The specific occasions for joyous feasting include consumption of the tithe (14.26), the feast of weeks (16.11), the feast of Sukkot (16.14–15), consumption of the first fruits (26.11), and inauguration of the first cultic site in the promised land (27.7)."[15] That festal joy was a ritual of the calendar in these ways shows how important it was for the regular, repeated realignment of the people with time and space—for their realignment, in other words, with creation, salvation history, and the land.

Fifth, with its roots in the connection between *joy and kingship*—for example, joy at the birth or accession of a king—joy takes on an eschatological dimension, coming also to be associated with the restoration of Israel. Many Isaianic texts speak along these lines. A classic expression is Isa 35:1–2, 10: "The wilderness and the dry land shall be glad, the desert shall rejoice and blossom; like the crocus it shall blossom abundantly, and rejoice with joy and singing. . . . And the ransomed of the Lord shall return, and come to Zion with singing; everlasting joy shall be upon their heads; they shall obtain joy and gladness, and sorrow and sighing shall flee away."

Finally, there is *joy of a more quotidian kind*. Here, joy and *merriment* (i.e., a form of joy connected less directly to transcendent realities) overlap. So, for example, there is joy associated with the everyday rites of passage, such as marriage (e.g., Song 3:11) and childbirth (e.g., Ps 113:9); joy associated with the seasons, especially harvesttime (e.g., Isa 9:2); and joy associated with the good things of life, like wine (e.g., Ps 104:15). In sum, joy is *the celebration of life and what is life-giving*. Not surprisingly, therefore, the practices of joy and rejoicing can be understood fully only in relation to their negative counterpart, especially the practices of

15. Anderson, *Time to Mourn*, 20.

mourning. Hence, eating and drinking have to be set over against fasting; sexual relations over against abstinence; praise over against lamentation; anointing with oil over against anointing with dust or ashes; and festal garments over against sackcloth.[16]

Overall, it may be said that joy and rejoicing in the Bible are expressions, in time and space, of *a profound sense of connectedness*—above all, connectedness with and between persons and things considered *transcendent and perduring*. This is a connectedness that links the heavens and the earth, God and God's elect people, God and the land, God and time, and God and value, in ways that are experienced as identity-defining, redemptive, and empowering. What is more, such joy is not just a matter of the emotions understood as expressions of a people's "inner life," though that is important: it is a matter also of *sociality and public performance*, including ritual performance. As a corollary—and because it is constitutive of the people's life—joy, like its counterpart mourning, can be *commanded* (cf. Deut 12:7, 12). Expressed in prescribed behaviors, it is a serious, social obligation pertaining to the cult and the offering of sacrifice. As such, joy is a fundamental, positive posture of piety and faith within the divine-human relation of covenant. It is a sharing in the very life of God.

3. Joy and Rejoicing among the Emotions in Early Christianity

Against this biblical background, I turn to articulations of joy in two New Testament texts, one narrative, the other epistolary: respectively, Luke-Acts and the Epistle to the Philippians. What I will demonstrate from these texts is that joy is a prime indicator of the first Christians' sense of (in Douglas' terms) "living the sacred order," of finding ultimate fulfillment in their new-found eschatological identity, faith, and practice. In the process, I will suggest also that joy and rejoicing appear to be among the *pre-eminent* emotions in early Christianity[17] and, as such, critical for the formation of early Christian (counter)culture. In comparison with the emotion of grief, for example, there is a striking contrast between an emotion requiring constraint and discipline, on the one hand, and an emotion allowed wide expression, on the other.[18] What constitutes the difference is the first

16. Cf. ibid., 49.

17. I note the prominence of joy as second only to love in the list of "fruits of the Spirit" in Gal 5:22.

18. On the constraint placed on grief by Paul in 1 Thess 4:13, see Barton, "Eschatology," 578–83.

Christians' "metaphysical horizon" of inaugurated eschatology with, as its corollary, a fundamental transformation in their emotional engagement with the world, including their sense of space, time, value, and persons. The coming of God's Messiah, the crucifixion and resurrection of the Messiah, and the coming of the Holy Spirit are salvific events that render grief otiose, inviting instead a kind of social and emotional *vitality* captured at least in part in the language, display, and perduring mood of joy.

3.1 Joy and Rejoicing in Luke-Acts

I take as a first case study that narrative text which is Luke-Acts. Here, joy and rejoicing are all-pervasive, so much so that Luke's Gospel has been called "the gospel of joy."[19] If we ask what it is to which joy is a characteristic response, the unequivocal answer is that, for Luke, joy is the emotional signifier of the discernment of the coming of salvation in fulfillment of God's plan for Israel and the nations. Put in terms of the programmatic announcement that Jesus makes in his inaugural speech at Nazareth (Luke 4:18–19; cf. Isa 61:1–2), joy is the characteristic individual and social response of those designated "the poor" to the messianic liberation and reversal of fortunes that constitute the eschatological Jubilee (cf. Lev 25:10).

Pertinent evidence from a plethora of possibilities may be drawn from the beginning and end of the Gospel, as well as from several points in between. First, in the opening two chapters, joy predominates in the narrative of the births of John and Jesus. It comes in angelic announcements (1:14; 2:10) and in responsorial songs (1:46f.), in the leaping "for joy" (*en agalliasei*) of Elizabeth's as yet unborn child (1:44), and in the rejoicing that accompanies John's birth (1:58). But the climactic joy is reserved for the birth of Jesus: "Be not afraid; for behold I bring you good news of a great joy [*charan megalēn*] which will come to all the people; for to you is born this day in the city of David a Savior, who is Christ the Lord" (2:10–11). In other words, joy marks this most dramatic turning point in the history of Israel and the nations, and it marks the moment positively as messianic and therefore salvific. Joy is an expression of *being in tune with what God is doing* as one epoch of salvation history gives way to another.

Noteworthy, in passing, is the countercultural potential of the fact that joy is not restricted to any particular category of person or place, even if there is a discernible bias. As to persons, there are typically the poor and humble, including even shepherds, and there are women as well as men;

19. Morrice, *Joy*, 91–99. According to Morrice, Luke-Acts contains 24 percent of the New Testament vocabulary for joy.

and there are also angelic hosts from heaven. As to places, there is Jeru-salem and the Temple; but there is also Judean hill country, Nazareth in Galilee, and Bethlehem and the surrounding countryside. Joy, we may say, is *unconfined*—to which we may add that, precisely as unconfined in the ways indicated, it stands over against "unconfined joys" of other kinds or joy restricted to particular people or places.[20]

If we move from the opening to significant points in the body of the narrative, we find joy and rejoicing inscribed indelibly in 10:17–24, the ac-count of the return from mission of the Seventy "with joy" (*meta charas*) from a successful mission of exorcising followed by, and climaxing in,[21] Jesus' exultant prayer of thanksgiving to the Father. Here, joy is the signifier of the disciples' conquest of Satan and the demons and an expression of the assurance of eschatological salvation thus guaranteed. As a close corollary, it is also a definitive mark of the sense of the presence of the eschatological Spirit, as the succeeding verses imply. The return of the Seventy causes Jesus himself joy in the Spirit: "In that same hour he rejoiced in the Holy Spirit [*ēgalliasato (en) tō pneumati tō hagiō*] . . ." (Luke 10:21; diff. Matt 11:25a). As the disciples' exorcising practice overflows in joy at their collaboration in the liberating work of the Messiah ("Lord, even the demons are subject to us *in your name* [*en tō onomati sou*]" [Luke 10:17]), so Jesus' exultant joy in the Holy Spirit—a feature unique to this Gospel—conveys his own alignment with, and sense of fulfillment in, God's saving work as the now-revealed Son of the heavenly Father (Luke 10:21–22, 23–24).[22]

Then there is the threefold sequence of parables of the Lost in chapter 15, told in response to the complaint against Jesus by the Pharisees, "This man receives sinners and eats with them" (15:1). Remarkable here is the deliberate and heavy repetition in all three parables of the motif of joy in the accounts of the emotional response of the main protagonists to the finding of that which was lost (15:5–6, 9, 22–24, 32). Remarkable also is the escha-tological insight offered by the first two parables. Joy is not just an earthly, human emotion but is characteristic of heavenly existence as well: joy on earth mirrors and is mirrored by joy "in heaven," or joy "before the angels of God" (15:7, 10). More specifically, heavenly joy is the response when sinners repent. Once again, joy is a key emotional corollary of a fundamental Lukan value: namely, salvation embodied in the Messiah's ministry of compassion

20. Cf. Neyrey, "Symbolic Universe."

21. Note the progression in "joy" from the *chara/chairō* terminology in 10:17, 20 to the more exuberant *ēgalliasato* in 10:21.

22. Cf. Voorwinde, *Jesus' Emotions*, 128–32.

for the poor and the lost. Joy and rejoicing mark a profound entry into, and participation in, that fundamental eschatological reality.

In the climactic and most elaborate of the three parables, the parable of the Two Lost Sons, there is a striking development in the deployment of emotional cues. On the one hand, the pitch of human joy is raised as the delight of the father in the return of the prodigal finds expression in the unexpected and unwarranted magnanimity of joyous welcome, feasting, and merrymaking.[23] On the other hand, joy is contrasted with anger and obstinate refusal (v. 28),[24] the response of the father finding no favor with the elder son, resentful as he is of behaviors open to interpretation as smacking of favoritism and threatening the delicate balance of traditional father-son reciprocity and elder brother-younger brother privileges and responsibilities. In the Lukan economy of salvation, the joy arising out of the freedom of gracious compassion practised by the father both provokes and trumps the joyless dutifulness of an elder son whose moral-emotional responses are constricted by unbending attachment to convention. As a response to the Pharisaic accusation that Jesus' indiscriminate table fellowship contravenes the law of purity (15:2), the parable invites the conclusion that, for the Lukan Jesus, joy is found, not in alignment with the law (as interpreted by the Pharisees), but in the acceptance of and participation in jubilar liberation.[25]

Joy and rejoicing are prevalent also in the ending of Luke's narrative. In 24:41, Luke has the Eleven and their companions curiously disbelieving "for joy" (*apo tēs charas*) when the risen Jesus appears miraculously at their gathering in Jerusalem. If earlier, when Jesus is at prayer prior to his arrest, Luke exculpates the disciples by saying that they were sleeping "for sorrow" (*apo tēs lypēs*) (22:45), here at Jesus' resurrection appearance, Luke absolves them of culpable disbelief by attributing their incredulity to joy and wonder! It is as if the emotions of joy and wonder were so overwhelming that the disciples were not able to give full credence to Jesus' real presence in their midst.[26]

Of even greater significance is the climactic final sentence of the Gospel describing the disciples' response to Jesus' ascension, an event narrated only

---

23. Note the repeated occurrences of *euphrainesthai* in vv. 23, 24, 29, and 32.

24. Note the correspondence between the anger of the elder brother in verse 28 and the "murmuring" of the Pharisees in verse 2a.

25. Indiscriminate table fellowship as an invitation to joyful, jubilary liberation is also a central motif of the Lukan story of Zacchaeus, another figure on the margins. At Jesus' startling offer to be a guest in Zacchaeus' own house, Zacchaeus "received him joyfully [*chairōn*]" (Luke 19:6).

26. Compare Acts 12:14, where again *apo tēs charas* is the reason given to explain Rhoda's surprised and surprising behavior in not opening the gate to Peter recently and miraculously released from prison.

by this Evangelist: "And they returned to Jerusalem with great joy [*meta cha-ras megalēs*], and were continually in the temple blessing God [*eulogountes ton theon*]" (24:52–53). The Gospel begins with joy and ends with joy. It begins and ends with joy over the fulfillment of God's plan of salvation in, respectively, the birth of the Messiah and the death, resurrection, and ascension of the Messiah. Significantly also, Jerusalem and the Temple are common to both (1:8–11, 21–23; 24:33, 52–53). Joy, in Luke, has a definite *topography*. As well as marking the fulfillment of salvation in time, it also marks the fulfillment of salvation in space. Salvation in Luke is, literally, an event that *takes place*. By taking place in (or near) Jerusalem and by being celebrated in the Temple,[27] the universal significance of salvation, beginning with the redemption of Israel (cf. 24:21; and earlier, 1:68; 2:38), even in spite of Israel's rejection of the Messiah, is made plain. Joy, in Luke's ending, is the discernment of God's plan of salvation, in spite of appearances to the contrary. It arises out of the recognition that the suffering of the Messiah was not some disastrous defeat, but "was necessary" (24:26; cf. 24:44b, 46) and was the prelude to his entry into glory. *Joy is an oppressed, sin-sick people's delight in the sovereignty of God who triumphs over his enemies and brings salvation.*

But joy is not limited to the time of salvation inaugurated in Jesus' earthly ministry. The Holy Spirit present in Jesus (cf. Luke 3:16, 22; 4:1, 14) is the same "power from on high" that inspires joy in the apostles and the faithful in the period after the resurrection (cf. Luke 24:49; Acts 1:4–5). Thus, in Luke's second volume, joy continues to appear as a prime emotion signifying recognition of and response to the dawning of salvation. First, in Peter's inaugural public speech in Jerusalem on the Day of Pentecost, the psalmist is enlisted as a joyful witness to the eschatological reality of Jesus' resurrection: "I saw the Lord always before me, for he is at my right hand that I may not be shaken; therefore my heart was glad, and my tongue rejoiced [*dia touto euphranthē hē kardia mou kai ēgalliasato hē glōssa mou*] . . ." (Acts 2:25–28; cf. Ps 16:8–11).

Second, in the cameo of utopian life consequent on the conversion and baptism of the three thousand that same Day of Pentecost, the mood of exuberant joy is all-pervasive: "And day by day, attending the temple together and breaking bread in their homes, they partook of food with glad and generous hearts [*en agalliasei kai aphelotēti kardias*], praising God and having favor with all the people" (Acts 2:46–47). Here is a resumption and augmentation of elements from the Gospel: the mapping of joy onto Jerusalem and the Temple as the prime symbolic loci of universal salvation

27. On the Temple as the "navel" of the world in biblical and early Jewish cosmology, see Hayward, *Temple*.

history, and the mapping of joy onto people's homes and table fellowship as the prime loci of redeemed sociality at the local level.

Third, similar to the joy that characterizes the triumphant exorcistic mission of the Seventy in Luke 10 is the joy in a city of Samaria where Philip preaches, exorcises, and heals (Acts 8:4–7). In a lapidary statement, Luke comments: "So there was much joy [*chara megalē*] in that city" (Acts 8:8). Following hard on the account of the martyrdom of Stephen, who is buried amid "great lamentation" (*kopeton megan*) (Acts 8:2), and the persecution of the church in Jerusalem (Acts 6:8—8:3), the "much joy" resulting from the mission of Philip in Samaria constitutes a powerful theological and socio-rhetorical contrast. The forces of opposition, human and divine, are not allowed the last word. Rather, victory is signalled in the idiom of joy and its social corollary (noting *homothymadon* in 8:6), unity.

Not surprisingly, then, as the narrative continues, joy and rejoicing continue to mark reception of the gospel and initiation into the Christian "way." Significantly, like the gospel proclamation itself, as it progresses territorially and providentially from Jerusalem to Rome, the joy that accompanies its positive reception has *a boundary-transcending quality*. It is as if joy and rejoicing are emotions that celebrate and simultaneously *give permission* for boundaries to be crossed and individual and social transformations to occur. Thus, on the liminal space of the desert road going from Jerusalem to Gaza, an Ethiopian eunuch receives the gospel, is baptized, and goes on his way "rejoicing" (*chairōn*) (Acts 8:39). In Pisidian Antioch, in response to the announcement of salvation, even amidst fierce opposition from the Jews, it is Gentiles who "were glad [*echairon*] and glorified the word of God" and who, even after the expulsion of Paul and Barnabas, "were filled with joy and with the Holy Spirit [*eplērounto charas kai pneumatos hagiou*]" (Acts 13:48, 52). Finally, and not dissimilarly, in the story of the jailer and his household in the Roman colony of Philippi, conversion and baptism find outworking in acts of hospitality and expressions of joy: "Then he brought them up into his house, and set food before them; and he rejoiced with all his household [*kai ēgalliasato panoikei*] that he had believed in God" (Acts 16:34).

Taken overall, then, it may reasonably be concluded that joy and rejoicing in Luke-Acts are all-pervasive emotional signifiers of the recognition of the dawning of salvation for Israel and the nations with the coming of God's Messiah as savior and liberator. *Joy is the embodied, performed delight that arises from discernment of and participation in the eschatological transformations of time, space, value, and persons consequent upon the coming of Christ and the Spirit.* Among these transformations, law and Temple are relativized in terms of their traditional roles in forming identity and shaping feelings and behavior. That which offers the joyous fulfilment for which one might be willing to die is no longer the law and the Temple but the risen and ascended Lord. As Paul says to the assembly of believers at Caesarea seeking, through mortal fear, to dissuade him from going to Jerusalem: "What are you doing, weeping and breaking my heart? For I am ready not only to be imprisoned but even to die at Jerusalem for the name of the Lord Jesus" (Acts 21:13). That phrase, "for the name of the Lord Jesus" (*hyper tou onomatos tou kuriou Iēsou*), expresses the change in a nutshell. Signifying the sovereignty of the risen and ascended Lord and the salvation he bestows (cf. Acts 2:21, citing Joel 2:32), "the name of the Lord Jesus" constitutes the transcendent "metaphysical horizon" of those expressions of early Christian joy that are displayed so vividly in Luke's two-volume work.

3.2 Joy and Rejoicing in Paul

From this latter reference to the narrated Paul of Acts we turn to the Paul of Paul's own letters, in particular to the Epistle to the Philippians, described by one commentator as "an epistle of joy tested and refined."[28] This is a kind of "family letter"[29] expressive of a profound relation of friendship.[30] It was written to report on Paul's own situation of imprisonment and its implications, to encourage the Philippians in their faith and common life, to warn against potential threats, to commend Epaphroditus for services rendered as he returns to Philippi, and to thank the Philippians for the financial aid which had come to him through Epaphroditus' agency. We find here one of the greatest concentrations of "joy" language in the Pauline corpus.[31] Given that the letter is written from the generally appalling conditions of a first-century prison (cf. Phil 1:13), it would be natural to expect expressions of fear and anxiety. Instead, Philippians displays repeated and profound expressions of joy (cf. 1:18, 25; 2:2, 17, 18, 28, 29; 3:1; 4:1, 4, 10).

In what follows I will seek to show both that this is the case and why. Among other things, we will see that there is more to what Paul says about joy than is covered by the common rubric, "joy in the midst of affliction." That joy can find expression in a letter from the privations of imprisonment is undoubtedly important,[32] but joy is inflected here in other ways as well: for

28. Bockmuehl, *Philippians*, 1.

29. See Alexander, "Hellenistic Letter-Forms."

30. Cf. Stowers, "Friends and Enemies."

31. The relevant statistics are given in Morrice, *Joy*, 112, 116.

32. This aspect is emphasized in the essay by Bloomquist, "Subverted by Joy," 274–75.

what Paul offers the Philippians is spiritual guidance, *a pedagogy in joy*.[33] In general, it may be said that *joy, for Paul, reflects an experience of profoundly uplifting spiritual and material partnership (koinōnia) in an inhospitable social environment set against the vivid, felt horizon of participation in the life of heaven*. The importance of that latter element—"the vivid, felt horizon of participation in the life of heaven"—cannot, in my opinion, be overestimated. The experience of deep mutuality between Paul and the Philippians is an experience of joy *because they know that their story is part of a larger story*: the story of salvation, as yet unfinished, but whose ending—because it is the story of God, Christ, and the Spirit—is sure. In describing how the theology of the letter shapes the friendship relation of Paul and the Philippians, Stanley Stowers makes a similar point:

> The fundamental theological tactic of the letter's discourse interprets the Philippians' experience by means of a larger narrative about God, Christ, and Paul. The experience of community resulting from Paul's missionary work is part of a grand drama beginning with Christ's decision to live as a servant and reaching its goal with Christ's return. The letter treats the experience of the Philippian community as a process and holds forth a clear goal that coincides with the resolution of the grand narrative. Paul describes the Philippian community as a good work that will be brought to completion on the day of Jesus Christ (1:6).[34]

As early as the letter's introduction (1:1–11), Paul draws attention to the fact that his prayerful remembrance of the Philippian believers is made "with joy" (*meta charas*) (1:4). The ground for this joy is revealed in what follows: Paul is thankful for the Philippians' "partnership in the gospel [*tē koinōnia hymōn eis to euangelion*] from the first day until now" (1:5). This partnership (*koinōnia*) has a spiritual dimension, since the Philippians are partners with Paul in the gospel and (as he goes on to say) they are partners also in grace (1:7). But it is also material—more precisely, monetary—as becomes clear in the letter's conclusion (4:15ff.), where partnership language recurs explicitly in the context of arrangements concerning apostolic subsistence: *oudemia moi ekklēsia ekoinōnēsen eis logon doseōs kai lēmpseōs ei mē hymeis monoi*. So Paul's joy in the Philippians, expressed in prayerful remembrance to God, arises from his recognition of a deep-rooted *connectedness over time* ("from the first day until now") *in matters both spiritual and material*. Put in brief, Paul's joy comes from their living the gospel together in partnership.

---

33. Cf. Stowers, "Friends and Enemies," 108–9, where Paul is described as a "psychagogue."

34. Ibid., 117.

In 1:12–26, Paul proceeds to give an account and an explanation of his current situation. He does so no doubt in part because, in an agonistic cultural context of intense interpersonal rivalry and competition for social dominance, his imprisonment renders him vulnerable by giving his competitors the advantage (cf. 1:15–17). Not only are his public presence and freedom to move about and preach denied, but the very fact of imprisonment will have attracted social opprobrium in the form of shame. Be that as it may, what is notable is that Paul is able to interpret his circumstances in terms of what we may call a *hermeneutic of joy*. He rejoices in the fact that his imprisonment has so emboldened the church—presumably by his personal example of courage and wholehearted commitment—that it has had the beneficial consequence of advancing the gospel (1:14). Whether it is his friends or his rivals who are so engaged, one thing is important for Paul: "Christ is proclaimed; and in that I rejoice" (*kai en toutō chairō*) (1:18). It is as if Paul can *rise above his circumstances* of shame and suffering because his sights are set, not on personal advantage in a competition for glory, but on the fulfillment that comes through the advance of the gospel in service of his risen Lord. A word for that fulfilment is *joy*.

Strikingly, Paul appears to have a penchant for (so to speak) *double* joy, for joy piled upon joy. Hence, "in that I rejoice. Yes, and I shall rejoice" (*kai en toutō chairō. Alla kai charēsomai*) (1:18b–19a; cf. 4:4). For Paul goes on to rejoice in the assurance that his imprisonment for the sake of Christ will bring a benefit additional to the advance of the gospel—the eschatological benefit, no less, of heavenly vindication (*moi apobēsetai eis sōtērian*) (1:19). Invoking the pivotal social values of honor and shame, Paul expresses his confidence that, whether his incarceration ends in life or death, he himself "will not be at all ashamed" (*en oudeni aischynthēsomai*), and, more importantly, Christ "will be honored" (*megalynthēsetai Christos*) in what is done to him (1:20; lit. "in my body"). Here is precisely the kind of profound joy that Mary Douglas refers to: that which arises from living in, and being willing to die for, what she calls "the sacred order." Put in Pauline terms, what fulfills Paul, what he lives for and is willing to die for, what gives him joy, is *that complex of personal allegiance, belief, and practice*, all summed up in the name of Christ, the ministry of partnership in the gospel, and participation in the life of heaven both now and at the day of resurrection (cf. 3:11, 14, 20–21).

The fact that joy is no mere epiphenomenon but integral to the faith Paul seeks to display and impart is then conveyed in a startling hendiadys: if Paul remains alive and continues in ministry among the Philippians, it will be "for your *progress and joy* in [lit. "of"] the faith [*eis tēn hymōn prokopēn kai charan tēs pisteōs*]" (1:25). The "progress" of the gospel which, paradoxically, has been advanced by his imprisonment (of which he has spoken in verse 12) is now applied to what Paul hopes to enable if he can be with the Philippians once again. Significantly, however, it is progress of a particular kind, progress "of faith" that has a particular corollary—namely, joy. Bockmuehl puts it well: "Progress is the objective quality, while joy is its appropriation in personal experience. . . . The twin themes of Christian progress and joy, which have characterized Paul's description of his own situation since 1.12 . . . will also guide his concern for the Philippians throughout the remainder of the letter."[35]

In 1:27—2:18, Paul goes on to offer paraenesis on how to "be citizens worthy of the gospel of Christ" (1:27), not least in a setting of (potential or actual) persecution. Here, using an imperative expressive of the relationship of partnership and patronal friendship he shares with the Philippians, he says, "Complete my joy [*plērōsate mou tēn charan*] by being of the same mind, having the same love, being in full accord and of one mind" (2:2). The ground of that joy is *eschatological*: what he refers to in 2:1 as "encouragement in Christ," "incentive of love," and "participation in the Spirit." But its expression is *social*, bound up with the quality of ecclesial sociality, in particular, the church's unity and countercultural ethic of humility (2:3–11).

As the climax of this section makes clear, however, Paul's joy is also bound up with the quality of his own relation of reciprocity with the Philippians: "Even if I am to be poured as a libation upon the sacrificial offering of your faith, I am glad and rejoice with you all [*chairō kai synchairō pasin hymin*]. Likewise you also should be glad and rejoice with me [*to de auto kai hymeis chairete kai synchairete moi*]" (2:17–18). Paul expresses joy in being able to complement the faith-sacrifice they have made with his own self-sacrifice, possibly (we may reasonably assume) in martyrdom. He also exhorts them to follow his example of sharing his joy with them by reciprocating in sharing their joy with him. Paul's letter, therefore, is both a display of joy and a pedagogy in joy.

Furthermore, given Mary Douglas' observation that joy in a religion manifests what its members are willing to die for, it may not be coincidental that the language of joy is concentrated in this central section (1:27—2:18) around expressions of self-abnegation. Thus, there are exhortations to self-denial, a core narrative of Christ as Lord in his self-emptying in death on a cross, metaphors of cultic sacrifice applied to the life of the faithful, and, in the section that follows (2:19–30), an account of the near-death experience on account of "the work of Christ" (2:30) of Paul's fellow-worker Epaphroditus, whom the Philippians are told to "receive . . . in the Lord with all joy [*meta pasēs charas*]" (2:29a). With Douglas, then, we may observe that, perhaps paradoxically, joy is *a language and experience of profound religious*

35. Bockmuehl, *Philippians*, 94.

and existential seriousness. It is an individual and social manifestation of, and response to, *things that matter most.* In Paul, that has to do with the progress of the eschatological gospel of Christ and the progress in faith of those who have come to acknowledge Christ as merciful Lord.

The preponderant language of joy that brings the preceding sections (1:27—2:18, at vv. 17–18; 2:19–30, at v. 29) to a close provides the link with the "interim conclusion" to the letter at 3:1a: "Finally, my brethren, rejoice in the Lord [*chairete en kyriō*]." Here Paul places right at the center of his letter an exhortation to joy that unites the letter as a whole. Important is that the exhortation is to rejoice *en kyriō*. Running throughout the letter, and fundamental to Paul's pedagogy in joy, is a comparison between those who put their own interests first and those whose interests are identified with the service of Christ (cf. 2:4, 21).[36] The comparison reaches its peak in 3:2—4:1, where Paul offers a highly polemical contrast between (most likely) judaizing missionaries whose confidence is "in the flesh" and those, like Paul himself, who have no confidence in the flesh, but who "boast" (i.e., rejoice[37]) in Christ (3:2–4). Interestingly, in drawing the comparison to a close, Paul uses contrasting emotional signifiers: of the "enemies of the cross of Christ" he speaks "even with tears" (*de kai klaiōn*) (3:18); of his brothers and sisters in the Lord in Philippi he speaks in terms of eschatological approbation as his "joy and crown" (*chara kai stephanos mou*) (4:1; cf. 1 Thess 2:19).

An ancient letter's final section provides the opportunity to recapitulate important themes as well as deal with matters still outstanding, often of a practical nature. That is certainly the case with this letter's ending (which constitutes 4:4–23),[38] not least in respect of the theme of joy. Remarkably, at its very opening (4:4), the prior exhortation to "rejoice in the Lord," which occurs at the interim conclusion in 3:1, is repeated, but also doubled, as well as being augmented with the important qualifier "always": "Rejoice in the Lord always; again I will say, Rejoice" (*Chairete en kyriō pantote; palin erō, chairete*). It is as if Paul cannot resist a final pedagogy in joy. Once more, it is the eschatological horizon that provides the essential underpinning ("The Lord is at hand"; 4:5b)—all this within the overarching conviction of the active agency of God as the source and guarantee of that close corollary of joy that is "peace" (4:7, 9b; cf. Gal 5:22).

---

36. See further Stowers, "Friends and Enemies," 114–17, with discussion of Paul's use of the rhetorical trope of *synkrisis.*

37. On "boasting" (*kauchēsis*) as a synonym for joy, see Morrice, *Joy,* 54–55.

38. This is to take 4:2–3 as belonging to the previous section (3:2ff.) where Paul is dealing with threats to the harmony and unity of the church, both external and, in this case, internal.

But even this is not the last invocation of joy: for having exhorted the Philippians always to "rejoice in the Lord," Paul now testifies to his own example. Introducing the delicate subject of the Philippians' provision, via Epaphroditus, of material and financial support, Paul says, "I rejoiced in the Lord greatly [*Echarēn de en kyriō megalōs*]" (4:10).[39] If we ask why Paul rejoiced greatly, the answer Paul intends—though expressed with due circumspection so as not to give oxygen to any suggestion that Paul is in it for the money (cf. v. 17a)—lies in what the gift represents. On the one hand, it represents the Philippians' partnership (noting *synkoinōnēsantes* in v. 14 and *ekoinōnēsen* in v. 15) in Paul's trials and tribulations for the gospel. On the other hand, it represents their identity under God: the gifts are "a fragrant offering, a sacrifice acceptable and pleasing to God" (4:18b).

In sum, and drawing the threads together, Paul can rejoice greatly because he belongs with the Philippians in *a great three-way partnership in the gospel that embraces earth and heaven*. Paul has met the need of the Philippians for "progress and joy in the faith" (cf. 1:24–26), the Philippians have met his need for financial and personal support (4:11, 14, 16, 18; cf. 2:25), and now Paul is able to invoke ongoing reciprocity toward the Philippians, not (or not only) from himself, but (far better) from "his" God: "And *my* God will supply every need of yours according to his riches in glory in Christ Jesus" (4:19). Such a *beneficent circle of grace and gift* uniting Paul, the Philippians, God, and God's Christ is a cause for doxology, a cause for joy: "To *our* God and Father be glory for ever and ever. Amen" (4:20).

4. Conclusion

What I have attempted in this essay is to reach an understanding of early Christian joy against a biblical background and through an exegetical analysis of its inflections in two New Testament texts: Luke-Acts and the Letter to the Philippians. If we take these two substantial texts—one narrative, the other epistolary—as at least in some way representative evidence of the emotional culture of early Christianity, a number of tentative conclusions and extrapolations may be drawn.

First, expressions of joy constitute a pervasive, even predominant, cognitive-evaluative feature of *early Christian self-definition*, of how the first Christians articulate their self-understanding in response to, alignment with—even possession by—what we may simply call *eschatological reality*. Having to do with space, time, value, and persons, reality is understood now as having been radically transformed for the good of the whole creation

---

39. Note that RSV translates the aorist *echarēn* with a present tense: "I rejoice."

by the revelation of salvation as the end-time gift of God in the life, death, and resurrection of the Messiah and the inauguration of the new age of the eschatological Spirit. Hence, joy is the believer's *condition*.[40] As an interpretation of—a reception of—*power*, joy is an expression of a newfound *authority*.[41] It communicates who they are, to whom they belong, and their sense of final destiny in God.

Second, and related, joy is *associated with key generative and sustaining Christian experiences*. As such, it is both punctiliar and perduring: it is an embodied response to grace both unexpected and intense, and, in the form of what we today might call a *mood*, it is a long-lasting condition of existence. Marking the *generative* work of the eschatological Spirit—for example, in Luke's accounts of the conception and birth of the Messiah or of the "birth" of the church on the Day of Pentecost—expressions of joy communicate the recognition of points of turning in human destiny and their reception as salvific. They both signal change and offer an interpretation of change as *for the good*. Marking the *sustaining* work of the same eschatological Spirit, especially in circumstances of suffering and persecution, the call to joy as a discipline of individual and communal life communicates the fundamental conviction that Christian hope is not illusory, that "whether we live or die, we are the Lord's" (Rom 14:8b).

Third, the first Christians' joy has points both of *continuity and discontinuity with their biblical and Jewish inheritance* briefly characterized earlier. As in Scripture, early Christian joy has a fundamentally theocentric and soteriological focus. It is joy in God and God's work of salvation—joy in the victory of God—brought to fulfilment by God's Messiah. On the other hand, joy in early Christianity is mediated somewhat differently. It loses Judaism's concentration on Torah obedience and related matters, including the Temple cult and the festivals governed by the calendar. Instead, early Christian joy is mediated through Christ and the Spirit. As such, it is intensely eschatological and boundary-transcending. In the light of the Messiah's coming, death, and resurrection, joy is the manifestation of the coming of the Holy Spirit and the anticipation of the life of heaven in novel, mixed groups open to all. As Paul writes to the groups of Jewish and Gentile Christians in Rome, "For the kingdom of God is not food and drink but righteousness and peace *and joy in the Holy Spirit* [*kai chara en pneumati hagiō*]" (Rom 14:17). Here, traditional repositories of power, identity, and

40. In the apt phrase of Nicholas Lash, in his *Seeing in the Dark*, 201, joy is "the felt form of Christian hope."

41. The relation between joy and power deserves further attention (cf. Rom 14:17).

emotion—food and drink and associated rules and rituals—have been displaced by eschatological realities understood as having far greater worth.

Fourth, joy is *an experience of revitalization*, that is, of the fulfillment and empowerment that the first Christians find in *the felt knowledge of what really matters*. And what really matters is entry into, and participation in, the eschatological practice of the life of heaven. This revitalizing experience is so profound, so touched by transcendence, that it makes possible the transcendence of suffering, grief, shame, and all that is death-dealing, even and especially death itself. Put another way, and invoking Mary Douglas again, joy makes the new way of life worth dying for, since dying is not the end but is itself (through union with Christ) a further entry into—even and especially *an enactment of*—the heavenly life.

It is worth adding, fifth, that the experience of joy-inspired revitalization, precisely because it makes possible the transcending of shame and death-dealing patterns of superordination and subordination, opens the way for a renegotiation of society's traditional fault-lines. Put another way, it opens the way for *new ways of classifying the world* and therefore new ways of being in the world. In relation to traditional classifications of persons according to *gender*, for example, the thrust of eschatological joy is towards inclusion in place of exclusion and unity in place of separation. Luke draws noteworthy attention to female characters in the narrative as well as male;[42] Paul reinterprets Gen 1 in order to stress the eschatological unity of male and female in Christ (Gal 3:27–28). In relation to classifications of persons according to *status*, the thrust of joy is towards status reversal, sometimes symbolic, sometimes expressed in practice. The apostles in Luke are accused of "turning the world upside down" (Acts 17:6); Paul invites Philemon to receive back the runaway slave Onesimus, "no longer as a slave but more than a slave, as a beloved brother . . . both in the flesh and in the Lord" (Phlm 16).

Sixth, and understandable in relation to the tensions inherent in practicing new ways of classifying the world, early Christian joy can justly be described as a *discipline*—an aspect of discipleship—*that has to be learned*. Coming from God as a gift and therefore constitutive of Christian identity, joy becomes a *responsibility*. As suggested earlier, joy is a serious business! That is why, in New Testament texts, joy can be requested and is the repeated subject of pedagogy, whether implicit in narrative or explicit in epistolary paraenesis. In the form of feelings, behavior-rules, and symbols, it helps constitute an ethos and culture distinctive in certain respects from the surrounding world, *even resistant to it*. Just as practices of grief can be

42. See Seim, *Double Message*.

constrained in the light of the new eschatological reality, over against "those who have no hope" (cf. 1 Thess 4:13b), so, contrariwise, feelings and practices of joy can be inculcated and nurtured in ways that are identity-defining and identity-transforming, as well as constituting a powerful witness to a new, life-giving way of being.

Seventh, such joy is an experience of transcendence *both individual and communal. Individually*, it expresses the major transition, characteristic of personal conversion, from being lost to being found, from infirmity to health, ignorance to knowledge, doubt to faith, despair to hope, weakness to strength-in-weakness, alienation to integration. *Communally*, joy and rejoicing express social relations transformed for the good by virtuous citizenship of the kingdom of God, where virtuous citizenship is the fruit of ever-deepening life in the Spirit (cf. Gal 5:22–23). Joyous life in the Spirit is itself nurtured by such spiritual disciplines as prayer and acts of solidarity following the teaching and example of Jesus and the apostles. It finds quintessential expression in hospitality to friends and enemies alike, in ministries of healing and release, in the signifying ritual practices of baptism and the common meal, in the thankful voicing of "psalms, hymns, and spiritual songs" (Col 3:16), and in the solidarity of shared feelings—as when Paul instructs his Roman readers to "rejoice with those who rejoice [and] weep with those who weep" (Rom 12:15).

Finally, this rejoicing is both *intensive and extensive*. It is *intensive* in that it is (as it were) a "movement of the soul" (invoking Woodhead and Riis) within a person or within the "corporate soul" of a group, a movement in the direction of depth (or height), a more profound engagement with what really matters—life in tune with God, Christ, the Spirit, the people of God, and the order of creation. But it is also *extensive* in the sense that joy is a witness to others and a sharing with others in eschatological delight. In brief, eschatological joy is *catching* (cf. Acts 2:46–47a).

In sum, I have argued for a greater recognition of the contribution of the emotions—in particular the emotion of joy—to the first Christians' practical understanding of existence as a sharing in what for them had become their "ultimate value": the revelation of eschatological reality christologically defined and pneumatologically received. The task for contemporary spirituality is to inquire into the ways in which the joy to which the New Testament bears witness may be entered into more fully in human life today.

This task is by no means impossible. In his recent, formidable attempt to express the condition to which human beings in a secular age aspire, Charles Taylor gives prime place to the metaphor of "fullness." He says:

We all see our lives, and/or the space wherein we live our lives, as having a certain moral/spiritual shape. Somewhere, in some activity, or condition, lies a fullness, a richness; that is, in that place (activity or condition), life is fuller, richer, deeper, more worthwhile, more admirable, more what it should be. This is perhaps a place of power: we often experience this as deeply moving, as inspiring. Perhaps this sense of fullness is something we just catch glimpses of from afar off; we have the powerful intuition of what fullness would be, were we to be in that condition, e.g., of peace or wholeness; or able to act on that level, of integrity or generosity or abandonment or self-forgetfulness. But sometimes there will be moments of experienced fullness, of joy and fulfilment, where we feel ourselves there.[43]

I note that Taylor speaks here of moments of "joy and fulfilment" as indicative of life's potential for "fullness." In my view, part of the privilege and responsibility of Christian witness—drawing upon its scriptural, theological, liturgical, and practical resources—is to embody that joy and fulfillment in ways that point to its true source in God, in the conviction that God's life overflows perpetually in grace to all creation.

43. Taylor, *Secular Age*, 5.

11

Love in the Letter to the Galatians

Pieter G. R. de Villiers
University of the Free State

1. Introduction

BIBLICAL SPIRITUALITY[1] IS A relatively new area of research in the fields and interface of spirituality and biblical studies. It shares a historical-critical approach to the Bible (including developments such as narratology, rhetorics, and intertextuality)[2] and also overlaps with a growing number of theological interpretations of the Bible.[3] One of its seminal characteristics is that it wishes to account for the transformational impact of biblical texts. In this sense, it also overlaps and continues with contextual readings of the Bible as another significant trend in biblical scholarship that wants to move beyond descriptive, historically distanced readings of biblical texts in order

1. For this term and an extensive discussion, cf. Waaijman, *Spirituality*, 685–766. Waaijman's phenomenological study of spirituality in various religious traditions is a comprehensive investigation of its forms, foundations, and methods. As part of spirituality's methods, Waaijman analyzed spiritual forms, configurations, topics, processes of transformation, and the interpretation of spiritual texts. He links the latter with spiritual hermeneutics, which is the theoretical reflection on how sacred texts were understood and interpreted spiritually. Biblical spirituality should be understood in this context.

2. Cf., e.g., Green, "This Old Text," 72–83 for a discussion of the relationship between these methods and biblical spirituality.

3. Many examples of such theologies from various traditions and countries can be mentioned. These include Strecker, *Theologie*; Stuhlmacher, *Theologie*; Gnilka, *Theologie*; Hübner, *Theologie*; Hahn, *Theologie*; Schnelle, *Theologie*; Marshall, *Theology*; Dunn, *Theology*. For other examples, cf. Morgan, "New Testament Theology" and the discussions in Rowe, "Revival," Carson, "New Testament Theology," and Carson, "Locating."

to express and illustrate their "efficacious," transformative consequences and implications for later readers.[4] The interest in biblical spirituality, finally, also continues hermeneutical reflections by influential authors such as Ricoeur on meaning as reference and Gadamer on the fusion of horizons where the world of the text and the world of the reader intersect to generate continuously new and various interpretations.[5]

Biblical spirituality is interested in how biblical texts formally and materially reflect and effect the transformational and ongoing divine-human relationship both in biblical texts and through the reception of these texts.[6] In doing so, it focuses on three major formal dimensions in biblical texts. They are the divine-human relationship, transformation, and growth.

Biblical spirituality is also interested in tracing key themes, spelled out as characteristic of spirituality, in and of a biblical text. This material aspect of spirituality includes notions like fear/awe of God, piety, holiness, and perfection.[7] In a Christian and biblical context, these notions can be extended to include others like love, peace, grace, and justice. This essay wishes to

4. Such readings address topical issues like gender, race, colonialism, and sociopolitical issues. Tolmie, "Research," described a large number of publications on the Letter to the Galatians from this perspective. For a similar position, but more from a traditional New Testament perspective, cf. Mattison, "Summary." Mattison reacts against Stowers' remark that "if I challenge the historical accuracy of some standard interpretations of the letter [Romans], it does not mean that I intend to denigrate the contributions of its great commentators. But my purposes as a historian of early Christian literature differ from the purposes of the theologians and churchmen." He continues, "Instead we must ask how Paul's original meaning, in its historical context, can be appropriated by contemporary theology. In so doing we affirm that New Testament theology is very much alive and a tenable undertaking in the twenty-first century; that the canon of Scripture has continuing relevance as an authoritative guide in matters of Christian faith."

5. An example of the way in which these dimensions are present in biblical spirituality is to be found in the work of Schneiders. Cf. Schneiders, *Revelatory Text*, 16. She draws attention to some implications of the focus on the spiritual understanding of biblical texts: "To engage the meaning of the text at this level is to court conversion." In her other major publication, *Written*, she showed how an appropriation of John's Gospel challenges existing power structures and invites readers to participate in the transformative dynamics that Scripture promotes. Schneiders' approach is influenced by, amongst others, Ricoeur and Gadamer. She continuously stresses appropriation that promotes an awareness of the ongoing, transformational impact of the biblical text.

6. For some examples of essays on biblical spirituality, cf. De Villiers, "Love in the Revelation of John"; De Villiers, "Peace in Luke-Acts"; De Villiers, "Peace in the Pauline Letters"; De Villiers, "Eschatology of 1 Thessalonians"; and De Villiers, "Love in the Letter to Philemon."

7. Waaijman, *Spirituality*, 320ff. Waaijman's work on the formal and material nature of biblical spirituality and spiritual hermeneutics forms the background to and framework for some insights in this essay.

contribute to this reflection on the material contents of biblical spirituality by discussing the key notion of love in Paul's Letter to the Galatians. This will be done against the background of some recent developments. In biblical scholarship, love has been considered a major motif in New Testament texts.[8] There is a growing awareness of its varied character. Certain texts speak in a radical manner about love for the enemy (Luke 6:27–36). Others (like John 13:34) speak only of love for other believers.[9] Paul's famous chapter on love in 1 Cor 13, again, is different from its discussion in Rom 12–13. Any discussion of love will gain clarity, therefore, when it is read in terms of its literary and social context. In addition, one should reflect on love in terms of recent linguistic insights that indicate that too often love has been studied in terms of a particular word rather than in terms of the semantic field of love, affection, and compassion.[10] The notion of love will also be illuminated by terms that indicate the lack of love and are therefore its antonyms, such as, for example, hatred. This essay on love will therefore take into consideration its varied character and will investigate all words belonging to the semantic field of love.[11]

2. Love in Galatians?

There is little doubt, given the textual evidence, that the love motif occupies a seminal place in some Pauline letters. If there is one author in the New Testament who understands that love is the highest state attainable in this

8. Cf. e.g., Schrage, *Ethics*, 213 (n.16) for examples of the central position of love in Pauline texts. Cf., in contrast, Houlden, *Ethics*, 73, who comments that not all early Christian circles were as single-mindedly dedicated to a "love morality" as is often supposed, and that even those that might be thus described meant by it many different things, ranging from the intra-community love of the Fourth Gospel to the devotion to the Torah in Matthew. Hays, *Moral Vision*, 274–75, also does not regard love as a unifying image in the New Testament or a central thematic emphasis.

9. On the different nuances or uses of words like *phileō* and *agapaō*, cf. Louw and Nida, *Lexicon*, 294, and also Spicq, *Lexique*, 15 and 20, who lists four Greek words for love. They are *storgē* (referring to tender feelings between, e.g., parents and children), *erōs* (not used in the New Testament; indicating irrational passion or desire), *philia* (friendship, affection, benevolence), and *agapē*. Cf. also Wheaton, "Love," 408, who links *agapē* with "unmerited, self-giving love" and *philia* with warm, merited love—that is, affectionate love characteristic of friendship.

10. Louw and Nida, *Lexicon*, 288–96.

11. Cf. two previous articles of mine in which I investigated love in Philemon and in Revelation (De Villiers, "Love in the Revelation of John" and "Love in the Letter to Philemon." A third article on love in Romans is in print. I hope to synthesize my findings of these and other Pauline letters at a later stage.

life, it is Paul.[12] He knows, as 1 Cor 13 indicates, that the loving touch of God can transform a deformed relationship into an intimate union of love that transcends time and all forms of negativity. Of the three seminal notions of faith, hope, and love in this chapter, Paul stresses that love is the greatest. In Rom 12–13 there is another example of the significant role of love in Paul's understanding of faith. Love is for him the one word that expresses the nature of the relationship between God and humanity and the continuous, intimate bond that results from this relationship.

This special role of love in Pauline letters seems to be in contrast to the letter of Galatians. On the face of it, Galatians does not seem to be one of Paul's most loving letters. It is read by many as a bitter, even hostile dispute with his opponents, as is evident from its aggressive language and tone.[13] Written in a vitriolic polemical style, Paul strongly attacks the other gospel of some false (2:4; 5:10, 12) opponents of his gospel of grace (esp. 2:16), of Christ (1:2), and of freedom (5:13). This gospel, to his mind, threatens his own gospel, which is "a heavenly revelation of Christ Jesus" (1:12). In addition, Galatians is well known in the history of biblical interpretation as the letter that especially focuses on motifs such as faith and justification.

And yet, a closer reading of Galatians will reveal the foundational place of love in it and the other, gentler side of the author's relationship with his readers. Paul refers to love (*agapē*) at five seminal places in Galatians: 2:20; 5:6, 13, 14, and 22. If Louw and Nida's semantic field of love, affection, and compassion is taken as a guideline,[14] other words and motifs can be added, making love stand out more prominently. They all point to a central[15] and seminal place of love in Galatians, as now needs to be explained in more detail.

3. Divine Acts of Love

In the history of its reception, Galatians is regarded as a letter that focuses on justification as the divine act of reconciliation with humanity. Paul speaks

12. Waaijman, *Spirituality*, 469. Jaquette, *Discerning*, 215, includes love, together with faith, freedom, and the faith community as four items that stand out as most important in Paul's ethical reflection.

13. Tolmie, *Persuading*, 74, noted that "from a rhetorical perspective, one of the conspicuous aspects of the letter is its aggressive tone." For verbal violence in Galatians, cf. Tolmie, "Violence."

14. Louw and Nida, *Lexicon*, 288–96. The subdomain of love, affection, and compassion is part of the domain of attitudes and emotions. Note their observation that of all domains, this one is most likely to consist of numerous idomatic and figurative expressions.

15. Cf. Schrage, *Ethics*, 213, for other examples of the central position of love in Pauline texts.

about these salvific actions of God in some key passages (e.g., 1:1–4, 16–21). In Gal 1:16 Paul belabors his statement about the truth of the gospel (1:14) by repeatedly referring to justification through faith in Christ without the works of the law. God liberated humanity from slavery and sin in order to restore the relationship with humanity and to restore humanity to mutual harmony and oneness (e.g., 3:28). One becomes a child of God not because one belongs to the Jewish race through circumcision. One is justified and becomes a member of God's family because of the divine grace and love.[16]

A close reading of the letter will show, however, that one should account for the more fundamental framework of love in which Paul embeds his remarks about justification. This motif of justification is, namely, linked with and represents the outcome of the divine love for humanity. Galatians 1:16 with its emphasis on justification is, for example, formally and materially intricately linked with Gal 2:20–21 where Paul explains in greater depth the link of justification with the death and love of Christ. These verses contain the first reference to love (2:20) as divine action, and deserve more attention now.

3.1 The Originary Nature of Love as Divine Action

In a seminal location of Galatians, Paul's remarks about justification and faith are framed by references to love. Having discussed justification in Gal 2:15–19, Paul speaks in Gal 2:20 in personal terms[17] of his faith in the Son of God. He mentions faith briefly in verse 20, but speaks in more depth about his participation in the death of Christ on the cross. His use of descriptions for Christ is striking. As in the preceding verses, he refers to "Christ" again when he discusses justification by faith in Christ. Here in Gal 2:20, however, he, surprisingly, refers to Christ as "the Son of God" who loved him and gave himself to Paul (*en pistei zō tē tou hyiou tou theou agapēsantos me kai paradontos heauton hyper emou*). This is the only time that Paul uses the term in Galatians (cf. 4:4, 6, 23).

---

16. *Justification* is one of the most controversial terms in New Testament studies. A vast number of publications have been published on it. Mattison, "Summary," gives a useful, short overview of some recent interpretations on justification and the rise of the "new perspective" on Paul. Restricted space does not allow for this debate to be evaluated here.

17. De Boer, *Galatians*, 163, notes that although Paul refers to himself in this passage, "he expects the new preachers and the Galatians to say it after him and to apply it to themselves." Though this is certainly true, it remains striking that Paul here speaks in such an individualistic mode, especially after the more general "we" language in the preceding passage. The tone is much more intimate, even mystical, than it would have been had he used the plural.

The reference to the divine sonship emphasizes that Paul sees love and justification in terms of the divine relationship with Paul: love, as the aorist participles indicate, was shown by the Son of God to Paul in past actions. With this observation the salvific actions of God in Christ are inextricably linked with divine love. Christ's act of love lies behind the divine action of redemption. In terms of the two poles in the divine-human relationship,[18] love, therefore, belongs first and foremost to the divine pole. It is part of the sphere of the divine in an originary sense of the word. It frames, but also qualifies the salvific actions of God.

The initiative and its origins of love remain with God, stressing that no one can claim or do anything to receive or earn the gracious love of God.[19] Redemption is given out of love to those who were prisoners of sin (3:22). Paul offers another perspective on this when he writes in Gal 3:9 about the Galatians "who know God," but then adds, "or rather having become known by God." De Boer has described Paul's correction of himself in this verse as "most fascinating." Paul is aware that his first expression may reflect contemporary thought about "the religious quest for a proper relationship with God." By correcting himself, Paul shows not only his sensitivity for language, but also his choice for language that speaks "of God's own initiative, of God's invasive self-disclosure on the earthly stage."[20] This is also what is suggested in Paul's reference to Christ's self-giving love.

3.2 Intimate Love

More formal and material remarks about Paul's first explicit reference to love in Gal 2:19–20 will further reveal its importance and explain its nature. Formally, this reference to love appears in a location that is filled with rich thoughts about the foundational events of Paul's gospel. Paul describes the divine-human relationship in a most intimate manner that illuminates his explicit reference to love. The divine-human relationship in this passage is namely characterized as a transformative, mystical union that is initiated by

18. Spirituality is about the divine-human relationship. The distinction of these two poles is seminal. Though the two are intricately interrelated, the distinction indicates that spirituality is about growing toward an ultimate goal that is not found in oneself.

19. References are often made to the fact that love in Greco-Roman times reflects a bond of friendship between people who share mutual affinity and care. In Paul's case love is not dependent on qualities in other people. It is given to sinners (Gal 3:22) and those who are not likely objects or who do not necessarily deserve it. This is not only true of love in the divine-human relationship, but also of love between people who have been touched by the divine love.

20. De Boer, *Galatians*, 273.

God in Christ and that is characterized by mutuality and reciprocity.[21] It is, furthermore, an intimate giving of Godself to humanity.[22]

In this passage Paul speaks about the human response to the self-giving of God. He describes the relationship from the human perspective: he has been crucified with Christ, adding with emphasis the phrase in which the "I" is foregrounded (*zō de ouketi egō*). The death of Christ on the cross brings about Paul's death, and, thereby, a nothingness. He no longer lives. His participation in the cross points to the moment of transformation that is anchored in the Christ event and that results in his no longer living.[23]

The other side of the picture confirms the death and nothingness of Paul. The relationship, Paul argues from a divine perspective, is focused on God. Human existence becomes oriented towards God. The dead Paul now lives "for God" (2:20) and no longer for himself. It becomes even more intense when Paul remarks that Christ lives in him (*zē en emoi Christos*). This mystical description indicates the divine indwelling in humanity. Christ becomes an abiding presence in the life of Paul, bringing him to become completely at "rest" in the divine.[24] The divine love does not go unanswered. In return Paul gives himself or lets himself go. This is about mutuality. Both the human and the divine "give possession of the self to the other . . . and both are one in the transformation of love." It is about being overcome "by the activity of the fathomless love of God."[25] It comprises the unmediated, ongoing divine presence, that is, Christ living in the believer. God entered the existence of humanity so that humanity displays the image of God. What makes this so intimate is the movement between the divine and human: the divine transforms the human being, but, at the same time, the human being is open to and transparent to the divine. God resides in him or her, so that the person is occupied with nothing else but God and gives him or herself completely to God.[26]

---

21. Duncan, *Galatians*, 73, explains Paul's remark that "I live in faith of the Son of God" as an example of Christ-mysticism, indicating Paul's reliance on Christ's unseen presence and fellowship. Ridderbos, *Paulus*, 255, rejects a reading that implies a mystical "depersonalization." A mystical union need not, however, necessarily imply a depersonalization.

22. Waaijman, *Spirituality*, 474.

23. Cf. here the remarks of Dunn, *Galatians*, 119, about Gal 2:20. "The old 'I' has died and been replaced by a new focus of personality, Christ himself. The 'I' which found social identity 'in Judaism' now finds personal meaning and identity in Christ and those who are also 'in' Christ."

24. Waaijman, *Spirituality*, 469.

25. Ibid., 471.

26. Ibid., 469–76, esp. 471.

Paul then links this ongoing indwelling of "Christ" with faith in the "Son of God."[27] This familial term provides a further clue to understand the divine-human relationship.[28] It is helpful to understand this language in the light of previous parts of the letter. Familial language is used to qualify the salvific actions of God in the prominent opening remarks of Gal 1:4. There, in another description of the redeeming work of Christ, Paul links salvation with the will of "our God and Father" (1:3). The qualification of God as Father and the reference to "our" (*apo theou patros hymōn*) introduces familial language right at the beginning of this letter, setting its tone and providing the framework within which his writing should be understood. With such familial language he suggests intimacy and love as the driving force behind, and motivation for, the redemptive acts and the divine relationship with humanity.[29]

It is this familial language that Paul develops further in Gal 2:20. Here the intimate relationship which in itself already suggests divine love, is not merely expressed in familial metaphors, but is explicitly linked with love. The pronouncements about Christ who lives "in" the believer and the life "for God," mentioned in the beginning of the verse, are explicitly linked with the love of the Son of God who "gave himself" to the sinner. In both these passages Paul shows that the family of God is about the divine Father

---

27. Galatians 4:1–7 concentrates on the sonship of Jesus in a striking manner. Here, too, the redemptive work of the Son is in focus. Note also Gal 1:16 where Paul refers to God who "reveals his Son in me" and where the close relationship between God and Christ is evident from the reference to the grace of Christ (1:6).

28. Cf. Aasgard, *Siblingship*, 308–10, for the link between sibling language and love, as well as for its importance in Pauline letters.

29. The debate about the use of *Father* in biblical texts cannot be discussed here. The notion of Father has become hugely controversial as a result of gender studies and its critique of patriarchy. The debate has made contemporary readers more aware of the problem of male language in the Bible and the way in which it may impede spiritual experiences. Here the term is understood as suggesting intimacy and love without necessarily legitimizing patriarchy and sexist language. Cf. Hamerton-Kelly, *God the Father*, 81, for the link between the description of God as Father and intimacy. He writes that the word *Father* suggests and evokes the loving relationship with God (100–101). This goes back to Jesus' experience of an intimate relationship with God that made "Father" the appropriate symbol of his existence. Through this, "He invited his followers to share in it by giving them the privilege of invoking God as 'Abba,' and that privilege became the creative center of Christian worship" (103). Cf. also Aasgard, *Siblingship*, 244 (cf. also 311), who describes siblingship as "a fundamental perspective," noting that "clearly [Paul] wants to create an 'atmosphere of love' in connection with this letter." Although it is clear that God can be called Father as Creator too, the link between Father and salvation is so dominant in Galatians that the term *Father* is used first and foremost in terms of intimate, loving relationships. For a discussion of Jesus as Son of God and his loving relationship with the Father, cf. also Bauckham, "Sonship," 259–60.

and Son lovingly desiring and initiating an intimate relationship with humanity and with believers as the family of God.[30]

Paul thus integrates his reference to love in Gal 2:20 within the framework of his discussion about the personal, intimate divine-human relationship in Gal 1–2. Both the beginning and end of Gal 1–2 as introduction to the letter, offers divine love as the driving force behind the salvific actions of God which bring about an ongoing, intimate relationship with humanity. Love indicates an affectionate divine attitude that is expressed towards humanity as its object in order to bring about a transformative and life-giving relationship with the divine and with others.[31]

Later parts in Galatians confirm the intimacy of the divine-human relationship, as is shown by a passage about the Spirit as a divine gift (4:4–7).[32] This discussion of the Spirit as the embodiment of the divine is, once again, part of a passage found in a significant location, that is, in "the theological center of the entire epistle."[33] This passage, like Gal 2:19–20, also speaks of the salvific events and also contains traditional christological statements, once again linked with familial language, to speak in a formulaic, solemn manner[34] about God "sending out" the Spirit of "his Son into our hearts" (cf. also 3:3, 5–6).[35] Here the divine initiative is once again spelled out. The intimate nature

---

30. This explicit reference to love is illuminated further by other remarks in Galatians that contrast divine love with human behavior. In Gal 1:13–15 Paul describes how he zealously persecuted the church out of love for the law. In personal, experiential terms he speaks of the gift that came to him in his calling by God (1:15) and that transformed him from a violent, hateful person with a destructive attitude and lifestyle (1:13) to one who lives "for God" and who is constantly aware of the love of Christ.

31. Through this focus on the originary, divine initiative of love, the nothingness of humanity and the ongoing indwelling of the divine, Paul further illustrates his often repeated argument in Galatians that the divine-human relationship is not dependent on human endeavor. This language further appeals to the relationship between God and humanity as having special consequences for the relationship between human beings. This emphasis provides an argument against the unloving exclusion of others on the basis of race, gender, and social standing (3:26–29). All are children of God in faith, transformed by the divine love and intimately bound to each other (cf. further below). Cf. Rom 8:37, but also 2 Cor 5:14: "The love of Christ compels us, because we are convinced that one died for all, and therefore all died." On Christ as mediator, cf. Gal 3:20. Cf. Gal 4:9 for the divine initiative.

32. Note the focus on the divine action in this passage. In the phrase *exapesteilen ho theos to pneuma tou hyiou autou eis kardias hēmōn* (v. 6), the *ho theos exapesteilen* stands out. It repeats the phrase also found in verse 4. The divine gift of the Spirit of the Son is again embedded in love, as is clear from the beginning of verse 6: *hoti de este hyioi*. God shares the Spirit of the "Son" with the other "sons."

33. Martyn, *Galatians*, 406.

34. Betz, *Galatians*, 205; Martyn, *Galatians*, 389, 406.

35. Betz, *Galatians*, 210, explains the "traditional idea" of the Spirit in the human

of the divine-human relationship is characterized as the Spirit's indwelling in the heart as the innermost being of humanity which steers its mind and life. The relational nature of this gift is expressed with a further insight when the Spirit is said to bring believers to respond to God, crying out prayerfully, "Abba, Father."[36] Once again salvation is about the gift of an intimate, transformative relationship. Once more it is linked with and qualified by the language of love through the endearing terms *Father* (which is emphasized by being mentioned twice), *Son*, and *sons*.

This passage also depicts the relationship between the divine and human as reciprocal and mutual.[37] The faithful are given the Spirit to love God, are granted sonship to call God lovingly and prayerfully Father, and are adopted to act as true heirs. The faithful thus are in their sonship transformed into the image of Christ, the Son of God. As Christ is the Son of God, so they have become sons of God[38] who call God their "Father." It is, after all, the Spirit of the Son of God (4:4) who loved humanity, who enters their existence and transforms them into becoming like Christ.[39] The bond between Christ and humanity is thus depicted once again as intimate and loving to the extent that humanity is "transformed in the Beloved: not because the nature of the soul is replaced by the nature of the Beloved but because the soul is conformed to him." "God *in*forms the soul with his grace and *con*forms it to himself; it is now *re*confirmed to his image and likeness."[40] This bond transforms them also in their mutual relationships with each other.[41]

heart thus: "The heart was considered the organ responsible for the control of the will."

36. Though the unusual repetition of the term in Greek and Aramaic could reflect the bilingual character of the early church, it is also, as Betz observes, an "inspired acclamation" that shows "both the inspiration of those who pray and their self-understanding as sons by those who address him as 'Father'" (*Galatians*, 211).

37. Martyn, *Galatians*, 392: "One sees, then, the folly of asking whether this vocal cry is an act of the Spirit or of the baptizands. It is the act of the Spirit just sent into their hearts, and in this way it is their act."

38. Waaijman, *Spirituality*, 462, 472–73.

39. Dunn, *Galatians*, 120, succinctly notes: "The objective of Paul's missionary and pastoral exertions is that the Galatians display more and more the character of Christ. In all three texts the unspoken assumption is that the risen Christ is the image of God, that is, the pattern of what God intended for humankind. In terms of simple piety, the objective of believers going on in the Christian life is that they become like Jesus."

40. Waaijman, *Spirituality*, 472.

41. Hays, "God of Mercy," 123–43.

3.3 The Self-Giving Nature of Love

The reference to the love of Christ in Gal 2:20 is linked with a phrase that further explains its nature. Paul describes the love of Christ for him with an aorist participle (*tou agapēsantos*), but adds another participial expression: "who gave himself" (*kai paradontos heauton*).[42] In the context of this passage, these phrases refer to the cross of Christ, which liberates humanity from the curse of the law. De Boer correctly notes that the second participle is explanatory of the first, so that one will have to translate: "the one who loved me, that is, gave himself up for me."[43] The love of Christ, therefore, is carefully characterized by self-giving.

Christ's giving of himself for humanity is an important motif in the letter. Paul thus describes Christ at the beginning of the letter as the one who gave himself for our sins (1:4). His death for others is also spelled out when he is portrayed as the one who redeemed us by becoming a curse for us (3:13). Elsewhere in the Pauline letters the presentation of Christ's death on behalf of others is also linked with divine love, as happens in Gal 2:20. Christ's death illustrates the divine love in Rom 5:8 when he writes, "God demonstrates God's love for us in this: While we were still sinners, Christ died for us." This verse also reflects the originary and radical nature of the divine love, since God reached out in love to those who have been "enemies of God" (Rom 5:10).

The spirituality in Galatians is, therefore, first and foremost about divine love, given unconditionally to humanity, without any merit on their side and irrespective of gender, status, and race. Love is about a close relationship between God and humanity that transforms them to live in inclusive, radically transformative relationships with each other (cf. further below).[44] Most telling is, however, that love is radical, representing the gift of the divine itself to humanity. It happens at all costs, even unto death.

---

42. Cf. Eph 5:2, 25.

43. De Boer, *Galatians*, 163. He adds that the love was not a disposition, but a concrete act of self-sacrifice. Though this may be the primary meaning of Gal 2:20, the divine disposition of love is certainly assumed in the rest of the letter, and is also present here.

44. For the affectionate and relational nature of familial terms in Galatians, cf. also Julien, "Coming Home." Scott, *Epistemology*, 270, argues (in support of Hays) that the love as expressed in Jesus' passion is the reason why the faith community lives a life of serving others. There is no reference to teachings of Jesus on humility or servanthood. The cross is thus the substance of Paul's love ethic.

4. Love as a Characteristic of Christian Identity and the Spiritual Way

The special role of divine love in the Letter to the Galatians is underlined with the equally important role Paul allocates to love in the life of the faith community. Though Paul describes the identity of followers of Christ primarily in terms of the key motif of faith, seminal remarks in key locations suggest that love is another profound marker of their identity.[45]

Galatians 2:15–20 (cf. also 3:1–5; 5:2–6) is especially relevant, showing how the Galatians' "earthly lives are characterised by faith in the Son of God."[46] In Gal 5:2–12[47] Paul summarizes all his arguments in the previous chapters against the opponents. In verses 2–4 he, first of all, warns the Galatians three times that human attempts to achieve righteousness through the law break off the relationship with Christ. He then, in verse 5, contrasts such attempts (once again in summarizing fashion) with faith, which is the only way of achieving righteousness. The statement in verses 5–6 "is a very concise summary of Paul's basic argument in the letter. He repeats several concepts that played a key role in his argument in the previous phase, namely Spirit, righteousness and faith."[48]

In his discussion of faith there is an unexpected but significant turn when he writes, *en gar Christō Iēsou oute peritomē ti ischyei oute akrobystia alla pistis di'agapēs eneryoumenē*[49] (5:6b). Here Paul develops his notion of faith in more detail by linking it with the love. The middle *energoumenē* means to become effective, to come to expression. It is thus about faith working through love.[50] Faith comes to expression and has love as its effect. Love, in other words, is the face of faith.[51]

45. Hahn, *Theologie*, 289, is one of several scholars who underlines that the link between faith and love is constitutive for Pauline ethics: "Lebendiger Glaube konkretisiert sich notwendigerweise im Tun der Liebe."

46. Tolmie, "Ethics," 248.

47. Cf. Tolmie, "Persuading," 177–79, for a discussion of the place of this passage in the letter as a whole. De Boer, *Galatians*, 315, notes, "The summarizing quality of these two verses [5–6] is indicated by the complete absence of the definite articles in the Greek text; the nouns are all anarthrous. Paul here uses shorthand formulations as a way to drive the central message of the letter home."

48. Tolmie, "Persuading," 181. On the importance of these three motifs, cf. Tolmie, "Ethics," 247–50.

49. Martyn, *Galatians*, 474. The participle can be either passive (faith that is activated by love) or middle ("faith is actively expressing itself through love"). Though patristic fathers supported the passive translation, the middle reading is to be preferred.

50. Betz, *Galatians*, 262; Tolmie, "Persuading," 182.

51. Spicq, *Agape*, 222: "Since faith arises and acts through *agape*, its effectiveness shows clearly that *agape* is inherent in St. Paul's conception of faith."

With this remark the full circle is completed: the divine love that lies behind justification and the gift of love transforms humanity to a life of faith, which works through love. At this seminal moment in his letter, Paul presents the notion of love differently than in the first part of the letter. This time it does not refer to divine love, but to love that believers have for God[52] and others. With this expression Paul paves the way for the last chapters in the letter in which he mentions love three times as a key characteristic of the spiritual way of believers (5:6, 13–14, and 22).

Once again a complex of motifs about the family of God confirms this. Paul speaks of his readers as "children of God" (3:26; cf. 4:5–6), even addressing them as "my" children (4:19). In one instance he explicitly speaks of "the household of faith" (6:10, *pros tous oikeious tēs pisteōs*; cf. Eph 2:19; 1 Tim 3:15; 5:8). Paul continues with this metaphorical language when he addresses his community ten times as "brothers."[53] The connotation of this address is explained by Paul's reference to "brotherly love" in 1 Thess 4:9–10 where he reminds the Thessalonians that they have been taught by God to love each other. It is further emphasized when Paul speaks of the Galatians as "sons of God through faith in Jesus Christ" (3:26, repeated in 4:5–6) and as "heirs" to the promise given to Abraham (3:29). All of these insights illuminate the loving and intimate character of the faith community as family.

5. Sharing Love

Love is a powerful presence among the faithful that needs to be revealed in their mutual relationships. Just as the divine love reaches out to humanity, their love has an outgoing nature. This becomes a major theme of the last part of Galatians, but it is qualified in another manner as necessary and as a sharing love. This is significant because it illuminates love as much more than a sentimental feeling of goodwill towards others. This love has, as the divine love also has, a relational character. It is directed at the other. Love is about connecting people of different persuasions, as Spicq indicated,[54] with an attitude of helping, supporting, and serving them.

52. Spicq, *Agape*, 387, notes that love in Gal 5:6 cannot be restricted to fraternal love. It refers "just as much to love of God as it does to love of neighbor."

53. In the first half of the letter he does so only a few times, but the references become more frequent as the letter progresses and its tone becomes less strict (1:1, 11; 3:15; 4:12, 28, 31; 5:11, 13; 6:1, 18). Paul is careful in the way he addresses his readers. The friendly letter to the Romans with its strong focus on love (Rom 12–13), for example, is the only one of Paul's letters in which he addresses his readers as those "who are loved by God" (*pasin tois housin en Rhōmē agapētois theou*; Rom 1:7).

54. Spicq, *Lexique*, 19.

5.1 Enslaved in Love

One of the striking aspects of Galatians is that Paul portrays love as a necessary condition and as an enduring law in the dispensation of the Spirit. This is remarkable, given his emphasis on the dispensation of the Spirit as a dispensation of freedom, particularly from the law. After his remarks about love as the face of faith in Gal 5:6, Paul, angry about the legalism of his opponents, continues with a digression[55] in Gal 5:7–12, attacking with rather violent language those who mislead the Galatians.[56] In Gal 5:13–14 he returns to the notion of freedom that he mentioned in Gal 5:1, when he reminds the readers that it is "for freedom that Christ has set us free." The freedom that Christ acquired should not be given up by believers. They should be free, not to indulge in sin, but to love like Christ did and to obey the love commandment (5:14). Paul feels strongly about this; believers should use their freedom to serve one another in love: *Hymeis gar ep'eleutheria eklēthēte, adelphoi. Monon mē tēn eleutherian eis amorphmēn tē sarki, alla dia tēs agapēs[57] douleuete allēlois* ("but through love become slaves of one another"). The passage thus functions like an oxymoron.

The Greek word *douleuete* is much stronger than *diakoneō*, which means to care for someone's needs. This word does not speak about serving others, but, strongly and even offensively, means to serve as a slave.[58] Paul speaks of the *necessity* of upholding loving relationships between believers when he writes that they should become slaves through love. To love is to be a slave, to be subject to. It does not mean that one should become a helper of another. Though it suggests being exposed to a different form of slavery than that of the law, it is still slavery. The slavery under the law with fear, submission, suppression, and scrupulosity as its consequences stands in contrast with the other slavery which is the "free and voluntary act of love."[59]

This intensifies Paul's appeal to his readers in their situation. To be asked to love each other amidst the hostility among groups in Galatia is demanding. Paul, referring to the tense situation in Galatia with its vicious infighting, admonishes them not to keep on biting and devouring each other (5:15). Paul thus contextualizes love and spells out its relational

55. De Boer, *Galatians*, 328, argues that this digression expresses Paul's exasperation with the formidable opposition in Galatia.

56. It is understandable that so many scholars note that this passage seems to interrupt the flow of the letter. Cf. the discussion in Tolmie, "Persuading," 190–91.

57. Spicq, *Lexique*, 19, wrote that *agapē* differs from other words on love insofar as it asks to be manifested, demonstrated, exhibited.

58. De Boer, *Galatians*, 328.

59. Betz, *Galatians*, 274: "Obviously, this juxtaposition is intended."

nature: it is that attitude and behavior of mutual affection that should replace the existing hatred, hostility, and lack of love among believers in Galatia. For Paul it is characteristic of love that it manifests itself even in the most difficult of situations to be shown even to opponents.[60] Love is needed and it is to be given unconditionally.

That Paul sees love as necessary, is further clear from Gal 5:14 where he sees love as the fulfillment of the law and appeals to the love commandment as valid for the Galatian community[61] (*ho gar pas nomos en heni logō peplērōtai, en tō Agapēseis ton plēsion sou hōs seauton*). The spiritual journey requires of the community to do good works, expressing their love to others.[62] It is not moralistic in nature, but has a christological basis. To love the other is a form of participation in the antecedent love of Christ.[63]

5.2 Unifying Love

Paul, finally, allocates a special place to love in the spiritual life when he describes it as the first of the "fruit" of the Spirit; in his enumeration Paul places love at the very beginning (Gal 5:22, *ho de karpos tou pneumatos estin agapē chara eirēnē, makrothymia chrēstotēs agathōsynē, pistis prautēs enkrateia*). He does so as part of the conclusion to the letter with an extensive discussion of the new dispensation of the Spirit in which believers find themselves since the death and resurrection of Christ and that displaced the time of the law. Scott has indicated that love as the first fruit seems to be the point of reference for the rest of the list.[64] Most of the other fruits bear a strong resemblance to Paul's description of love in 1 Cor 13:4–8.

The Spirit, having inaugurated the new dispensation of freedom and equality (3:26–29), is at work in the life of love of the faith community. Those who live by the Spirit should keep in step with the Spirit (5:25). Even the list of vices seems to reflect the lack of love. Believers should not gratify

60. Paul also allocated an important role to love in 1 Cor 13 in a letter in which bitter divisions in the faith community is a major point of discussion.

61. Cf. De Boer, *Galatians*, 332ff.; Dunn, *Theology*, 115–18, for a discussion of the tension between Paul's rejection of the law and his retention of the law of love. It remains confusing to many that Paul draws his first ethical exhortation from the law.

62. Note similar remarks in Rom 3:31 where Paul stresses that the law is not overthrown, but upheld, and regards love as the fulfillment of the law (Rom 13:8–10). As Hahn, *Theologie*, 290, notes, "Die 'Agape' ist Grundprinzip und Kriterium des Gesetzes." It is not the words of the law that are the norm, but the will of God for salvation in it. Love reveals the inner structure of the law.

63. De Boer, *Galatians*, 328.

64. See Scott, *Epistemology*.

the desires of the sinful nature (5:16, cf. 19–21) with the vices "hatred, discord, jealousy, fits of rage, selfish ambition, dissensions, factions, and envy." These are acts that represent the opposite of acts of love.[65] All of them indicate that love is a most important virtue, indicative of the presence of the Spirit, which restores and transforms relationships between members of the community.

If a characteristic of divine love is that it seeks to restore and transform relationships and to unite God and humanity through the redemptive work of Christ, the same can be said about love among those who are part of the faith community. This is most clear when the situation of the Galatian community is analyzed. Paul stresses that the false gospel of the hypocritical apostles (2:13) separates groups and alienates people from each other. Peter, afraid of the Jewish Christians, began to withdraw from the Gentile Christians by refusing to eat with them (2:12–13). Peter is afraid of "those who belonged to the circumcision group" (2:12).

The opposite of such divisive action is to seek to become the family of God in which loving relationships exist. Love is about building up the community of faith (1 Cor 8:1; Phil 2:2) and a lack of selfishness (1 Cor 10:23–24; Phil 2:1–4; Rom 15:1—16:7).

These remarks are part of a wider framework. Crocker drew attention to two trajectories, which can be described in terms of two groups of related concepts "that are central for discerning and deciding things within the body of Christ."[66] The theme of newness (the new creation, knowing one's new identity and freedom from old conventions) is such a group, while "the trajectory of inclusivity and love, of peace and unity, of the commandments of God and the law of Christ" form another group. Of special interest is the "law of Christ,"[67] which is "inherent in the gift of God's love, to which faith working in love is the appropriate response"[68] (5:6, 13–14; 1 Cor 9:21). It is, therefore, once again similar to the sharing, self-giving nature of divine love. The responsibility to act lovingly toward others reflects one's identity in Christ as the One who acted lovingly.[69]

---

65. Cf. ibid., 264.

66. Crocker, *Reading*, 195.

67. On the close relationship between the law of Christ and love, cf. Hays, "Christology," 274–75.

68. Crocker, *Reading*, 195.

69. Martyn, *Galatians*, 524, writes that the law of love "does nothing other than reflect the preeminence of Christ's love." Cf. also Spicq, *Lexique*, 19, about love that is driven by God's love, referring to Rom 5:8.

6. Conclusion

Love, in Galatians, is about a loving relationship with humanity, initiated by the divine. It is, however, more than an initiative. It is also about moving towards and "giving" Godself. Christ, in Paul's words, gave and let go of himself, and thus reached out and "moved" toward humanity to enter their existence, to dwell with them in an intimate union and in an ongoing process of spiritual growth. Christ "lives" in Paul and takes up residence in him (2:20). The beloved, one may say, desires to be with the loved one and becomes one with the loved one. It is from love as such a movement that the gift of justification flows.

At the same time, Paul, the earlier enemy of Christ and the church, speaks of his outgoing movement toward the divine. Without having anticipated it in any way, he enters into the relationship begun by Christ and makes it his own. This relationship brings to an end his earlier existence without the beloved.[70] With this he can leave behind his previous, hateful rejection of and hostility towards Christ. Paul no longer regards himself as alive. Christ has drawn Paul away from himself. He now "lives for" God (2:20).

This act of divine indwelling brings about a complete rest in each other, mutual acceptance and affection. As a result of this mutual giving, living for/in, and reaching out, there is such an intimate bond that the divine and the human are one in love, that they share a likeness in love.[71] It is a secure, trusting relationship of Father, Son, and children in the new family and household of God. They are brought together in an intimate, spiritual union so that the Spirit prays in them and they pray to the Father. The family of God shares an intimate reality, a spiritual bond that binds them in such a way that they are in perfect harmony and that they are one in likeness. If they live in this love, they will be formed in the likeness of Christ (4:19). In loving each other, they undergo "a moral transformation in which they become more and more like Christ."[72]

Paul's remarks on love in some ways equal his profound remarks about love in 1 Cor 13. Like in 1 Corinthians, which extols love as the highest good in a situation of bitter division and enmity, Galatians too insists on the necessary and important role of love in difficult times. Believers live in hateful, hostile times when the community itself is torn apart by strife and tension (5:19–21). Despite these trying times the community must be

---

70. It represents a "destruction" of Paul and the becoming nothingness of a form of existence. Paul shows how he has been moved away from himself to live for God. With this verse he shows how he lets himself go. Waaijman, *Spirituality*, 470.

71. Cf. the remarks on the notion of "transformation in love" in ibid., 469.

72. Scott, *Epistemology*, 270.

slaves of a love that seeks the well-being of the other, just as they themselves, when still enemies of God, received a self-giving Love. Love does not come easily. It comes to those who understand how divine it is in nature and how rewarding it is in reconciling humanity.

In the light of this role of love, it is striking that Paul's Letter to the Galatians is so permeated by violent rhetoric. Even though Paul's violent rhetoric is a product of rhetorical practices of his day, and even though such language shows how the opponents may have been a real threat to the truth and liberty of the gospel, it remains puzzling that the apostle seemed not to have practiced what he preached when he wrote this letter. Though this letter helps contemporary readers understand the divine nature of love and the way in which it can overcome division and hatred, it also helps us recognize the many hidden ways in which the lack of love can reassert itself within the faith community.

12

The Spiritual Wisdom
of Colossians in the Context
# of Graeco-Roman Spiritualities

Andrew T. Lincoln
University of Gloucestershire

1. Colossians as Spiritual Wisdom Document

HOW ARE THE SCRIPTURES to be seen when interpreted for spirituality? As "spiritual wisdom documents" is Philip Sheldrake's proposal.[1] If there is a general sense in which all scriptural texts fall into this category, then the argument of the present essay will be that the letter to the Colossians is one of those documents that fit it more specifically than others and that this means its wisdom was in dialogue, both consciously and unconsciously, with other wisdoms of its day. Three major themes within that dialogue will then be explored in order to highlight the distinctive aspects of Colossians' contribution.[2] Inevitably, however, such an exploration is also colored by assumptions about what is meant by "spirituality" in our own time. Here spirituality is understood both in a more

1. Sheldrake, "Interpretation," 459. He goes on to argue that the study of such classics entails a self-involving critical dialogue, seeking not only information but also transformation with its elements of judgment and appropriation.

2. I have reflected on appropriation of aspects of the spirituality of Colossians for the present day elsewhere in Lincoln, "Colossians," esp. 607–11, 618–19, 627–30, 635–37, 639–41, 649–51, 658–60. This paper engages in a different exercise—the attempt to see Colossians in its context in the ancient world as part of a broader discussion of spirituality.

general sense as the aspiration toward a fully flourishing life[3] and, recognizing that the full life takes particular shapes in religious traditions, in a more specific sense as "the divine-human relational process as transformation."[4]

Reading Colossians as a document of spiritual wisdom with these lenses is in fact in line with what the letter suggests from its outset. In his intercessory prayer report within an extended thanksgiving (1:3–23), which anticipates major themes in the body of the letter, the writer[5] indicates that his concern for the addressees is that they "be filled with the knowledge of God's will in all spiritual wisdom and understanding, so that you may lead lives worthy of the Lord, fully pleasing to him, as you bear fruit in every good work and as you grow in the knowledge of God" (1:9, 10). Clearly the knowledge and understanding desired for the addressees are to be transformative of their everyday living, and immediately striking is the combination of language about spiritual wisdom with that of fullness and of flourishing by growing and bearing fruit. Equally clearly, the letter's one mention of the Spirit in the previous verse—"your love in the Spirit"—means that "spiritual" is to be understood in relation to the divine Spirit and, together with the references here to knowledge of God and being pleasing to the Lord, signals that the writer's interest will not simply be in a wisdom that is an innate capacity of the human spirit but in a wisdom that is provided by a relationship to God in Christ.

1.1 Spiritual Wisdom and Epistolary Genre

The articulation of the spiritual wisdom presented in Colossians, however, is by no means unrelated to the human wisdom of its day, with which it is in dialogue and by which it is shaped. The very form the letter takes confirms this. It is distinctive within the Pauline corpus for being primarily a series of exhortations. On an epistolary analysis, the letter's body-middle is 2:6—4:6, which is structured around twenty-four imperatives, and this constitutes Colossians as a paraenetic letter, providing encouragement and admonition directed towards a specific way of life. As such, it most closely resembles the paraenetic letters of the ancient philosophical schools, such as Stoicism, Epicureanism, Cynicism, and Middle Platonism, which provided advice on the wisdom necessary for living a full and good life. Corresponding to the

---

3. Cf. esp. Taylor, *Secular Age*, 5–20.

4. Waaijman, *Spirituality*, 6, 312, 424.

5. Though some scholars opt for a form of Pauline authorship during his lifetime, the stance assumed here is that the writer was a later follower of Paul. For justification of that assumption, see Lincoln, "Colossians," 577–83.

three types of paraenesis in Colossians—affirmation (1:3—2:7), correction (2:8—3:4), and more general exhortations (3:5—4:6)—the letters of the schools would affirm their students' progress, correct erroneous or rival views and conduct, and provide exhortation, giving selective reminders of what was most relevant to students' needs, highlighting key principles and showing their benefits.[6] In commending the superiority of their particular school's wisdom, they reinforced commitment to it and helped students to reorientate their lives to its goals. Significantly, such letters were frequently pseudonymous. They employed the names of leading teachers and philosophers who were dead and addressed figures from the past, while clearly having a contemporary audience in view.

Among recent writers Pierre Hadot has done most to emphasize that the teaching of the schools was not simply theoretical or ethical but transformative and spiritual in the broader sense. In fact, he calls their instructions about learning to live "spiritual exercises"[7] and argues that "spiritual" is the most appropriate adjective because what is advocated corresponds to "a transformation of our vision of the world, and to a metamorphosis of our personality . . ."[8] So, for example, Plutarch, in arguing that philosophizing, as opposed to indulging in rhetoric, should be allowed at table, states that philosophy "is the art of living, and therefore must be admitted into every part of our conversation" (*Quaest. Conv.* 1.1; *Mor.* 623B), while Epictetus holds that philosophy is not about the promise of external rewards but instead "the subject-matter of the art of living [i.e., philosophy] is the life of every individual" (*Diatr.* 1.15). The philosophical movements aimed not merely to pass on tradition or impart intellectual enlightenment but "sought from their initiates a personal 'turning'—a moral transformation that accompanied a new intellectual and spiritual orientation."[9] Seneca, for example, writes explicitly, "I feel, my dear Lucilius, that I am being not only reformed but transformed. . . . I therefore wish to impart to you this sudden change in myself" (*Ep.* 6.1). Like the writers of the letters in the philosophical schools, the author of Colossians thinks of the wisdom to be conveyed as spiritually transformative.

6. For a detailed discussion of the similarities between Colossians and the exhortations of the Graeco-Roman philosophical schools, see Wilson, *Hope of Glory*, esp. 10–131, 219–29. For one example of a letter with this three-part structure, see Seneca, *Ep.* 16 and for Seneca's reflections on the three functions, cf. e.g., *Ep.* 94–95.

7. Hadot, *Philosophy as a Way of Life*, 81–125.

8. Ibid., 82.

9. Wilson, *Hope of Glory*, 255.

1.2 Spiritual Wisdom and the Content of Colossians

In line with its genre, Colossians has the theme of spiritual wisdom consistently to the fore. It is worth noting briefly both its overall prominence and the explicit references to it in each of the major sections of the letter's persuasive argument. After indicating that its goal is that the readers be filled with spiritual wisdom (1:9–10), the thanksgiving section's affirmation of them in terms of what God has done for them in Christ is dominated by the use of hymnic material with its unmistakable application to Christ of the language and concepts associated with Wisdom in the Hellenistic Jewish tradition (1:15–20). This is no more than one would expect from a writer who will go on to assert that the content of the knowledge of God's mystery is "Christ himself, in whom are hidden all the treasures of wisdom and knowledge" (2:2–3). In stressing the reliability and quality of the wisdom that it passes on to its recipients, Colossians presents its human source, Paul, as the wisdom teacher par excellence, not just for those students in the churches in Colossae and Laodicea (cf. 2:1; 4:16), who have learned Pauline wisdom from Epaphras (1:7), but for all people—"warning every one and teaching every one in all wisdom" (1:28). This teaching activity has the goal of presenting everyone mature or complete in Christ and is depicted as part of a struggle or *agōn* (1:28—2:1). The *agōn* terminology, originating in an athletic context, was used primarily for the sage's struggle for truth and virtue but also for the contest with rival views within which this took place.[10] Pauline wisdom teaching, then, was not a peaceful detached enterprise but a passionate, costly debate about what was necessary for living well and maturely. The philosopher, as spiritual director, claimed to be able to handle adversity and even rejoice in it, because it strengthened virtue (cf. e.g., Marcus Aurelius, *Ad Se Ipsum* 11.16). Similarly the mediator of the wisdom conveyed in Colossians is a sage who has experienced and rejoices in the suffering brought about by fierce dispute, a suffering that is for the sake of his converts, is in service of the church, and plays a unique role in the same pattern of suffering experienced by Christ (1:24–25). The later references to the chains of his imprisonment (4:3, 18) serve as a poignant reminder of this suffering servant's vocation in relation to his gospel's wisdom.

In offering correction about the attractions of a rival philosophy (2:8), the writer evaluates it in terms of its wisdom and concludes that its teachings about "worship of angels," observance of festivals, fasting, and severe treatment of the body may have "the appearance of wisdom" but are of no

10. The undisputed Paul sees himself as engaged in just such a battle in 2 Cor 10:3–5. For differing analyses of this motif in Hellenistic philosophy, see Pfitzner, *Paul*, 23–72; Brändl, *Agon*, 32–70.

value for genuinely living to the full, since they serve only to fulfil or satisfy the negative sphere of "the flesh" (2:23). In the more general exhortations, he then provides his own practical wisdom designed to deal with this sinful sphere of the life of the old humanity and, among his positive instructions, underlines that in the community of the new humanity believers are expected to become wisdom teachers themselves: "teach and admonish one another in all wisdom" (3:16). Finally, in the concluding exhortations, he can summarize the practical advice he has given, particularly to the various members of the household, in terms of living wisely in relation to outsiders (4:5). Wisdom, then, operates on and integrates all three levels of relationship that are significant for the readers—the cosmic, the apostolic, and the local. It sums up God's relation to the cosmos in terms of its embodiment in and revelation through Christ, which, in turn, is mediated through Paul's carrying out of his apostolic commission as wisdom teacher for the Gentiles, among whom are the letter's addressees (cf. 1:13, 21, 27; 2:13; 3:7), now instructed to appropriate, teach, and exhibit the same spiritual wisdom in their own local setting through moral renewal, their assemblies for worship, and their everyday living within society.

2. The Spiritual Wisdom of Colossians in Dialogue

In considering other versions of spirituality with which Colossians might be in dialogue, scholarly literature continues to devote its attention almost exclusively to reconstructing the origins and details of the rival philosophy in view in 2:8–23 and indeed makes much of its interpretation of the letter dependent on such reconstructions. It should be clear, however, that we have only this writer's negative perspective on a few selected features and catchwords of the alternative spirituality, employed in the knowledge that his readers would be familiar with what was being indicated. Not surprisingly, despite numerous attempted analyses of its background and details, no consensus on the precise nature of this rival wisdom is in view.[11] Some pin their hopes on further excavation of the site of Colossae providing more clues, but, if in fact the letter is pseudepigraphical, the particular addressees are part of the writer's attempt at verisimilitude and probably chosen because, although there is no evidence for Colossae existing for a considerable period of time after the earthquake that destroyed it in 61 CE, it was known

11. For a recent review of a range of proposals about the nature of the teaching and his own addition of yet another, see Smith, *Heavenly Perspective*; cf. also Rowland, *Mystery*, 156–65, for a further attempt to see it as a version of so-called merkabah mysticism.

there was a church there in Paul's lifetime. The real recipients may perhaps be glimpsed, despite the pseudepigraphical device, through the mention of Laodicea and Hierapolis in 4:13–16 or may be churches in the Pauline tradition beyond the Lycus Valley in the more general area of Asia Minor. Recognition of this factor also undermines the view of those who distance the recipients of the letter from any influence from the concerns of Hellenistic philosophy on the grounds of the likely low level of sophistication of the inhabitants of rural Colossae.

Since Colossians has chosen to articulate the Pauline gospel in the form of the paraenetic letters of the Graeco-Roman philosophical schools, we are on firmer ground if we set its themes in the context of the concerns those schools were addressing, of which we know considerably more. Their paraenetic texts were in turn part of "an ongoing discussion taking place in the wider culture concerning worldview and ethics, but this participation constitutes a critical engagement that is informed by each thinker's special ideological assumptions."[12] The appropriateness of approaching Colossians in this way receives further confirmation through its writer drawing on Hellenistic Jewish wisdom traditions, particularly in the hymnic material about Christ in 1:15–20 and in the household code of 3:18—4:1, which were already in dialogue with the broader Graeco-Roman culture. What Colossians tells us about the teaching that is deemed to be leading readers astray can then be seen as some key characteristics of yet another specific philosophy attempting to address the similar broader concerns that occupied the philosophical movements.[13] Only one further observation about the rival teaching is necessary here. It differs significantly from the other philosophical movements because it appears already to include faith in Christ. A clear inference from 2:18–19—which speak of the person or persons advocating its wisdom as "not holding fast to the head, from whom the whole body grows"—is that they thought of themselves as in relationship to Christ and so were promoting a wisdom they considered to be fully compatible with belief in Christ. Whether its other characteristics derived from Judaism, the cosmological concerns of Hellenistic philosophical movements, mystery cults, or local folk religion, or, most likely, involved a syncretistic combination from all these sources, for the purposes of this essay it is sufficient to work with how these are depicted in the text. The encounter of Pauline wisdom with that of the rival teaching may well provide the immediate impetus for the letter's production but we do not need to be able to pin down the

12. Wilson, *Hope of Glory*, 105–6.

13. This approach should not be confused, then, with attempts to identify the rival philosophy with any one particular philosophical school, such as Middle Platonism (e.g., DeMaris, *Colossian Controversy*) or Cynicism (e.g., Martin, *By Philosophy*).

precise nature of that teaching in order to be able to appreciate aspects of the more general "social imaginary" that writer and readers shared with others in their culture—the taken-for-granted assumptions about their world, their place within it, and what was necessary for a full and virtuous life.[14]

Three overlapping *topoi* shared by the philosophical schools and Colossians will be sketched briefly in order to examine such assumptions about spirituality. A more adequate investigation would need to take account of the variations within different writers and schools and the complexities of the relation among them. All that can be done here is to make some general remarks about the broader discussion of each theme, situate the writer's comments about the specific rival philosophy within these, and then observe the distinctive contribution of Colossians' spiritual wisdom.[15] The sketch of the first theme will be somewhat more extensive in order to explore the elusive and complicated force of the notion of fullness, on which it focuses.

2.1 Cosmic Spirituality and Fullness

In their different ways all the philosophical schools claimed that, in order to know how to live fully, humans needed to be aware of their role in and relation to the cosmos of which they were a part. For the Stoics the cosmos possessed a rational order resulting from its divine principle, and humans, endowed with the gift of reason, function as they are meant to when they live in harmony with that rational order. The refrain in Epictetus' instructions is "unless we act . . . conformably to the nature and constitution of each thing, we shall never achieve our true end" and "the law of life" is "that we must act conformably to nature" (*Diatr.* 1.9, 26). Alignment with the reality of the cosmos is essential to human well-being. In Marcus Aurelius' words, "All that is in harmony with you, O universe, is in harmony with me" (*Ad Se Ipsum* 4.23).

In Epicureanism understanding the nature of the cosmos is also crucial. Lucretius spends much time arguing that the cosmos and its matter have no coherent principle but are the result of a blind process of atomic conglomeration (cf. *De rer. nat.* 5.91–770). It is this view of the cosmos that frees humans from unreasonable fear of the gods, who do not intervene in

14. On the notion of "social imaginary," see Taylor, *Secular Age*, 171–76, who allows that what may start off as the ideas of an educated few then infiltrate the social imaginary, becoming part of the background understanding of much larger groups within a society or of a society as a whole.

15. For more detailed justification of the exegetical conclusions assumed here, some of which are inevitably contested, see Lincoln, "Colossians." For more recent commentary discussion, cf. esp. MacDonald, *Colossians*; Wilson, *Colossians*; Thompson, *Colossians*; Talbert, *Ephesians*; Moo, *Letters*; Sumney, *Colossians*.

the world but exist in a serene detachment, and that indicates that the goal of philosophy is to achieve just such happiness and tranquillity (cf. e.g., *De rer. nat.* 6.43–95). Indeed, he can say of Epicurus, "As soon as your philosophy issuing from a godlike intellect has begun with loud voice to proclaim the nature of things, the terrors of the mind are dispelled, the walls of the world part asunder, I see things in operation throughout the whole void; the divinity of the gods and their tranquil abodes . . ." (*De rer. nat.* 3.16–17). It should be no surprise that Hadot can assert that "wisdom is nothing more than the vision of things as they are, the vision of the cosmos as it is in the light of reason, and wisdom is also nothing more than the mode of being and living that should correspond to this vision" and then later declare, "this cosmic dimension is . . . essential to the antique sage."[16]

It is within this stress on wisdom as cosmic attunement that Colossians' notion of fullness or *plērōma* has its roots. It is significant that in its first reference to fullness (1:19), despite some translations (e.g., NRSV), "all the fullness" is not explicitly linked to deity and stands in its own right as the subject of the clause, suggesting the term *plērōma* would have been expected to be recognized as already significant in a cosmological context such as this. Its connotations are hard to pin down precisely, but ideas of filling and plenitude appear to have become associated with thinking about the relation between a transcendent source of reality and the immanence of that reality within the cosmos. From Plato onwards, and in a variety of different forms, it was common to hold that if the world or nature was perfect, it must also be full, that in fact the universe was filled with all possible forms of being in gradation according to degrees of perfection and that this abundance in creation was commensurate with its inexhaustible source of plenitude. The movement of ceaseless outflowing or emanation from the One, the Creator, called for the necessity of a corresponding ascending movement of humans from the lower level of cosmic energy and sense reality back to the higher invisible reality in order to achieve plenitude and contemplate the One.

Within this chain of being there should be no deficiencies, no lacks in terms of empty space, including between the source of being and the created world. In the Platonism that built on the *Timaeus* the latter space is filled by a world of ideas or forms, the content of the mind of the Creator, from which the created world is generated and copied. This noetic world contains within it archetypes of the four cosmic elements of fire, air, water, and earth (cf. *Tim.* 39E).[17] Philo, who articulated his Jewish beliefs through

16. *Philosophy*, 58, 252. Cf. also Pénin, "Cosmic Piety," 408: "cosmic religion was, in fact, . . . the concern of the greatest philosophers of the Greek tradition."

17. For discussion of the relation between the noetic cosmos and the notion of pleroma, see Dillon, "*Pleroma*," 99–110.

a Stoicized Middle Platonism, takes up this notion of plenitude and a noetic cosmos.[18] In the Jewish Scriptures God can be depicted as filling heaven and earth (e.g., Jer 23:24) and Wisdom as "the spirit of the Lord" that "has filled the world" (Wis 1:6–7). Building on the basic convictions that God fills the all or the cosmos (cf. e.g., *Leg. Alleg.* 1.44; 3.4; *Post.* 6.14; *Somn.* 2.221) and, therefore, the divine dynamic presence constitutes space, Philo could designate God as "the place" (cf. e.g., *Conf.* 96; *Somn.* 1.64, 67, 182). At the same time he applies this designation to the Logos who contains within himself and sums up the world of ideas (cf. e.g., *Opif.* 16–20; *QE* 2.39; *Somn.* 1.61–71, 116–19). In discussing the Logos as this transcendent place in the cosmos, Philo speaks of "the divine Word which God himself has filled wholly and entirely with incorporeal powers" (*Somn.* 1.62). What is more, the divine Logos in turn fills the cosmos and thereby brings about harmony and peace: "The divine Logos, inasmuch as it is appropriately in the middle, leaves nothing in nature empty, but fills all things and becomes a mediator and arbitrator for the two sides which seem to be divided from each other, bringing about friendship and concord, for it is always the cause of community and the artisan of peace" (*QE* 2.68).

Such references employ the verb "to fill" rather than the noun "fullness." The noun does occur in later syncretistic literature with a Gnosticizing tendency such as *Corpus Hermeticum* (e.g., 6.4; 16.3) and the *Odes of Solomon* (e.g., 7.11, 13; 16.3; 17.7; 36.1–2) but plays its most significant role in second-century Gnostic writings, where it refers to the fullness of the world of ideas now represented by the Aeons seen as "the thoughts of the Father" (*Tri. Trac.* 60). Endowed with intellect, they become self-subsistent entities and their pleroma is filled out with a variety of "thrones, powers, and glories" (*Tri. Trac.* 54). The precise relation between God and the noetic cosmos or pleroma of emanations from God is not always clear within this development of Middle Platonic ideas. Sometimes it is identified with God and sometimes separate but in the closest proximity, and frequently this sphere of perfection and salvation is opposed to the lower material realm (e.g., *Gos. Truth* 16, 34–36, 41; *Tri. Trac.* 70, 75, 77, 78, 80). In this cosmic context "fullness" in Col 1:19 constitutes the first extant use of the noun, where it has connotations somewhere within the development between Hellenistic Jewish cosmological speculation and Gnostic usage, and Colossians' usage may well have served as the catalyst for its later more frequent occurrence.[19]

18. Philo appears to have done his teaching in the synagogues, which, in an intentional comparison to the philosophical schools, he describes as "the schools of Moses" (cf. *Spec.* 2.62; *Hypoth.* 7.14; *Mos.* 2.215–16).

19. Cf. also Dillon, "*Pleroma*," 108.

Talk of the Logos was a way of articulating the presence of the Creator God in the cosmos while at the same time preserving this God's transcendence. In maintaining that transcendence, various schools of thought proposed further mediation with the world of the senses. Plato had already done so with his distinction between the demiurge and lesser gods (e.g., *Tim.* 42E). Plutarch refers to the existence of daemons, divine entities inferior to the first God or the One, who are said to be "by nature on the boundary between gods and humans" (*Def. orac.* 416C). The daemons can mediate in either a beneficial or hostile manner towards humans, by communicating God's will (*Amat.* 758E; *Gen. Socr.* 580C; *Fac.* 944C–D) and offering them care and protection (*Amat.* 758A–B) or by punishing them (*Def. orac.* 417A–B), and can be influenced or won over by gifts, prayers, and ceremonies. They are also closely associated with the four cosmic elements—water, earth, fire, and air—and were thought by some to be made out of fire or air. In Stoicism and Middle Platonism the further one got from the plenitude of the noetic cosmos into the material world and from the absolute Logos or Mind into the realm of sense perception, the greater the likelihood of experiencing irrational forces and disharmony. But what was wrong with the world could be traced not only to the changeableness and corruption that resulted from the mingling and separating of the material elements of the world but also to their source in the cosmic powers. Hellenistic Judaism already had in its tradition a belief in intermediaries in the heavenly world, the angels, and these were readily linked with the daemons and their functions in Graeco-Roman philosophy. Both Philo and Plutarch can employ the terms *archai*, rulers, and *dunameis*, powers, used in Jewish apocalyptic writings to designate angelic beings, for the forces underlying the elements of the cosmos (*ta stoicheia tou kosmou*). Wisdom of Solomon states that Gentiles "supposed that either fire or wind or swift air, or the circle of the stars, or turbulent water, or the luminaries of heaven were the gods that rule the world" (13:2; cf. also Philo, *Contempl.* 3; *Decal.* 53)

This, of course, provides a link to the cosmic dimension of the rival spirituality mentioned in Colossians, whose writer condemns it as "according to the elemental spirits of the universe" (*ta stoicheia tou kosmou*), and not "according to Christ" (2:8). While there is no clear evidence that the actual term *fullness* was prominent in its teaching, the writer clearly thinks the notion of cosmic plenitude is relevant to its concerns, because he decides to draw on this notion again immediately after this note of censure (2:9–10a) and to follow the mention of Christ's fullness by depicting him as "the head of every ruler and authority" (2:10b). In this section of correction (2:8–23) he also talks of Christ's defeat of the rulers and authorities (2:15) and associates the rival wisdom's regulations with the elemental spirits of the cosmos

(2:20). In addition, two of the practices, on which it insists, are related to the cosmic dimension. "Observing festivals, or new moons, or sabbaths" lists calendrical features that are found together in the Jewish Scriptures (cf. LXX Ezek 45:17; 1 Chr 23:31; 2 Chr 2:3; 31:3; Hos 2:13), but there is no hint here that such special days are being observed because of the desire to obey Torah or because keeping them was a special mark of Jewish identity. The first two terms were just as much part of Graeco-Roman calendars, and Elchasai taught his followers that the Sabbath was to be observed because it was one of the days controlled by the course of the stars (cf. Hippolytus, *Haer.* 9.16.2–3). It is probable, then, that in the rival spirituality observance of such days was linked to a desire to please the "elemental spirits of the universe" held to rule the heavenly bodies and therefore in control of the calendar. The other practice involves "worship of angels," a phrase that has given rise to much debate, but where the most plausible interpretation is that it is the writer's derogatory way of describing the well-attested practice of invoking angels to ward off other evil spirit powers and to provide special knowledge.[20] Angels and other spirit powers needed to be placated if there was to be any hope of both security in an unstable world and participation in the fullness of the divine presence.

In this context Colossians offers its own wisdom about the cosmos in which its readers find themselves. As is made explicit in 2:9, the transcendent source of its plenitude is not a cosmic sphere of ideas or forms separate from or in some ambiguous relation to God but is to be identified with God: "all the fullness of deity." "Fullness" already indicates completeness or totality, so this tautological expression emphasizes that there is nothing outside the divine presence and power. If achieving a full life is the goal of wisdom teaching, then the wisdom of Colossians claims that believers already have this fullness in Christ: "you have been filled in him" (2:10a). Both the preceding—"in him the whole fullness of deity dwells bodily" (2:9)—and the following—"who is the head of every ruler and authority"(2:10b)—statements underline that its source is Christ, and both point back to the Christ-hymn, which is now being applied to believers' lives. There too it is stated that thrones, dominions, rulers, and powers are subordinated to Christ through both creation and reconciliation (1:16, 20) and that "in him all the fullness was pleased to dwell" (1:19). In its context this talk of believers having been filled is meant to undercut the rival Christian spirituality. Since

20. The evidence for taking the phrase as a subjective genitive, where it would refer to worship performed by angels, is very weak, and Arnold, *Colossian Syncretism*, esp. 8–102, convincingly makes the case for the objective genitive and its reference to calling on angels to influence one's own fate favorably through protection and provision of revelations and the fate of others malevolently through curses.

the totality of deity is embodied in Christ, there can be no grounds for a person who confesses Christ seeking God or cosmic plenitude elsewhere or thinking that the way to divine fullness was through cosmic intermediaries. Indeed, if Christ's fullness entails his headship over these powers, then to participate in that fullness is to make any ascetic and cultic observances designed to appease the rulers and powers completely redundant. And if the fullness dwells in Christ bodily and not just in the noetic cosmos, then there is none of the dualism, found in some versions of the tradition that built on Plato, between the God of the higher world and the human body viewed as an impediment to the ascent of the soul from the lower world.

In many ways the hymnic material's statement about all the fullness being in Christ sums up the thrust of its praise as a whole. Whoever composed it originally has taken Hellenistic Jewish thought about the relation between God's transcendence of and yet immanence in the cosmos in terms of Wisdom and the Logos and adapted it in the light of belief in Christ. Virtually all its language can be found in relation to Sophia in Proverbs and Wisdom and to Sophia and the Logos in Philo. As in the philosophical schools, the Christ-hymn presupposes some major disruption in cosmic harmony but shows little interest in explaining how this occurred. It focuses on Christ not only as the divine agent in the creation and maintenance of the cosmos but also, as in the case of Philo's Logos, as the one through whom the fullness reconciles and restores harmony to the cosmos. Since, in the present form of the hymnic material, 1:19 is most immediately a supporting statement for a previous assertion that began with a reference to Christ's status by virtue of the resurrection and since 1:20 goes on to speak of reconciliation through the cross, the claim is that in Christ's existence as a whole, culminating in the death and resurrection, the divine fullness can be seen to have been displayed. The conviction that Christ's identity by virtue of the resurrection meant that he must always have had this status, and thus he pre-existed as the creative and sustaining principle of the cosmos, is built into this praise of the cosmic Christ. Christ in his fullness now sums up all that God is in interaction with the cosmos.

In the spirituality of Colossians Christ's identity and the pattern of what has taken place in him are imprinted on the cosmos and radically shape the experience of humans in this cosmos. As the point of union between the transcendent source of the world's life and that world's physical and sensible reality, Christ is the energizing principle of the cosmos. That principle is no longer thought of as reason or pure intellect or even as the personified figure of Wisdom but as the exalted Christ who remains the crucified Jesus. The plenitude of the cosmos is not impersonal but has a human face, that of Jesus Christ, and the corollary is that human participation in plenitude is not only for the intellect, residing in the soul, but for the whole of embodied existence. Such participation in plenitude also embraces the experience of pain and suffering, because the fullness that resided in Christ has restored cosmic harmony precisely in his suffering and death. Colossians underscores this point by bringing together in 1:20 two images the undisputed Paul had employed separately—"blood" to denote Christ's violently taken life in contexts where the sacrificial nature of his death was to the fore, and "cross," the more general image, to convey the ignominy of this death by Roman execution. Paradoxically, in this cosmic spirituality the achievement of cosmic harmony and peace is accomplished through absorbing the worst consequences of cosmic disharmony—the irrationality of violent passions and the dissolution of death. Quite distinctively from that of any other ancient wisdom, that of Colossians integrates in a remarkable fashion statements about Christ's cosmic and universal significance with the particulars of his death as a victim, bleeding and suffocating in humiliation on a cross.

The addressees are reminded that they have already been filled through their relation to this Christ (2:10). They are attuned to the plenitude of the cosmos, the abundant fullness of its source of life, a life characterized by the one who fills it. They have already been filled but they also need to continue to appropriate this fullness, to be further filled with knowledge of God's will (1:9; 2:2), to grow communally (1:10; 2:7, 19), and thereby to reach completion or maturity (1:28; 4:12). The relation between the fullness of Christ in creating, sustaining, and reconciling the cosmos and his fullness in the life of believers is not spelled out precisely, but it is made clear that it is exhibited in the church as his body in a special way (cf. 1:18), presumably because this is where its relational and moral qualities should come to expression. For Colossians, if Christ's fullness pervades and permeates the cosmos, nothing less can be the case within the community of the new humanity, where he is all in all (3:11).

2.2 Spirituality as Learning to Die

Closely associated with the imaginary about the cosmos in ancient philosophy is another major theme—wisdom as training for death through the liberation of the soul from its bodily passions in order to be able to contemplate the whole.[21] Plato's *Phaedo* was particularly influential in the promotion of this spirituality through its claim that "those who pursue philosophy aright study nothing but dying and being dead" (64). Since the full life is possible only when the soul is separated from the body at death, what is being called for is a program of *askesis* enabling that future liberation

21. On this, see e.g., Hadot, *Philosophy*, 93–101; Aune, "Human Nature," 305–12.

ahead of time in this life (cf. *Phaed.* 61C–69E; 80C–84B). This is what Plato's Socrates calls "the practice of dying" or "the study of death" (*Phaed.* 81A). In Ps.-Plato, *Axiochus* 370E, Socrates' approach to the whole matter of dying frees Axiochus from his fear of death and enables him to say, "I have become a new person." "Death is therefore both a biological phenomenon, and more importantly, a way of living in this world in which the self is transformed."[22] In the Platonic tradition, then, the spiritual exercise of training for death was a process of purification, the stripping away of the passions that hamper the soul, so that human affairs and death itself are seen to be insignificant as the soul is freed to experience the life of the intellect that leads to the reality of universal Reason. Epicurus did not believe in the continuation of the soul after death; death, therefore, should not produce fear but be seen as the appropriate ending of a flourishing and good life. In this sense he too held that the philosopher's vocation entailed training for dying, "because to practice living well and to practice dying well are one and the same" (*Ep. ad Men.* 126). In commenting on the Epicurean slogan "Think on death," the Stoic Seneca explains, "The meaning is clear—that it is a wonderful thing to learn thoroughly how to die. . . . In saying this, he bids us think on freedom. . . . He who has learned to die has unlearned slavery" (*Ep.* 26.8).

There are indications that a similar program of mortification was part of the rival philosophy in view in Colossians. This included abstinence in regard to food and drink (2:16a) with its accompanying taboos, which are caricatured as "do not handle, do not taste, do not touch" (2:21). In 2:18 the insistence on *tapeinophrosunē* is mentioned. This Greek term could have more positive (humility) or more negative (humiliation) connotations, and in this polemical context the latter—"self-abasement" (NRSV)—is the more plausible. It was frequently associated with fasting and, in its mention immediately before the worship of angels and visions, this also appears to be the case here.[23] The term is listed again as the second of three features of the asceticism promoted by this spirituality—self-imposed piety, self-abasement/fasting, and severity to the body—judged by the writer to have only the appearance of wisdom (2:23). When these ascetic regulations are linked to other clues about the teaching, then abstaining from certain foods

22. Aune, "Human Nature," 306.

23. It is employed as a technical term for fasting in the Shepherd of Hermas (*Vis.* III, 10.6; *Sim.* V, 3.7) and Tertullian (*Jejun.* 12). Cognate terms are also employed in the LXX for fasting, where the practice is an expression of abasement before God (cf. e.g., Lev 16:29, 31; 23:27, 29, 32; Isa 58:3, 5; Ps 34:13–14). Fasting was also frequently a preparation for visionary experience and the reception of divine revelations (cf. Dan 10:2–9; 4 Ezra 5:13, 20; 9:23–25; 2 Bar 5:7–9; 12:5–7). Sometimes it is the preparation specifically for entrance into the heavenly realm (cf. Philo, *Mos.* 1.67–70; *Somn.* 1.33–37).

and drink at particular times is likely to have been seen as necessary for the soul's subduing or escaping from the physical body in order to achieve a state of purity in readiness for visionary experience and access to the heavenly realm. In this section that corrects the opposing spirituality, the writer twice uses the imagery of "stripping off" in unusual ways (2:11, 15), suggesting he may well have been using that spirituality's own terminology. In the first usage the language of "the stripping off the body of the flesh" would be an allusion to the way the alternative wisdom described its spiritual exercises of mortification.

When in his own wisdom paraenesis in 3:5 the writer instructs, "Put to death, therefore, your members that are on the earth," this sounds for all the world like a straightforward endorsement of such a program of training for death, one that needs to deal with the members of physical bodies dependent on the lower material realm.[24] But then comes a list, not of physical parts of the body, as he has led readers to expect, but of vices. This is more like the apprenticeship for death in the wisdom of the philosophical schools that focuses on dealing with the passions. In fact, the first list of five vices to be mortified includes passion and evil desire. A further list of five vices to be put off follows in 3:8, underlining that the impediment to a flourishing life is neither ignorance nor irrationality nor the downward drag of the body but sinful practices. Virtually all the vices and all the virtues that follow in 3:12–14 are familiar from the ethical advice offered by the philosophical schools, where as we noted, they can also be associated with the transformation to a new self. Here in 3:9–10 the translation of *anthrōpos* by "self" (NRSV, NIV) is too narrowly individualistic. In line with the Pauline tradition, the "old person" is the person as identified with the old humanity, living under the present evil age and its powers, while the "new person" is the believer as identified with the new humanity, the new order of existence inaugurated by Christ's death and resurrection. In their new context the vices and virtues selected are primarily those that will either disrupt or enhance the life of the new corporate humanity. The emphasis on sins of speech, which comes to the fore at the end of the catalogue of vices, is continued in the prohibition of lying. Its warrant is formulated in terms of the transformation believers have already undergone. They have "stripped off" (not simply "put off," which would correspond to the following "put on") the old person and its practices. The ascetic terminology of the alternative spirituality for acts of severity in relation to the physical body is again given an ethical twist. For Colossians the *askesis* of practicing dying is not accomplished simply through a process of education enabling detachment from the body and its

24. Both NRSV and NIV miss the force of this with their paraphrases of 3:5a.

passions through the heightening of the soul's capacity for reasoning. Nor is its basis the achievement of insight into one's own future death. Its source and motivation come rather from understanding and appropriating one's identification with a past death, that of Christ.

This has been made clear earlier in the letter. The readers' past act of "stripping off" the old humanity took place at the time they were "circumcised" in Christ (2:11–12). Instead of talking about their union with Christ in his death, burial, and resurrection, as does Paul in Rom 6, the writer speaks of their union with Christ in his circumcision, burial, and resurrection. The use of the metaphor of circumcision for Christ's death enables the writer to deal with the rival perspective on spirituality. Readers need to realize that the decisive "stripping off" occurred in the circumcision Christ underwent in his death, which was not merely the stripping off of a token part of the flesh, the foreskin, but a cutting off of his whole fleshly body from life. Believers' identification with Christ in the circumcision of his death is a spiritual ("made without hands") circumcision that needs to be appropriated for its ethical consequences (cf. 3:9). According to 2:15, in Christ's death God also "stripped off" the hostile cosmic intermediaries, the rulers and authorities, exposing them to public shame. The significance of these metaphors for the readers is spelled out in 2:20. Since Christ's death was the event in history at which the powers' domination was decisively brought to an end and since believers have died with Christ, they have also died to the powers of the old order, the elemental spirits of the universe. Both the powers and the regulations designed to appease them can have no hold over those, who, while living in the world, have experienced the liberating effect of having died in union with Christ. To learn to die in the spirituality of Colossians, then, is to recall the significance of baptism, in which believers not only died but were also buried with Christ (2:12). And since baptism signified also being made alive with Christ (2:12–13), it is to recall the role of this death to the old order in experiencing the fullness and flourishing of the new and thus to see mortification as part of the larger process of vivification.

2.3 Spirituality as "the View from Above"

"All the while the soul yearns after and is athirst for its native heavenly aether, always striving for the life there and the divine choral dance" (Ps.-Plato, *Axiochus* 366A). While the purified soul was usually held to ascend after death and remain above, the philosophical schools cultivated in their different ways an ascent in one's lifetime, predominantly through the faculty of the intellect, but also occasionally through ecstatic experiences (cf. e.g., Plutarch, *Def. orac.* 39, 40; Philo, *Opif.* 69–71; *Her.* 257, 265). In this wisdom the thinking soul was seen as able to overcome its attachment to the body and to ascend to the realm above from where it could achieve a total and universal perspective on the cosmos and the affairs of humans.[25] Not surprisingly this theme was frequently linked with that of training for death. Indeed Marcus Aurelius can cite Plato to the effect that "he who is discoursing about men should look also at earthly things as if he viewed them from some higher place," urge "look down from above on the countless herds of men and their countless solemnities," and then state "you can strip off the many useless things that are obstacles to you, for they depend entirely on your opinion; you will then gain for yourself a vast space by comprehending the whole universe in your mind" (*Ad Se Ipsum* 7.48; 9.30, 32). The well-known passage in Plato about the pair of winged horses and the charioteer indicates what is involved. The horse of noble breed, the divine part of the soul, soars upward to the heaven of heavens, while the horse of ignoble breed, the lower part of the soul, if not properly trained, drags against this, weighing the charioteer down to the earth (*Phaedr.* 247). Plato's Socrates says of the philosopher that "the outer form of him only is in the city: his mind disdaining the littlenesses and the nothingnesses of human things, is . . . measuring earth and heaven and the things which are under and on the earth and above the heaven, interrogating the whole nature of each and all in their entirety" (*Theaet.* 173). To ascend into the heights and view things from above is to attain a universal perspective, to see the life of the world for what it is, to realize the insignificance of human passions, worldly affairs, and death, and to experience serenity and joy. Philo sums it up well:

> For all those, whether among the Greeks or among the barbarians, who practise wisdom, . . . admire . . . a life of peace and tranquillity, contemplating nature and all the things in it, investigating earth and sea, and the air, and the heaven, and all the different natures in each of them, dwelling in their minds with the moon, and the sun, and the rest of the stars, both wandering and fixed. Their bodies, indeed, are firmly planted on the earth, but their souls are furnished with wings, so that, rising into the ether, they may closely survey all the powers above. . . . Being, therefore, full of all kinds of excellence, they are accustomed to disregard all those things which affect the body and external circumstances, practised in looking upon things indifferent as really indifferent, and armed by study against the pleasures and appetites, and, in short, always striving to raise themselves

25. See esp. Hadot, *Philosophy*, 238–50, a chapter titled "The View from Above."

above the passions. . . . Such people, who are made joyful by
their virtues, celebrate the whole of their lives as a festival.[26]

In the spirituality against which the writer of Colossians warns the
concern to subdue the body in order to experience the heavenly world has
already been noted. Its preoccupation is with an "above" similar to the realm
of the planets and stars and their daemons explored by the mind in the
other philosophies. It seeks out the heavenly intermediaries—the rulers and
powers, the spirits controlling the elements of the cosmos, the angels—who
are also a means of ascending further to knowledge and experience of the
divine. From the writer's perspective, the ascent of the soul in this spirituality led to its insistence on visionary experiences—"which he has seen when
entering" the above—and to arrogant claims that the mind had thereby
achieved special insight (2:18b).

Given the dangers the writer perceives in such preoccupations, it is
all the more remarkable that his own spiritual wisdom appears to endorse
emphatically the same concerns: "Seek the things that are above" (3:1b),
"set your minds on things that are above" (3:2).[27] The transcendent realm
remains of paramount significance, but in the spirituality of Colossians
this is because it is "where Christ is" at present (3:1c). The above is the
locus of the risen and exalted Christ, "seated at the right hand of God"
(3:1d). Believers in Christ already have access to this realm above, because
just as their baptism signified a union with him in his death, so also it
signified a participation with him in his risen and exalted life (3:1a, cf.
2:11–12). To seek and to set one's mind on things above are, on this view,
to appropriate the access to the above that one already has in union with
Christ. They are not activities needed in addition to belief in Christ but
the outworkings of what God has graciously provided in Christ. The view
from above that this entails further underscores believers' status in relation to the powers. Not only does having died with Christ free them from
bondage to the elemental spirits of the cosmos, but having been raised with
the one who has the position of authority over the cosmos also confirms
that such powers have no hold over humans because they are subordinate
to Christ's sovereign purposes. The instruction to set one's mind on things
above is strengthened by the contrast added: "not on things that are on
earth" (3:2). Is this in order to cultivate the indifference to human affairs
that often accompanies the view from above in philosophical spiritualities
or even the disdain of the physical found in some cases there and certainly

26. *Spec.* 2.44–46.

27. See the complementary discussion of this passage in this volume by Gorman,
"This-Worldliness." Cf. also Smith, *Heavenly Perspective*, 173–84.

in the rival wisdom in view here? That would be to put this exhortation in contradiction to other emphases in the letter and, as noted earlier, the writer will immediately gloss "your members that are on the earth" as the vices of the old humanity (3:5). The contrast, then, appears to be shaped by an eschatological perspective and to have an ethical dimension. Because of Christ's exaltation, the designation "the things above" highlights the life and rule of the age to come already present in heaven with Christ (3:1). The phrase "the things on earth," on the other hand, refers to the earth as the arena of this present evil age, the sphere of the flesh (2:18, 23), where life is still in subjection to the cosmic powers (2:20).

The spirituality of Colossians assumes the importance of experience of the transcendent realm but gives both the realm and the experience of it a distinctive christological content. This amounts to a redirection of the ascent of the soul or the mind. In the various philosophies, including the one specifically in view in the letter, the starting point is the earthly situation of the wise, from which by their own efforts and techniques they will move beyond the body, either training the mind to contemplate the cosmos or subduing the body to gain visionary experience, thereby achieving their privileged insight on reality from above. The writer has already aimed barbed comments at this approach in 2:18, claiming that its advocate's attitude is evidence that, far from ascending into heaven, the mind has remained firmly bound to the sphere of the flesh. The wisdom proposed by Colossians moves in the reverse direction, seeing the starting-point and source of the believer's life in the resurrected Christ in heaven, from where it will eventually be publicly revealed (cf. 3:4) and from where in the meantime it works itself out in earthly life (cf. 3:5—4:6). Believers' lives are so bound up with Christ's that Christ can be called "our life" and they can be said to be "hidden with Christ in God" (3:3b–4a). The latter phrase has a threefold significance for the readers. (i) They do not need to strive to ascend to the transcendent God; their relationship to Christ is such that they *already* participate in the life of God. (ii) The lives they live on earth from their source above have a hidden aspect; their union with Christ is a reality accessible to faith not sight. (iii) As in apocalyptic writings, what is at present hidden and secure in heaven is to be revealed at the end of history; the true nature of their relationship with Christ in the above will become manifest at the consummation when they participate in Christ's revelation from above in glory.

The issue for the philosophical schools was how the vision from above, from the standpoint of universal nature, could be lived out in the world with its customs and conventions, how the tension between the ideal perspective of noetic wisdom and daily life could be resolved.[28] In Colossians the view from above is a view of life in the world under the lordship of Christ. Spiritual wisdom entails conduct that is worthy of this Lord (1:10). Life in the community of believers is to display the loving, forgiving, and peaceful qualities of his rule (3:12–16). The exhortation "And whatever you do, in word or deed, do everything in the name of the Lord Jesus . . ." (3:17) makes unmistakably clear that the scope of Christ's lordship extends from community life and worship to encompass all of life. It provides an appropriate transition to the household code, where the title "Lord" occurs seven times in nine verses (3:18—4:1). Having a Lord in heaven should motivate masters to pursue justice and fairness (4:1), while the fear of the Lord, to which slaves are exhorted for their motivation, is of course at the heart of spiritual wisdom in the scriptural tradition (cf. e.g., Prov 9:9; Sir 1:14, 27; 19:20).[29]

3. Spirituality in Dialogue

The definitions of spirituality in our own time, with which this essay began, raise the question of how the broader cultural sense of a full life and the more specific religious sense that invokes the divine as transformative might be in dialogue.

In the case of Colossians its spiritual wisdom engages some of the major aspirations for human flourishing of its day but, in doing so, brings to bear the resources of its own Pauline tradition about the gospel of the crucified and risen Christ. The engagement leads to new applications and expressions of that gospel, to a development of the Pauline tradition, and at the same time to a distinctive contribution to the wider conversation, as it radically reconfigures and redirects common aspirations from within its own perspective. In affirming those aspirations, Colossians also accepts basic aspects of the cosmological thinking of the day and contains considerable overlap with the virtues that others considered to be necessary for a full life. But its distinctiveness, produced by its christological convictions, is also considerable. It recognizes that for humans to have a wise, responsible and flourishing relation to the cosmos, they have to be able to imagine their place within it. This cosmos, however, is one informed and permeated by God's creative and reconciling purposes displayed in history in the decisive events of Christ's death and resurrection. It recognizes that humans have to

---

28. Cf. Hadot, *Philosophy*, 56–59, 103–4.

29. For more detailed analysis of Colossians' views on household management, see esp. the complementary treatments of Lincoln, "Household Code," and Barclay, "Ordinary but Different."

deal with evil passions and subservience to death, fate, and power structures beyond the human. The resource for dealing with these, however, is again what God has done in Christ, in the death and resurrection in which believers participate, and not simply human efforts in moral training for death or techniques of appeasement. It recognizes that humans aspire to a comprehensive vision of life and its meaning that somehow transcends their physical and finite limitations. But its own view "from above" is not that offered by disembodied universal reason but that provided through participation in God's action in raising and exalting Christ, which enables all of life to be seen in the light of Christ's lordship.

For those interested in the dialogue and debate between Christian spirituality and other spiritualities in our own time this wisdom of Colossians can remain highly instructive in its combination of affirmation and radical critique. It also offers a clear reminder that Christian spirituality is itself contested and that judgments have to be made whether some versions of it have become too greatly assimilated to aspects of culture that are in conflict with faithful appropriation of the gospel. Finally, there can be no mistaking that for Colossians, as for other ancient philosophies, the dialogue about spiritual wisdom is not simply about words or ideas but about living a transformed life. It measures wisdom not merely by its claims but by the quality of life it produces. Its own cosmic wisdom is to be displayed in wise living in local worshipping communities and in society. How far the proponents of a particular spirituality exhibit the transformative wisdom it advocates remains a hugely significant factor in contemporary dialogue about transcendence and immanence, renunciation and flourishing.

13

2 Timothy 3:10–17
and a Spirituality of Persecution

Lloyd K. Pietersen
University of Gloucestershire

1. Introduction

FOR THE PURPOSE OF this essay I am not primarily interested in a detailed exegesis of the text to seek to ascertain the spirituality of its author, but rather in both the spirituality advocated within the text of 2 Timothy and, in particular, in the kind of spirituality(ies) produced by the text. I am, therefore, focusing on Schneiders' "third meaning" of biblical spirituality:

> A third meaning of biblical spirituality, which comes closer to what I am particularly interested in, is not so much the spirituality(ies) that produced the Bible insofar as historical and literary critical methods can establish that, nor in the spirituality(ies) we find in the Bible, but the spirituality that the Bible *produces* in readers by their contact/interaction with it.[1]

This approach to biblical spirituality is therefore primarily concerned with the reception history of texts attuned to its effects on the spirituality of readers both in the first century CE and subsequently. By "spirituality" I mean the lived experience of readers, which will be profoundly shaped by the social imaginaries they inhabit.[2] This lived experience, for biblical spiritual-

1. See the chapter by Schneiders in this volume, 132.
2. For the concept of "social imaginary" I am deeply indebted to Charles Taylor

ity, focuses on the transformational process involved in the divine-human relationship.[3] This essay, therefore, explores first, the kinds of spirituality advocated by the text of the Pastoral Epistles (PE), particularly 2 Timothy, and second, the ways in which readers' experiences of persecution have shaped the way they have lived their lives before God. Within the confines of this chapter I necessarily have to be selective, so I shall focus on the immediate first-century context of persecution together with the ways in which this text was read in the first few centuries. I then turn to a much neglected area in mainstream biblical scholarship—namely, the reception of this text by sixteenth- and seventeenth-century Anabaptists for whom 2 Tim 3:12 particularly resonated with their experience of persecution by both Protestants and Catholics. I conclude with some brief reflections on contemporary interactions with the text.

2. The Spirituality Advocated by the PE

The authenticity of the PE has been the primary issue in their interpretation since the rise of historical-critical biblical scholarship. Of all the epistles in the Pauline corpus these are the ones whose Pauline authorship is most contested. The scholarly consensus, although challenged by a number of recent commentaries, is that they are late and reflect "an ecclesial situation in which the communities for which they were written were trying to find a niche in the Greco-Roman world; and their eschatology has lost its urgency because the expectation of an imminent Parousia has long since waned."[4] This results in a particular view of the spirituality of the PE, characterized especially by the key word *eusebeia*, that suggests an accommodation to wider society and the adoption of Hellenistic notions of piety. A key advocate of this position was Dibelius, who famously described the outlook of the Pastorals as "the ideal of good Christian citizenship" (*christliche Bürgerlichkeit*).[5] However, this view fails to take sufficient account of 2 Tim

---

whose concept concerns the ways in which ordinary people imagine their world, and this is usually "carried in images, stories, legends, etc." See Taylor, *Secular Age*, 171–76.

3. So Waaijman, *Spirituality*, 6, 312, 424.

4. Collins, *1 & 2 Timothy and Titus*, 9. Recent commentaries advocating Pauline authorship include Johnson, *First and Second Letters to Timothy*; Mounce, *Pastoral Epistles*; Towner, *Timothy and Titus*. Marshall, *Pastoral Epistles*, advocates the notion of "allonymity"—the view that, although not written by Paul, they were written soon after his death by someone close to him so that they faithfully represent his thought. Prior, *Paul the Letter Writer,* and O'Connor, "2 Timothy," argue for the authenticity of 2 Timothy but not the other letters.

5. For a critique of Dibelius' position, see Pietersen, "Spirituality."

3:10–17, which clearly envisages a climate in which believers continue to face persecution.

2.1 Timothy as Paul's Last Will and Testament

Whatever one makes of the authorship of the Pastoral Epistles, and I remain convinced of their pseudonymity, there is a recent trend in PE scholarship to treat 2 Timothy particularly as an individual letter rather than as a component of a corpus.[6] Second Timothy purports to be written by Paul, who is in prison in Rome (1:8, 17), chained like a criminal (2:9), and expecting imminent death (4:6). At the literary level, therefore, it is best to regard 2 Timothy as a testamentary letter functioning as Paul's "last will and testament." The following characteristics are typical of the testamentary genre:

1. Paul's life functions paradigmatically (1:13; 3:10–12).

2. Paul is concerned that his ministry is passed on to others who will be faithful guardians of the tradition (2:2–3).

3. There are predictions about the future success of heretical teachers (2:20—3:9), and this serves as a warning to Timothy to continue as a faithful teacher in the Pauline tradition (4:1–5).

4. Paul assures his readers that God's will will ultimately prevail, rewarding the faithful and punishing the opponents (2:11–13; 4:8).

5. Finally, and typical of the testamentary genre, there is a statement concerning Paul's impending death (4:6).[7]

As Bauckham notes, the form of the testamentary letter enables the author to "communicate at a distance *in space* (like all letters) and also at a distance

6. See, e.g., Prior, *Paul the Letter Writer*, 168; Murphy-O'Connor, "2 Timothy," 403–10; Johnson, *First and Second Letters to Timothy*, 63–64; Towner, *Timothy and Titus*, 27–31; Zehr, *1 & 2 Timothy, Titus*, 18–20. For a recent commentary continuing to regard the PE as a corpus, see Fiore, *Pastoral Epistles*, 5–7. With the exceptions of Prior and O'Connor, it is virtually undisputed that a single author wrote the PE.

7. So, Fiore, *Pastoral Epistles*, 8–9. See especially Martin, *Pauli Testamentum*; Wolter, *Die Pastoralbriefe*, 222–41; Redalie, *Paul après Paul*, 101–7, and also Bassler, *1 Timothy, 2 Timothy, Titus*, 22–23; Fee, *1 and 2 Timothy, Titus*, 13; Quinn and Wacker, *First and Second Letters to Timothy*, 566–67. For dissenting views, regarding 2 Timothy as a personal paraenetic letter, see Johnson, *First and Second Letters to Timothy*, 320–24; Marshall, *Pastoral Epistles*, 12; Prior, *Paul the Letter Writer*, 110–12, and Towner, *Timothy and Titus*, 79. Whatever decision is taken on genre, the significant point for this essay is that for the majority of Christian history 2 Timothy has been received both as genuinely Pauline and, therefore, as Paul's last will and testament. Biblical spirituality that seeks to engage with this text takes this reception of authorship and situation seriously.

in time, for in a written testament it is possible explicitly to address not only those who read it immediately but also those who will read it after the testator's death."[8] The purpose, therefore, of such a testamentary letter is to ensure that Paul's normative teaching is interpreted for a new situation/generation. In our text, therefore, it is imperative to note that persecution is the expected outcome for believers intent on imitating Paul. Furthermore, the author draws on events narrated in Acts to infer that persecution involves the likelihood of expulsion (Acts 13:50—Antioch), attempted stoning (Acts 14:5—Iconium), and actual stoning to the point of near death (Acts 14:19—Lystra). Although the author, again drawing on these events, can confidently assert that "the Lord rescued [Paul] from all of [these persecutions]" (2 Tim 3:11), nevertheless the reader of the letter is well aware that Paul's current situation when writing is one of imprisonment and certain death (2 Tim 4:6)—not all persecution does, in fact, result in deliverance.

2.2 Does Persecution Imply Martyrdom?

The reference to Paul's death raises the question as to whether the author has martyrdom in mind when he refers to persecution. The notion of suffering and persecution pervades the New Testament. Every letter in the generally accepted Pauline corpus refers to this theme. In Romans Paul speaks of boasting in suffering (*en tais thlipsesin*) because it produces endurance (5:3) and considers that "the sufferings [*ta pathēmata*] of this present time are not worth comparing with the glory about to be revealed in us" (8:18). In 1 Corinthians he speaks of being beaten, homeless, reviled, and persecuted (*diōkomenoi*) (4:11–12). Second Corinthians exhorts the Corinthian believers to "patiently endure the same sufferings [*tōn autōn pathēmatōn*] that we are also suffering [*kai hēmeis paschomen*]" (1:6) and reminds them that Paul suffered persecution (*diōkomenoi*) (4:9), beatings, imprisonments, riots, and punishment (6:4–10); the catalogue of hardships in 11:22–29 includes numerous imprisonments and floggings, being close to death often, receiving thirty-nine lashes five times, being beaten with rods three times, and being stoned once. Galatians rebukes those who seek to escape persecution (*mē diōkōntai*) for the cross of Christ (6:12). In Philippians Paul is in prison and speaks of the privilege of suffering (*paschein*) for Christ (1:29). First Thessalonians praises the believers for receiving the word with joy despite persecution (*en thlipsei pollē*) (1:6), speaks of Paul suffering (*propathontes*) and being shamefully mistreated at Philippi (2:2), and highlights

8. Bauckham, *Jude, 2 Peter*, 133. As well as 2 Peter, Bauckham categorizes 2 Timothy as another example of the testamentary letter in the NT.

the solidarity of the Thessalonian believers with the churches in Judea due to their common experience of suffering (*epathete*) at the hands of compatriots (2:14). Finally, in Philemon, Paul writes from the experience of being imprisoned (1, 9–10, 13).

The theme of suffering, persecution, and imprisonment is also found in the deuteropaulines (e.g., Eph 3:1, 13; Col 1:24; 2 Thess 1:4–6) and in Heb 10:32–36; 1 Pet 3:14; 4:12–19; 5:9–10. In all these texts suffering and persecution are very real and the threat of possible death is undoubtedly present, but none of them speak of actual martyrdom.[9] Nevertheless, as Middleton notes with reference to Paul in particular, such texts provide the framework in which subsequent emphasis on Christian martyrdom could develop.

> Paul is not a radical martyr, nor does he advocate radical martyrdom, though he does develop many of the theological concepts that enabled radical martyrology to develop. Three important aspects of radical martyrdom are crucially developed by Paul. First, the idea that suffering was the only way to demonstrate one was an authentic believer. Secondly, Paul advances the example of Jesus as the model of suffering to be imitated by Christians. Thirdly, not only did the believer imitate Jesus but also the participation theology pioneered by Paul could easily be transformed into the means by which the martyr could contribute to the cosmic war effort in later Christian martyrology. This development takes another dramatic turn in the Gospel of Mark.[10]

The reference to Mark above points to accounts in the Synoptic Gospels that could well be construed as a call to embrace martyrdom. The paradigmatic text is Mark 8:34–38 (parallels Matt 10:38–39; Luke 9:23–26), in which willingness to undergo crucifixion (taking up the cross) seems to be a condition of discipleship. That this is the likely import of Mark 8:34 is reinforced by the Lukan redaction which adds *kath' hēmeran* ("daily") to the injunction to take up the cross, thus softening its impact (although even Luke has a version of this saying without the addition in 14:27). Furthermore, the apocalyptic discourse of Mark 13 reflects the position of Jesus' disciples where they can expect to be put on trial, beaten, and delivered up to death (Mark 13:9–13). The parallel in Matt 24:9–14 has disciples tortured and put to death and Luke 21:12–19, which follows Mark more closely, has

9. However, the reference to "those who have died [*peri tōn koimōmenōn*]" in 1 Thess 4:13 may refer to martyrdom. This is the same verb as is used as a euphemism for the death of Stephen in Acts 7:60. See the discussion in Middleton, *Radical Martyrdom*, 143. Middleton also discusses the possibility of Philippians as a martyrological treatise (143–45).

10. Ibid., 146.

some disciples put to death. The Synoptics, therefore, reflect a situation where followers of Jesus can expect persecution, with death as a possible, even likely, outcome.[11] Finally, the last book of the Bible clearly portrays a situation where some Christians are facing persecution, as reflected in the letters to the churches at Smyrna (Rev 2:10–11) and Pergamum (2:13). Furthermore, Rev 6:9–11 and 11:7 specifically refer to martyrs.

In conclusion, most of the material in the New Testament suggests a context in which Christians can expect suffering, persecution, and death. However, the expectation of death should not be construed at this stage as "radical martyrdom"—those who subsequently actively sought death, even if that meant provoking their own arrest. The only named Christian martyrs in the entire New Testament are Stephen (Acts 7:54–60), James (Acts 12:1–2), and Antipas (Rev 2:13).[12]

2.3 Persecution in the First Century

The pervasive emphasis on suffering and persecution found in the New Testament is somewhat surprising given what we know historically about the persecution of Christians in the first century. Apart from the scapegoating, torturing, and killing of Christians by Nero in 64, as recorded by Tacitus, *Annals* 15.44 (and which was unlikely to have spread beyond Rome), there is little evidence of sustained state persecution in the first century. Even the previous widely held view that Revelation reflects subsequent state persecution of Christians by Domitian no longer holds sway among biblical scholars.[13] This lack of state persecution is substantiated by the famous letter from Pliny to Trajan in 113 concerning Christians in Bithynia, of which I shall say more below. This letter, written less than twenty years after the reign of Domitian ended, clearly demonstrates that there was no empire-wide edict against Christians. Trajan's response specifically indicates that Christians

11. For a detailed discussion of the various interpretations of these texts and a compelling argument that they do envisage martyrdom, see ibid., 146–58.

12. For a nuanced argument demonstrating that "the New Testament stands as a crucial transition between the theology of martyrdom found in Judaism and that of the Christian radical martyrs," see ibid., 134–71 (171).

13. A significant number of recent commentaries on Revelation agree that there was no systematic state persecution by Domitian. Even Beale, who remains convinced of persecution under Domitian as the backdrop for Revelation, admits that the evidence only points to "the plausibility of selective yet significant persecution under Domitian. Therefore, later Christian sources referring to persecution under Domitian should not be wholly discounted, though some may overemphasize the programmatic nature and the severity of the persecution." Beale, *Revelation*, 13–14.

are not to be sought out and that Pliny should not accept unsubstantiated anonymous charges. So, how do we account for the extensive New Testament language concerning persecution? This surely must reflect in some way the actual experiences of first century Christians? It seems to me that the best way to account for the language in the light of the lack of evidence of systematic state persecution of Christians at this time is that "Christians, however much they may have wished, *could* not be good citizens of the Roman Empire. The standard for even the most nominal display of good citizenship was set far in excess of what the Christians could meet."[14] The significant issue concerns the Christian response to the impact of the imperial cult in the local regions. The primary impetus for the rise of the cult, especially in Asia Minor, did not come from the center but rather from the provinces themselves. The combination of informal cultural pressure generally and specific civic pressure at important festivals would have made the position of Christians intolerable. For example, "festivals were held both in temples and in civic centers, and civic mandates to participate extended even to people being required to offer sacrifices outside their houses as the festival procession passed by toward its final destination."[15] In addition, the influence of local cults such as that of Artemis in Ephesus, reflected in Acts 19, should not be underestimated.[16] Furthermore, and fundamentally, Christians' allegiance to Christ subverted all totalizing claims of the imperial cult. For them there was one Lord, one God and one Savior and so they could never accept the claims to either deity or salvation of the emperor or the local gods. Of course, they were not in a position to demonstrate publicly against either imperial or local cults—the first-century Greco-Roman world was no democracy! But refusal to participate in sacrifices offered at local festivals would have been noticed by their pagan neighbors, and this meant that Christians must have lived continually with the realization that they could be denounced before the authorities. This is precisely what happened in the case of Pliny, who writes of "those who were accused before me as Christians" (*Ep.* x.96.2). Those who confessed were executed (so Christians did have to live with an expectation of death as the ultimate penalty for their faith), but, significantly, those who denied the charge had to prove it by praying to the gods, making supplication to Trajan's statue and images of other gods, and cursing Christ—which, Pliny recognizes, genuine Christians would not do.[17]

14. Middleton, *Radical Martyrdom*, 40.

15. Beale, *Revelation*, 14. For the impact of the imperial cult on local regions, see especially Price, *Rituals and Power*, and Friesen, *Twice Neokoros*.

16. See Pietersen, "Spirituality," 157–59.

17. Pliny, *Ep.* x.96.5.

2.4 Christian Spirituality
in the Light of First-Century Persecution

Second Timothy 3:12 states emphatically that "all who want to live a godly life in Christ Jesus will be persecuted." The *kai . . . de* construction serves to emphasize the intervening word, *pantes*. It is *all* Christians, not just leaders, who can expect persecution if they lead a godly life.[18] This focus on the godly (*eusebōs*) life is significant for spirituality.

> Christian spirituality can best be understood using Waaijman's definition of spirituality as "the divine-human relational process . . . which is viewed as a layered process of transformation."[19] Waaijman emphasises four key divine-human relational moments: creation; humanity as God's representative; humanity as pupils of God; and humanity as covenant partners.[20] In the context of the Pastorals, with their clear emphasis on teaching and instruction, it is the third of these relational aspects that is primarily in view. For Waaijman the process of transformation consists of five layers: from non-being to being; from being malformed to being re-formed; becoming conformed to Christ; transformation in love; and final transformation in glory.[21] Although all layers are referred to in the Pastorals (e.g., 1 Tim 6:13a; Titus 3:3–5; 2 Tim 1:13–14; 1 Tim 6:18–19; 2 Tim 4:8), *eusebeia* as devotion to Christ focuses on the third process of conformation. We can see this by examining *eusebeia* and its cognates in 1 and 2 Timothy. The word group is used 11 times in these two letters (1 Tim 2:2; 3:16; 4:7, 8; 5:4; 6:3, 5, 6, 11; 2 Tim 3:5, 12). 1 Tim 4:7–8 is particularly significant. Godliness here is quite clearly not seen as a state of reverence or as cultic worship. It needs to be continually worked at (present tense imperative) and, using the well known analogy of physical training drawn from athletics, spiritual discipline is encouraged with a clear notion of "fullness" also being highlighted: "godliness is valuable *in every way, holding promise* for both the present life and the life to come." This way of life holds the promise of fulfillment both in the present and also eschatologically. 1 Tim 5:4 admit-

18. Persecution can thus be construed as an indication of the authentic Christian life. For an illuminating discussion of the power of the rhetoric of withstanding persecution to function as a form of cultural capital providing legitimacy to those persecuted, see Kelhoffer, *Persecution*.

19. Waaijman, *Spirituality*, 425.

20. Ibid., 446–54.

21. Ibid., 455–81.

tedly comes closest to the Greek concept of *eusebeia* as respect for the orders of life but this also reflects Hellenistic Jewish use of the concept. "For Paul, 'godliness' is the integration of the inward faith-commitment and outward faith-response that should characterize belief in God."[22] In other words, godliness represents authentic Christian existence. In 1 Tim 6:11 *eusebeia*, along with righteousness, faith, love, endurance, and gentleness, is to be pursued as part of the lifelong process of being conformed to Christ so that one becomes a person of God. 2 Tim 3:5 contrasts an outward form of godliness with true godliness which has transformative power.[23]

The choice of *eusebeia* to represent conformation to Christ is significant.[24] This subverts notions of *eusebeia* as reverence to the emperor and, in the context of Ephesus (to which at least 1 Timothy is addressed), as reverence to Artemis.[25] This is why Christians can expect persecution—their devotion to Christ manifestly prohibits a lifestyle of devotion to the emperor and the local gods. So, whenever their piety towards the emperor, Artemis, or whoever is questioned, their single-minded devotion to Christ inevitably brings them into conflict with the authorities.

Waaijman draws attention to the significance of the word *piety* for spirituality. He notes that in its basic Hellenistic context it is equivalent to our notion of "reverence." However, in the Middle Ages, writers such as Bonaventure and Aquinas no longer viewed piety as a virtue but as a gift of the Holy Spirit. Finally, he notes that the German *Frömmigkeit*, and the Dutch *vroomheid*, tend to translate the Latin *pietas* in the sense of an upright life validating itself in the life of everyday from the sixteenth century onwards. However, *Fromm* and *vroom* "go back to the basic meaning of 'standing out in front.' Hence also: leading the way, magnanimous, plucky, brave, upright."[26] I suggest this notion of bravery also forms part of the first-century Christian understanding of *eusebeia*.

22. Towner, *Timothy and Titus*, 339.

23. Pietersen, "Spirituality," 161–62.

24. The word group is found elsewhere in the New Testament only in Acts and 2 Peter.

25. For example, a second-century inscription inscribed on three sides of the base of a statue testifies to imperial involvement in the cult of Artemis at Ephesus and speaks specifically of devotion (*eusebeian*) to the goddess. See Horsley, *New Documents 4*, 74–82. A mid-first-century inscription on the base of a statue in Sardis speaks of piety (*eusebeias*) and thanksgiving (*eucharistias*) toward Tiberius Caesar, who is hailed as god and benefactor of the whole world. See Llewelyn, *New Documents 9*, 22.

26. Waaijman, *Spirituality*, 349–50. For the whole discussion on piety, see 348–51.

In the context of devotion to Christ inevitably leading to persecution, the author of 2 Timothy deliberately invokes the righteous sufferer of the Psalms. The language of 2 Tim 3:11 (*hoious diōgmous hypēnenka; kai ek pantōn me errysato ho kyrios*) echoes that of Ps 33:18 LXX = Ps 34:19 MT (*kai ek pasōn tōn thlipseōn errysato autous*). So the believer is to adopt the same attitude in the face of persecution as the righteous sufferer in the Psalms who waits on the Lord for deliverance. The prime spiritual qualities required of the believer are thus *endurance* (*hypopherō/hypomenō/hypomonē* [2 Tim 3:11; 2:10, 12; cf. Rom 5:3]) in the face of suffering and *hope* in the God who delivers. In this context it is instructive to note the specific addition to the salutation in 2 Tim 1:1, "for the sake of the promise of life that is in Christ Jesus" (*kat' epangelian zōēs tēs en Christō Iēsou*). The hope of the promise of life is to characterize the believer facing persecution. The phrase "promise of life" is found elsewhere in the New Testament only in 1 Tim 4:8, where it is linked specifically with *eusebeia* as noted above. Furthermore, as noted in the Middle Ages according to Waaijman, spirituality is a *gift of the Spirit* and, in the terms of 2 Timothy, this is precisely the "spirit of power and of love and of self-discipline" in place of "a spirit of cowardice" in the face of persecution (2 Tim 1:6–7). Finally, to nurture this kind of spirituality, believers are instructed to immerse themselves in the Scriptures (2 Tim 3:14–17). The spiritual discipline of *reading the sacred texts*, however this is employed, is designed to equip believers to function effectively in the world. The inspired text enables teaching, conviction of sin, correction, and training in righteousness.

However, the invocation of the righteous sufferer of the Psalms by the writer leads to the question, what should be the response of the persecuted toward their persecutors? For the psalmist there is frequently the desire for retribution (e.g., Pss 34:16, 21; 35:4–8; 69:22–28; 137:8–9), and this is a far cry from the gospel imperative to "love your enemies and pray for those who persecute you" (Matt 5:34). In the PE, Paul is presented as the archetypal persecutor and sinner (1 Tim 1:13–15), but he received mercy and an experience of the overflowing grace of God (1 Tim 1:13–14). In the light of this Timothy is exhorted to be "kindly to everyone" and to engage in gentle correction of opponents in the hope that they too will come to repentance (2 Tim 2:24–25). So, unlike the psalmist, the spirituality of persecution advocated by the PE involves a transformative response on behalf of the persecuted that is in keeping with the words of Jesus in the Sermon on the Mount.

3. Reception of 2 Timothy 3:12

The recognition that living a godly life inevitably leads to persecution (understood as real physical suffering that could lead to martyrdom) changes over time. Particularly instructive are modern commentators on the passage.

3.1 Commentators on 2 Timothy 3:12

3.1.1 Modern Commentators

Dibelius dismisses this verse with the following comment: "The apostle's experience of suffering is applied to all Christians in the form of a general thesis. Thus the verse expresses the intention of these biographical allusions."[27] He makes no attempt to relate this intention to the rest of the material in the Pastorals. Collins views this verse as part of the apocalyptic scheme begun in 2 Tim 3:1. It is characteristic of this scheme that the last days will be a period of terrible evil and suffering and the author simply "capitalizes on this Pauline tradition."[28] Nearly all commentators note that the author echoes Jesus' and/or Paul's comments concerning persecution.[29] Bassler suggests that persecution here arises from within the church.[30] However, no commentator attempts to link this verse, and the preceding ones concerning persecutions suffered by Paul, with the rest of the Pastorals.

3.1.2 Earlier Commentators

Origen cites 2 Tim 3:12 in the course of commenting on Matt 13:57. Writing in the period before Christendom emerged in the fourth century, he acknowledges that it is still possible for Christians of his day to be "hated and attacked" for seeking to imitate the prophetic life.[31] Theodoret sees the accusations made against him of unorthodoxy concerning the person of

---

27. Dibelius and Conzelmann, *Pastoral Epistles*, 119.

28. Collins, *1 & 2 Timothy and Titus*, 259.

29. E.g., Guthrie, *Pastoral Epistles*, 161; Kelly, *Pastoral Epistles*, 200; Fee, *1 and 2 Timothy, Titus*, 277; Knight, *Pastoral Epistles*, 440–41; Davies, *Pastoral Epistles*, 80; Marshall, *Pastoral Epistles*, 786–87; Mounce, *Pastoral Epistles*, 559; Quinn and Wacker, *First and Second Letters to Timothy*, 744–45; Johnson, *First and Second Letters to Timothy*, 418.

30. Bassler, *1 Timothy, 2 Timothy, Titus*, 165.

31. Origen, *Comm. Matt.* X.18.

Christ as persecution and cites 2 Tim 3:12 in this context.[32] Athanasius writes in the context of persecution arising from conflict within the church. He cites our text in connection with the Arian controversy, considers the struggle against heresy as equivalent to martyrdom, and defends his flight from the Arians, fearing capital punishment if he had been discovered.[33]

Leo the Great, however, reinterprets the verse as concerning temptations that beset the believer,[34] or slander from others.

> And it is not only to be reckoned persecution, when sword or fire or other active means are used against the Christian religion; for the direst persecution is often inflicted by nonconformity of practice and persistent disobedience and the barbs of ill-natured tongues: and since all the members of the Church are always liable to these attacks, and no portion of the faithful are free from temptation, so that a life neither of ease nor of labor is devoid of danger, who shall guide the ship amidst the waves of the sea if the helmsman quit his post?[35]

This interpretive move, or something like it, is made regularly by subsequent commentators. For example, Chrysostom states:

> "But martyrdom is not to be had nowadays." True, but there are contests to be had, as I have often told you, if we had the mind. "For they that wish", says the Apostle, "to live godly in Christ Jesus, shall suffer persecution" (2 Tim. iii. 12). They that live godly are always undergoing persecution, if not from men, at any rate from evil spirits, which is a more grievous persecution.[36]

And again:

> Each one that will live godly will be persecuted. Here he calls afflictions and sorrows, "persecutions," for it is not possible that a man pursuing the course of virtue should not be exposed to grief, tribulation, and temptations.[37]

Augustine states:

> Persecution, therefore, will never be lacking. For, when our enemies from without leave off raging and there ensues a span of

---

32. Theodoret, *Letters* 109.

33. Athanasius, *Ep. fest.* XI.9; *Ep. Aeg. Lib.* II.20–21; *Fug.* 3, 21.

34. Leo, *Sermons* LXXXV.4.

35. Leo, *Letters* CLXVII.2.

36. Chrysostom, *Hom. Act.* XXIV.

37. Chrysostom, *Hom. 2 Tim.* VIII; see too *Hom. 1 Thess.* III; *Hom. Heb.* V.7.

tranquility—even of genuine tranquility and great consolation at least to the weak—we are not without enemies within, the many whose scandalous lives wound the hearts of the devout. . . . So it is that those who want to live piously in Christ must suffer the spiritual persecution of these and other aberrations in thought and morals, even when they are free from physical violence and vexation.[38]

Luther refers to 2 Tim 3:12 twelve times and, on all but one occasion, equates persecution either with temptation, false teaching, or the burdens Christians have to bear.[39]

Calvin, in his commentary on 2 Timothy, also transforms persecution into slander and general opposition.

But it is asked, Must all men be martyrs? For it is evident that there have been many godly persons who have never suffered banishment, or imprisonment, or flight, or any kind of persecution. I reply, it is not always in one way that Satan persecutes the servants of Christ. But yet it is absolutely unavoidable that all of them shall have the world for their enemy in some form or other, that their faith may be tried and their steadfastness proved; for Satan, who is the continual enemy of Christ, will never suffer any one to be at peace during his whole life; and there will always be wicked men that are thorns in our sides. Moreover, as soon as zeal for God is manifested by a believer, it kindles the rage of all ungodly men; and, although they have not a drawn sword, yet they vomit out their venom, either by murmuring, or by slander, or by raising a disturbance, or by other methods. Accordingly, although they are not exposed to the same assaults, and do not engage in the same battles, yet they have a warfare in common, and shall never be wholly at peace and exempt from persecutions.[40]

3.1.3 Summary

All commentators, ancient and modern, link 2 Tim 3:12 to Jesus' and Paul's comments on persecution. Some, particularly modern commentators, are

38. Augustine, *City of God* 18.51.2.

39. Luther, *Luther's Works,* 6:99; 9:57; 10:51, 289; 11:307, 365; 12:216; 14:58; 20:41; 21:46; 43:171, 184. The exception is 14:58 where Luther, commenting on Ps 118:4, states that those who honor God "must truly suffer and endure mockery, shame, hurt, hatred, envy, defamation, fire, sword, death, and every other calamity . . ."

40. Calvin, *Calvin's Commentaries: 2 Timothy* (no pages).

content to leave the observation there and make no attempt to link it with the rest of the Pastorals. Others seek to transform the meaning of persecution into general trials suffered by Christians, slander, and/or demonic attacks. On only three occasions reference is made of persecution in the sense of actual, or threatened, bodily harm facing contemporary believers. Luther's comment appears to be general in the context of commenting on Ps 118; there does not seem to be any specific persecution in mind. Athanasius fears capital punishment, but this is at the instigation of Arian Christians. Only Origen appears to refer to the possibility of persecution in his day from outsiders. There appears to be a distinct lack in the subsequent reception of this text of reflection on the type of spirituality required in the face of actual persecution.

3.2 *Martyrs Mirror*

3.2.1 *Introduction*

By way of contrast to the lack mentioned above, sixteenth-century Anabaptists developed a distinct spirituality of martyrdom, referring often to this text, and based on their experiences of persecution from both Catholics and Protestants. As Snyder states, "martyrdom came to define the very essence of the Anabaptist spiritual tradition."[41] In contrast to the commentators above, the seventeenth-century text *Martyrs Mirror*[42] takes the persecution mentioned in 2 Tim 3:12 as referring to actual, physical persecution. *Martyrs Mirror* is *the* Anabaptist martyrology and is of comparable size to the French Calvinist Jean Crespin's *Histoire des Martyrs*, published in Geneva in 1554; the Flemish minister van Haemstede's *History and Deaths of the Devout Martyrs*, published in 1559; and John Foxe's *Acts and Monuments of the English Martyrs*, first published in 1563. For Anabaptism it contains the same mélange of interpretation and historical sources as these other martyrologies, and is one of the great sources for Anabaptism. It also was the largest book to have been published in pre-Revolutionary America. This specific verse is mentioned no less than twenty-five times and there are a further three references to 2 Tim 3:12–13. I set out below a number of accounts where our text is significant.

41. Snyder, *Following*, 161.

42. First published in 1660 by the Dutch Mennonite Thieleman J. van Braght; translated into German in the 1740s and into English (from this German edition) in 1837. The second English edition was published in London in 1853. The third English edition, published in 1886, was translated from the original Dutch edition of 1660. This edition has subsequently gone through a number of printings. The edition quoted here is the twentieth printing, published by Herald Press in 1998.

3.2.2 Walter of Stoelwijk

Walter of Stoelwijk, from Brabant in Belgium, was imprisoned for three years, interrogated, and tortured by the Catholic authorities. He was burned to death on 24 March 1541. Writing from prison he understands our text as stating that "it must incontrovertibly follow, that all servants of God, all godly men, all disciples of Jesus Christ must suffer persecution for His name's sake and be tried through manifold temptations."[43] He deplores the fact that those who profess to be Christians in his day "have the least thought of suffering anything for the name of Christ Jesus"[44] and accuses them of being "wicked hypocrites."[45] In a section reminiscent of Heb 11 he lists characters from the Old Testament, Tobit, and 2 Maccabees who faced imprisonment and death rather than disobey God.[46]

3.3.3 Jacques D'Auchy

Jacques D'Auchy was imprisoned in 1557 and finally put to death in 1559. While in prison he writes about a series of interrogations. In his third interrogation (the second by the inquisitor appointed by the king of Spain) the inquisitor insists that the biblical texts concerning suffering were spoken to the apostles only. Jacques, in reply, quotes 2 Tim 3:12, emphasizing "all." Interestingly, the inquisitor then makes the same move as many of the commentators examined above; he states that "this means that the devil will always cause them enough temptation and affliction." Jacques retorts that "Paul speaks of persecution, and not of temptation."[47]

3.3.4 Jan van Hasebroeck

Twelve people, including van Hasebroeck, were arrested, interrogated, tortured, and put to death at Antwerp in 1569 by being burned alive after having their mouths screwed together so that they could not testify from the stake. Three letters from van Hasebroeck to his wife from prison are preserved in *Martyrs Mirror*. In the third letter he states: "my mind is still unchanged to go on in that which I unworthy one declared and confessed in His name.

43. Braght, *Martyrs Mirror*, 456.
44. Ibid.
45. Ibid., 457.
46. Ibid.
47. Ibid., 602.

I also hope to seal the same with my blood, and I trust that the Lord will help me in my extremity." He then cites a number of New Testament texts concerning suffering, including 2 Tim 3:12, and closes with an exhortation to instruct their two children "in the obedience of truth" and always to associate with true believers.[48]

3.3.5 *Clement Hendrickss*

Hendrickss was a sail maker who had not been able to get baptized as a believer before he was arrested. Five letters of his from prison remain. In the second, using typical language, he quotes a number of texts concerning suffering and persecution, including 2 Tim 3:12. He was tortured and burned at the stake on 12 March 1569 at Amsterdam. His case is particularly interesting, as *Martyrs Mirror* preserves the text of his sentence:

> Whereas Clement Hendrickss, sail maker, citizen of this city, at present a prisoner here, unmindful of his soul's salvation, and the obedience which he owed to our mother, the holy church, and to his imperial majesty, as his natural lord and prince, has so apostatized from the holy church, that he, despising her ordinances, has for five years and longer been neither to confession nor to the holy sacrament, and has at three different times attended the assembly of the reprobated and accursed sect of the Mennonists, the last time about a year ago; and is so hardened in said sect, that even while a prisoner he has declared that he is sorry that he is not rebaptized, and has not received the breaking of bread; and has also repeatedly attended the meetings; to which above-mentioned reprobated sect of Mennonists, he, the prisoner, still persistently clings, refusing to return to our mother, the holy church, notwithstanding he has repeatedly, by divers clerical persons as well as by the court of this city, been urged thereto and instructed; so that the prisoner, according to what has been mentioned, has committed crime against divine and human majesty, as disturbing by his sect the common peace and welfare; therefore, my lords of the court, having heard the demand of my lord the bailiff, and seen the confession of the prisoner, and having had regard to his great stubbornness and obstinacy, and duly considered everything, have condemned said prisoner, and by these presents do condemn him to be executed with fire, according to the decrees of his majesty; and declare all his property confiscated for the benefit of his majesty

48. Ibid., 773–74.

aforesaid without prejudice to the privilege of this city in all other matters.[49]

3.3.6 Janneken Munstdorp

Janneken was executed at Antwerp in 1573, shortly after her husband. She was not executed with him, as she was heavily pregnant. She gave birth to a daughter in prison and managed to get the infant to some friends before she could be baptized by the priests. Just before she died she wrote a testament to her daughter, who at this time was about one month old. In a very moving text she informs her daughter that she and her husband had only been together six months before they were arrested because "they sought the salvation of [their] souls." She speaks of the pain of seeing her husband die, then giving birth to the child and having her taken away from her. She states that she now waits, "expecting death every morning." She stresses that they were not imprisoned and executed for any evil they had done and urges her daughter to investigate the matter herself when she reaches the age of understanding so that she is not ashamed of them. The text goes on to provide a wealth of information as to how young children were brought up in Anabaptist communities. After this detailed instruction, she states:

> Dear Janneken, we have not left you much of this world's goods, and I have now not much to give you, but what I have I give you. However, we leave you a good example to fear God, which is better than much of the temporal goods of this world. Only follow us, and you shall have wealth enough; true, you are poor here, but you shall possess much wealth, if only you fear God and shun sin. . . . [M]y dear lamb, cease not, because of the cross, to fear God, for a Christian is not made meet except by much tribulation and persecution upon this world, and we must through much tribulation enter into the kingdom of God; for Paul says: "All that will live godly in Christ Jesus shall suffer persecution."[50]

3.3.7 Martyrs in England

On 3 April 1575 a gathering of Dutch Anabaptists was discovered in a house near Aldgate in London. Seventeen were arrested and four subsequently

49. Ibid., 834.
50. Ibid., 984–87 (986).

imprisoned. On 22 July two were burned to death at Smithfield. Two letters from those imprisoned survive. The first is particularly interesting as it begins by echoing the language of 1 Tim 2:2—the very text that Dibelius highlighted as supporting his view of the Pastorals as advocating "the ideal of good Christian citizenship." The letter begins: "We poor and despised strangers, who are in persecution for the testimony of Jesus Christ, wish all men, of whatever race or office, from God, that the Lord would grant them a long peace, so that we may live in peace among one another, *in all godliness*, to the praise and glory of the Lord, and the salvation of the soul."[51] The letter goes on to state, quoting 2 Tim 3:12, "that those who have the true evangelical doctrine and faith will persecute no one, but will themselves be persecuted."[52] Here is a text that echoes 1 Tim 2:2 in the context of real persecution.

3.4 Summary

It is clear, from the evidence above, that sixteenth-century Anabaptists found 2 Tim 3:12 particularly relevant in facing persecution. Many more examples of the significance of this text could have been provided.[53] This, and many other New Testament texts concerning suffering and persecution, resonated with their own experience. They were marginalized Christian communities suffering persecution from both Catholics and Protestants. What is most surprising is that, in their context, they could also freely make use of 1 Tim 2:1–2. For example, the Anabaptist confession *Scriptural Instruction*, drawn up on 27 September 1627 at Amsterdam, states in the section on magistrates:

> [W]e must submit ourselves to every ordinance of man for the Lord's sake, and pray to Almighty God for [the secular power]; also to give our greatest thanks to the Lord for good and reasonable authorities.[54]

In addition, Article XXVII of the Mennonite *Confession of Faith*, dated around 1600, also refers to 1 Tim 2:2 in connection with response to the governing authorities.[55] Finally, not only the Dutch Anabaptist martyrs in England, but also Jacques D'Auchy, mentioned above, could refer to 1 Tim 2:2, stating: "I also confess that the higher powers are ordained of God . . . to which

51. Ibid., 1012, my italics.

52. Ibid., 1013.

53. Some ten more were included in the original presentation of this paper.

54. Braght, *Martyrs Mirror*, 32.

55. Ibid., 403.

powers the Scriptures command us to be subject, and instruct us to pray for them, in order that, as Paul says, we may lead a quiet and peaceable life."[56]

Martyrs Mirror thus bears eloquent testimony to the power of 2 Tim 3:12 to speak to a persecuted minority who, at the same time, can pray for the authorities and seek a quiet and peaceful life. The prevailing scholarly interpretation—that the PE represent Christian communities that have accommodated themselves to the wider Greco-Roman culture—fails to see that the desires expressed in 1 Tim 2:1–2 can be those of a community facing persecution in the way suggested by 2 Tim 3:12. Furthermore, even a cursory glance at *Martyrs Mirror* quickly highlights how much emphasis Anabaptists placed on memorizing the Scriptures to such an extent that they formed their lives and witness. Time and again they astounded their interrogators, both Catholic and Protestant, with their biblical knowledge. Their testimony reminds us how closely linked the injunction to pay attention to the sacred writings in 2 Tim 3:14–17 is to the notion of facing persecution in 2 Tim 3:11–12. This is particularly relevant when this text is uprooted from its clear context and made to serve debates about biblical inerrancy.

The early Anabaptists saw persecution as a hallmark of true discipleship. For example, Menno Simons lists persecution as the sixth and last sign that distinguishes the true church from the false.[57] Similarly, Dietrich Philips, writing around 1560, cites persecution as the seventh and last ordinance of the true church.[58]

4. Concluding Thoughts

As I write there has recently been an outcry from some conservatives that Christians are being deliberately persecuted in Britain. George Carey, the former archbishop of Canterbury, has been at the forefront of such claims. By persecution he seems to mean issues such as Christians being banned from wearing crosses at work and a court decision to prohibit a local council from opening its council meetings with prayers.[59] This is a far cry from the persecution faced by first-century Christians, Anabaptists, and many others

56. Ibid., 592.

57. His six signs are a correct doctrine of Scripture; the proper administering of the sacraments of baptism and Eucharist; Christian piety and obedience; love; confession of Christ; and persecution. Simons, *Complete Works*, 2:81–82.

58. Philips' seven ordinances are a correct doctrine of Scripture; the proper administering of the sacraments of baptism and Eucharist; foot-washing; separation and the exercise of church discipline; love; Christian piety and obedience; and persecution. Williams, *Spiritual and Anabaptist Writers*, 240–55.

59. See, for example, Carey, "Heavy-Handed Courts."

throughout church history who have had to face beatings, imprisonment, and death. It should also give us pause for thought at a time when claims are being made that there were more Christian martyrs in the twentieth century than in the previous nineteen centuries combined.[60] Perhaps in the twenty-first century if Western Christians were truly to live out a spirituality that claims in every area of life "there is another king named Jesus" (Acts 17:7) there would be a rediscovery that "the unconditional validity of God's rule" clashes with the totalizing claims of much contemporary discourses of power. In this case we might also rediscover "that the spirituality of the martyrs belongs to the very core of Christian spirituality."[61]

---

60. See, for example, Barrett, Kurian, and Johnson, *World Christian Encyclopedia*. The claims made here are disputed as exaggerated, but nevertheless the scale of Christian martyrdom in the twentieth century is widely recognized.

61. Waaijman, *Spirituality*, 276.

Bibliography

Aasgard, Reidar. *"My Beloved Brothers and Sisters!" Christian Siblingship in Paul.* JSNTSup 265. London: T. & T. Clark, 2004.

Abarbanel, Isaac. *Commentaries on the Torah.* 3 vols. Jerusalem: Benei Arabel, 1964.

Abelard, Peter. *Dialogue of a Philosopher with a Jew and a Christian.* Translated by P. J. Payer. Toronto: Institute for Mediaeval Studies, 1979.

Alexander, Loveday. "Hellenistic Letter-Forms and the Structure of Philippians." *JSNT* 57 (1989) 87–101.

Allen, Leslie C. *Psalms 101–150.* WBC 21. Waco, TX: Word, 1983.

Allister, John. "The Amalekite Genocide." *Churchman* 124 (2010) 217–26.

Alter, Robert. *The Book of Psalms.* New York: Norton, 2007.

———. *The Pleasures of Reading in an Ideological Age.* New York: Simon & Schuster, 1989.

———. *The Wisdom Books.* New York : Norton, 2010.

Alves, R. A. *The Poet, the Warrior, the Prophet.* London: SCM, 2002.

Amichai, Yehuda. "Jerusalem 1967." In *Poems of Jerusalem,* translated by Stephen Mitchell, 38–63. New York: Harper & Row, 1988.

Anderson, Gary A. "Redeem Your Sins by the Giving of Alms: Sin, Debt, and the 'Treasury of Merit' in Early Jewish and Christian Tradition." *Letter and Spirit* 3 (2007) 39–69.

———. *Sin: A History.* New Haven: Yale University Press, 2009.

———. *A Time to Mourn, a Time to Dance: The Expression of Grief and Joy in Israelite Religion.* University Park: Pennsylvania State University Press, 1991.

Anderson, Paul. "Genocide or Jesus: A God of Conquest or Pacificism?" In *The Destructive Power of Religion: Violence in Judaism, Christianity, and Islam,* edited by J. Harold Ellens, 4:31–52. Westport, CT: Praeger, 2004.

Andersson, Greger. *Untamable Texts: Literary Studies and Narrative Theory in the Books of Samuel.* LHBOTS 514. London: T. & T. Clark, 2009.

Aravamudan, Srinivas. "Introduction: Perpetual War." *Publications of the Modern Language Association* 124 (2009) 1505–14.

Armstrong, K. *The Case for God.* New York: Knopf, 2009.

Arnold, Bill T. "The Amalekite's Report of Saul's Death: Political Intrigue or Incompatible Sources?" *JETS* 32 (1989) 289–98.

Arnold, C. E. *The Colossian Syncretism.* Tübingen: Mohr, 1995.

Aune, David E. "Following the Lamb: Discipleship in the Apocalypse." In *Patterns of Discipleship in the New Testament*, edited by Richard N. Longenecker, 269–84. Grand Rapids: Eerdmans, 1996.

―――. "Human Nature and Ethics in Hellenistic Philosophical Traditions and Paul: Some Issues and Problems." In *Paul in His Hellenistic Context*, edited by T. Engberg-Pedersen, 305–12. Edinburgh: T. & T. Clark, 1994.

Bacevich, Andrew. *The New American Militarism*. New York: Oxford University Press, 2005.

Barclay, J. G. "Ordinary but Different: Colossians and Hidden Moral Identity." *ABR* 49 (2001) 34–52.

Barrett, D., G. Kurian, and T. Johnson. *World Christian Encyclopedia*. 2nd ed. Oxford: Oxford University Press, 2001.

Barth, Karl. *Church Dogmatics, I/1: The Doctrine of the Word of God*. 2nd ed. Translated and edited by G. W. Bromiley. Edinburgh: T. & T. Clark, 1975.

―――. *Church Dogmatics, III/3*. Translated and edited by G. W. Bromiley and R. J. Ehrlich. Reprint. Peabody, MA: Hendrickson, 2010.

―――. *Church Dogmatics, IV/3*. Translated and edited by G. W. Bromiley and T. F. Torrance. Edinburgh: T. & T. Clark, 1961.

Barton, John. "The Dark Side of God in the Old Testament." In *Ethical and Unethical in the Old Testament: God and Humans in Dialogue*, edited by Katharine J. Dell, 122–34. LHBOTS 518. New York: T. & T. Clark, 2010.

―――. "Theological Ethics in Daniel." In *Understanding Old Testament Ethics: Approaches and Explanations*, 154–61. Louisville: Westminster John Knox, 2003.

Barton, Stephen C. "Eschatology and the Emotions in Early Christianity." *JBL* 130 (2011) 571–91.

Bassler, J. M. *1 Timothy, 2 Timothy, Titus*. ANTC. Nashville: Abingdon, 1996.

Bauckham, R. J. *Jude, 2 Peter*. WBC 50. Dallas: Word, 1983.

―――. "The Sonship of the Historical Jesus in Christology." *SJT* (1978) 245–60.

Beale, G. K. *The Book of Revelation: A Commentary on the Greek Text*. NIGTC. Grand Rapids: Eerdmans, 1999.

Bellah, R. N. *Religion in Human Evolution: From the Paleolithic to the Axial Age*. Cambridge: Belknap, 2011.

The Benedictine Handbook. Norwich, UK: Canterbury, 2003.

Berquist, Jon L., and Claudia V. Camp. *Constructions of Space II: The Biblical City and Other Imagined Spaces*. LHBOTS 490. London: T. & T. Clark, 2008.

Betz, Hans Dieter. *Galatians: A Critical and Historical Commentary on the Bible*. Hermeneia. Philadelphia: Fortress, 1979.

Beyreuther, E., and G. Finkenrath. "Joy, Rejoice." In *NIDNTT* 2:352–61.

Bipartisan Policy Center, National Security Preparedness Group. "Tenth Anniversary Report Card: The Status of 9/11 Commission Recommendations." Online: http://www.bipartisanpolicy.org/sites/default/files/CommisionRecommendations.pdf.

Bird, Michael F. *Colossians and Philemon*. NCCS 12. Eugene, OR: Cascade Books, 2009.

Bloomquist, L. Gregory. "Subverted by Joy: Suffering and Joy in Paul's Letter to the Philippians." *Int* 61 (2007) 270–82.

Blount, Brian K. *Revelation: A Commentary*. NTL. Louisville: Westminster John Knox, 2009.

Bockmuehl, Markus. *The Epistle to the Philippians*. London: A. & C. Black, 1997.

Boda, Mark J. *A Severe Mercy: Sin and Its Remedy in the Old Testament.* Siphrut 1. Winona Lake, IN: Eisenbrauns, 2009.

Boda, Mark J., et al., editors. *Seeking the Favor of God.* SBLEJL 21–23. Atlanta: SBL, 2006–8.

Bonhoeffer, Dietrich. *Letters and Papers from Prison.* Translated by Isabel Best. Edited by John W. De Gruchy. Dietrich Bonhoeffer Works 8. Minneapolis: Fortress, 2009.

———. *Ethics.* Translated by N. Horton-Smith. 2nd impression. London: SCM, 1971.

Borg, Marcus. *Meeting Jesus Again for the First Time: The Historical Jesus and the Heart of Contemporary Faith.* San Francisco: HarperSanFrancisco, 1994.

Boring, M. Eugene. "Matthew: Introduction, Commentary, and Reflections." In *NIB* 8:87–505.

Boxall, Ian. *The Revelation of Saint John.* BNTC. London: Continuum, 2006.

Boyle, B. "Ruination in Jerusalem: Narrative Technique and Characterisation in Jeremiah 37–38." *Compass Theology Review* 32 (1998) 38–45.

Braght, T. J. van. *The Bloody Theater: Or, Martyrs Mirror of the Defenseless Christians.* Scottdale, PA: Herald, 1998.

Brändl, M. *Der Agon bei Paulus: Herkunft und Profil paulinischer Agonmetaphorik.* Tübingen: Mohr Siebeck, 2006.

Briggs, R. S. *The Virtuous Reader: Old Testament Narrative and Interpretive Virtue.* Studies in Theological Interpretation. Grand Rapids: Baker Academic, 2010.

Brown, R. E. *The Virginal Conception and Bodily Resurrection of Jesus.* New York: Paulist, 1973.

Brown, William P. *Seeing the Psalms: A Theology of Metaphor.* Louisville: Westminster John Knox, 2002.

Brueggemann, W. *A Commentary on Jeremiah: Exile & Homecoming.* Grand Rapids: Eerdmans, 1998.

———. *Finally Comes the Poet: Daring Speech for Proclamation.* Minneapolis: Fortress, 1989.

———. *Praying the Psalms: Engaging Scripture and the Life of the Spirit.* 2nd ed. Eugene, OR: Cascade Books, 2007.

———. *The Prophetic Imagination.* Philadelphia: Fortress, 1978.

———. "Psychological Criticism: Exploring the Self in the Text." In *Method Matters: Essays on the Interpretation of the Hebrew Bible in Honor of David L. Petersen,* edited by Joel M. Lemon and Kent Harold Richards, 213–32. SBLRBS 56. Atlanta: SBL, 2009.

Burton-Christie, D. *The Word in the Desert: Scripture and the Quest for Holiness in Early Christian Monasticism.* New York: Oxford University Press, 1993.

Bychkov, O. V., and J. Fodor, editors. *Theological Aesthetics after von Balthasar.* Aldershot, UK: Ashgate, 2008.

Callaway, M. C. "Telling the Truth and Telling Stories: An Analysis of Jeremiah 37–38." *USQR* 44 (1991) 253–65.

Calvin, J. *Calvin's Commentaries: 2 Timothy.* Electronic ed. Logos Library System. Albany, OR: Ages Software, 1998.

———. *Sermons on Job.* Edinburgh: Banner of Truth, 1993.

Caputo, J. D., and C. Keller. "Theopoetic/Theopolitic." *Cross Currents* 56 (2007) 105–11.

Carey, George. "Heavy-Handed Courts Are Persecuting Christians and Driving Them Underground." *Daily Mail Online,* April 13, 2012. Online: http://www.dailymail.

co.uk/news/article-2129593/Heavy-handed-courts-persecuting-Christians-driving-underground-says-Carey.html.

Carmy, Shalom. "The Origin of Nations and the Shadow of Violence: Theological Perspectives on Canaan and Amalek." *Tradition* 39 (2006) 57–88.

Carson, Donald A. "Locating Udo Schnelle's *Theology of the New Testament* in the Contemporary Discussion." *JETS* 53 (2010) 133–44.

———. "New Testament Theology." In *DLNT* 797–814.

Charry, Ellen. *God and the Art of Happiness*. Grand Rapids: Eerdmans, 2010.

Childs, Brevard S. *Introduction to the Old Testament as Scripture*. Philadelphia: Fortress, 1979.

Chittister, Joan. *The Rule of Benedict: Insights for the Ages*. New York: Crossroad, 2005.

Clanchy, M. T. *Abelard: A Medieval Life*. Oxford: Blackwell, 1997.

Clines, David J. A. "'The Fear of the Lord Is Wisdom' (Job 28:28): A Semantic and Contextual Study." In *Job 28: Cognition in Context*, edited by Ellen van Wolde, 57–92. Leiden: Brill, 2003.

———. *Job 1–20*. WBC 17A. Dallas: Word, 1989.

Coats, George W. *Exodus 1–18*. FOTL 2A. Grand Rapids: Eerdmans, 1999.

Cohen, Joshua. "The Remembrance of Amalek: Tainted Greatness and the Bible." In *Tainted Greatness: Anti-semitism and Cultural Heroes*, edited by Nancy A. Harrowitz, 289–301. Philadelphia: Temple University Press, 1994.

The Collected Works of St. John of the Cross. Translated by K. Kavanaugh and O. Rodriguez. Rev. ed. Washington, DC: Institute of Carmelite Studies, 1991.

Collins, J. J. *The Apocalyptic Visions of the Book of Daniel*. HSM 16. Missoula, MT: Scholars, 1977.

———. *Daniel*. Hermeneia. Minneapolis: Fortress, 1993.

Collins, J. J., and P. W. Flint, editors. *The Book of Daniel: Composition and Reception*. 2 vols. VTSup 83.1–2. Leiden: Brill, 2001.

Collins, R. F. *1 & 2 Timothy and Titus: A Commentary*. Louisville: Westminster John Knox, 2002.

Coloe, M. *Dwelling in the Household of God: Johannine Ecclesiology and Spirituality*. Collegeville, MN: Liturgical, 2007.

Conzelmann, H., and W. Zimmerli. χαίρω κτλ. In *TDNT* 9:362–66.

Copan, Paul M. *Is God a Moral Monster? Making Sense of the Old Testament God*. Grand Rapids: Baker Academic, 2011.

Corrigan, John. "Amalek and the Rhetoric of Extermination." In *The First Prejudice: Religious Tolerance and Intolerance in Early America*, edited by Chris Beneke and Christopher S. Grenda, 53–72. Early American Studies. Philadelphia: University of Pennsylvania Press, 2011.

Cox, John, Alastair V. Campbell, and Bill (K. W. M.) Fulford. *Medicine of the Person: Faith, Science and Values*. Philadelphia: Kingsley, 2007.

Craigie, P. C. *Psalms 1–50*. WBC 19. Waco, TX: Word, 1983.

Crocker, Cornelia C. *Reading 1 Corinthians in the Twenty-First Century*. New York: Continuum, 2004.

Cromer, Gerald. "Amalek as Other, Other as Amalek: Interpreting a Violent Biblical Narrative." *Qualitative Sociology* 24 (2001) 191–202.

Culpepper, R. Alan. "Luke: Introduction, Commentary, and Reflections." In *NIB* 9:1–490.

Daniélou, Jean. *From Shadows to Reality: Studies in the Biblical Typology of the Fathers.* 1960. Reprint, Eugene, OR: Wipf & Stock, 2003.

Davies, Eryl W. *The Immoral Bible: Approaches to Biblical Ethics.* London: T. & T. Clark, 2010.

Davies, M. *The Pastoral Epistles: I and II Timothy and Titus.* Epworth Commentaries. London: Epworth, 1996.

Davies, Philip R. *In Search of "Ancient Israel."* JSOTSup 148. 1992. Reprint, Sheffield, UK: Sheffield Academic, 1995.

Davis, S. T., D. Kendall, and G. O'Collins, editors. *The Resurrection: An Interdisciplinary Symposium on the Resurrection of Jesus.* New York: Oxford University Press, 1997.

De Boer, Martinus C. *Galatians: A Commentary.* Louisville: Westminster John Knox, 2011.

DeMaris, R. E. *The Colossian Controversy: Wisdom in Dispute at Colossae.* Sheffield, UK: JSOT, 1994.

De Villiers, Pieter G. R. "The Eschatology of 1 Thessalonians in the Light of Its Spirituality." *Acta Theologica* 28 (2008) 1–32.

———. "The Glory of the Son of Man in Revelation 1–3: Reflections on Mysticism in the New Testament." *Acta Theologica* 29 (2009) 17–39.

———. "Love in the Letter to Philemon." In *Philemon in Perspective: Interpreting a Pauline Letter*, edited by D. Francois Tolmie, 181–203. BZNW 169. Berlin: de Gruyter, 2010.

———. "Love in the Revelation of John." In *Seeing the Seeker: Explorations in the Discipline of Spirituality*, edited by Hein Blommestijn et al., 155–68. Studies in Spirituality 19. Leuven: Peeters, 2008.

———. "Peace in Luke-Acts: A Perspective on Biblical Spirituality." *Acta Patristica et Byzantina* 19 (2008) 110–34.

———. "Peace in the Pauline Letters: A Perspective on Biblical Spirituality." *Neotestamentica* 43 (2009) 1–26.

———. "Towards a Spirituality of Peace." *Acta Theologica Supplementum* 11 (2008) 20–58.

Diamond, A. R. P. "Portraying Prophecy: Of Doublets, Variants and Analogies in the Narrative Representation of Jeremiah's Oracles—Reconstructing the Hermeneutics of Prophecy." *Journal for the Study of Old Testament Theology* 57 (1993) 99–119.

Dibelius, M., and H. Conzelmann. *The Pastoral Epistles.* Hermeneia. Philadelphia: Fortress, 1972.

Dietrich, Walter, and Christian Link. *Die dunklen Seiten Gottes.* 3rd ed. 2 vols. Neukirchen-Vluyn: Neukirchener, 2000.

Dillon, J. M. "*Pleroma* and Noetic Cosmos: A Comparative Study." In *Neoplatonism and Gnosticism*, edited by R. T. Wallis, 99–110. Albany: State University of New York Press, 1992.

DiVito, Robert A. "Old Testament Anthropology and the Construction of Personal Identity." *CBQ* 61 (1999) 217–38.

Douglas, Mary. "The Cosmic Joke." In *Thought Styles: Critical Essays on Good Taste*, 193–212. London: Sage, 1996.

Duncan, G. S. *The Epistle of Paul to the Galatians.* London: Hodder & Stoughton, 1944.

Dunn, James D. G. *The Theology of Paul the Apostle.* Grand Rapids: Eerdmans, 2006.

———. *The Theology of Paul's Letter to the Galatians.* Cambridge: Cambridge University Press, 1993.

————. *Unity and Diversity in the New Testament.* London: SCM, 1977.

Eagleton, Terry. *The Event of Literature.* New Haven: Yale University Press, 2012.

Edelman, Diana. "Saul's Battle against Amaleq (1 Sam 15)." *JSOT* 35 (1986) 71–84.

Eisen, Bruce. *The Peace and Violence of Judaism: From the Bible to Modern Zionism.* New York: Oxford University Press, 2011.

Ellul, Jacques. *The Presence of the Kingdom.* Translated by Olive Wyon. 2nd ed. Colorado Springs, CO: Helmers & Howard, 1989.

Fee, Gordon D. *1 and 2 Timothy, Titus.* NIBCNT 13. Peabody, MA: Hendrickson, 1988.

Feldman, Louis H. *"Remember Amalek": Vengeance, Zealotry and Group Destruction in the Bible according to Philo, Pseudo-Philo, and Josephus.* Cincinnati, OH: Hebrew Union College Press, 2004.

Fiore, B. *The Pastoral Epistles: First Timothy, Second Timothy, Titus.* SP 12. Collegeville, MN: Liturgical, 2007.

Firestone, Reuven. "Holy War in Modern Judaism? 'Mitzvah War' and the Problem of the 'Three Vows.'" *JAAR* 74 (2006) 954–82.

Fishbane, Michael. *The Exegetical Imagination.* Cambridge: Harvard University Press, 1998.

Ford, David F. *Self and Salvation: Being Transformed.* Cambridge: Cambridge University Press, 1999.

Fountain, David. *Isaac Watts Remembered.* Worthing, UK: Walter, 1974.

Fowl, Stephen E., and L. Gregory Jones. *Reading in Communion: Scripture and Ethics in Christian Life.* 1991. Reprint, Eugene, OR: Wipf & Stock, 1998.

Freedman, David Noel. *Psalm 119: The Exaltation of Torah.* BJS 6. Winona Lake, IN: Eisenbrauns, 1999.

Frei, Hans. *The Eclipse of Biblical Narrative: A Study in Eighteenth and Nineteenth Century Hermeneutics.* New Haven: Yale University Press, 1974.

————. "The 'Literal Reading' of the Biblical Narrative in the Christian Tradition: Does It Stretch or Will It Break?" In *Theology and Narrative: Selected Essays*, edited by George Hunsinger and William C. Placher, 117–52. Oxford: Oxford University Press, 1993.

————. *Types of Christian Theology.* Edited by George Hunsinger and William C. Placher. New Haven: Yale University Press, 1992.

Fretheim, Terence E. "*byn*." In *NIDOTTE* 1:652–53.

————. *Exodus.* Interpretation. Louisville: John Knox, 1991.

————. "God, Creation, and the Pursuit of Happiness." In *The Bible and the Pursuit of Happiness*, edited by Brent A. Strawn, 44–79. New York: Oxford University Press, 2012.

Friesen, S. *Twice Neokoros.* Leiden: Brill, 1993.

Furnish, Victor Paul. *II Corinthians.* AB 32A. Garden City, NY: Doubleday, 1984.

————. *The Love Commandment in the New Testament.* Nashville: Abingdon, 1972.

Gammie, J. G. "A Journey through Danielic Spaces: The Book of Daniel in Theology and Piety in the Christian Community." *Int* 39 (1985) 144–56.

Garber, Zev. "Amalek and Amalekut: A Homiletic Lesson." In *Jewish Bible Theology: Perspectives and Case Studies*, edited by Isaac Kalimi, 147–60. Winona Lake, IN: Eisenbrauns, 2012.

Garber, Zev, and Bruce Zuckerman. *Double Takes: Thinking and Rethinking Issues of Modern Judaism in Ancient Contexts.* Studies in the Shoah 26. Lanham, MD: University Press of America, 2004.

Gavrilyuk, Paul L., and Sarah Coakley, editors. *The Spiritual Senses: Perceiving God in Western Christianity.* New York: Cambridge University Press, 2012.

Gerstenberger, Erhard S. *Psalms Part 2, and Lamentations.* FOTL XV. Grand Rapids: Eerdmans, 2001.

Gemser, B. "The *RIB-* or Controversy-Pattern in Hebrew Mentality." In *Wisdom in Israel and in the Ancient Near East: Presented to Professor Harold Henry Rowley,* edited by M. Noth and D. W. Thomas, 120–37. VTSup 3. Leiden: Brill, 1960.

Giddens, Anthony. *Modernity and Self-Identity: Self and Society in the Late Modern Age.* Stanford: Stanford University Press, 1991.

Gillingham, Susan. *The Poems and the Psalms of the Hebrew Bible.* OBS. Oxford: Oxford University Press, 1994.

Gnilka, Joachim. *Theologie des Neuen Testaments.* Freiburg: Herder, 1994.

Goetz, Ronald. "Joshua, Calvin, and Genocide." *ThTo* 32 (1975) 263–74.

Goldingay, John E. *Daniel.* WBC 30. Dallas: Word, 1987.

———. *Old Testament Theology.* Vol. 3, *Israel's Life.* Downers Grove, IL: InterVarsity, 2009.

———. *Psalms.* Vol. 2, *Psalms 42–89.* Baker Commentary on the Old Testament Wisdom and Psalms. Grand Rapids: Baker, 2007.

Good, Edwin. *In Turns of Tempest: A Reading of Job.* Stanford: Stanford University Press, 1990.

Gordis, Robert. *The Book of Job: Commentary, New Translation, and Special Studies.* New York: Jewish Theological Seminary of America, 1978.

Gorman, Michael J. *Apostle of the Crucified Lord: A Theological Introduction to Paul and His Letters.* Grand Rapids: Eerdmans, 2004.

———. *Cruciformity: Paul's Narrative Spirituality of the Cross.* Grand Rapids: Eerdmans, 2001.

———. *Inhabiting the Cruciform God: Kenosis, Justification, and Theosis in Paul's Narrative Soteriology.* Grand Rapids: Eerdmans, 2009.

———. *Reading Revelation Responsibly: Uncivil Worship and Witness—Following the Lamb into the New Creation.* Eugene, OR: Cascade Books, 2011.

———. "Romans: The First Christian Treatise on Theosis." *JTI* 5 (2011) 13–34.

Goulder, Michael. *The Psalms of the Sons of Korah.* JSOTSup 20. Sheffield, UK: JSOT, 1982.

Green, Barbara. *Jonah's Journeys.* Collegeville, MN: Liturgical, 2005.

———. *Plans of Well-Being: Jeremiah as Literary Persona.* Columbia: University of South Carolina Press, 2013.

———. "This Old Text: An Analogy for Biblical Interpretation." *BTB* 36 (2006) 72–83.

———. *What Profit for Us? Remembering the Story of Joseph.* Lanham, MD: University Press of America, 1996.

Gregorius Magnus. *Moralia in Iob.* CCSL 143, 143A, 143B. Turnhout: Brepols, 1979–85.

Gunn, David M. *The Fate of King Saul: An Interpretation of a Biblical Story.* JSOTSup 14. Sheffield, UK: JSOT, 1980.

Guthrie, Donald. *New Testament Theology: History, Method and Identity.* Leicester, UK: InterVarsity, 1981.

———. *The Pastoral Epistles: An Introduction and Commentary.* TNTC. Leicester, UK: InterVarsity, 1957.

Guyn, M. "Theopoetics: The Dead May Become Gardeners Again." *Cross Currents* 56 (2006) 98–109.

Habel, Norman C. *The Book of Job: A Commentary*. London: SCM, 1985.

Hadot, P. *Philosophy as a Way of Life*. Oxford: Blackwell, 1995.

Hahn, Ferdinand. *Theologie des Neuen Testaments, 1/2*. Tübingen: Mohr-Siebeck, 2005.

Hamerton-Kelly, Robert. *God the Father: Theology and Patriarchy in the Teaching of Jesus*. Philadelphia: Fortress, 1979.

Hardt, Michael, and Antonio Negri. *Multitude: War and Democracy in the Age of Empire*. New York: Penguin, 2005.

Hart, R. L. *Unfinished Man and the Imagination: Toward an Ontology and a Rhetoric of Revelation*. New York: Seabury, 1968.

Hays, Richard B. "Christology and Ethics in Galatians: The Law of Christ." *CBQ* 49 (1987) 268–90.

———. "The God of Mercy Who Rescues Us from the Present Evil Age." In *The Forgotten God: Perspectives in Biblical Theology: Essays in Honor of Paul J. Achtemeier on the Occasion of His Seventy-Fifth Birthday*, edited by A. A. Das and F. J. Matera, 123–43. Louisville: John Knox 2002.

———. *The Moral Vision of the New Testament: A Contemporary Introduction to New Testament Ethics*. Edinburgh: T. & T. Clark, 1996.

———. "What Is 'Real Participation in Christ'? A Dialogue with E. P. Sanders on Pauline Soteriology." In *Redefining First-Century Jewish and Christian Identities: Essays in Honor of Ed Parish Sanders*, edited by Fabian E. Udoh et al., 336–51. Notre Dame: University of Notre Dame Press, 2008.

Hayward, C. T. R. *The Temple: A Sourcebook*. London: Routledge, 1996.

Hebbard, A. B. *Reading Daniel as a Text in Theological Hermeneutics*. PTMS 109. Eugene, OR: Pickwick, 2009.

Hirsch, Samson Raphael. *The Hirsch Chumash: The Five Books of the Torah*. 5 vols. Translated by Daniel Haberman. New York: Judaica, 2005.

Holder, Arthur, editor. *The Blackwell Companion to Christian Spirituality*. Oxford: Blackwell, 2005.

Holland, N. N., P. K. Kugler, and M. Grimaud. "Psychological Criticism." In *The New Princeton Encyclopedia of Poetry and Poetics*, edited by A. Preminger and T. G. A. Brogan, 997–1002. Princeton: Princeton University Press, 1993.

Holland, S. "Theology Is a Kind of Writing: The Emergence of Theopoetics." *Cross Currents* 47 (1997) 317–31.

Hopper, S. R. "The Literary Imagination and the Doing of Theology." In *The Way of Transfiguration: Religious Imagination as Theopoiesis*, edited by R. M. Keiser and T. Stoneburner, 207–29. Louisville: Westminster John Knox, 1992.

Horsley, G. H. R., editor. *NewDocs* 4. Grand Rapids: Eerdmans, 1987.

Hossfeld, Frank-Lothar, and Erich Zenger. *Psalms 2: A Commentary on Psalms 51–100*. Hermeneia. Minneapolis: Fortress, 2005.

Houlden, J. L. *Ethics and the New Testament*. London: T. & T. Clark, 1992.

Houtman, Cornelis. *Exodus*. Translated by Johan Rebel and Sierd Woudstra. 4 vols. Historical Commentary on the Old Testament. Kampen: Kok, 1993–2002.

Howard, David M., Jr. "The Psalms and Current Study." In *Interpreting the Psalms: Issues and Approaches*, edited by Philip S. Johnston and David G. Firth, 23–40. Leicester, UK: Apollos, 2005.

Howard-Brook, W. *"Come Out, My People!" God's Call Out of Empire in the Bible and Beyond*. Maryknoll, NY: Orbis, 2010.

Howard-Brook, W., and A. Gwyther. *Unveiling Empire: Reading Revelation Then and Now*. Maryknoll, NY: Orbis, 1999.

Hubner, Hans. *Biblische Theologie des Neuen Testaments*. 2 vols. Göttingen: Vandenhoeck & Ruprecht, 1990–93.

Humphrey, Edith. *Ecstasy and Intimacy: When the Holy Spirit Meets the Human Spirit*. Grand Rapids: Eerdmans, 2006.

Humphreys, W. L. "A Life-Style for Diaspora: A Study of the Tales of Esther and Daniel." *JBL* 92 (1973) 211–23.

Hunter, Alastair G. "(De)Nominating Amalek: Racist Stereotyping in the Bible and the Justification of Discrimination." In *Sanctified Aggression: Legacies of Biblical and Post-biblical Vocabularies of Violence*, edited by Jonneke Bekkenkamp and Yvonne Sherwood, 99–105. London: T. & T. Clark, 2003.

Jacob, Benno. *Das Buch Exodus*. Edited by Shlomo Mayer. Stuttgart: Calwer, 1997.

Jaquette, James L. *Discerning What Counts: The Function of the Adiaphora Topos in Paul's Letters*. Atlanta: Scholars, 1995.

Jenkins, Philip. *Laying Down the Sword: Why We Can't Ignore the Bible's Violent Verses*. New York: HarperOne, 2011.

Johnson, L. T. *The First and Second Letters to Timothy*. AB 35A. New York: Doubleday, 2001.

———. *Prophetic Jesus, Prophetic Church: The Challenge of Luke-Acts to Contemporary Christians*. Grand Rapids: Eerdmans, 2011.

Jones, Gareth Lloyd. "Sacred Violence: The Dark Side of God." *Journal of Beliefs and Values* 20 (1999) 184–99.

Josipovici, Gabriel. *The Book of God: A Response to the Bible*. New Haven: Yale University Press, 1988.

Julien, Sarah. "Coming Home: Adoption in Ephesians and Galatians." *Quodlibet Online Journal of Christian Theology and Philosophy* 5 (2003). Online: http://www.quodlibet.net/articles/murray-adoption.shtml.

Just, Arthur A., Jr., editor. *Luke*. ACCS New Testament III. Downers Grove, IL: InterVarsity, 2003.

Kang, Sa-Moon. *Divine War in the Old Testament and in the Ancient Near East*. BZAW 177. Berlin: de Gruyter, 1989.

Kangas, David. "Kierkegaard." In *Oxford Handbook of Religion and Emotion*, edited by John Corrigan, 380–403. Oxford: Oxford University Press, 2008.

Keefe-Perry, L. B. C. "Theopoetics: Process and Perspective." *Christianity and Literature* 58 (2009) 579–601.

Kelhoffer, J. A. *Persecution, Persuasion and Power: Readiness to Withstand Hardship as a Corroboration of Legitimacy in the New Testament*. WUNT 270. Tübingen: Mohr Siebeck, 2010.

Kelly, A. *The Resurrection Effect: Transforming Christian Life and Thought*. Maryknoll, NY: Orbis, 2008.

Kelly, J. N. D. *A Commentary on the Pastoral Epistles: I Timothy, II Timothy, Titus*. London: A. & C. Black, 1963.

Kelsey, David. "On Human Flourishing: A Theocentric Perspective." Online: http://www.yale.edu/faith/rc/rc-ghf-cons-2008.htm.

Kerr, Fergus. *Thomas Aquinas: A Very Short Introduction*. Oxford: Oxford University Press, 2009.

Bibliography

Kierkegaard, Søren. *Eighteen Upbuilding Discourses.* Translated by H. Hong and E. Hong. Princeton: Princeton University Press, 1992.

———. *Fear and Trembling/Repetition.* Translated by H. Hong and E. Hong. Princeton: Princeton University Press, 1983.

Kirk, J. R. Daniel. *Unlocking Romans: Resurrection and the Justification of God.* Grand Rapids: Eerdmans, 2008.

Knibb, Michael. "The Book of Daniel in Its Context." In *The Book of Daniel: Composition and Reception,* edited by J. J. Collins and P. W. Flint, 1:16–35. Leiden: Brill, 2001.

Knight, G. W. *The Pastoral Epistles: A Commentary on the Greek Text.* NIGTC. Grand Rapids: Eerdmans, 1992.

Knight, Henry F. "Coming to Terms with Amalek: Testing the Limits of Hospitality." In *Confronting Genocide: Judaism, Christianity, Islam,* edited by Steven Leonard Jacobs and Marc I. Sherman, 223–37. Lanham, MD: Lexington, 2009.

Knowles, Michael P. "'Christ in You, the Hope of Glory': Colossians." In *Patterns of Discipleship in the New Testament,* edited by Richard N. Longenecker, 180–202. Grand Rapids: Eerdmans, 1996.

———. *We Preach Not Ourselves: Paul on Proclamation.* Grand Rapids: Eerdmans, 2008.

Kourie, Celia. "Reading Scripture through a Mystical Lens." In *The Spirit that Inspires: Perspectives on Biblical Spirituality,* edited by P. G. R. de Villiers and Lloyd K. Pietersen, 132–53. Acta Theologica Supplementum 15. Bloemfontein, South Africa: University of the Free State Press, 2011.

Kraus, H.-J. *Psalms 60–150: A Commentary.* Translated by Hilton C. Oswald from the 5th German ed., 1978. Minneapolis: Augsburg, 1989.

Kugel, James L. *The Bible as It Was.* Cambridge: Belknap, 1997.

Langner, Allan M. "Remembering Amalek Twice." *JBQ* 36 (2008) 251–53.

Lapsley, Jacqueline E. "Feeling Our Way: Love for God in Deuteronomy." *CBQ* 65 (2003) 350–69.

Lash, Nicholas. *Seeing in the Dark.* London: Darton, Longman & Todd, 2005.

Leibowitz, Yeshayahu. *Judaism, Human Values, and the Jewish State.* Edited by Eliezar Goldman. Translated by Eliezar Goldman et al. Cambridge: Harvard University Press, 1992.

Leung Lai, B. M. *Through the "I"-Window: The Inner Life of Characters in the Hebrew Bible.* HBM 34. Sheffield, UK: Sheffield Phoenix, 2011.

Levenson, Jon D. "Is There a Counterpart in the Hebrew Bible to New Testament Anti-Semitism?" *JES* 22 (1985) 242–60.

———. *Sinai and Zion: An Entry into the Jewish Bible.* San Francisco: Harper & Row, 1985.

Levinson, Stephen C. *Pragmatics.* Cambridge: Cambridge University Press, 1983.

Lieu, Judith. *The Gospel of Luke.* Epworth Commentaries. Peterborough, UK: Epworth, 1997.

Lincoln, Andrew T. "The Household Code and the Wisdom Mode of Colossians." *JSNT* 74 (1999) 93–112.

———. "The Letter to the Colossians: Introduction, Commentary, and Reflections." In *NIB* 11:551—669.

———. *Paradise Now and Not Yet: Studies in the Role of the Heavenly Dimension in Paul's Thought with Special Reference to His Eschatology.* Cambridge: Cambridge University Press, 1981.

————. "Spirituality in a Secular Age: From Charles Taylor to Study of the Bible and Spirituality." In *The Spirit that Inspires: Perspectives on Biblical Spirituality*, edited by P. G. R. de Villiers and Lloyd K. Pietersen, 61–89. Acta Theologica Supplementum 15. Bloemfontein, South Africa: University of the Free State Press, 2011.

Lipton, Diana. "Remembering Amalek: A Positive Biblical Model for Dealing with Negative Scriptural Types." In *Reading Texts, Seeking Wisdom: Scripture and Theology*, edited by David F. Ford and Graham Stanton, 139–53. Grand Rapids: Eerdmans, 2003.

Litwa, M. David. *We Are Being Transformed: Deification in Pauline Soteriology*. BZNW 187. Berlin: de Gruyter, 2012.

Llewelyn, S. R., editor. *NewDocs* 9. Grand Rapids: Eerdmans, 2002.

Louw, Johannes P., and Eugene Nida. *Greek-English Lexicon of the New Testament Based on Semantic Domains*. New York: United Bible Society, 1988.

Lüdemann, Gerd. *The Unholy in Holy Scripture: The Dark Side of the Bible*. Translated by John Bowden. Louisville: Westminster John Knox, 1997.

Lundbom, J. R. *Jeremiah 1–20: A New Translation with Introduction and Commentary*. AB 21A. New York: Doubleday, 1999.

————. *Jeremiah 37–52: A New Translation with Introduction and Commentary*. AB 21C. New York: Doubleday, 2004.

Luther, M. *Luther's Works*. 55 vols. American ed. St. Louis: Concordia, 1957–86.

Lux, Richard. *The Jewish People, the Holy Land, and the State of Israel: A Catholic View*. New York: Paulist, 2010.

MacDonald, Margaret Y. *Colossians and Ephesians*. 2nd ed. Collegeville, MN: Liturgical, 2008.

MacDonald, Nathan. "Anticipations of Horeb: Exodus 17 as Inner-Biblical Commentary." In *Studies on the Text and Versions of the Hebrew Bible in Honour of Robert Gordon*, edited by Geoffrey Khan and Diana Lipton, 7–19. VTSup 149. Leiden: Brill, 2012.

————. *Not Bread Alone: The Uses of Food in the Old Testament*. Oxford: Oxford University Press, 2008.

Magonet, Jonathan. *The Subversive Bible*. London: SCM, 1997.

Maier, Christl M. *Daughter Zion, Mother Zion: Gender, Space, and the Sacred in Ancient Israel*. Minneapolis: Fortress, 2008.

Mandolfo, Carleen. "Feminist Enquiry into the Psalms and Book of Lamentations." A paper given at SBL in San Francisco, November 2011, and forthcoming in a volume edited by Susanne Scholz and F. Rachel Magdalene.

Marcus, Joel. *Mark 8–16*. AYB. New Haven: Yale University Press, 2009.

Marshall, I. H. *A Critical and Exegetical Commentary on the Pastoral Epistles*. ICC. Edinburgh: T. & T. Clark, 1999.

————. *The Gospel of Luke: A Commentary on the Greek Text*. NIGTC. Exeter, UK: Paternoster, 1978.

————. *New Testament Theology: Many Witnesses, One Gospel*. Downers Grove, IL: InterVarsity, 2004.

Martin, Dale. "Paul's Disciples." Online lecture: http://oyc.yale.edu/religious-studies/rlst-152/lecture-17.

Martin, S. C. *Pauli Testamentum: 2 Timothy and the Last Words of Moses*. Rome: Editrice Pontifice Universita Gregoriana, 1997.

Martin, T. W. *By Philosophy and Empty Deceit: Colossians as Response to a Cynic Critique.* Sheffield, UK: Sheffield Academic, 1996.

Martyn, James Louis. *Galatians.* AB 33A. New York: Doubleday.

Matera, Frank J. *New Testament Theology: Exploring Diversity and Unity.* Louisville: Westminster John Knox, 2007.

Mathews McGinnis, C. "Swimming with the Divine Tide: An Ignatian Reading of 1 Samuel." In *Theological Exegesis: Essays in Honor of Brevard S. Childs,* edited by Christopher Seitz and Kathryn Greene-McCreight, 240–70. Grand Rapids: Eerdmans, 1999.

Mattison, Mark M. "A Summary of the New Perspective on Paul." The Paul Page. Online at http://www.thepaulpage.com/a-summary-of-the-new-perspective-on-paul/.

May, M. A. *A Body Knows: A Theopoetics of Death and Resurrection.* New York: Continuum, 1995.

McCarter, P. Kyle, Jr. *1 Samuel: A New Translation and Commentary.* AB 8. Garden City, NY: Doubleday, 1980.

McConville, J. Gordon. "Forgiveness as Private and Public Act: A Reading of the Biblical Joseph Narrative." *CBQ,* forthcoming.

———. "Happiness in the Psalms." In *The Spirit that Inspires: Perspectives on Biblical Spirituality,* edited by Pieter de Villiers and Lloyd K. Pietersen, 81–100. Acta Theologica Supplementum 15. Bloemfontein, South Africa: University of the Free State, 2011.

———. "Righteousness and the Divine Presence in Psalm 17." In *The Centre and the Periphery: A European Tribute to Walter Brueggemann,* edited by Jill Middlemas, David J. A. Clines, and Else K. Holt, 193–207. Hebrew Bible Monographs 27. Sheffield, UK: Sheffield Phoenix, 2010.

McGinn, Bernard, and John Meyendorff, editors. *Christian Spirituality: Origins to the Twelfth Century.* New York: Crossroad, 1985.

McKane, W. *A Critical and Exegetical Commentary on Jeremiah.* Vol. 2, *Jeremiah XXVI–LII.* ICC 19/2. Edinburgh: T. & T. Clark, 1996.

Metzger, James A. "Where Has Yahweh Gone? Reclaiming Unsavory Images of God in New Testament Studies." *HBT* 31 (2009) 51–76.

Meyer, Paul W. "The This-Worldliness of the New Testament." In *The Word in This World: Essays in New Testament Exegesis and Theology,* edited by John T. Carroll, 5–18. Louisville: Westminster John Knox, 2004.

Middleton, P. *Radical Martyrdom and Cosmic Conflict in Early Christianity.* LNTS 307. London: T. & T. Clark, 2006.

Miller, Patrick. "Kingship, Torah Obedience, and Prayer." In *Neue Wege der Psalmenforschung,* edited by K. Seybold and E. Zenger, 127–42. Freiburg: Herder, 1995.

Moberly, R. W. L. *Old Testament Theology: Reading the Hebrew Bible as Christian Scripture.* Grand Rapids: Baker Academic, 2013.

Moo, Douglas J. *The Letters to Colossians and to Philemon.* Grand Rapids: Eerdmans, 2008.

Moore, Stephen D. *Empire and Apocalypse: Postcolonialism and the New Testament.* Bible in the Modern World 12. Sheffield, UK: Sheffield Phoenix, 2006.

Morgan, Robert. "New Testament Theology in the Twentieth Century." In *Biblical Theology: Introducing the Conversation,* edited by Leo G. Perdue, Robert Morgan, and Benjamin D. Sommer, 137–208. Library of Biblical Theology. Nashville: Abingdon, 2009.

Morray-Jones, C. R. A. "Paradise Revisited (2 Cor 12:1–12): The Jewish Mystical Background of Paul's Apostolate, Part 1: The Jewish Sources." *HTR* 86 (1993) 177–217.

———. "Paradise Revisited (2 Cor 12:1–12): The Jewish Mystical Background of Paul's Apostolate, Part 2: Paul's Heavenly Ascent and Its Significance." *HTR* 86 (1993) 265–92.

Morrice, William. *Joy in the New Testament.* Grand Rapids: Eerdmans, 1985.

Morriston, Wes. "Ethical Criticism of the Bible: The Case of Divinely Mandated Genocide." *Sophia* 51 (2012) 117–35.

Mounce, W. D. *Pastoral Epistles.* WBC 46. Nashville: Thomas Nelson, 2000.

Murdoch, Iris. *The Black Prince.* 1973. Reprint, Harmondsworth, UK: Penguin, 1975.

Murphy-O'Connor, J. "2 Timothy Contrasted with 1 Timothy and Titus." *RB* 98 (1991) 403–18.

Neufeld, Thomas R. *"Put on the Armour of God": The Divine Warrior from Isaiah to Ephesians.* JSNTSup 140. Sheffield, UK: Sheffield Academic, 1997.

Neyrey, Jerome H. "The Symbolic Universe of Luke-Acts: 'They Turn the World Upside Down.'" In *The Social World of Luke-Acts,* edited by Jerome H. Neyrey, 271–304. Peabody, MA: Hendrickson, 1991.

Niditch, Susan. *War in the Hebrew Bible: A Study in the Ethics of Violence.* New York: Oxford University Press, 1993.

Nolan Fewell, Danna. *Circle of Sovereignty: Plotting Politics in the Book of Daniel.* Nashville: Abingdon, 1991.

———. *Circle of Sovereignty: A Story of Stories in Daniel 1–6.* JSOTSup 72. Sheffield, UK: Almond, 1988.

Noort, Ed. "Josua und Amalek: Exodus 17:8–16." In *The Interpretation of Exodus: Studies in Honour of Cornelis Houtman,* edited by Riemer Roukema, 155–70. Leuven: Peeters, 2006.

Novick, Tzi. "Amaleq's Victims in Dtn 25,18." *ZAW* 119 (2007) 611–15.

Nunberg, Geoffrey. "Indexicality and Deixis." *Linguistics and Philosophy* 16 (1993) 1–43.

Nysse, Richard. "The Dark Side of God: Considerations for Preaching and Teaching." *WW* 17 (1997) 437–46.

O'Brien, Julia, and Chris Franke, editors. *Aesthetics of Violence in the Prophets.* JSOTSup 517. London: T. & T. Clark, 2010.

O'Collins, G. *Believing in the Resurrection: The Meaning and Promise of the Risen Jesus.* New York: Paulist, 2012.

Oden, Thomas C., and Christopher A. Hall, editors. *Mark.* ACCS New Testament III. Downers Grove, IL: InterVarsity, 1998.

Ollenburger, Ben C. "Gerhard von Rad's Theology of Holy War." In Gerhard von Rad, *Holy War in Ancient Israel,* translated by Marva J. Dawn, 1–33. Grand Rapids: Eerdmans, 1991.

Otto, Rudolf. *The Idea of the Holy* [1917]. Translated by John Harvey. London: Oxford University Press, 1923.

Patton, Kimberley, and John Hawley, editors. *Holy Tears: Weeping in the Religious Imagination.* Princeton: Princeton University Press, 2005.

Peels, Eric. *Shadow Sides: God in the Old Testament.* Carlisle, UK: Paternoster, 2003.

Penchansky, David. *The Betrayal of God: Ideological Conflict in Job.* Louisville: Westminster John Knox, 1990.

Bibliography

_____. *What Rough Beast? Images of God in the Hebrew Bible.* Louisville: Westminster John Knox, 1999.

Pénin, J. "Cosmic Piety." In *Classical Mediterranean Spirituality: Egyptian, Greek, Roman,* edited by A. H. Armstrong, 408–35. London: Routledge & Kegan Paul, 1986.

Peplau, H. E. *Interpersonal Relations in Nursing.* New York: Putnam, 1952.

Perrin, David B. "Mysticism." In *The Blackwell Companion to Christian Spirituality,* edited by Arthur Holder, 442–58. Oxford: Blackwell, 2005.

Pfitzner, V. C. *Paul and the Agon Motif: Traditional Athletic Imagery in the Pauline Literature.* Leiden: Brill, 1967.

Pietersen, Lloyd K. "Spirituality as 'Good Christian Citizenship' in the Pastoral Epistles?" In *The Spirit that Inspires: Perspectives on Biblical Spirituality,* edited by P. G. R. de Villiers and Lloyd K. Pietersen, 154–66. Acta Theologica Supplementum 15. Bloemfontein, South Africa: University of the Free State Press, 2011.

Pope, Marvin H. *Job: Introduction, Translation and Notes.* Rev. ed. New Haven: Yale University Press, 2008.

Potkay, Adam. *The Story of Joy: From the Bible to Late Romanticism.* Cambridge: Cambridge University Press, 2007.

Price, S. R. F. *Rituals and Power: The Roman Imperial Cult in Asia Minor.* Cambridge: Cambridge University Press, 1984.

Prior, M. *Paul the Letter Writer and the Second Letter to Timothy.* JSNTSup 23. Sheffield, UK: JSOT, 1989.

Quinn, J. D., and W. C. Wacker. *The First and Second Letters to Timothy.* Eerdmans Critical Commentary. Grand Rapids: Eerdmans, 2000.

Redalie, Y. *Paul après Paul: Le Temps, le Salut, la Morale selon les Épîtres à Timothée et à Tite.* Geneva: Labor et Fides, 1994.

Ricoeur, Paul. *The Conflict of Interpretations.* Evanston, IL: Northwestern University Press, 1976.

_____. *Interpretation Theory: Discourse and the Surplus of Meaning.* Fort Worth, TX: Texas Christian University Press, 1976.

_____. *Oneself as Another.* Translated by Kathleen Blamey. Chicago: University of Chicago Press, 1992.

Ridderbos, Herman. *The Epistle of Paul to the Churches of Galatia.* NICNT. Grand Rapids: Eerdmans, 1953.

_____. *Paulus. Ontwerp van zijn Theologie.* Kampen: Kok, 1966.

Riesenfeld, Harald. "Faith and Love Promoting Hope: An Interpretation of Philemon v. 6." In *Paul and Paulinism: Essays in Honour of C. K. Barrett,* edited by Morna Hooker and S. G. Wilson, 251–57. London: SPCK, 1982.

Robbins, Bruce. *Perpetual War: Cosmopolitanism from the Viewpoint of Violence.* Durham, NC: Duke University Press, 2012.

Robertson, David. *The Old Testament and the Literary Critic.* Philadelphia: Fortress, 1977.

Robinson, Bernard P. "Israel and Amalek: The Context of Exodus 17:8–16." *JSOT* 32 (1985) 15–22.

Roncace, M. *Jeremiah, Zedekiah, and the Fall of Jerusalem.* London: T. & T. Clark, 2005.

Rooze, Egbert. *Amalek: Over gewald in het Oude Testament.* Kampen: Kok, 1997.

Rowe, C. Kavin. *Early Narrative Christology: The Lord in the Gospel of Luke.* Grand Rapids: Baker Academic, 2009.

266

————. "New Testament Theology: The Revival of a Discipline—A Review of Recent Contributions to the Field." *JBL* 125 (2006) 393–419.

Rowland, Christopher C. "The Book of Revelation: Introduction, Commentary, and Reflections." In *NIB* 12:501–736.

Rowland, Christopher C., and Christopher R. A. Morray-Jones. *The Mystery of God: Early Jewish Mysticism and the New Testament.* Leiden: Brill, 2009.

Rudavsky, Dahlia C. "In Defense of Tradition: Haftarat Zachor in the Light of Purim." *Judaism* 47 (1998) 80–87.

Runions, Erin. *Changing Subjects: Gender, Nation and Future in Micah.* Sheffield, UK: Sheffield Academic, 2001.

Rush, O. *The Eyes of Faith: The Sense of the Faithful and the Church's Reception of Revelation.* Washington, DC: Catholic University of America Press, 2009.

Sagi, Avi. "The Punishment of Amalek in Jewish Tradition: Coping with the Moral Problem." *HTR* 87 (1994) 323–46.

Schaefer, Konrad. *Psalms.* Berit Olam. Collegeville, MN: Liturgical, 2001.

Scheetz, J. M. *The Concept of Canonical Intertextuality and the Book of Daniel.* Eugene, OR: Pickwick, 2011.

Schiffmann, Lawrence H., and Joel B. Wolowelsky, editors. *War and Peace in the Jewish Tradition.* New York: KTAV, 2007.

Schmitt, Hans-Christoph. "Die Geschichte vom Sieg über die Amalekiter Ex 17,8–16 als theologische Lehrerzählung." *ZAW* 102 (1990) 335–44.

Schneiders, Sandra M. "Approaches to the Study of Spirituality." In *The Blackwell Companion to Christian Spirituality,* edited by A. Holder, 15–33. Oxford: Blackwell, 2005.

————. "Biblical Spirituality." *Interpretation* 56 (2002) 133–42.

————. "Christian Spirituality: Definition, Methods and Types." In *The New Westminster Dictionary of Christian Spirituality,* edited by P. Sheldrake, 1–6. Louisville: Westminster John Knox, 2005.

————. *The Revelatory Text: Interpreting the New Testament as Sacred Scripture.* 2nd ed. Collegeville, MN: Liturgical, 1999.

————. "The Study of Christian Spirituality: Contours and Dynamics of a Discipline." *JSSCS* 6 (1998) 1, 3–11.

————. *"Written That You May Believe": Encountering Jesus in the Fourth Gospel.* New York: Crossroad, 2003.

Schnelle, U. *Theologie des Neuen Testaments.* 2 vols. Tübingen: Mohr Siebeck, 2001–2005.

Schrage, Wolfgang. *The Ethics of the New Testament.* Philadelphia: Fortress, 1988.

Schreiner, Susan E. *Where Shall Wisdom Be Found? Calvin's Exegesis of Job from Medieval and Modern Perspectives.* Chicago: University of Chicago Press, 1994.

Schrenk, Gottlob. "Father." In *TDNT* 5:1011–13.

Schuil, Auke. *Amalek: Onderzoek naar oorsprong en ontwikkeling van Amaleks rol in het Oude Testament.* Zoetermeer: Boekencentrum, 1997.

Scott, Ian W. *Implicit Epistemology in the Letters to Paul: Story, Experience and the Spirit.* WUNT 2.205. Tübingen: Mohr, 2006.

Seibert, Eric A. *Disturbing Divine Behavior: Troubling Old Testament Images of God.* Minneapolis: Fortress, 2009.

Seim, T. K. *The Double Message: Patterns of Gender in Luke-Acts.* Edinburgh: T. & T. Clark, 1994.

Bibliography

Seligman, Martin. *Flourish*. Boston: Nicholas Brealey, 2011.

Severin-Kaiser, Martina. "Gedenke dessen, was dir amalek antat . . . Auslegungen zu Exodus 17, 8–16 und Deuteronomium 25, 17–19." In *(Anti-)Rassistische Irritationen: Biblische Texte und interkulturelle Zusammenarbeit*, edited by Sylvia Wagner et al., 151–66. Berlin: Alektor, 1994.

Seybold, Klaus. *Die Psalmen*. HAT 1/15. Tübingen: Mohr-Siebeck, 1996.

Sheldrake, Philip. "Interpretation." In *The Blackwell Companion to Christian Spirituality*, edited by A. Holder, 459–77. Oxford: Wiley-Blackwell, 2005.

Siegel, Daniel. "Amalek: Internalizing the External, Externalizing the Internal." *Conservative Judaism* 56 (2004) 55–59.

Simonetti, Manlio, editor. *Matthew 14–28*. ACCS New Testament 1b. Downers Grove, IL: InterVarsity, 2002.

Simons, Menno. *The Complete Works of Menno Simons*. Vol. 2. Elkhart, IN: Funk, 1871.

Smith, I. K. *Heavenly Perspective: A Study of the Apostle Paul's Response to a Jewish Mystical Movement at Colossae*. London: T. & T. Clark, 2006.

Smith-Christopher, Daniel L. *A Biblical Theology of Exile*. OBT. Minneapolis: Fortress, 2002.

———. "Daniel." In *NIB* 7:17–194.

———. "The Quiet Words of the Wise: Biblical Developments towards Nonviolence as a Diaspora Ethic." In *Character Ethics and the Old Testament: Moral Dimensions of Scripture*, edited by M. David Carroll R. and J. E. Lapsley, 129–51. Louisville: Westminster John Knox, 2007.

Snyder, C. A. *Following in the Footsteps of Christ: The Anabaptist Tradition*. Traditions of Christian Spirituality. London: Darton, Longman & Todd, 2004.

Soja, Edward W. *Thirdspace: Journeys to Los Angeles and Other Real-and-Imagined Places*. Cambridge: Blackwell, 2000.

Sommer, Benjamin. *A Prophet Reads Scripture: Allusion in Isaiah 40–66*. Stanford: Stanford University Press, 1998.

Sparks, Kenton L. *Sacred Word, Broken Word: Biblical Authority and the Dark Side of Scripture*. Grand Rapids: Eerdmans, 2012.

Spicq, Ceslas. *Agape in the New Testament*. Vol. 2. St. Louis: Herder, 1965.

———. *Lexique Theologique du Nouveau Testament I*. Göttingen: Vandenhoeck, 1978.

Sprinzak, Ehud. *The Ascendance of Israel's Radical Right*. New York: Oxford University Press, 1991.

Stark, Thom. *The Human Faces of God: What Scripture Reveals When It Gets God Wrong*. Eugene, OR: Wipf & Stock, 2011.

Stern, Philip. "1 Samuel 15: Towards an Ancient View of the War-Ḥērem." *UF* 21 (1989) 413–20.

———. *The Biblical Ḥērem: A Window on Israel's Religious Experience*. BJS 211. Atlanta: Scholars, 1991.

Sternberg, Meir. *The Poetics of Biblical Narrative*. Bloomington: Indiana University Press, 1985.

Stowers, Stanley K. "Friends and Enemies in the Politics of Heaven." In *Pauline Theology, Volume 1: Thessalonians, Philippians, Galatians, Philemon*, edited by Jouette M. Bassler, 105–21. Minneapolis: Fortress, 1991.

Strawn, Brent, editor. *The Bible and the Pursuit of Happiness*. Oxford: Oxford University Press, 2012.

Strawn Brent A., and Brad D. Strawn. "Prophecy and Psychology." In *DOTPr* 610–23.

Strecker, Georg. *Theologie des Neuen Testaments.* Berlin: de Gruyter, 1996.

Stuhlmacher, Peter. *Biblische Theologie des Neuen Testaments.* 2 vols. Göttingen: Vandenhoeck & Ruprecht, 1991–99.

Stulman, L. *Jeremiah.* Nashville: Abingdon, 2005.

Stump, Eleonore. "The Problem of Evil and the History of Peoples: Think Amalek." In *Divine Evil? The Moral Character of the God of Abraham,* edited by Michael Bergmann et al., 179–91. New York: Oxford University Press, 2011.

Sumney, J. L. *Colossians.* Louisville: Westminster John Knox, 2008.

Swinton, John. *Spirituality and Mental Health Care: Recovering a "Forgotten" Dimension.* Philadelphia: King, 2001.

Symonds, Gwyn. *The Aesthetics of Violence in Contemporary Media.* New York: Continuum, 2008.

Talbert, C. H. *Ephesians and Colossians.* Grand Rapids: Baker Academic, 2007.

Tamir, Yael. "Remember Amalek: Religious Hate Speech." In *Obligations of Citizenship and Demands of Faith: Religious Accommodation in Pluralist Democracies,* edited by Nancy L. Rosenblum, 321–34. Princeton: Princeton University Press, 2000.

Tanner, Hans Andreas. *Amalek—der Feind Israels und der Feind Jahwes: eine Studie zu den Amalektexten im Alten Testament.* Zurich: Theologischer, 2005.

Taylor, Charles. *A Secular Age.* Cambridge: Belknap, 2007.

Thomas Aquinas. *Expositio super Iob ad litteram.* Opera Omnia. Iussu Leonis XIII P.M. edita, vol. 26. Rome: Ad Sanctae Sabinae, 1965.

Thompson, Marianne Meye. *Colossians & Philemon.* THNTC. Grand Rapids: Eerdmans, 2005.

Ticciati, Susannah. *Job and the Disruption of Identity: Reading beyond Barth.* London: T. & T. Clark, 2005.

Tiede, David L. *Luke.* ACNT. Minneapolis: Augsburg, 1988.

Tolmie, D. Francois. "Ethics and Ethos according to the Letter to the Galatians." In *Identity, Ethics and Ethos in the New Testament,* edited by Jan G. van der Watt, assisted by Francois S. Malan, 240–55. BZNW 141. Berlin: de Gruyter, 2006.

———. *Persuading the Galatians.* WUNT 2.190. Tübingen: Mohr Siebeck, 2005.

———. "Research on the Letter to the Galatians: 2000–2010." Paper read at a conference on Galatians, University of the Free State, Bloemfontein, 2012. Forthcoming in *Acta Theologica* (2013).

———. "Violence in the Letter to Galatians?" In *Coping with Violence in the New Testament,* edited by Pieter G. R. de Villiers and Jan-Willem van Henten, 69–82. STAR 16. Leiden: Brill, 2012.

Tournier, Paul. *Médecine de la personne.* Neuchâtel: Delachaud et Niestlé, 1940.

Towner, Philip H. *The Letters to Timothy and Titus.* NICNT. Grand Rapids: Eerdmans, 2006.

Trend, David. *The Myth of Media Violence: A Critical Introduction.* Malden, MA: Blackwell, 2007.

U.S. Department of Homeland Security. "Implementing 9/11 Commission Recommendations: Progress Report 2011." Online: http://www.dhs.gov/xlibrary/assets/implementing-9-11-commission-report-progress-2011.pdf.

Van Ness, P. H. "Introduction." In *Spirituality and the Secular Quest,* edited by P. H. Van Ness, 1–17. New York: Crossroad, 1996.

Venema, G. J. *Reading Scripture in the Old Testament: Deuteronomy 9–10; 31—2 Kings 22–23—Jeremiah 36—Nehemiah 8.* OTS 47. Leiden: Brill, 2004.

Venter, P. M. "Daniel 9: A Penitential Prayer in Apocalyptic Garb." In *Seeking the Favor of God*, edited by Mark J. Boda et al., 2:33–50. Atlanta: SBL, 2007.

Voorwinde, Stephen. *Jesus' Emotions in the Gospels*. London: T. & T. Clark, 2011.

Waaijman, K. *Spirituality: Forms, Foundations, Methods*. Leuven: Peeters, 2002.

———. "Spirituality—A Multi-faceted Phenomenon: Interdisciplinary Explorations." *Studies in Spirituality* 17 (2007) 1–113.

Walker-Jones, Arthur. *The Green Psalter: Resources for an Ecological Spirituality*. Minneapolis: Fortress, 2009.

Wellman, James K., Jr. "Is War Normal for American Evangelical Religion?" In *Belief and Bloodshed: Religion and Violence across Time and Tradition*, edited by James K. Wellman Jr., 195–210. Lanham, MD: Rowman & Littlefield, 2007.

Wheaton, D. H. "Love." In *Evangelical Dictionary of Theology*, 2nd ed., edited by Walter A. Elwell, 408–9. Grand Rapids: Baker, 2001.

Wierzbicka, Anna. *Emotions across Languages and Cultures: Diversity and Universals*. Cambridge: Cambridge University Press, 1999.

Wilder, A. N. *Theopoetic: Theology and the Religious Imagination*. Philadelphia: Fortress, 1976.

Williams, G. H. *Spiritual and Anabaptist Writers: Documents Illustrative of the Radical Reformation*. Philadelphia: Westminster, 1957.

Wilson, Gerald H. *The Editing of the Hebrew Psalter*. SBLDS 76. Chico, CA: Scholars, 1985.

———. "The Prayer of Daniel 9." *JSOT* 48 (1990) 91–99.

Wilson, R. McL. *Colossians and Philemon*. London: T. & T. Clark, 2005.

Wilson, W. T. *The Hope of Glory: Education and Exhortation in the Epistle to the Colossians*. Leiden: Brill, 1997.

Wink, Walter. *The Bible in Human Transformation: Toward a New Paradigm for Biblical Study*. Rev. ed. Minneapolis: Fortress, 2010.

———. *Engaging the Powers: Discernment and Resistance in a World of Domination*. Philadelphia: Fortress, 1992.

———. *Naming the Powers: The Language of Power in the New Testament*. Philadelphia: Fortress, 1984.

———. *Unmasking the Powers: The Invisible Forces that Determine Human Existence*. Philadelphia: Fortress, 1986.

Wolter, M. *Die Pastoralbriefe als Paulustradition*. FRLANT 146. Göttingen: Vandenhöck & Ruprecht, 1988.

Woodhead, Linda, and Ole Riis. *A Sociology of Religious Emotion*. Oxford: Oxford University Press, 2010.

Wright, N. T. *The Climax of the Covenant: Christ and the Law in Pauline Theology*. Edinburgh: T. & T. Clark, 1991.

Younger, K. Lawson. "Some Recent Discussion on the Ḥērem." In *Far from Minimal: Celebrating the Work and Influence of Philip R. Davies*, edited by Duncan Burns and J. W. Rogerson, 505–22. LHBOTS 484. London: T. & T. Clark, 2012.

Zehr, P. M. *1 & 2 Timothy, Titus*. BCBC. Scottdale, PA: Herald, 2010.

Zuckerman, Bruce. *Job the Silent: A Study in Historical Counterpoint*. Oxford: Oxford University Press, 1991.

Scripture and Ancient Writings Index

Old Testament

Verses in [ ] refer to the equivalent reference in MT unless otherwise stated.

New Testament

Galatians *(cont.)*

1:16	198, 201 n.27
2:4	197
2:12–13	209
2:12	209
2:13	209
2:15–20	205
2:15–19	198
2:16	197
2:19–20	159 n.33, 199, 202
2:20–21	198
2:20	197, 198, 200, 200 n.23, 201, 202, 204, 204 n.43, 210
3:1–5	205
3:1	162
3:3	202
3:5–6	202
3:9	199
3:13	204
3:15	206 n.53
3:20	202 n.31
3:22	199, 199 n.19
3:26–29	202 n.31, 208
3:26	206
3:27–28	191
3:28	198
3:29	206
4:1–7	201 n.27
4:4–7	202
4:4	198, 202 n.32, 203
4:5–6	206
4:6	198, 202 n.32
4:9	202 n.31
4:12	206 n.53
4:19	206, 210
4:23	198
4:28	206 n.53
4:31	206 n.53
5:1	207
5:2–12	205
5:2–6	205
5:2–4	205
5:5–6	205, 205 n.47
5:5	205
5:6	197, 206, 206 n.52, 207, 209
5:6b	205
5:7–12	207
5:10	197

5:11	206 n.53
5:12	197
5:13–14	206, 207, 209
5:13	197, 206 n.53
5:14	197, 207, 208
5:15	207
5:16	209
5:19–21	209, 210
5:22–23	192
5:22	178 n.17, 188, 197, 206, 208
5:25	208
6:1	206 n.53
6:10	206
6:12	236
6:18	206 n.53

Ephesians

2:12	90
2:17	90
2:19	206
3:1	237
3:13	237
4:2	90
4:31—5:2	165 n.49
5:2	204 n.42
5:18–21	89
5:21–25	90
5:25	204 n.42
6:12	15

Philippians

1:1–11	185
1:4	185
1:5	185
1:6	185
1:7	185
1:12–26	186
1:12	186, 187
1:13	184
1:14	186
1:15–17	186
1:18	184, 186
1:18b–19a	186
1:19	186
1:20	186
1:24–26	189
1:25	184, 186

Author index

Author index